Women and Russian Culture

Studies in Slavic Literature, Culture, and Society
General Editor: Thomas Epstein

Vladimir Odoevsky and Romantic Poetics: Collected Essays
    Neil Cornwell
Women and Russian Culture: Projections and Self-Perceptions
    Edited by Rosalind Marsh
Russian Postmodernism: New Perspectives on Post-Soviet Culture
    Mikhail Epstein, Alexander Genis, and Slobodanka Vladiv Glover
Sight and Sound Entwined: Studies of the New Russian Poetry
    Gerald Janecek
Mikhail Lermontov: From Russia to the Caucasus
    Robert Reid
Voices from the Void: The Genres of Liudmila Petrushevskia
    Sally Dalton-Brown
Cold Fusion: Aspects of the German Cultural Presence in Russia
    Edited by Gennady Barabtarlo

WOMEN AND RUSSIAN CULTURE
Projections and Self-Perceptions

Edited by Rosalind Marsh

Berghahn Books
New York • Oxford

First published in 1998 by
Berghahn Books

© 1998 Rosalind Marsh

All rights reserved.
No part of this publication may be reproduced in any form or by any means without the written permission of Berghahn Books.

Library of Congress Cataloging-in-Publication Data
Women and Russian culture : projections and self-perceptions / edited by Rosalind Marsh.
      p. cm. -- (Studies in Slavic literature, culture, and society ; v. 2)
    Includes bibliographical references and index.
    ISBN 1-57181-913-4 (alk. paper)
    1. Russian literature--20th century--History and criticism.
2. Russian literature--19th century--History and criticism.
3. Women in literature.   4. Russian literature--Women authors--History and criticism.   5. Russia--Intellectual life.   I. Marsh, Rosalind.   II. Series
PG3026.W6W64   1998
891.709'352042--dc21   98-16216
                                                                                  CIP

British Library Cataloguing in Publication Data
Women and Russian culture : projections and self-perceptions. - (Studies in Slavic literature, culture and society ; v. 2)
    1. Women – Russia – Social conditions 2. Russian literature – Women authors – History and criticism 3. Russian literature – History and criticism
I. Marsh, Rosalind J.
891.7'09'352042

ISBN 1571819134

CONTENTS

Acknowledgements		vii
Note on the Text		viii
Introduction *Rosalind Marsh*		ix

Part One: Theoretical Perspectives

1	An Image of Their Own?: Feminism, Revisionism and Russian Culture *Rosalind Marsh*	2
2	Reading the Texts – Rereading Ourselves *Adele Barker*	42

Part Two: Women and Russian Culture: from the Nineteenth Century to the Revolution

3	The Benevolent Matriarch in Elena Gan and Mar'ia Zhukova *Joe Andrew*	60
4	Mid-Nineteenth-Century Domestic Ideology in Russia *Diana Greene*	78
5	Criticism and Journalism at the Turn of the Century on the Work of Russian Women Writers *Irina Kazakova*	98
6	Actresses, Audience and Fashion in the Silver Age: a Crisis of Costume *Catherine Schuler*	107

Part Three: Women Writers from the Revolution to the Present

7	The Art of Suggesting More: Akhmatova and the Diaphoric Manner *Sheelagh Graham*	124
8	Under an Unwomanly Star: War in the Writing of Ol'ga Berggol'ts *Katharine Hodgson*	134

9	A Difficult Journey: Evgeniia Ginzburg and Women's Writing of Camp Memoirs *Natasha Kolchevska*	148
10	Women Memoirists on Pasternak *Neil Cornwell*	163
11	Iuliia Voznesenskaia: a Fragmentary Vision *Julie Curtis*	173
12	The Other Woman: Character Portrayal and the Narrative Voice in the Short Stories of Liudmila Petrushevskaia *Monika Katz*	188
13	Contemporary Women Poets in the Metropolis and Diaspora *Marina Ledkovsky*	198

Part Four: The Image of Women in Twentieth-Century Russian Literature

14	Gaps in the Cosmogony: Witchcraft Imagery in Andrei Bely's *Kotik Letaev* *Peter I. Barta*	212
15	The Romantic Presentation of the Heroine in Selected Works of Aleksandr Grin *Anna Darmodekhina*	227
16	Is Village Prose Misogynistic? *David Gillespie*	234
17	Real and Unreal Women in the Works of Chingiz Aitmatov *Natal'ia Zhuravkina*	244
18	The Image of Women in the Prose of Sergei Dovlatov *Boris Lanin*	252
19	In the Shadow of a Prominent Partner: Educated Women in Literature on the *shestidesiatniki* *Svetlana Carsten*	259
20	Russian Women in Anatoly Kurchatkin *Arch Tait*	275
	Notes on Contributors	281
	Index	286

ACKNOWLEDGEMENTS

I gratefully acknowledge the financial support offered by the British Academy, the Ford Foundation, the ESRC, the British Council in Russia and Ukraine, South West Arts, and the Council for Co-operation in Russian and Soviet Education for the conference on 'Women in Russia and the Former USSR' held at the University of Bath in March-April 1993, at which earlier versions of some of the chapters in this volume were presented. Special thanks are due to Celia Dyer for ensuring the efficient organisation of the conference. I should also like to thank the British Academy for enabling me to conduct research in Moscow in September 1995, and St Antony's College, Oxford, for making me a Senior Research Associate.

I should like to express my gratitude to all the contributors to this volume for their co-operation and courteous responses to my queries. The comments of Robert Porter have been particularly helpful in preparing this collection. For useful references and assistance on a number of specific points, I am indebted to Joe Andrew, William Brooks, Peter Olf Møller, David Howells and the staff of the Taylor Institution, Oxford.

I am also grateful for the insights of my colleagues in the Women's Studies Centre of the University of Bath, and for the technical assistance of James Davenport, Icarus Sparry and Christopher Williams. Finally, I should like to thank all the participants in the 'Women in Russia' conference, as well as Peter Barta and Linda Edmondson, the organisers of two 1996 conferences on gender and Russian culture which helped to stimulate debate and further reflection on many issues discussed below.

NOTE ON THE TEXT

Translations are by the contributors, unless otherwise stated. The transliteration of Cyrillic follows a modified Library of Congress system, including soft and hard signs but omitting diacritics on the letter 'ë'. In the text, proper names ending in 'ii' or 'i' (such as Dostoevsky or Tolstoy) are rendered in a simplified form ending in 'y', although in specific references they appear in their fully transliterated form. Titles of Russian texts will be given initially in transliteration, using italic script for novels, novellas (*povesti*), plays and narrative poems, and roman type for short stories (*rasskazy*), stories in collections and lyric poems. If the work has been published in an English translation, the Russian title will be followed in parenthesis by the title of the published translation in the same format; if no translation has been published, the translation of the title will appear in roman. The date in parenthesis refers to the first publication of the work, normally in Russian.

INTRODUCTION

Rosalind Marsh

From the origins of modern Russian literature in the eighteenth century until the Revolution of 1917, women have been a source of fascination for Russian writers and critics,[1] many of whom, in the 1840s and 1850s, began to participate in the public discussion of the so-called *zhenskii vopros* (woman question).[2] In the nineteenth century, articles by such prominent radical critics as Belinsky, Dobroliubov and Pisarev on the portrayal of women characters in literature helped to form the opinion of a large part of the Russian reading public.[3] After the Bolshevik Revolution, however, and particularly after Stalin's rise to power in the late 1920s, public discussion of the representation of women in literature rapidly declined, since rigid gender roles were established by the Soviet regime, and in 1930 the woman question was declared to have been 'resolved'.[4] Whereas in Britain, western Europe and the United States, the new wave of the feminist movement in the 1960s promoted what Elaine Showalter has called 'the feminist critique' – 'revisionary readings' of masculine texts and criticism[5] – it was only in the late 1980s that a feminist reinterpretation of Russian literature got seriously under way in the West,[6] with the publication of the pioneering works by Barbara Heldt and Joe Andrew.[7] In the 1990s, major nineteenth-century Russian writers such as Dostoevsky, Pushkin and Turgenev have been reread from a feminist standpoint,[8] although ample scope still remains for further research in this area.

In recent years, influenced by changing trends in feminist criticism as a whole,[9] the attention of western Slavists has begun to shift from the feminist critique to 'gynocritics', the rediscovery and analysis of literature by Russian women.[10] Within Russia, under the influence of glasnost, Russian women themselves began to reclaim their own feminine literary tradition, initially republishing some important, hitherto neglected texts by Russian women of the nineteenth and early twentieth centuries,[11] and subsequently, collections of stories by contemporary Russian women writers.[12] In the 1990s, several important general works of bibliography and criticism on Russian women writers have appeared,[13] revolutionising our understanding of Russian culture as a whole. Nevertheless, much work still remains to be done, especially in relation to twentieth-century women writers. Although in recent years some interesting critical works focusing on contemporary Russian women writers have appeared,[14] there have hitherto been relatively few extensive studies of individual Russian women authors whose writings were published before the era of glasnost, other than Anna Akhmatova and Marina Tsvetaeva.[15]

The aim of this book is to make a contribution to both the feminist critique and the gynocritics of Russian literature.[16] This comparative approach reflects the contemporary direction in feminist literary criticism, which tends to focus on gender – cultural constructions of masculinities and femininities – rather than specifically on women writers.[17] In the case of Russian literature, it is particularly important to look at both male and female-authored literature together, in order that literature by Russian women should not simply be regarded as an autonomous cultural experience, marginal to Russian literary history as a whole. This is still an essential task for feminist critics because, although the invaluable *Dictionary of Russian Women Writers* has at long last enabled at least 448 women writers to take their place in the Russian historical record, this does not imply that women's writings are now in the 'canon' (that is, the collection of literary works deemed superior and worthy of study),[18] or, *a fortiori*, that the whole concept of a 'canon' of Russian literature has been exploded.[19]

Although the validity of the feminist critique of English and American literature has been called into question by feminist theorists in recent years,[20] the study of the image of women in Russian literature remains an innovative and valuable critical activity. In the first place, the literary representation of Russian women possesses an influence transcending the world of literature, exerting a profound impact on the way in which women have been, and still are, regarded in Russian society. Secondly, it is still important for western critics to explore this subject, because within Russia itself there has been a persistent reluctance to acknowledge and investigate the patriarchal nature of the Russian cultural tradition. Preconceptions about western-style feminism[21] have prevented many Russian women from acknowledging or analysing the second-class status which has been allotted to them as a 'muted group'[22] in Russian culture as a whole.

It is also important to pursue research into gynocritics, since critics of Russian literature are still faced with three fundamental tasks: to provide more detailed analysis of the work of many women writers, and, where appropriate, to reinterpret them from a feminist point of view; to analyse the disparity between the notion of 'woman', defined as the representation of women in Russian culture, and that of 'women', interpreted as real historical women; and to investigate further the relationship between literature by women and the changing position of women in Russian society.

The chapters in this book concerned with Russian women writers focus to a significant degree on the first stage of this process of rediscovery: the attempt by feminist critics to establish a more accurate and systematic literary history for Russian women writers and to read their work in its entirety before passing judgement on them. It is hoped that this collection will help to redress some of the imbalances of Russian cultural history, both by examining gender stereotypes and by giving full weight to aspects of women's writing and women's experience which have hitherto frequently been ignored or undervalued.

Whereas most previous studies have concentrated on the aesthetic qualities of works by women writers, this collection includes both close textual analysis and the discussion of biographical, historical and political questions relating both to the representation of women and women's culture in Russia. The aim is not to present a unified manifesto, but rather to bring together a spectrum of approaches and positions within their common focus on the relationship between women and culture in Russia. Contributions differ widely, not only in critical method and in the material they draw upon – novels, poetry, drama, film, autobiography, journalism by and for women, both 'high' and 'popular culture' – but also in their theoretical and political stance. The collection contains a variety of feminisms,[23] and many definitions of the relationship between women and their representation in Russian culture. The hope is that these different approaches might fruitfully play off against one another, initiating debate within the book's covers as well as indicating some of the main questions which animate current criticism and theory in relation to gender and Russian culture.

Each essay is written from the individual standpoint of its author and speaks for itself, but raises issues that are of common concern for the collection as a whole, ranging from the extent to which cultural representation has oppressed Russian women to the ways in which such representations may be challenged and transformed by women themselves. The essays dealing with Russian women writers pose questions about the nature of their relationship with the dominant masculine culture, the specificity of women's language and experience, and the validity, or otherwise, of western feminist approaches to Russian women's writings.

The book combines a discussion of some key theoretical issues with an overview of some important aspects of women's culture in various periods of nineteenth- and twentieth-century Russian history, and more detailed studies of individual authors, both male and female.

In the first, theoretical part of the book, my chapter provides an overview of the representation of women in Russian literature since the late eighteenth century, endorsing some points made by previous critics, while contesting others. I emphasise the continuing value of using the insights of feminist theory, where appropriate, to analyse Russian literature, and argue against the current fashion for 'revisionism' which seeks to diminish the significance of the feminist critique. Adele Barker adopts a rather different approach, pointing out that western literary theory cannot always be applied unproblematically to Russian texts. She argues that it is necessary to be selective in the use of western feminist concepts, and suggests that insights from cultural studies theory may be of more value in interpreting the work of Russian women writers than postmodernist criticism. Barker proposes that critics should pay more attention to works written within, rather than outside, the Soviet system, since many Soviet women writers of the Stalin and post-Stalin periods – notably Berggol'ts, Panova, and Grekova – cannot be assigned unambiguously to the category of either Soviet hack or critical outsider.

The majority of essays in Parts Two and Three are devoted to Russian women writers of the nineteenth and twentieth centuries. Joe Andrew and Irina Kazakova provide general discussions of writing by and about women in the nineteenth century and the Silver Age; Sheelagh Graham offers new insights into the gender implications of Akhmatova's stylistic techniques; while Katharine Hodgson, Julie Curtis, Monika Katz and Marina Ledkovsky explore the life and work of individual twentieth-century women writers who still remain insufficiently studied in both Russia and the West. One writer to receive a detailed reassessment is Ol'ga Berggol'ts, who rose to great prominence during the siege of Leningrad (1941-1944); other essays provide close readings of the work of contemporary women writers, such as the well-known prose writers Iuliia Voznesenskaia and Liudmila Petrushevskaia, and a number of talented, hitherto neglected poets, Ina Bliznetsova, Elena Ignatova, Ol'ga Rozhanskaia and Irina Znamenskaia.

Natasha Kolchevska and Neil Cornwell explore two different kinds of autobiographical writing by Russian women – the memoir of a woman's own life, and the memoir about a famous man. These writings illustrate some of the specific features of women's autobiography, which in Russia, as in other cultures, tends to focus on relationships, rather than on the intellectual and spiritual development of the writer herself.[24] However, as Cornwell demonstrates, some of Pasternak's female memoirists were able to exploit the authority invested in the conventional Russian genre of the biography by the 'great writer's widow' to write about themselves, as well as about their famous dead husband or lover.

Hitherto, the study of the cultural construction of women's identity by Russian men has tended to focus on nineteenth-century literary texts, on Soviet socialist realism and socio-political conditioning by the Soviet regime.[25] Studies of Russian cultural history rarely contain references to conduct manuals for women, although they, as well as literature, have been integral to the history of gender and sexuality in Russian society.[26] Diana Greene engages with this important subject, demonstrating how in nineteenth-century Russia, as in the United States, women's journals and conduct manuals (many of them written by men)[27] attempted to impose on women a narrow conception of domestic ideology which aimed at keeping them in their place. Catherine Schuler explores another unusual facet of women's cultural construction in Russia: the impact that an excessive emphasis on the richness and variety of women's theatrical costumes had on actresses of the Silver Age, turning many of them into prostitutes. As in other countries, fashion in Russia was frequently related to a prescriptive articulation of female roles, constituting yet another form of women's oppression.[28]

Hodgson's study of Berggol'ts analyses the roles of women writers in wartime, demonstrating that in the USSR, as in other cultures, they were conditioned by broader perceptions of gender espoused by their society as a whole.[29] Russian women writers were able to assume an important role during the Second World War, not because of the actual convergence of women's work with that of men, but because of women's special identity in Russian culture as the 'weaker sex' whom men were supposed to protect, as a source of consolation, voice of the nation, and custodians of the values for which the soldiers were allegedly fighting. Although Berggol'ts was sometimes able to subvert the imagery expected of women war poets in order to tell some of the truth about women's suffering, neither she nor other Russian women writers went as far as some western feminists, who have postulated a necessary connection between patriarchy and militarism,[30] or regarded national security as not only 'the protection of the state and its citizens from external foes', but also, and 'perhaps even primarily, the preservation of the existing, male-dominant social order'.[31] Yet Berggol'ts's post-war writings, which highlight the problem of women exhausted by heavy physical labour, illustrate her increasing understanding of the authoritarian and masculinist nature of the Soviet system.[32]

Whereas the feminist critique of Russian literature has previously concentrated on the depiction of women in the works of classical male writers of the nineteenth and early twentieth centuries,[33] or on the stereotypes of women as worker, soldier, political activist, or wife and mother in socialist realist literature of the 1930s to the 1980s,[34] the essays in Part Four will help to redress the balance by focusing on the image of women in twentieth-century literature outside the socialist realist mainstream. They demonstrate that conventional, often misogynistic images of women as Madonna, Witch and Whore inherited from classical models also existed in twentieth-century Russian literature long before the inception of socialist realism, continued in underground and émigré literature during the Soviet period, and still hold sway, in different permutations, in 'alternative prose' of the post-Communist period.

Feminist critics have noted the powerful masculinist and misogynistic current within the modernist movement in other cultures, with its emphasis on masculine sexuality, the experience of war, work, politics and an urban environment.[35] Such an interpretation has rarely been applied to Russian literature of the Silver Age, although it is relevant to many Russian modernists, such as Andreev and Blok. Andreev's 1902 stories 'Bezdna' (The Abyss) and 'V tumane' (In the Fog), for example, despite all the controversy provoked by their outspoken treatment of sexual themes, simply present an updated version of the conventional representation of women as victims or corrupters of young men.[36] Peter Barta's essay contributes to the further study of the Silver Age, exploring the stereotyped portrayal of elderly women as witches in the work of the major Symbolist writer Andrei Bely.

In the section devoted to post-Stalin literature, David Gillespie investigates the allegations of misogyny levelled against 'village prose' published from the 1960s to the 1980s; while the essays on recent fiction by Boris Lanin, Svetlana Carsten and Arch Tait suggest that glasnost served to intensify the innate sexism of many Russian male writers, which was already in evidence in dissident and émigré fiction. Many writers have simply shifted their focus from woman as mother or symbol of virtue to a more explicit portrayal of woman as sexual object, even as victim of rape. Much contemporary Russian literature, like Andreev's stories in the Silver Age, confirms the view that when male discourse 'abjures the erotics of virtue, it tends to replace it by the erotics of rape or captivity'.[37]

There is some disagreement in this book about the idealisation of women in Russian culture. Whereas several male contributors perceive a positive side to the depiction of women as beautiful objects, perfect mothers, symbols of moral purity or Mother Russia, female critics tend to problematise these images, emphasising the 'terrible perfection' to which women characters are supposed to conform, and the fact that such idealised female characters are rarely to be encountered in the works of women writers. Nevertheless, the essays by two Russian contributors, Natal'ia Zhuravkina and Anna Darmodekhina, emphasise the poetic beauty and mythological significance of images of women in the works of two highly individual twentieth-century male writers of different periods, Aleksandr Grin and Chingiz Aitmatov, serving to counter the suggestion by some radical western feminists that male writers' use of female characters to symbolise the 'eternal feminine' or the Motherland must inevitably imply an unremittingly negative view of women.

Notes

1. Both Nikolai Karamzin (1766–1826) and his opponent in the linguistic controversies of the late eighteenth and early nineteenth centuries, Admiral Aleksandr Shishkov, believed that women should act as arbiters of good writing: see N.M. Karamzin, 'Poslanie k zhenshchinam' (1796), in Karamzin, *Polnoe sobranie stikhotvorenii*, ed. Iu.M. Lotman (Moscow-Leningrad: Biblioteka poeta, 1966), pp. 169–79; A. Shishkov, 'Rech' pri otkrytii Besedy liubitelei russkogo slova', in his *Sobranie sochinenii i perevodov*, vol. 4 (St Petersburg, 1825), p. 143.
2. See Richard Stites, *The Women's Liberation Movement in Russia: Feminism, Nihilism and Bolshevism 1860–1930* (Princeton, NJ: Princeton University Press, 1978); G.A.Tishkin, *Zhenskii vopros v Rossii, 50-60-e gody XIX v.* (Leningrad: Izdatel'stvo Leningradskogo universiteta, 1984). Although issues of concern to women had been discussed in literature far earlier, from the end of the eighteenth century, the formulation of the *zhenskii vopros* by social theorists such as Mikhail Mikhailov did not take place until the period of eased censorship inaugurated by the death of Nicholas I in 1855.
3. See, for example, V. Belinskii's article on the work of Elena Gan, 'Povesti Zeneidy R–voi' (1842), in *Polnoe sobranie sochinenii*, 13 vols (Moscow: Akademiia Nauk SSSR, 1953–1959), vol. 7, pp. 648–78; N. Dobroliubov's article on Turgenev's *On the Eve*, 'Kogda zhe nastupit nastoiashchii den'?', *Sovremennik* (March 1860), in Dobroliubov, *Pervoe polnoe sobranie sochinenii* (St Petersburg, 1911), vol. 4, p. 63; and D. Pisarev's article, 'Zhenskie tipy v romanakh i povestiakh Pisemskogo, Turgeneva i Goncharova' (1861), in Pisarev, *Sochineniia v chetyrekh tomakh* (Moscow: Gosudarstvennoe izdatel'stvo khudozhestvennoi literatury, 1955–1956) vol. 1, pp. 231–73.

4. Mary Buckley, *Women and Ideology in the Soviet Union* (New York and London: Harvester Wheatsheaf, 1989), pp. 108-60.
5. Elaine Showalter, 'Towards a feminist poetics', in Mary Jacobus (ed.), *Women Writing and Writing about Women* (London: Croom Helm, 1979), p. 25.
6. Earlier western critical works had been devoted to the portrayal of women characters in the works of individual Russian writers and in Russian and Soviet literature in general, although such studies had not always been presented from an overtly feminist standpoint. See, for example, Xenia Gasiorowska, *Women in Soviet Literature, 1917-1964* (Madison, WI: Wisconsin University Press, 1968); Temira Pachmuss (trans. and ed.), *Women Writers in Russian Modernism* (Urbana, IL: University of Illinois Press, 1978); Carolina de Maegd-Soëp, *The Emancipation of Women in Russian Literature and Society* (Ghent: Ghent State University, 1978).
7. See, for example, Joe Andrew, *Women in Russian Literature, 1780-1863* (Basingstoke: Macmillan, 1988); Barbara Heldt, *Terrible Perfection: Women and Russian Literature* (Bloomington and Indianapolis: Indiana University Press, 1987).
8. Recent general works include Joe Andrew, *Narrative and Desire in Russian Literature, 1822-49: The Feminine and the Masculine* (Basingstoke: Macmillan, 1993); Sona Stephan Hoisington (ed.), *A Plot of her Own: The Female Protagonist in Russian Literature* (Evanston, IL: Northwestern University Press, 1995). On film, see Lynne Attwood, *Red Women on the Silver Screen: Soviet Women and Cinema from the Beginnning to the End of the Communist Era* (London: Pandora, 1993). Book-length studies of individual writers include Carolina de Maegd-Soëp, *Chekhov and Women: Women in the Life and Work of Chekhov* (Columbus, OH: Slavica, 1987); Nina Pelikan Straus, *Dostoevsky and the Woman Question* (New York: St Martin's Press, 1994); Jane Costlow, *Worlds within Worlds: The Novels of Ivan Turgenev* (Princeton, NJ: Princeton University Press, 1990); Stephanie Sandler, *Distant Pleasures: Alexander Pushkin and the Writing of Exile* (Stanford, CA: Stanford University Press, 1989). Rosalind Marsh (ed.), *Gender and Russian Literature: New perspectives* (Cambridge: Cambridge University Press, 1996) contains feminist readings of works by Leonid Andreev, Daniil Kharms and Aleksandr Velichansky.
9. See, for example, Elaine Showalter, 'Feminist Criticism in the Wilderness', in Elaine Showalter (ed.), *The New Feminist Criticism: Essays on Women, Literature, and Theory* (London: Virago, 1985), pp. 243-70. On the three phases of feminist criticism, see Gayle Austin, *Feminist Theories for Dramatic Criticism* (Ann Arbor, MI: University of Michigan Press, 1990), p. 17.
10. For western collections of contemporary women's fiction, see Helena Goscilo (ed.), *Balancing Acts: Contemporary Stories by Russian Women* (Bloomington and Indianapolis: Indiana University Press, 1989); Helena Goscilo (ed.), *Lives in Transit* (Ann Arbor: University of Michigan Press, 1993); Jacqueline Decter (ed.),*Soviet Women Writing* (New York, 1990); 'Women's View', *Glas: New Russian Writing*, no.3, 1992. Recent collections include Catriona Kelly (ed.), *An Anthology of Russian Women's Writing, 1777-1992* (Oxford: Oxford University Press, 1994); Joe Andrew (ed.), *Russian Women's Shorter Fiction: An Anthology 1835-1860* (Oxford: Oxford University Press, 1996).
11. See the four volumes compiled by V. Uchenova, *Dacha na Petergofskoi doroge: Proza russkikh pisatel'nits pervoi poloviny XIX veka* (Moscow: Sovremennik, 1986); *Svidanie: Proza russkikh pisatel'nits 60-80-kh godov XIX veka* (Moscow: Sovremennik, 1987); *Tol'ko chas: Proza russikh pisatel'nits kontsa XIX - nachala XX veka* (Moscow: Sovremennik, 1988); *Tsaritsy muz: russkie poetessy XIX-nachala XX vv* . (Moscow: Sovremennik, 1989).
12. See, for example, L.V. Stepanenko and A.V. Fomenko (eds), *Zhenskaia logika* (Moscow: Sovremennik, 1989); Larisa Vaneeva (ed.), *Ne pomniashchaia zla* (Moscow: Moskovskii rabochii, 1990); Svetlana Vasilenko (ed.), *Novye Amazonki*

(Moscow: Moskovskii rabochii, 1991). In the post-Communist period another collection has appeared, Elena Trofimova (ed.), *Chego khochet zhenshchina* ... (Moscow: Linor, 1993).
13. Marina Ledkovsky, Charlotte Rosenthal and Mary Zirin (eds), *A Dictionary of Russian Women Writers* (Westport, CT: Greenwood Press, 1994); Catriona Kelly, *A History of Russian Women's Writing, 1820–1992* (Oxford: Clarendon Press, 1994); Toby W. Clyman and Diana Greene (eds), *Women Writers in Russian Literature* (Westport, CT: Greenwood Press, 1994); Helena Goscilo (ed.), *Fruits of her Plume: Essays on Contemporary Russian Women's Culture* (Armonk, NY and London: M.E. Sharpe, 1993); Helena Goscilo, *Dehexing Sex: Russian Womanhood during and after Glasnost* (Ann Arbor, MI: University of Michigan Press, 1996).
14. See, for example, Helena Goscilo (ed.), 'Introduction', in *Balancing Acts,* pp. xiii–xxvii; Barbara Heldt, 'Gynoglasnost: writing the feminine', in Mary Buckley (ed.), *Perestroika and Soviet Women* (Cambridge: Cambridge University Press, 1992), pp. 160–75; Goscilo, *Fruits of her Plume.*
15. Recent exceptions are Beth Holmgren, *Women's Works in Stalin's Time: On Lidiia Chukovskaia and Nadezhda Mandelstam* (Bloomington, IN: Indiana University Press, 1993); Sonia I. Ketchian, *The Poetic Craft of Bella Akhmadulina* (University Park, PA, 1993); Diana Burgin, *Sophia Parnok: The Life and Work of Russia's Sappho* (New York: New York University Press, 1994); Helena Goscilo, *Tatyana N. Tolstaya's Fiction* (Armonk, NY: M.E.Sharpe, 1996). This lacuna has also been partially filled by the detailed chapters on individual authors in Catriona Kelly's *History of Russian Women's Writing*; Joe Andrew, *Narrative and Desire*; and by studies of Anna Bunina, Nadezhda Khvoshchinskaia, Lidiia Zinov'eva-Annibal, Anna Mar, 'A.Mire', Anastasiia Verbitskaia and Lidiia Ginzburg in Marsh, *Gender and Russian Literature.*
16. Most previous works have concentrated either on the image of women in Russian fiction, for example Andrew, *Women in Russian Literature*; Andrew, *Narrative and Desire in Russian Literature*; Sigrid McLaughlin, *The Image of Women in Contemporary Soviet Fiction* (Basingstoke: Macmillan, 1989); or on the rediscovery of texts by Russian women (see notes 7, 10–15 above). Barbara Heldt's *Terrible Perfection* ventures into both fields, although it concentrates on the feminist critique of nineteenth-century Russian literature. Collections of conference papers which touch on both these subjects, among other historical themes, are Linda Edmondson (ed.), *Women and Society in Russia and the Soviet Union* (Cambridge: Cambridge University Press, 1992); Marianne Liljeström, Eila Mäntysaari, and Arja Rosenholm (eds), *Gender Restructuring in Russian Studies,* Slavica Tamperensia, no. 2 (Tampere, Finland: University of Tampere, 1993); Jane Costlow, Stephanie Sandler and Judith Vowles (eds), *Sexuality and the Body in Russian Culture* (Stanford, CA: Stanford University Press, 1993); Pamela Chester and Sibelan Forrester (eds), *Engendering Slavic Literatures* (Bloomington: Indiana University Press, 1996). Marsh, *Gender and Russian Literature* discusses both the works of women writers and the image of women in fiction, but lays greater emphasis on the former.
17. On the value of such a comparative approach, see Annette Kolodny, 'Some notes on defining a "feminist literary criticism"', *Critical Inquiry*, vol. 2, no. 1 (1975), p. 78; Myra Jehlen, 'Archimedes and the paradox of feminist criticism', *Signs*, vol. 6, no. 4 (1981), p. 584.
18. On this distinction, see Jacobus, *Women Writing and Writing about Women,* p. 178; Nina Baym, *Woman's Fiction. A Guide to Novels by and about Women in America, 1820-79*, 2nd edition (Urbana and Chicago, IL: University of Illinois Press, 1993), p. xii.
19. Austin, *Feminist Theories for Dramatic Criticism*, p. 17 defines the explosion of all canons as the third phase of feminist criticism.

20. Showalter, 'Feminist criticism in the wilderness'.
21. For a powerful recent expression of this viewpoint, see Larissa Lissyutkina, 'Soviet Women at the Crossroads of Perestroika', in Nanette Funk and Magda Mueller (eds), *Gender Politics and Post-Communism: Reflections from Eastern Europe and the Former Soviet Union* (New York and London: Routledge, 1993), pp. 274–86. For a critique of the 'imperialistic' approach of western feminism in dealing with a very different culture, see Gayatri Chakravorty Spivak, 'French Feminism in an International Frame', *Yale French Studies*, no. 62 (1981), pp. 154–80. For further discussion, see Marsh, *Gender and Russian Literature*, pp. 14–17.
22. See Shirley Ardener's introduction to Edwin Ardener's theory in Shirley Ardener (ed.), *Perceiving Women* (London: Malaby Press, 1977), pp. 3–4, and Edwin Ardener's 'Belief and the problem of women', in ibid., pp. 5-19.
23. On the diversity of current approaches to feminist criticism and theory, see Robyn R. Warhol and Diane Price Herndl (eds), *Feminisms* (New Brunswick, NJ: Rutgers University Press, 1991). It is the existence of such a plurality of views in western feminist thought which is rarely appreciated by Russian women writers.
24. Compare the 'relational' memoirs of Evgeniia Ginzburg and Nadezhda Mandel'shtam with the author-centred autobiographies of Solzhenitsyn, Siniavsky, Shcharansky and other male authors. For recent theoretical discussion of women's autobiographical writing, see the works cited in Natasha Kolchevska's essay, note 5.
25. See the works mentioned in notes 4, 6–8 above, and Lynne Attwood, *The New Soviet Man and Woman: Sex-Role Socialization in the USSR* (Basingstoke: Macmillan, 1990). One recent exception is Helena Goscilo and Beth Holmgren (eds), *Russia, Women, Culture* (Bloomington and Indianapolis: Indiana University Press, 1996).
26. Nancy Armstrong and Leonard Tennenhouse, 'The literature of conduct, the conduct of literature, and the politics of desire: an introduction', in Armstrong and Tennenhouse (eds), *The Ideology of Conduct: Essays on literature and the history of sexuality* (New York and London: Methuen, 1987), p. 1.
27. Baym, *Women's Fiction*, points out that in the United States men wrote many female conduct books, but avoided women's fiction because its challenge to the male-defined status quo made them feel uncomfortable (p. xi).
28. For further discussion, see Anne Hollander, *Seeing through Clothes* (Berkeley: University of California Press, 1978); Eugene M. Waith, 'Heywood's Women Worthies', in Norman T. Burns and Christopher J. Reagan (eds), *Concepts of the Hero in the Middle Ages and the Renaissance* (Albany: State University of New York, 1975), pp. 234, 236; Susan Brownmiller, *Femininity* (New York: Fawcett Columbine, 1984), pp. 79–102. Lindsey Hughes, in her paper 'From Kaftans to Corsets: Petrine Dress Code' (Guildford, June 1996), has shown how Peter the Great's attempt to bring women out of the seclusion of the *terem* by making them wear low-cut European-style dresses did not appeal to all Russian women (but, of course, Peter's dress reforms affected both sexes equally).
29. See, for example, Sharon Macdonald, Pat Holden and Shirley Ardener (eds), *Images of Women in Peace and War: Cross-cultural and Historical Perspectives* (Basingstoke: Macmillan, 1987).
30. Virginia Woolf, *Three Guineas* (Harmondsworth: Penguin, 1977).
31. Cynthia Enloe, *Does Khaki Become You? The Militarization of Women's Lives* (London: Pluto Press, 1983), p. 11.
32. Katharine Hodgson, 'Kitezh and the Commune: Recurrent Themes in the Work of Ol'ga Berggol'ts', *Slavonic and East European Review*, vol. 74, no. 1 (January 1996), pp. 1–18.
33. Exceptions include the critique of Pasternak's *Doctor Zhivago* and Rasputin's *Zhivi i pomni* (1975) in Heldt, *Terrible Perfection*, pp. 146–50; the critique of the stereo-

typed images of women in Solzhenitsyn's *First Circle* in Rosalind Wells, 'The Definitive Solzhenitsyn?', *Irish Slavonic Studies,* no. 1 (1980), p. 118; McLaughlin, *The Image of Women,* which focuses on fiction of the 1980s by both male and female authors. Andrew, *Narrative and Desire* deals with Odoevsky and Herzen; Tatyana Mamonova, *Russian Women's Studies: Essays on Sexism in Soviet Culture* (Oxford: Pergamon, 1989) considers Gor'ky, Kuz'min and Bunin.

34. Gasiorowska, *Women in Soviet Literature 1917-1964*; Vera Sandomirsky Dunham, 'The Strong-Woman Motif', in Cyril E. Black (ed.), *The Transformation of Russian Society* (Cambridge, MA: Harvard University Press, 1960), pp. 459-83; Rosalind Marsh, *Soviet Fiction since Stalin: Science, Politics and Literature* (London and Sydney: Croom Helm, 1986), pp. 110-15; Mary Seton-Watson, 'Myth and Reality in Recent Soviet Fiction', *Coexistence. An International Journal,* vol. 19 (1982), pp. 213-19.

35. Janet Wolff, *Feminine Sentences* (Oxford: Polity, 1991), pp. 38-40, 51-66. However, Julia Kristeva, *Revolution in Poetic Language* (New York: Columbia University Press, 1984) has established a connection between 'the feminine' and the crisis which produced the language of modernism, which may help to interpret the explosion of Russian women's poetry and Symbolist drama in the Silver Age.

36. I am indebted to Peter Ulf Møller, 'Leonid Andreev on Sexual Morality', conference paper (University of Birmingham, July 1996).

37. Naomi Segal, 'Sexual politics and the avant-garde: from Apollinaire to Woolf', in Edward Timms and Peter Collier (eds), *Visions and Blueprints: Avant-garde Culture and Radical Politics in Early Twentieth-century Europe* (Manchester: Manchester University Press, 1988), p. 235. On pornography in contemporary Russia, see Goscilo, *Dehexing Sex,* pp. 135-70.

Part One

THEORETICAL PERSPECTIVES

Chapter 1

AN IMAGE OF THEIR OWN?: FEMINISM, REVISIONISM AND RUSSIAN CULTURE

Rosalind Marsh

The aim of this chapter is to reconsider the representation of women in Russian literature, in order to focus on key issues in the current debate, enter into dialogue with previous scholars, and contribute to an ongoing discussion. While sharing many of the assumptions and interpretations elaborated more fully in previous feminist critiques of Russian literature, notably those by Joe Andrew and Barbara Heldt, I will, nevertheless, point to some exaggerations or debatable conclusions in their work. However, this analysis will primarily take issue with one recent book, Sona Stephan Hoisington's *A Plot of her Own* (1995), which claims to be a 'revisionist' study of female characters in Russian fiction, and especially with one essay in that collection, Gary Rosenshield's, 'Afterword' (Hoisington: 114–27). One of the most controversial aspects of Hoisington's book is that it appears somewhat premature to engage in a 'revisionist' approach to the image of women in Russian literature when the feminist critique is still in a relatively early stage in the West, and is practised so little within Russia itself. Such revisionism overlooks or underestimates a number of strikingly phallocentric or misogynistic features in many texts currently belonging to the Russian literary and critical canon, and leaves the feminist critique itself half-finished, not open to discussion or change.

This chapter makes no claim to be comprehensive, and does not wish to be reductive in its brief survey of two hundred years of Russian literature. It is an attempt to counter a fully fledged revisionism in the study of gender and Russian culture, not by picking easy targets – dwelling on obviously stereotyped representations of women – but by discussing some of the more complex feminine images in Russian literature. It will begin by exploring some of the principal features of the masculinist literary tradition, then explain why it is still vital to pursue the feminist critique of Russian literature.

How Central is the Image of Woman?

The subtitle of Hoisington's book is 'The Female Protagonist in Russian Literature'. The use of the term 'protagonist' ('main hero'), while avoiding the potentially pejorative connotations of the term 'heroine',[1] is, however, misleading, since it ignores the fact that the image of woman is not central to the majority of Russian writers. For the most part, except in some texts by women writers, the main female character in a work of Russian literature is defined almost solely through her relations to men. In Russian culture, as in other cultures, as Virginia Woolf suggested, 'women have served all these centuries as looking-glasses possessing the magic and dubious power of reflecting the figure of man at twice his natural size'.[2]

The role of many female characters in male-authored Russian literature is to act as the Other, as 'touchstone for the man',[3] or 'noncognating phenomenon for the hero to test himself against as he would against hurricane or high mountain or disease'.[4] This was generally true in Russian literature from the early nineteenth century to the 1917 Revolution, whether the text featured the Byronic hero of Pushkin's *Evgenii Onegin* (*Eugene Onegin*, 1833) and Lermontov's *Geroi nashego vremeni* (*A Hero of our Time*, 1840), the 'superfluous men' of Turgenev, Goncharov and Ostrovsky, or the 'underground men' of Dostoevsky and his successors Andreev, Sologub and Garshin.[5] This phenomenon finds its most widespread expression in the novels of Turgenev, who is usually regarded as one of the nineteenth-century Russian writers most sympathetic to the 'woman question'. Even Anna Odintsova in *Ottsy i deti* (*Fathers and Sons*, 1862), one of Turgenev's most interesting female characters, who fully deserves her recent reassessment by Jane Costlow,[6] is not as important to the novel as the male protagonist, Bazarov – indeed, she represents just one phase of the hero's development. Similarly, even in the major novels of Dostoevsky, whose technique of polyphony enables women's individual voices to be heard more clearly than in many other masculine texts, the principal function of such striking 'new women' as Nastas'ia Filippovna and Aglaia in *Idiot* (*The Idiot*, 1868) and Katerina Ivanovna in *Brat'ia Karamazovy* (*The Brothers Karamazov*, 1880) is to illuminate or influence the consciousness of a more important male character.[7] Although there are some sections of Russian novels where a female character does play a significant role, or is sometimes allowed to move the plot forward (as in Turgenev's *Pervaia liubov'* [*First Love*, 1860], Dostoevsky's *The Idiot* [Part 1: Chapter 16], or Tolstoy's *Anna Karenina* [1875–1877, Part 4: Chapter 17]),[8] Rachel Brownstein's comment still applies: 'perhaps a suggestion of parody hangs over the head of every heroine, as woman's traditional powerlessness and unremarkable, predictably generic nature is set up against the importance, clarity and transcendent meaning of a central character in a literary work.'[9]

Another misleading assumption is that if a female character can be interpreted as embodying the author's main ideas or ideals, she necessarily becomes the central focus of the text. Such an interpretation overlooks the essentialist or misogynistic features which may also characterise such female images, or the stereotypical depiction of other minor female characters in the same texts. Hoisington, in her study of Zamiatin's *My* (*We*, 1924), for example, appears to assume that if I-330, rather than D-503, can be presented as the main character of the novel (a highly debatable issue, since the entire narrative is filtered through D-503's consciousness), the whole work should be regarded as female-centred. Although I-330 undoubtedly expresses many of Zamiatin's own most cherished ideas, such an interpretation ignores Zamiatin's stereotyped representation of I-330 as Eve, the temptress, the serpent in the Garden of Eden, the enigmatic woman whose eyebrows form an 'x', the incarnation of nature and sensual delight. The character of I-330 is thus firmly rooted in the age-old masculine tradition of the *femme fatale,* exemplified by Turgenev's predatory villainesses, such as Mar'ia Polozova in *Veshnie vody* (*The Torrents of Spring*, 1872), and Dostoevsky's 'demonic women'. Moreover, for all her strength and intellectual superiority, I-330 eventually falls into the conventional category of female victim, and her death – even if it could be construed as heroic – is described in orgasmic terms ('her head fell back, her half-closed eyes, her clenched lips – reminded me of something' [Entry 40]); while the principal significance of the female survivor, O-90, is that she is about to fulfil her traditional female role of giving birth.[10]

Another interesting female character afforded detailed analysis in Hoisington's book, Sonia in Chekhov's *Diadia Vania* (*Uncle Vania,* 1899), may well be the bearer of the dramatist's *moral* values, yet it is the semi-autobiographical Astrov who embodies the author's *intel-*

lectual values. Moreover, although *Uncle Vania* contains no single protagonist, Sonia is not the central character from a dramatic point of view – it is Vania's tribulations which create the main dramatic tension in the play. Gary Saul Morson's interpretation of Sonia's significance in the play, while possessing considerable validity, does nothing to undermine the conventional stereotype of the woman as moral paragon in male-authored Russian literature, or to counteract the clichéd portrayals of other women in the same play. Whereas Sonia (whose full name, Sof'ia, refers to Sophia, or divine wisdom) is one of the few important young female characters in male-authored Russian texts who is explicitly plain, albeit spiritually beautiful, she is accompanied by other, more stereotyped images: Elena, the incarnation of physical beauty, whose name echoes the age-old archetype of female beauty, Helen of Troy, and Uncle Vania's mother Mariia Vasil'evna, a caricature of the 'emancipated woman', who is obsessed by her brochures on the 'woman question'.

Although, as Amy Mandelker contends, Anna Karenina can certainly be interpreted as the 'tragic heroine' of the novel that bears her name,[11] and is arguably as important, if not more, to the plot than Tolstoy's semi-autobiographical male protagonist Levin, this does not alter the fact that Anna still remains a female character in a fundamentally patriarchal narrative. Anna is presented in a highly attractive fashion in Part One, where her charm at times appears to enchant the author himself, outweighing the burden of his moral disapproval. Yet even in Part One her beauty is presented as 'strange, diabolical and enchanting' (Chapter 23), and her initial love-making with Vronsky, which is compared to a murder, provokes in her a mixture of 'shame, rapture and horror' (Chapter 11). In Part Two Anna is obliged to bear the full weight of the author's opprobrium, when she begins to use drugs and contraceptives, and is not permitted to love her daughter by Vronsky as much as her son by Karenin, or even to contemplate the possibility of divorce.[12] Anna, like all Tolstoy's female characters, is not allowed to be both a sexual being and a mother, 'la mère qui jouit', in the words of Julia Kristeva.[13] Thus, even if Tolstoy's depiction of Anna Karenina has correctly been regarded as one of the most successful portraits of a female character in nineteenth-century Russian literature, she too can be interpreted as a combination of 'several conflicting stereotypes' rather than a realistic, well-rounded depiction of a woman.[14] Female characters in Tolstoy's works are generally judged by the author according to whether they fulfil or betray his own definition of the feminine at any given period of his personal artistic and spiritual development.

There are few works of classical Russian literature which bear titles referring to the female protagonist: notable exceptions include

Anna Karenina, Dostoevsky's unfinished *Netochka Nezvanova* (1849), Vladimir Odoevsky's *Kniazhna Mimi (Princess Mimi,* 1834) and *Kniazhna Zizi (Princess Zizi,* 1836/1839), and the stories 'Bela' and 'Kniazhna Meri' ('Princess Mary') in Lermontov's *Hero of Our Time* (although these women are the objects of Pechorin's seduction rather than the subjects of their own stories, and it is significant that the general title of this novel refers to the male protagonist).[15] Sometimes, titles of male-authored Russian texts define a woman in relation to men, as in the case of Karamzin's *Bednaia Liza (Poor Liza,* 1792), Pushkin's *Kapitanskaia dochka (The Captain's Daughter,* 1833–1836), Dostoevsky's 'Krotkaia' ('The Meek One', 1876), or Gor'ky's *Mat'* *(Mother,* 1906).

Even fewer male-authored texts in Russia are actually presented, or partially presented, through a woman's consciousness. Exceptions include Dostoevsky's *Netochka Nezvanova,* whose somewhat dubious claims to being a female-authored text have rightly been called into question due to Dostoevsky's focus on paternal incest and child abuse;[16] Anna Karenina's final monologue during her last journey to her suicide; and Viktor Erofeev's *Russkaia krasavitsa (Russian Beauty,* 1990), an extended example of female*skaz* allegedly presented from the point of view of a nymphomaniac, which actually panders to male desire and voyeurism. Thus, in the exceptional cases when female characters in male-authored Russian literature are allowed to tell their own stories, women still emerge largely as victims of male use and abuse, rather than as independent, autonomous human beings.

A related aspect of masculine literary texts in Russia is that, whereas the psychology of the male protagonist is frequently portrayed with great detail and complexity, female characters are generally depicted from the outside, seldom described in detail, and largely presented through male eyes. As Heldt and Andrew have demonstrated, the Russian heroine is often described in clichés – as an animal (the eyes of Lermontov's Bela resemble those of a horse or a gazelle), a vulnerable child (the heroine is often 'pale', 'blushing', or has 'little feet'), an angel or a demon.

There are few female *Bildungsromane* by nineteenth-century Russian male writers.[17] Male writers are rarely interested in the intellectual development of their female characters: a woman's love of reading is usually emphasised in male-authored texts only in so far as it helps to form her attitudes to men and love, as in the case of Tat'iana in Pushkin's *Evgenii Onegin,* who has been influenced by French and English Sentimentalism and Romanticism (Chapter 2: XXIX; Chapter 3: IX-X; Chapter 4, XXIV).[18] Success in male terms is generally regarded as failure for women in male-authored Russian literature, reflecting the fact that the woman intellectual or professional was not perceived as an ideal to aspire to in prerevolutionary Russian culture. This is dramatised in Dostoevsky's *Brothers Karamazov* by the scene in which the sexually active, traditionally 'feminine' Grushen'ka gets the better of the intellectual, Katerina Ivanovna (Part 3: Chapter 10). On the other hand, there are numerous female *Bildungsromane* by Russian women writers, such as Elena Gan's *Naprasnyi dar* (A Futile Gift, 1842), Nadezhda Khvoshchinskaia's *Pansionerka* (The Boarding-School Girl, 1861), and many of Anastasiia Verbitskaia's early novels, for example *Pervye lastochki* (First Signs, 1900), *Osvobodilas'!* (She Was Liberated!, 1898) and *Istoriia odnoi zhizni* (Story of a Life, 1903).[19] Women writers frequently suggest in memoirs and fiction that reading played a major part in developing their minds;[20] and it is often mothers who bestow the gift of reading and intellect on their daughters, as in Gan's *Ideal* (*The Ideal*, 1837) and *Sud sveta* (*Society's Judgement*, 1840). In Russia, as in nineteenth-century American literature, 'Only a woman, it seems, can write realistically about the awakening of woman to her own identity'.[21]

If male authors do pay some attention to the intellectual development of their principal female character, as in the case of such Turgenevan heroines as Natal'ia in *Rudin* (1856) and Elena in *Nakanune* (*On the Eve*, 1860), they generally describe her consciousness being raised by a male character; her only heroic act is to choose a husband for herself (that is, like Jane Austen's heroines, to operate as freely as possible within the bounds of the current patriarchal system). However, the reality of nineteenth-century Russia was that some women writers were leading more adventurous lives than the passive heroines usually depicted in masculine literature, and that some portrayed independent women who read, travelled and strove to obtain an education: prominent examples are the memoirs of Ekaterina Dashkova (written in French in 1804–1805) and Nadezhda Durova (*Kavalerist-devitsa* [*The Cavalry Maiden*, 1836]), and the lives of women writers and artists depicted by Gan, Pavlova and Nadezhda Khvoshchinskaia.

Nevertheless, one question posed by much fiction by Russian women, as by women's writing in other cultures, is: why do Russian women writers so rarely depict women as interesting and successful as they are themselves?[22] Some male writers, notably Turgenev and Chernyshevsky, present more positive images of women than their female contemporaries – even if men tend to stress women's emotional needs, rather than their intellectual achievements. This may be partly due to the 'anxiety of authorship'[23] experienced by many Russian women writers, who have been made to feel that it is 'presumptuous' to take up the pen,[24] and that intellectual women, especially women writers, are nothing but a freak, a 'crocodile in flannel or a dancing monkey' in Russian society.[25] Another possibility is that women writers have a more realistic view of the actual opportunities for most women in Russian society, and are sceptical of utopian solutions. Or perhaps Russian women writers, obliged to regard themselves as totally exceptional individuals, have been influenced by radical critics stressing the socio-political significance of literature, and prefer to write about ordinary female characters who can be interpreted as more representative of women in Russia as a whole, similar to the 'little man' in Russian masculine literature? This may well have been true of women populist, realist and feminist writers of the late nineteenth century, and of women writers, both official and unofficial, in the Soviet period. Such considerations may, for example, have prompted Lidiia Chukovskaia to write *Sof'ia Petrovna* (1937), whose female protagonist has come to embody the general plight of Russian women in the 1930s. An intellectual heroine, such as the narrator of Chukovskaia's second novel *Spusk pod vodu* (*Going Under*, 1949) could not be seen as so representative of Soviet women as a whole. Since it is mainly in lyric poetry and autobiography that Russian women write directly from their own experience, about the rich complexity of an exceptional woman's life, these have generally been regarded as the most important and successful literary genres for Russian women.[26]

Woman as Ideal and Sign

It is generally agreed that the most widespread images in nineteenth-century Russian literature are those of the morally strong woman who acts as mentor or Muse to the weak 'superfluous man'. Owing to the prevalence of the 'strong-woman motif' in Russian literature,[27] many Russian critics insist that the Russian novelistic tradition in no way denigrates women, but, on the contrary, places them on a pedestal. Likewise, Rosenshield has argued that the main problem for a feminist deconstruction of Russian literature is that women characters are so often held up as models to inspire both men and women to social action.[28] However, an entirely positive view of the idealisation of women characters by Russian male writers overlooks the fact that idealisation may be merely the other side of the coin of the denigration of women: 'Earth Mother, Muse, love goddess, siren, nymph, angelic maiden, in one form or another, all the feminine qualities have been elevated to the highest cultural status...Mythologising woman has been a standard method of gilding her cage'.[29] Both idealisation and denigration are forms of sexism, limiting the roles women are allowed to play and ignoring their reality as unique individuals. The idealised woman in male-authored Russian literature emerges not as a real woman, but as a fictional construct, a sign, a projection of male fantasy and desire.[30]

In Russia the binary oppositions related to gender which feminist critics have perceived as universal in other cultures are also ubiquitous. Much of Russian literature reflects the dualistic assumptions of patriarchal ideology – the perception of woman as object, 'immanence', 'nature', passivity, or death, as opposed to man as subject, 'transcendence', 'culture', activity and life.[31] As Siniavsky has ironically pointed out, in nineteenth-century Russian literature 'woman is a sort of vague, pure and lovely thing. There's no need for her to be more concrete and more defined; it is enough for her (does one ask much of women?) to be pure and lovely to save man'.[32]

Moreover, as Barbara Heldt has shown, virtuous female characters are often used by nineteenth-century male authors to highlight a debate about socio-political issues, rather than sexual relations, to exemplify 'a standard not met by Russian society as a whole'.[33] The heroine frequently becomes a 'non-cognating' symbol of the Russian soul: Pushkin's Tat'iana, for example, is 'Russian in her soul, without knowing why herself' (Chapter 5: IV), and Turgenev says of Liza in *Grazhdanskoe gnezdo* (*Nest of the Gentry*, 1859): 'It would never have occurred to Liza that she was a patriot; but she found Russian people to her liking; the Russian way of thinking delighted her' (Chapter 34).

Since, according to some commentators, women are more liable to be influenced by literary images than male readers,[34] it is probable that ordinary Russian women have felt oppressed by the need to live up to 'heroinic'[35] stereotypes of women as virtuous paragons or self-sacrificing mothers. This cannot, however, be proved conclusively, since Russian women, like women in other cultures, have often found it difficult to express their own identity and needs.[36] Some women writers have attempted to circumvent this problem by providing their own new, more empowering interpretations of classic female images.[37]

The representation of women in male-authored Russian literature depends on images in other texts as much as on the relationship of authors with the outside world. Many twentieth-century writers portray new incarnations of the epic Russian heroines of Pushkin or Tolstoy (such as Tonia and Lara in Pasternak's *Doktor Zhivago* [*Doctor Zhivago*, 1957]),[38] or of Dostoevsky's female characters (such as Zamiatin's I-330). Such influences continue in contemporary masculine literature: in Vladimir Kunin's *Interdevochka* (*Hard Currency Prostitute*, 1988), the female protagonist Tania combines the age-old stereotypes of the 'prostitute with the heart of gold' and the 'woman as nurse', harking back to Dostoevsky, or even to Karamzin's *Poor Liza*.[39]

Contributors to Hoisington's book correctly note that female characters often bear alternative symbolic meanings in masculine literature, in addition to their obvious role in the hero's love plot. This does not, however, necessarily invalidate a feminist critique of such images. For example, even if the death of Karamzin's 'poor Liza' was primarily intended to evoke admiration for the narrator's aesthetic sensitivity rather than pity for the victimisation of the female peasantry,[40] this in no way contradicts a feminist analysis of the conventional elements in Karamzin's portrait of Liza,[41] or a recognition that her seducer Erast is a more fully developed character.[42] Caryl Emerson's complex interpretation of Pushkin's Tat'iana as a 'synaesthetic Muse',[43] whether or not it possesses some validity, does not alter the fact that Tat'iana has been regarded by generations of Russian men, and women too, as a symbol of self-sacrificing, morally pure Russian womanhood.[44]

As in other cultures, male writers in nineteenth-century Russia often chose to portray two contrasting types of female characters, who can be loosely interpreted in terms of the age-old opposition of Madonna and Whore, or as Russian variants of the stereotypical 'Angel in the House'[45] and 'Madwoman in the Attic'[46] depicted in nineteenth-century English literature. Sometimes these two polarised types feature in the same novel: Turgenev's *Nest of the Gentry*, for example, contrasts the pure, spiritual Liza with the loud, sexually voracious Varvara (whose name evokes the barbarity of her nature); many of Dostoevsky's heroines fall into the opposing categories of the 'meek woman' and the 'proud woman', or the respectable virgin and the sexually active woman; and in Tolstoy's *Voina i mir* (*War and Peace*, 1865–1869) Hélène is the incarnation of physical beauty, while Princess Mar'ia is the incarnation of spiritual beauty. This tradition persisted in the twentieth century: Olesha's *Zavist'* (*Envy*, 1927) is reminiscent of Gogol' in its polarised portraits of the youthful, idealised Valia and the repulsive, man-devouring, yet masochistic middle-aged widow Anichka; and Solzhenitsyn's *Rakovyi korpus* (*Cancer Ward*, 1968) follows Tolstoyan models in depicting Vega and Zoia as contrasting embodiments of spiritual and physical love.

The dual, or multiple, roles which female characters are asked to play in male-authored texts persist in twentieth-century Russian literature.[47] The portrait of Lara in Pasternak's *Doctor Zhivago* possesses many symbolic resonances – as Mary Magdalen, the Muse, and the spirit of Russia – but this does not preclude a feminist critique of Yury's passive observation of Lara as a domestic paragon at the ironing board (Chapter 13: Part 15), or of his praise of her ability to find starch during the Civil War while he writes poetry (Chapter 14: Part 8).[48] A wide reading of Russian literature would suggest that most female characters in male-authored texts are not *only* women – they are both more and less than women.

Woman as Mystery and Victim

As in other cultures, Russian male writers often perceive woman as an enigma which man must unravel in the course of a quest or a seduction, or as 'the unutterable which man must forever continue to try to utter'.[49] In Turgenev's *First Love*, for example, the young narrator attempts to fathom the mystery of Zinaida's character,[50] and when the shocking 'solution' (that she is his father's mistress) is ultimately disclosed, there is nothing more for Zinaida to do in the masculine text except die. An even more extreme incarnation of the notion of woman as mysterious, emotional, dangerously sexual Other is the 'demonic woman', who figures in many of Dostoevsky's novels as the object of male desire, curiosity and hostility:[51] for example, Polina in *Igrok* (*The Gambler*, 1867), who ultimately succumbs to 'temporary madness', and Nastas'ia Fillipovna in *The Idiot*, who invites her own death. Significantly, such a limited view of woman as a natural, instinctive creature, an unfathomable enigma, or a passionate hysteric[52] is rarely found in female-authored Russian literature.

Another related, patriarchal feature of Russian literature, as of the literature of other countries, is that women are often presented as silent, passive or suicidal victims of male abuse.[53] Karamzin's *Poor Liza*, which contains one of the first examples of such a figure, provides an endorsement of the view that: 'Sentimentalism ... asserts that the values a society's activity denies are precisely the ones it cherishes.'[54] Karamzin's story, which emphasises the value of a tale told by a male narrator to other men about his compassion for the plight of a gullible peasant girl, was produced in a society which in reality pursued 'masculine' goals involving damage to women from the peasantry and other classes, and generally ignored such 'feminine' emotions as compassion altogether.

In some later masculine fiction, such as Pushkin's *Kavkazskii plennik* (*Prisoner of the Caucasus*, 1822), Ostrovsky's *Groza* (*The Storm*, 1860), and Tolstoy's *Anna Karenina*, the danger posed by a woman's awakening to her own sexuality and the challenge she issues to the prevailing patriarchal order seemingly has to be punished by suicide or early death.[55] Such an emphasis on female suicide in male-authored literature is curious, in view of the statistics which suggest that in the nineteenth century, in Britain at least, men were actually more likely to commit suicide than women.[56] Some male writers express sympathy for their victimised female characters, emphasising the problems which a patriarchal society creates for women, and appearing to sanction their rebellion against masculine tyranny. However, the fact that such an attractive character as Katerina in Ostrovsky's *The Storm* is obliged to commit suicide because there is no place for her in Russian society appears to confirm the feminist view that woman's language lies mute in patriarchy, and that death may be her only form of expression.

In Russian literature, as in other cultures, women are frequently associated with closed spaces, or death.[57] As Hélène Cixous has perceptively commented: '[Men] need femininity to be associated with death: it's the jitters that give them a hard-on! for themselves!'.[58] At the end of Turgenev's *First Love*, the illusory nature of feminine power is highlighted by the narrator's final imaginary vision of Zinaida, inert in her coffin; while in the conclusion of Turgenev's *On the Eve*, the formerly powerful, independent Elena writes after her husband's death: 'Yesterday Dmitry died. Everything is finished for me', and acknowledges her own death wish: 'I sought happiness – and perhaps I will find death' (Chapter 35). Perhaps the most extreme examples of this association of women with death are found in Dostoevsky's 'The Meek One' and *The Idiot*, in which men discuss women (and ultimately fail to understand them) while sitting by their dead bodies.

Nina Auerbach has argued that the stereotyped representations in Victorian literature of women as victim and queen, domestic angel and domestic outcast, old maid and fallen woman can be seen as myths of transfiguration that glorified the women they seemed to suppress. Similarly, some critics of Russian literature claim that woman's very victimisation, or her dominant role in the love plot of nineteenth-century literature, give her a certain mythical status and power.[59] This view, however, overlooks several factors: firstly, some of the female characters in the texts which Auerbach uses to prove her point, such as Charlotte Brontë's *Villette* (1853), Rider Haggard's *She* (1887) and George du Maurier's *Trilby* (1896), do demonstrate far more female talent and empowerment than such Russian texts as *Poor Liza*, 'Bela', or Tolstoy's *Family Happiness* (1859); secondly, nineteenth-century Britain differed from Russia, because a powerful Queen-Empress was on the throne; and thirdly, Auerbach's argument is somewhat tortuous, since the 'myth of women' in nineteenth-century literature, even if it may sometimes bestow value and power upon women, is nevertheless largely a patriarchal myth. Much of Russian literature, like other masculine literary traditions, is concerned with the question 'What is femininity – for men?'.[60]

In the words of Laura Mulvey, 'Sadism demands a story, depends on making something happen, forcing a change in another person, a battle of will and strength, victory/defeat, all occurring in a linear time with a beginning and an end'.[61] The gender implications inherent in this view of narrative are evident in many works of Russian literature, in which male writers cannot resist victimising their most attractive female characters. Tolstoy, for example, allows the beautiful temptress Hélène in *War and Peace* to die after an abortion, and reduces the enchanting Natasha Rostova first to being seduced by the cad Anatoly Kuragin, then in the 'Epilogue' to becoming a plump, drab domestic 'female animal' (*samka*);[62] he kills Anna Karenina, and turns Katia in *Voskresenie* (*Resurrection*, 1899) into a 'fallen woman'. Similarly, even an attempted feminist reading of Dostoevsky cannot avoid the problem that in his works many female characters are humiliated, beaten, raped, driven to suicide, or murdered by men. Although Rosenshield is quite correct in emphasising that Dostoevsky presents the victimisation of women as a problem for men, as well as women,[63] his argument could be taken further: Dostoevsky's main interest appears to be in masculine psychology rather than in the feelings of the female victim. In his depictions of rape, particularly of a young girl, Dostoevsky does not present a detailed evocation of its effect on the victim; he is more concerned with exploring its impact on the rapist or potential rapist, such as Svidrigailov in *Prestuplenie i nakazanie* (*Crime and Punishment*, 1866) and Stavrogin in *Besy* (*The Devils*, 1872).

Dostoevsky's female suicides are generally depicted as victims rather than the attempted authors of their own fate, unlike such male intellectual suicides as Kirillov in *The Devils*. Although in reality Dostoevsky was fascinated by the triumphant and cynical suicide of the 'emancipated' Liza Herzen,[64] which he analysed in his *Dnevnik pisatelia* (*Diary of a Writer*) for 1876,[65] in his story 'The Meek One' he preferred to use a very different real-life story, the 'meek and humble' suicide of Maia Borisova, who jumped from a roof holding an icon of the mother of God.[66] It is surely significant that in Dostoevsky's fiction it is only men who are allowed to commit suicide for the sake of an idea.

The Old Woman and the Witch

Another patriarchal feature of Russian literature is that most of the sympathetic female characters in Russian novels are young – as Joe Andrew and Peter Barta demonstrate below, the middle-aged and elderly woman are generally presented in grotesque, caricatured terms. One classic image is Pushkin's depiction in *Pikovaia dama* (*The Queen of Spades*, 1833) of Hermann's voyeuristic scrutiny of the undressing of the old countess, in which disgust predominates. Pushkin's detailed portrayal of 'the revolting secrets of [the Countess's] toilette' (Chapter 3) leaves little room for compassion, and Pushkin provides no corresponding physical descriptions of old men, revolting or otherwise: Count Saint-Germain simply emerges as a wise, powerful custodian of a profound mystery. An even more repulsive image of an old woman is Dostoevsky's portrayal in *Crime and Punishment* of the elderly pawnbroker Alena, whom Raskol'nikov dismisses as 'vermin'. As Andrew's chapter in this volume demonstrates, nineteenth-century Russian women writers such as Elena Gan and Mar'ia Zhukova often implicitly contest such stereotypes, presenting their own more realistic or more benevolent portraits of elderly women.

As Barta suggests, the portrayal of older women in Russian literature is frequently misogynistic, related to the image of the witch in Russian and European folklore.[67] However, the older woman, or the mother, is a profoundly ambivalent figure in Russian culture.[68] The other side of the coin, as David Gillespie shows, is the idealisation of the wise old woman in some late twentieth-century literature, notably Matrena in Solzhenitsyn's 'Matrenin dvor' ('Matrena's Home', 1963) and Dar'ia in Rasputin's *Proshchanie s Materoi* (*Farewell to Matera*, 1976). Such portraits of elderly women, whose traditional moral values issue a challenge to Soviet ideology and the destructive aspects of modern technology, may be related to more beneficent images of the witch (Baba-Iaga) in Russian folklore, as well as to iconic views of motherhood in Soviet culture.

If a young witch is portrayed in literature, she is allowed to be sexy and forgiving, as in Bulgakov's *Master i Margarita* (*The Master and Margarita*), written from 1928 to 1940, and Konstantin Fedin's *Goroda i gody* (*Cities and Years*, 1924). However, although Bulgakov's Margarita can correctly be viewed as 'the bearer of energy and compassion in the novel' and 'the compositional element whose activity precipitates the final harmony',[69] it should not be forgotten that in her supernatural state Margarita still acts only as the handmaid of the demonic Woland, the source of her power, just as in her former life she played the role of Muse and handmaid to the Master whose manuscripts she preserved, rather than being an author in her own right. Her first action when she came to visit the writer was to cook a meal for him; subsequently, while he wrote, she read, or wiped 'the hundreds of dusty spines'; then, 'sensing fame, she drove him on and started to call him "the master"'; she lived vicariously through him, stating that 'the novel was her life' (Part 1: Chapter 13).[70]

The Beautiful Woman, the Plain Woman and the Unmarried Woman

Male writers in Russia, as in other cultures, have a tendency to depict women who are not only young, but also beautiful. These include the idealistic virgins and pure-hearted prostitutes of nineteenth-century literature; the 'beautiful lady' of the Symbolist period; attractive workers, soldiers and mothers in the works of Soviet socialist realism; and insatiably sexy, albeit independent young women in dissident, émigré or post-perestroika literature.[71] The depiction of woman as beautiful object is so widespread in male-authored Russian literature that the distinction between such images as the ethereal, yet erotic portrayal of Valia, the unattainable ideal woman, by Kavalerov, the narrator in Olesha's *Envy*, and Nabokov's depiction of the 'pubescent sweetheart' Lolita (Chapter 2: Section 2) with her 'apricot-coloured limbs' (Chapter 2: Section 20), pictured at the swimming pool and tennis court through the eyes of her paedophiliac stepfather Humbert Humbert, is only a difference of degree.

Only rarely, in male-authored literature of the twentieth century, do physically unattractive young or middle-aged women briefly constitute the focus of authorial attention, and when they do, as Boris Lanin and Svetlana Carsten demonstrate, Russian writers usually treat them with hostility, disapproval or pity: Sima and Muza in Solzhenitsyn's *V kruge pervom* (*The First Circle*, 1968), for example, are vulnerable objects of pity. By contrast, some Russian women writers select plain young women as their heroines: Mariia in Zhukova's story 'Medal'on' ('The Locket', 1837) is one prominent example. In the 1860s, a number of Russian women writers, influenced by Charlotte Brontë's *Jane Eyre* (translated into Russian in 1849), chose to depict a poor, plain, but independent woman striving to make a living through her work.[72] Subsequently, in some underground and post-glasnost writings, women writers began to deconstruct the stereotyped image of the beautiful woman in Russian culture. In 1980, the dissident feminist Tat'iana Mamonova, in her *samizdat* journal *Woman and Russia*, emphasised the impossible demands placed on the modern Soviet woman: 'Ideally, a woman is expected to have children, be an outstanding worker, take responsibility for the home, and, despite everything, still be beautiful'.[73] In 1985, Tat'iana Tolstaia, in her story 'Okhota na mamonta' ('Hunting the Woolly Mammoth'), subverted the notion of women using their attractiveness to catch a man.[74]

Russian male authors frequently regard single or childless women as figures of fun or objects of pity; it is as true in Russian literature, as in American fiction, that 'most male writers would rather write about vapid angels and malign temptresses than about what Louisa May Alcott called "good, useful women"'.[75] Portraits of such 'useful women' are indeed rare: Sonia, at the end of Tolstoy's *War and Peace*, is seen as a woman who is worthy of respect, but not of love (although it is only fair to say that Tolstoy's views subsequently changed, and that two unmarried women in his later novels, Varen'ka in *Anna Karenina* and Mar'ia Pavlovna in *Resurrection*, are more sympathetically presented).[76]

It was mostly in women's writings, such as Zhukova's *Moi kurskie znakomtsy* (*My Acquaintances from Kursk*, 1838), that some attempt was made to show that there could be a good life for women outside marriage (although Zhukova's conclusion belies this possibility, and the theme itself provoked Belinsky's ridicule).[77] Only very occasionally, in some women's texts of the 1970s and 1980s, such as the stories of Maia Ganina,[78] do we find positive images of women who either do not see their main aim as pleasing men, or have no relations with men and do not wish to have. However, even since the 1980s, not all women writers accept the diversity of female lives or choices which we take for granted in the West. In both Russian culture and the media, the childless or infertile woman is generally seen in negative terms, as a defective being, inferior to the single mother. The 'career woman' has been portrayed as a negative type, not only in recent works by conservative male writers, such as Vasily Belov's *Vse vperedi* (*The Best is Yet to Come*, 1986) and Anatoly Kurchatkin's *Vechernii svet* (Light of Evening, 1989) but also in some stories by women writers, such as Nadezhda Kozhevnikova's 'Vera Perova' (1983).

A new approach to 'writing the body' has been adopted by some Russian women writers in the latter half of the twentieth century. Women who have suffered themselves, such as Akhmatova and Chukovskaia, do not present women's endurance in the war, purges and prison camps as either heroic or ideal, as some male authors do, but instead dwell on the terrible physical effects of female suffering (including the loss of their looks, a subject which men tend to avoid). Likewise, as Katharine Hodgson's chapter shows, Berggol'ts did not shy away from realistic descriptions of starving women during the siege of Leningrad; while in their camp memoirs Evgeniia Ginzburg and Irina Ratushinskaia frankly depict the suffering and physical deterioration of women prisoners.[79] In contemporary Russia, instead of exalting female beauty and sexual desire (in contrast to some women writers during the Silver Age, an earlier period of relative literary freedom), many women writers, notably Iuliia Voznesenskaia, Liudmila Petrushevskaia, Elena Tarasova and Svetlana Vasilenko, have emphasised female physical suffering, depicting the female body in a distorted manner, or focusing on distressing aspects of women's sexual and reproductive experience, such as abortion and rape.[80]

The Emancipated Woman and the New Woman

Russian male writers often relate physical unattractiveness in women to intellectual activity or feminist activism. From the 1860s onwards, even writers ostensibly sympathetic to women's emancipation, such as Turgenev, painted damning pictures of the 'emancipated woman'. Evdoksiia Kukshina in *Fathers and Sons* has dishevelled blonde hair, wears a 'crumpled silk dress' and lives in an untidy room, where she rolls cigarettes between 'her fingers which were brown with tobacco stains' (Chapter 13).[81] The lower-class populist Mashurina in *Nov'* (*Virgin Soil*, 1877) is less pretentious and more hard-working, but she also smokes, has a 'broad red hand', a slovenly figure, and large lips, teeth and nose, which render her incapable of attracting Nezhdanov, the man she loves (Chapter 1). Other striking masculine satires on 'the emancipated woman' are Dostoevsky's portrait of Virginsky's nihilist 'student sister' in *The Devils*, Tolstoy's sketch of 'the lady' in *Kreitserova sonata* (*The Kreutzer Sonata*, 1889), and Chekhov's mockery of Gurov's black-browed, 'intellectual' wife in 'Dama s sobachkoi' ('The Lady with the Dog', 1899).

Dostoevsky's portrayal of the 'emancipated woman', however, sometimes transcends mere stereotypes. Some of his more complex female characters, such as Dunia in *Crime and Punishment*, Aglaia in *The Idiot*, and Katerina Ivanovna in *The Brothers Karamazov*, can justly be called 'proto-feminists', since they rebel against male abuse and patriarchal society. However, in contrast to his male intellectuals such as Ivan Karamazov, none of them is allowed to express any interesting ideas, their emotional, even 'hysterical' nature is emphasised, and they are presented in a less positive light than more sensual, or spiritual, lower-class women, such as Sonia or Grushen'ka. Dostoevsky is, nevertheless, successful in using his 'emancipated women' as a vehicle for raising questions about women's roles which are still of interest in the late twentieth century.[82]

It was the 'mannishness' of the 'new woman' (with its possible implications of lesbianism or bisexuality) which seemed particularly disturbing for Russian male writers and critics at the beginning of the twentieth century. Mar'ia, the heroine of Anastasiia Verbitskaia's *Po-novomu* (In a New Way, 1902), a 'new woman' who tries to establish a new type of marriage based on personal autonomy and mutual respect, was ridiculed by critics because she prefers not to look in the mirror, and gets married in a simple woollen skirt. Such preoccupations persisted after the Bolshevik Revolution, even in male-authored literary works of the 1920s ostensibly sympathetic to the 'new Soviet woman'. In Aleksei Tolstoy's 'Gadiuka' ('The Viper', 1928) for example, the heroine Ol'ga, who fought bravely alongside men in the Civil War, is depicted as incapable of adjusting to the requirement that she should wear dresses and stockings again during the period of the New Economic Policy. Solzhenitsyn continued the tradition in *Mart semnadtsatogo* (March 1917, 1988), with his biting satire on the prominent writer Zinaida Gippius (thinly disguised as 'the hostess'), who is described as 'a Symbolist poetess with a masterful character' and a 'masculine mind', although her total lack of understanding of the revolutionary situation is emphasised (Vol. 3: Chapter 634).

In the first edition of Fedor Gladkov's *Tsement* (*Cement*, 1925), the main female character, Dasha Chumalova, represents a more problematic image of the 'new woman' of the 1920s than is suggested by the 'revisionist' critic Thea Margaret Durfee.[83] At the beginning of the book, Dasha's changed way of life after the Civil War is seen through the eyes of her aggrieved husband Gleb, who dislikes her new tendency to pay no attention to her appearance or her home (Chapter 2: Section 1).[84] The shortcomings of the 'new woman' are initially evoked through male eyes; it is only later that we come to understand Dasha's point of view.

Dasha's role as mother is presented in a more negative light than Durfee implies. Although Dasha justifies her decision to put her daughter Niurka into a children's home by the desire not to give preference to her own child at the expense of other children, Gleb's first reaction – that this is insensitive and cruel – is also expressed, and the reader comes to feel that it is not necessarily 'politically correct' to subject children to privations that the parents themselves are not suffering. Although Dasha is presented in idealised terms as mother to all the children in the home rather than to her own child alone, the fact that Niurka eventually dies of starvation serves to condemn her in the eyes of both author and reader (significantly, we are never invited to condemn Gleb for failing even to consider taking Niurka out of the home and helping to look after her himself). This ambiguous, male-authored portrait of the 'new woman' as an unsatisfactory mother presents a contrast with the more positive images of motherhood in Aleksandra Kollontai's feminist fiction of the 1920s, such as *Vasilisa Malygina* (1923), which depicts, albeit in a simplistic, utopian light, a woman having a child on her own with the support of a Communist sisterhood.[85]

Gladkov's attitude to sexual relations is also problematic, to say the least. The information that Dasha herself was raped by the Whites during the Civil War and has also narrowly escaped rape by her Communist comrade Bad'in is not offered as a possible reason for her reluctance to sleep with her husband. And what are we to make of the fact that Gleb fails to show Dasha any understanding, and that her indifference drives him into the arms of Polia, the head of the Zhenotdel ('Women's section'), another more 'feminine' woman? Subsequently, when Polia herself is repeatedly raped by Bad'in, Gladkov appears to take the disturbing view that this is just deserts for Polia's excessive 'softness', her failure to become a strong 'new woman' like Dasha.[86] Eventually, even Polia's lover Gleb supports the decision to exclude her from the Party.

For all its artistic defects, the first edition of Gladkov's *Cement* does succeed in conveying the confusion of both Soviet men and women in the 1920s, the difficulty they both experienced in adjusting to their changing roles in the new era of female liberation. However, such realism and ambiguity in thinking about gender were not allowed to survive long in Soviet literature. In Soviet fiction of the 1930s, images of women became one-dimensional exemplars of the official ideology. The ideal Stalinist heroine, whether pure young girl or self-sacrificing mother, was also a worker participating actively in economic construction, but unlike the 'new woman' of the 1920s, was no longer assertive; her chief virtue was supposed to be modesty (*skromnost'*).[87] Taia, the modest, quiet bride of Pavel Korchagin in Nikolai Ostrovsky's *Kak zakalialas' stal'* (*How the Steel was Tempered*, 1932-1934) is an embodiment of the 1930s Stalinist ideal. At the same time, however, as Durfee correctly notes, the disturbing, misogynistic view of sexual relations characteristic of the 1920s still persisted: Ostrovsky implies that women who did not live up to the ideal were likely to be punished. Anna Borhart is raped by bandits, it is suggested, because she is cowardly enough to cling to the arm of the chaste hero when he is trying to shake her off, thus preventing him from protecting her. After the rape, Pavel shows little consideration for Anna, and Tsvetaev, a man who previously loved her, is primarily interested in finding out if she has been raped because of the shame this will bring on him; subsequently Anna disappears from the text.

Mothers and Daughters

The idealisation of the mother figure, with the mother often used to symbolise Mother Russia, is widespread in masculine twentieth-century Russian literature, most notably in war prose and village prose.[88] It was less evident in the nineteenth century, when most women of the upper classes (to which nearly all women writers and most female literary characters belonged) did not look after their children themselves, relying instead on a series of wet nurses and nannies. Belinsky, for example, does not idealise maternity, although he does regard it as woman's natural mission.[89] The roots of the mystique of motherhood, however, go back far deeper into folklore and the doctrine of the Russian Orthodox Church. It has not generally been acknowledged that such a reverential attitude to motherhood in Russian culture, which reflects profound needs on the part of male writers and

Russian men in general, could be oppressive and damaging to actual Russian women, since the real experience of motherhood has hardly been examined, and the female perspective on maternity has been consistently ignored. As feminist psychologists have noted, such officially sponsored idealisation of motherhood can have harmful effects: 'We are ... only now beginning to understand that the sanctification of motherhood, which prevented mothers from ever admitting to feelings of ambivalence toward their children, is not necessary for the child, but may induce profound anxiety'.[90]

The portrayal of the mother-daughter or father-daughter relationship is relatively uncommon in the Russian literary canon, compared with the numerous works treating relationships between fathers and sons or mothers and sons, which reflect the main concerns of male writers.[91] Although the title of Turgenev's classic novel on relations between the generations should be translated as *Fathers and Children*, rather than, as in the usual English translation, *Fathers and Sons*, the novel nevertheless focuses on the relationship of Bazarov and Arkady to the older generation rather than on the relationship of Kat'ia to her sister Odintsova or her dead father. It is predominantly in women's fiction and memoirs that the mother-daughter relationship is viewed in a more favourable, or more realistic, light.[92]

The majority of Russian writers, both male and female, have failed to provide a realistic exploration of the complex and contradictory nature of the mother-daughter relationship, as constructed by western feminist discourse, encompassing fascination and repulsion, identity and separation, competition and co-operation on the part of both mothers and daughters.[93] The continuing idealisation of motherhood in masculine culture of the post-Stalin period, which corresponded to demographic needs after the huge losses incurred by the Russian male population in the war, has helped to perpetuate the model of the conventional nuclear family, which, in the words of Nancy Chodorow, commonly operates 'with boys appropriating their masculine prerogatives and girls acquiescing in their feminine subordination and passivity'.[94]

One curious aspect of some Russian male-authored texts is that mothers and daughters (or two sisters) are sometimes presented as sexual rivals for the favours of the same man. This is not a particularly common theme in western European or North American literature, but figures in a number of well-known Russian texts, such as Turgenev's *Rudin*, Gogol''s *Revizor* (*The Inspector General*, 1836), Herzen's *Kto vinovat?* (*Who is to Blame?*, 1846), and Pasternak's *Doctor Zhivago*. In every case, the older woman is depicted as either pathetic or grotesque in her sexual desire and ambitions. The extraordinary nature of this theme is accentuated when it emerges that the prototype for the image of a young woman seduced by her mother's lover (Zina Pasternak in the case of Pasternak's Lara, as Neil Cornwell's later chapter demonstrates) did not compete with her mother in real life. The reverse situation – a father and son or two brothers competing for one woman – is rarely to be found in Russian literature, which contains many examples of male bonding.[95] (One prominent exception is Turgenev's *First Love*, but in this story the father proves to be completely dominant.) It could be argued that such female rivalry, and the general lack of female solidarity depicted in male-authored Russian texts, to some extent simply reflects the isolation of women in nineteenth-century patriarchal society, where 'the feminine heroine grows up in a world without female solidarity, where women in fact police each other on behalf of patriarchal tyranny'.[96] However, it is more likely that such images bear a closer resemblance to male misogynistic fantasies than to Russian reality, since the fiction and memoirs of many women writers depict devoted sisters or daughters, and place much greater emphasis on female friendship than masculine literature: examples in nineteenth- and early twentieth-century literature include Elena Gan's *The Ideal* and *Medal'ion* (*The Locket*, 1839); Nadezhda Sokhanskaia's *Posle obeda v gostiakh* (*A Conversation After Dinner*, 1858); Valentina Dmitrieva's novel *Tuchki* (Clouds, 1904) which focuses on the friendship between two educated women, a teacher and a doctor's assistant, in a remote part of rural Russia; and Anastasiia Verbitskaia's memoirs, *Moemu chitateliu* (To my Reader, 1908; 1911), which depict the close relationship between the author and her sister. Indeed, friendship between sisters or women friends appears to be quite a widespread theme in Russian literature, albeit one treated almost exclusively by women writers. The theme of female solidarity resurfaced in underground feminist writing of the Brezhnev era, notably in women's prison-camp memoirs, and Voznesenskaia's *Zhenskii dekameron* (*The Women's Decameron*, 1986), one of the few Russian literary works to depict an autonomous female community.

In Defence of the Feminist Critique

It has been the central argument of this chapter that the Russian literary canon represents a tradition of male-produced literature, rather than an expression of universal human values, since 'the idea that art is universal and thus potentially androgynous is basically an idealist notion.'[97]

Works currently shaping the classical Russian literary canon pay far more attention to the 'superfluous man' than the 'superfluous woman' in nineteenth-century Russian society (although the Russian term *lishnii chelovek* is non-gender-specific); express more interest in male pastimes such as hunting than female activities such as sewing or knitting; frequently ridicule the intellectual woman, the 'new woman' and the elderly woman; present more satires of domineering mothers, shrewish wives, dry old maids and treacherous mistresses than of tyrannical fathers, abusive husbands, eccentric bachelors or philandering seducers; offer more portraits of female victims than of female rebels, express a more exquisite compassion for male adolescent angst than for the similar tribulations of young women; are more prepared to depict the suicide of an adulteress than the early death of a talented woman writer; present more pictures of female rivalry than of female solidarity; and offer many examples of the 'rake's progress', but few of triumphant, independent female sexuality.[98]

Leaving aside such debatable questions as whether such female types could really have existed in nineteenth-century Russia, and whether literature is necessarily a reflection of life, is it even possible to imagine an alternative Russian literature, in which some of the most famous works would treat such themes as a heartless aristocratic vamp driving a male peasant to suicide; a fascinating, highly educated coquette who makes a career of breaking many male hearts; a lazy noblewoman who finds it difficult to get out of bed; a woman radical inspiring a younger male lover to socio-political action; a married man committing suicide because of an insoluble conflict between his mistress and his children; a female murderer redeemed by a male prostitute; a radical daughter who politicises her retrograde father during the 1905 Revolution?

The Phallocentric Tradition

It has generally been men who have defined the canon, themes and style of Russian literature. The critical tradition has been predominantly masculine: for example, Belinsky, the first Russian radical critic, defined attitudes to women writers in his day, whether he expressed essentialist views on the superiority of the male genius, as in his 1840 article on Mar'ia Zhukova, or was more supportive, as in his article of 1843 praising Elena Gan.[99] Even the 'woman question' in mid- and late nineteenth-century Russia was defined and publicised predominantly by radical men, who often failed to take account of the real experience and needs of Russian women.[100]

Major Russian writers, such as Pushkin, Turgenev, Dostoevsky and Chekhov, harboured ambivalent attitudes towards women writers of their time, frequently expressing misogynistic opinions, while on occasion championing the careers of certain individual women. Pushkin, for example, launched a conventional attack on 'academicians in bonnets' in *Evgenii Onegin* (Chapter 13: XXVIII), although he was also instrumental in securing the publication of Durova's memoirs, and gave support to Evgeniia Rostopchina and other female contemporaries.[101] Turgenev was quite willing to appropriate one of Evgeniia Tur's texts for his own purposes, while disparaging her work and women's writing as a whole for containing 'something not quite right, not literary, that rushes straight from the heart, something not thought through to the end' – that is, implicitly lacking in distance and irony, the essence of true (masculine) literary talent.[102] Similarly, Dostoevsky criticised Nadezhda Sokhanskaia's writing, while recognising that 'she has talent, sensibility, even some ideas'.[103]

Many philosophical texts which have exerted a great influence on Russian writers have also been highly misogynistic, such as Otto Weininger's *Geschlecht und Charakter* (*Sex and Character*, 1903; translated into Russian in 1909), which expressed such extreme opinions as: 'Women have no existence, no essence; they are not, they are nothing'.[104] In the Soviet period, the sexist views of officials in charge of literature, such as Trotsky and Zhdanov,[105] have frequently been emphasised. In the post-Communist period, leading critics have expressed anti-feminist views with renewed vigour: the iconoclastic spokesman of Russian postmodernism, Viktor Erofeev, refers to feminism as an 'ideology' from which contemporary Russian women writers are quite correct to keep their distance.[106]

The feminist critique is still highly relevant to a deconstruction of the misogynistic representation of women in much contemporary Russian culture. The principal advantage of the idealisation of women in male-authored nineteenth-century and socialist realist texts was that such portraits, albeit unrealistic and patriarchal, were at least flattering to Russian women – indeed, vastly preferable to the images which proliferate in literature and film of the late Gorbachev and post-Communist periods, where women are routinely depicted either as sexually voracious, or as victims of violence, rape and sexual abuse.[107] In masculine texts the lifting of censorship has led to numerous portrayals of the sexual exploitation of women, frequently bordering on pornography (as in the works of Eduard Limonov and Vladimir Sorokin). While male writers and film directors usually claim to be using female images to express wider ideas, such as the rape of Russia by the Communist Party or the disintegration of all moral values in contemporary society, woman is again being used as pure sign, albeit a sign which is now openly debased, rather than idealised as before.

In some recent male-authored texts which continue the Russian tradition of the weak, introspective man and the stronger, more active woman, sex and alcohol are presented as the male protagonist's main concerns. If so, as in Venedikt Erofeev's *Moskva-Petushki* (*Moscow to the End of the Line*, 1977) and the stories of Sergei Dovlatov, alcohol frequently takes pride of place, emphasising the subordinate position which women occupy in the Russian man's hierarchy of values. Such works confirm Siniavsky's view that 'Vodka is the Russian man's white magic – he decidedly prefers it to black magic – the female sex.'[108]

Biography and Misogyny

Well-known literary texts in Russia have frequently been created by men who held misogynistic views typical of their time; some even harboured pathological attitudes to women or had suffered at the hands of 'the new woman'. Although writers' biographies and their texts should not be simplistically equated, a brief summary of some salient features of the biographies of major Russian writers will demonstrate that their personal experience was hardly conducive to fostering a totally dispassionate view of women.

Pushkin and Lermontov were both children of their time who wrote pornographic juvenilia, including scenes of rape. Pushkin was a womaniser in his youth (as were many other Russian writers), and later contracted a troubled marriage to a much younger wife, Natal'ia Goncharova, whom he attempted to educate in the ways of propriety. His views on women were profoundly ambivalent: he could praise their cultivation in his work, while expressing disdain for them in his letters.[109] It has been suggested that Lermontov, who suffered from his mother's early death, may have felt insecure in relation to women because he was stoop-shouldered and bow-legged; his first love was unrequited, and he subsequently behaved cruelly towards other women.[110]

Gogol', who, according to modern biographers, was latently homosexual in orientation,[111] portrays women either as ethereal stereotypes, such as the governor's daughter in *Mertvye dushi* (*Dead Souls*, 1842), a 'young girl of sixteen with golden hair' and a pretty oval face like a white, transparent egg, who has as yet 'nothing womanly' about her (an image as near to an absence, a pure sign, as any significant character in a novel can be), or as grotesque caricatures, such as the mayor's wife in *The Inspector General* and the dim-witted Korobochka in *Dead Souls*. Some of Gogol''s male protagonists are bachelors who express an almost pathological fear of women and marriage, notably the reluctant bridegroom Podkolesin in the play *Zhenit'ba* (*Marriage*, 1842), and the eponymous hero of 'Ivan Fedorovich Shpon'ka i ego tetushka' ('Ivan Fedorovich Shpon'ka and his Auntie', 1832). Turgenev's attitude to women was also very unconventional, influenced by a brutal mother, a series of sexual liaisons which resulted in several illegitimate children, and a (possibly unconsummated) lifelong devotion to the opera singer Pauline Viardot.[112]

Leaving aside the controversial question of whether Dostoevsky himself was guilty of violating a young girl in a bath-house, as his friend Strakhov alleged (probably mischievously) in a letter of 1883,[113] it is certainly true that he was obsessed all his life by what he saw as the 'most fearful crime' – the rape and murder of a young girl, which destroys 'faith in love's beauty' [114] – and was fascinated by cases of suicide and murder of women. His unhappy first marriage was followed by a passionate affair with the writer Apollonariia Suslova (a prototype of Polina in *The Gambler*, who, along with another emancipated woman, the writer Anna Korvin-Krupovskaia (a possible model for the character of Aglaia in *The Idiot*), rejected his proposals of marriage, until he was ultimately taken in hand by his devoted, if dull, second wife Anna Snitkina.

Tolstoy seduced a peasant woman in his youth, as did many young noblemen; later he attempted to shape his young wife according to his own blueprint, then blamed her for not being able to adapt to his new ideas after his 'conversion': the vicissitudes of their stormy marriage are well documented.[115] It is generally agreed, even by critics who emphasise the alleged 'feminism' of some of his later texts, that his letters and diaries express many misogynistic views.[116]

Chekhov, according to recent archival research, visited brothels and had many affairs with women,[117] assiduously avoiding marriage until he met the actress Ol'ga Knipper late in life. Whereas previously he had written many stories disparaging women and marriage, such as 'Supruga' ('His Wife', 1895), which appeared to deny the possibility of a true and enduring love, the female characters in the works he wrote after his marriage in 1901 were generally more sympathetic, for example Nadia in 'Nevesta' ('The Betrothed', 1903), an attractive portrait of a 'new woman'.

Of major twentieth-century Russian writers outside the socialist realist mainstream, Pasternak, Bulgakov and Solzhenitsyn, all of whom were married several times, held sincere, if unconventional, religious views, and traditional patriarchal attitudes towards women which find reflection in their works. Solzhenitsyn, for example, expresses great respect for the simple, saintly woman of the people Matrena, but scorn for many women intellectuals. In *Avgust chetyrnadt-*

satogo (*August 1914*, 1983) he chooses to explore the Russian revolutionary tradition through satirical thumbnail sketches of a series of women terrorists, purportedly depicted through the eyes of two enthusiastic female supporters (Chapter 60). Solzhenitsyn's choice of women is designed to accentuate the iniquities of the nineteenth-century radical intelligentsia by suggesting that the revolutionary movement was not only wrong-headed and dangerous, but also responsible for leading women astray from their natural womanly mission.

These comments on the biographies and writings of Russian male authors are not designed to disparage them, or to condemn them ahistorically for a sexism based on the standards of our own very different time or culture; more comparative research is needed to establish whether Russian writers have been more, or less, misogynistic than male writers of their period in other countries. The aim is simply to point out that the images of women portrayed in the Russian literary canon are unlikely to be 'objective' or 'universally true', as is often assumed in Russia, but highly partial and individual, a product of the author's own time, culture and personal experience. If a Russian male writer does occasionally manage to portray a female character who transcends his own limited personal vision, this is a considerable achievement.

Feminine Approaches to Masculine Stereotypes

As Shoshana Felman has acutely commented: 'To the extent that women are the question, they cannot be the speaking subjects of the knowledge and the science which the question seeks'.[118] In the mid-nineteenth century it was necessary for Russian women (as for women in other cultures), to reformulate the 'woman question', to become, in the powerful words of the poet Adrienne Rich, 'the woman who asks the question', not 'the woman who is the question'.[119] Contrary to the opinions of Gary Rosenshield and Carolina de Maegd-Soëp,[120] who have argued that Russian women took no part in the discussion of 'the woman question' in the 1860s (echoing the complaint voiced by Nikolai Shelgunov in 1870[121]), in actual fact, as Arja Rosenholm has shown, women writers such as Nadezhda Khvoshchinskaia often expressed their aspirations and doubts through fiction, rather than in essays on socio-political questions, which they regarded as a predominantly masculine genre.[122]

From the 1860s to the 1917 Revolution, Russian women frequently tried to establish their own agenda in both fiction and criticism, but their needs were frequently ignored or misunderstood. Although it is true that Russian women at first lacked the education or confidence to play as prominent a part in the Russian women's liberation movement as radical men, it is certainly not true that there are no feminist writings by Russian women. From the 1860s onwards a number of women realist writers emerged, such as 'Marko Vovchok' (Mariia Markovich), Ol'ga Shapir, Anastasiia Verbitskaia, Valentina Dmitrieva and Tat'iana Shchepkina-Kupernik, who were sympathetic to women's emancipation, and later, to the women's movement, possessing a feminist agenda which differed considerably from that of men. At the same time, women writers of the alternative, Symbolist tradition, though not interested in the women's movement, were also concerned with themes which today would be interpreted as feminist, such as women's personal and sexual liberation.

In the twentieth century, particularly since the First Writers' Congress of 1934, Soviet women writers have not only been subject to the same oppressive cultural constraints as male writers, but also obliged to conform to conservative Soviet ideological assumptions about women's essential nature. During Stalin's time, although the relative freedom introduced by the Second World War enabled a few women writers such as Ol'ga Berggol'ts to express some truth about the experience of Russian women, the full extent of this reality could only be evoked in underground women's writings, such as Akhmatova's *Rekviem* (*Requiem*, mostly written in the 1930s, but not published in full in Russia until 1987) and Chukovskaia's *Sof'ia Petrovna*. After the cultural dislocation caused by Stalinism, some women writers began to discuss women's issues in print, with varying degrees of openness, from the 1960s to the end of the Brezhnev period, but it has been mainly in dissident and post-glasnost women's writings that genuinely autonomous female voices have again been heard in Russia.[123]

The relative rarity of such independent voices is due to the fact that in Russia, as in other cultures, many women have not challenged, but unconsciously internalised the sexist attitudes and desires prevalent in their culture.[124] It is as true in Russia as in the United States that 'As readers and teachers and scholars, women are taught to think as men, to identify with the male point of view, and to accept as normal and legitimate a male system of values, one of whose central principles is misogyny'.[125] Many Russian women writers have failed to acknowledge the patriarchal nature of the Russian literary canon, displaying an unwillingness to be categorised as a 'woman writer',[126] and positing a distinction between what they perceive as allegedly narrow 'women's themes' and ostensibly wider 'universal themes'. They are reluctant to admit that their treatment of supposedly 'universal themes' means that they are in fact choosing to become part of a male-dominated tradition. Deeply, if unconsciously, conditioned by the essentialism embedded in their culture, many Russian women writers seem not to realise that it is possible to articulate both 'feminist' and 'human' concerns simultaneously – indeed, most feminists would argue that the latter is impossible without the former. Even today, Russian women writers and critics still have to struggle to gain acceptance for the view that 'women's literature' exists as an autonomous concept worthy of understanding rather than denigration.[127]

The Russian woman reader's relationship to her 'great tradition' is made even more problematic by the fact that writers frequently dedicate their literature to defining what is peculiarly Russian about their experience and identity. Given the pervasive masculine bias of this literature, it is not surprising that the experience of being Russian is frequently equated with the experience of being a man. In Russian culture Russia is female, but to be Russian is predominantly male.

In the post-Stalin period, particularly in underground and post-glasnost literature, some women writers have attempted to deconstruct the female stereotypes prevalent in masculine literature. Natal'ia Baranskaia's *Nedelia kak nedelia* (*A Week Like Any Other*, 1969) exposes the reality of the Soviet woman's 'double burden'; I. Grekova's *Vdovii parakhod* (*Ship of Widows*, 1981) frankly describes the life of drudgery led by Russian mothers left on their own after the war, and their exploitation by unscrupulous sons; while, as Monika Katz demonstrates, Petrushevskaia contests the stereotype of the self-sacrificing mother in such bleak narratives as 'Svoi krug' ('Our Crowd', 1988). In contemporary Russia, too, some women writers have subverted the image of the wise old woman beloved of male-authored 'village prose', painting realistic portraits of elderly women in Russian society, emphasising their poverty, ill-health and loneliness. Two powerful recent examples are Marina Palei's story 'Evgesha i Annushka' (Evgesha and Annushka, 1990), in which the existence of two old women is reduced to little more than an endless cycle of bodily functions, and Petrushevskaia's harrowing portrait of the mentally ill, incontinent grandmother in *Vremia noch'* (*The Time: Night*, 1992).

One masculine stereotype has, however, been slow to change: there are still relatively few positive sexual images of women in Russian culture.[128] Male psychologists in contemporary Russia frequently take a negative view of female sexuality, regarding women's role as nothing but the satisfaction of men's needs;[129] similarly, many recent works of fiction by Russian men, such as Viktor Erofeev's *Russian Beauty* and Kurchatkin's *Strazhnitsa* (The Watchwoman, 1993), merely depict women fulfilling men's fantasies. Although some recent stories by women writers are beginning to treat women's sexuality in a non-judgemental way (for example, Valeriia Narbikova's

Ravnovesie sveta dnevnykh i nochnykh zvezd [The Equilibrium of Diurnal and Night-time Stars, 1988], Marina Palei's 'Kabiriia s Obvodnogo Kanala' ['Cabiria from the Bypass', 1991], and Liudmila Ulitskaia's 'Lialin dom' [Lialia's House] and 'Gulia' [1994]), such representations are relatively rare, and have often been critically received.[130]

Very few cultural representations of women by women in contemporary Russia can be called 'feminist' in a western sense. In the mid-1990s there is only one feminist journal in Russia, *Prosveshchenie*, which provoked an ironic review by a female critic.[131] One interesting development in contemporary women's fiction is that whereas in the past literature sometimes broke taboos on women's issues before the media (as in the case of Baranskaia's *A Week Like any Other* and Voznesenskaia's *The Women's Decameron*), the current literary treatment of certain controversial issues, for example rape (as in Tat'iana Nabatnikova's 'Shofer Astap' ['The Bus Driver Astap', 1989], Galina Shcherbakova's 'Tri liubvi Mashi Peredreevoi' ['The Three "Loves" of Masha Peredreeva', 1990], and Ulitskaia's 'Bron'ka' [1994]), is more ambiguous and problematic than some frank articles on this subject by women in the press.[132]

Shortcomings of the Feminist Critique

Sympathy for the feminist critique of Russian literature has not always been furthered by the expression of various extreme positions, which give hostile critics an excuse to attack feminist criticism as a prescriptive approach, akin to socialist realism, which allegedly urges readers to reject or ignore the traditional 'great works of Russian literature' and to read only women's writings. Such criticism, however, is misdirected in a variety of ways. In the first place, the feminist critique is primarily deconstructive, rather than prescriptive. It is important to analyse images of men and women in Russian literature, not to argue for the artistic superiority of feminist texts. Rosenshield is guilty of prescriptive criticism himself when he suggests that feminist critics of Russian literature should write only about women writers.

Secondly, it is totally unnecessary for feminist critics to overpraise mediocre novels with a feminist content, such as Chernyshevsky's *Chto delat?* (*What is to be Done?*, 1863). It is quite legitimate to argue that, although the content of Chernyshevsky's novel may have been very progressive for its time – indeed, inspirational for the Russian women's movement – in *What is to be Done?* interesting feminist ideas coexist with artistic mediocrity. (By the same token, in many other 'great works of Russian literature', artistic merit coexists with misogyny.) Similarly, some feminist literature of the 1920s, such as the novels and stories of Aleksandra Kollontai, while possessing considerable interest from a sociological point of view, cannot be viewed as sophisticated artistic texts, since they were written in a deliberately simple style in order to be understood by uneducated Russian women.

Thirdly, it is also unnecessary to posit feminism in texts usually read as profoundly misogynistic, as Barbara Heldt does in the case of Tolstoy's *Kreutzer Sonata*. Although Tolstoy's story contains some elements which today might be interpreted as feminist (such as the rejection of the double standard of morality, and the suggestion that women should not be regarded as sex objects), the work as a whole does not amount to a feminist text. Most modern feminists would advocate greater sexual and emotional freedom for women, rather than Tolstoy's extremist solution of radical chastity for both men and women. Likewise, Dostoevsky's texts yield valuable insights if they are read through the prism of feminist criticism, but a certain amount of sophistry is needed in order to claim him as a feminist.

It is also unnecessary for feminist critics to deny that some nineteenth-century male writers held views which were progressive for their time, or that images of women in male-authored literature could sometimes prove inspirational to real Russian women. It is well attested that some women revolutionaries were influenced by the representation of women in the works of Druzhinin, Nekrasov, Goncharov, Herzen and Turgenev.[133] In the context of a society in which there were few (if any) women writers who could write as powerfully and poetically about women's issues as Turgenev, the influence he exerted is hardly surprising. A recognition of this fact, however, is not to deny the restricted nature of the roles his female characters are allowed to play. In Turgenev's early novels *Rudin* and *Nest of the Gentry*, Natal'ia and Liza, albeit strong and morally pure, simply wish to choose their own husbands. In *On the Eve*, the more independent Elena is inspired to leave home, but only under the influence of her lover, the Bulgarian revolutionary Insarov; she is never depicted in action, only preparing for action. In *Virgin Soil*, Turgenev portrays a populist revolutionary, Marianna, whose work among the peasantry with the doomed Nezhdanov proves largely unsuccessful. Even in these supposedly 'feminist' texts, the 'Turgenevan maiden''s virtues of innocence, independence and self-reliance are only tested within prescribed, conventional limits, and she is always seen in relation to a man.[134]

It should also be recognised that the fiction of Turgenev and other male writers was not the only radical literary influence on nineteenth-century Russian women: a powerful impact was also exerted by the works of foreign women writers, particularly George Sand

and Charlotte Brontë.[135] It is also quite possible that some adventurous Russian women may have been inspired to follow male historical and literary models such as the Decembrists, rather than female ones such as the Decembrists' wives, as is suggested by Evdokiia Rostopchina's poems on the Decembrists, 'The Dream' ('Mechta', 1830) and 'To the Sufferers' ('K stradal'tsam', 1831).[136]

On the other hand, it would be erroneous to deny the complexity and subtlety displayed by the greatest Russian writers in their treatment of both male and female characters. Our discussion of images of women in Russian literature would be inadequate if we were to perceive only stereotypes; women characters sometimes surpass the so-called heroes in their moral complexity and human veracity.[137]

As both Rosenshield and Heldt point out, arguing from totally different premises, major writers such as Tolstoy, Dostoevsky and Chekhov problematise issues of gender, love and marriage as they affect both sexes. Although classical male authors idealise women, whilst limiting their role, at the same time they probe the assumptions about gender common in their literary tradition: for example, by depicting an unhappy marriage (as in *Anna Karenina*), which suggests that marriage may not be the correct, or only, goal for women; or by evoking men's abuse of power over women (as in Dostoevsky's 'The Meek One', and Stavrogin's 'Confession' in *The Devils*), which implicitly poses the question of whether more equal, humane relations between men and women might be possible.

The objections of Rosenshield and Mandelker that feminist criticism is necessarily 'ideological' or 'closed' overlook the fact that 'prescriptive criticism' is only one strand in contemporary feminist scholarship,[138] and one that is increasingly contested by feminist critics themselves. Emphasis is now laid on a variety of 'feminisms',[139] rather than on one single monolithic 'feminism'. Many modern feminist critics promote a recognition of diversity, stressing the 'jouissance' to be obtained from textual plurality. Annette Kolodny, for example, advocates 'a playful pluralism, responsive to the possibility of multiple critical schools and methods, but captive of none'.[140]

Conclusion

In Russian literature 'the male-authored canon contributes to the body of information, stereotypes, inference and surmise about the female sex that is general in the culture'.[141] It is fair to say that Russian literature is not as sexist or one-dimensional as some radical feminist critics might lead us to believe; but neither is it as free from stereotypes and misogyny as opponents of the 'feminist critique' of

Russian literature would like to think. In rereading Russian literature, it is important to remain open to the text and not try to minimise complexity – but it is equally vital to be prepared to deconstruct gender stereotypes and expose misogynistic attitudes, wherever they may be found. It should not be forgotten that classical literary texts have frequently been, and still are, used as propaganda for essentialist notions of gender in Russian society.

'Revisionism' can be valuable, in that it may remind feminist critics about historical and cultural diversity, thereby modifying the degree to which they perceive the representation of women at any given historical period to be essentialising or stereotypical, and emphasising the many gradations which can exist between misogyny and feminism. If the revisionist impulse springs not merely from a desire to 'correct' the alleged 'mistakes' of earlier feminist scholars, but rather from an attempt to add new dimensions and greater complexity to the feminist critique, it will succeed in furthering our understanding of the image of women in Russian literature. However, the insights that may be gained from a more nuanced rereading of individual literary texts do not necessarily invalidate the misogynistic burden of the accumulated Russian cultural tradition as a whole.

The feminist critique of Russian literature involves a re-examination of works by male authors which 'we loved, or hoped to love, and still do half love',[142] a process which, at least for female readers, inevitably raises controversial questions about whether the 'great works of Russian literature' are in fact as great as we had been led to believe. Unlike more radical feminist critics, I would contend that there is no need to 'throw out the baby with the bathwater' – it is unnecessary to reject out of hand major novelists such as Tolstoy or Dostoevsky, or to impugn the undoubted artistic merits of Pushkin, Lermontov, Turgenev, or Chekhov. What is desirable, however, is to confront the Russian literary canon as a rich source of motifs and myths about the two sexes, not in order to label and dismiss even the most misogynistic literary classics, but to apprehend them in all their human dimensions.

It is hoped that this volume will help to promote a belated acknowledgement that 'Russian literature' is not simply a collection of great texts, but of texts which have been deeply structured by sexist ideologies, and that many themes and images in Russian literature which have hitherto been unproblematically designated as 'universal' are actually parochial and phallocentric. Such an awareness, one of the basic premises of feminist criticism, is a view which still meets considerable resistance, both from western Slavists and within Russia itself.

Notes

References to parts and chapters of literary works will be given in the text.
1. For further discussion of this term, see Ellen Moers, *Literary Women* (Garden City, NY: Doubleday, 1976); Nancy K. Miller, *The Heroine's Text: Readings in the French and English Novel* (New York: Columbia University Press, 1980); Rachel M.Brownstein, *Becoming a Heroine: Reading about Women in Novels* (Harmondsworth: Penguin, 1984); Carolyn Heilbrun, *Reinventing Womanhood* (New York: Norton, 1979). For the defence of the term, see Amy Mandelker, 'The Judgement of *Anna Karenina*', in Sona Stephan Hoisington (ed.), *A Plot of her Own: The Female Protagonist in Russian Literature* (Evanston, IL: Northwestern University Press, 1995), pp. 36–37. An alternative term, 'woman as hero', is preferred in Carolyn Heilbrun, *Toward a Recognition of Androgyny* (New York: Knopf, 1973), p. 49; Lee R. Edwards, 'The Labors of Psyche: Towards a Theory of Female Heroism', *Critical Inquiry*, 6 (1979), pp. 33–49.
2. Virginia Woolf, *A Room of One's Own* (New York and London: Harcourt Brace Jovanovich, 1929), p. 35.
3. The term 'the Other' was coined by Simone de Beauvoir, *The Second Sex*, trans. and ed. H.M.Parshley (Harmondsworth: Penguin, 1988), pp. 97, 100–13; Abram Terts (Andrei Siniavskii), 'Chto takoe sotsialisticheskii realizm', in *Fantasticheskii mir Abrama Tertsa* (New York: Inter-Language Literary Associates, 1967), p. 427.
4. Susan Koppelman Cornillon (ed.), *Images of Women in Fiction: Feminist Perspectives* (Bowling Green, OH: Bowling Green University Popular Press, 1972), p. x.
5. This typology follows that used in Barbara Heldt, *Terrible Perfection: Women and Russian Literature* (Bloomington and Indianapolis: Indiana University Press, 1987), p. 13.
6. Jane Costlow, '"Oh-là-là" and "No-no-no": Odintsova as Woman Alone in *Fathers and Children*', in Hoisington, *A Plot of her Own*, pp. 21–32.
7. Nina Pelikan Straus, *Dostoevsky and the Woman Question* (New York: St Martin's Press, 1994) gives full weight to Dostoevsky's use of polyphony, but, in my opinion, overestimates the centrality of his female characters, which is hardly surprising in a book devoted entirely to this subject.
8. For further discussion, see Heldt, *Terrible Perfection*, p. 14.
9. Brownstein, *Becoming a Heroine*, p. 299.
10. I agree with Andrew Barratt, 'Introduction' to Evgenii Zamiatin, *My* (Bristol: Bristol Classical Press, 1994), p. xviii, who argues that the two women, I–330 and O–90, are 'presented very much in terms of competing male fantasies'. On the traditional association of sex and death in masculine culture, see Beth Ann Bassein, *Women and Death: Linkages in Western Thought and Literature* (Westport, CT: Greenwood, 1984).
11. Mandelker, 'The Judgement of *Anna Karenina*'; Mandelker, *Framing 'Anna Karenina': Tolstoy, the Woman Question, and the Victorian Novel* (Columbus: Ohio University Press, 1993).
12. For further discussion of Anna as a mother, see Naomi Segal, *The Adulteress's Child: Authorship and Desire in the Nineteenth-century Novel* (Cambridge and Oxford: Polity Press, 1992).
13. Julia Kristeva, *About Chinese Women [Des Chinoises]*, trans. Anita Barrows (London: Boyars, 1977), p. 32. 'Jouissance', in the works of French feminists, refers to the intense, rapturous pleasure which women know and men fear.
14. Joe Andrew, *Women in Russian Literature, 1780–1863* (Basingstoke: Macmillan, 1988), p. 6.
15. It is, however, possible that these outnumber the relatively few works by Russian women writers which bear the name of the male protagonist – many Russ-

ian women's texts are female-centred, and only a few stories by women, such as Mar'ia Zhukova's 'Baron Reikhman' (1837), Valentina Dmitrieva's 'Dimka' (1900), and N. Ol'nem's *Ivan Fedorovich* (1903), are entirely, or partially, devoted to an eponymous male protagonist.

16. Joe Andrew, *Narrative and Desire in Russian Literature, 1822-49: The Feminine and the Masculine* (Basingstoke: Macmillan, 1993), pp. 214-26.
17. However, Joanna Russ, 'What Can a Heroine Do? Or Why Women Can't Write', in Cornillon, *Images of Women in Fiction*, p. 9, argues that for nineteenth-century women protagonists, the love story includes the *Bildungsroman*.
18. Tat'iana's talent as a writer (as demonstrated by her letter to Onegin) and as a critic (exemplified by her response to Onegin's books) has recently been emphasised by some feminist critics: see, for example, Diana L. Burgin's ingenious article 'Tatiana Larina's *Letter to Onegin*, or *La Plume Criminelle*', *Essays in Poetics*, vol. 16, no. 2 (September 1991), pp. 12-23. I would, however, argue that such modern interpretations take us rather too far away from the author's ironic intentions. Even if there is some validity in these readings, it could be argued that Pushkin is simply expressing another conventional idea: that women's creativity springs from their love.
19. Discussed in Rosalind Marsh, 'Anastasiia Verbitskaia reconsidered', in Rosalind Marsh (ed.), *Gender and Russian Literature: New Perspectives* (Cambridge: Cambridge University Press, 1996), pp. 190-93.
20. On the importance of reading for women populists, see Hilde Hoogenboom, 'Vera Figner and revolutionary autobiographies', in Rosalind Marsh (ed.), *Women in Russia and Ukraine* (Cambridge: Cambridge University Press, 1996), pp. 88-89.
21. Judith Fyer, *Women in the Nineteenth-Century American Novel* (Oxford: Oxford University Press, 1976), p. 206.
22. Heilbrun, *Reinventing Womanhood*, pp. 71-92.
23. On this problem as it affected British and American women writers, see Sandra M. Gilbert and Susan Gubar, *The Madwoman in the Attic: the Woman Writer and the Nineteenth-Century Literary Imagination*, 2nd edition (New Haven: Yale University Press, 1984), pp. 45-92.
24. This is a familiar criticism levelled against women writers; for its use in a Russian context, see Marsh, *Gender and Russian Literature*, pp. 66-68, 204, n. 56.
25. These quotations are taken from Gan's letters of 1839, quoted in Joe Andrew, 'A Crocodile in Flannel or a Dancing Monkey', paper presented to V ICCEES World Congress (Warsaw, July 1995).
26. For an extended elaboration of this view, see Heldt, *Terrible Perfection*. Prominent examples are the poetry of Akhmatova and Tsvetaeva, and the autobiographies of Nadezhda Durova and Nadezhda Mandel'shtam. Following the model of Mariia Bakhkirtseva's diaries (published in Russian in 1889), the life and career of the 'exceptional woman' became a fashionable subject in women's popular novels of the Silver Age, such as Verbitskaia's *Kliuchi schast'ia* (The Keys to Happiness, 1908-1913) and Evdokiia Nagrodskaia's *Gnev Dionisa* (*The Wrath of Dionysus*, 1911).
27. Vera Sandomirsky Dunham, 'The Strong-Woman Motif', in Cyril E. Black (ed.), *The Transformation of Russian Society* (Cambridge, MA: Harvard University Press, 1960), pp. 459-83.
28. Gary Rosenshield, 'Afterword: The Problems of Gender Criticism; or, What Is to be Done about Dostoevsky?', in Hoisington, *A Plot of Her Own*, p. 117.
29. Theodore Roszak, 'The Hard and the Soft: the Force of Feminism in Modern Times', in Theodore and Betty Roszak (eds), *Masculine/Feminine: Readings in Sexual Mythology and the Liberation of Women* (New York: Harper and Row, 1969), pp. 91-92.

30. For further discussion, see Teresa de Lauretis, *Alice doesn't: feminism, semiotics, cinema* (Basingstoke: Macmillan, 1984), pp. 103–57. I am grateful to Joe Andrew for drawing this work to my attention.
31. Analyses of these issues are too numerous to mention, but the specific references are taken from Simone de Beauvoir, *The Second Sex*; Sherry Ortner, 'Is Female to Male as Nature is to Culture?', in Michelle Rosaldo and Louise Lamphere (eds), *Woman, Culture and Society* (Stanford: Stanford University Press, 1974), pp. 67–87; Hélène Cixous (with Catherine Clément), *La Jeune Neé* (Paris: Union géneral d'éditions, 1975), p. 115.
32. Terts, *Fantasticheskii mir Abrama Tertsa*, p. 427. See also the comment of Mary Jacobus (ed.), *Women Writing and Writing about Women* (London: Croom Helm, 1979), p. 10: 'woman as silent bearer of ideology (virgin, wife, mother) is the necessary sacrifice to male secularity, worldliness and tampering with forbidden knowledge. She is the term by which patriarchy creates a reserve of purity and silence in the materiality of its traffic with the world and its noisy discourse'.
33. Heldt, *Terrible Perfection*, p. 4.
34. Brownstein, *Becoming a Heroine*, p. xviii.
35. The term 'heroinic' was coined in Moers, *Literary Women*.
36. For further discussion, see Tillie Olsen, 'The Fiction of Fiction', in Cornillon, *Images of Women in Fiction*, pp. 113–30. She also suggests that women often feel unable to live up to their culture's image of the feminine, but usually consider themselves, not their culture, to be at fault.
37. See, in particular, the reinterpretations of Pushkin's Tat'iana by Karolina Pavlova in her long poem *Kvadril'* (*Quadrille*, 1843-1857), and by Marina Tsvetaeva in her essay 'Moi Pushkin' ('My Pushkin', 1937), discussed in Olga Hasty, 'The Woman Poet's Tat'iana', conference paper (Guildford, June 1996).
38. On Tonia and Lara as the heroines of classical epic and Russian national epic, see Edith Clowes, 'Characterization in *Doktor Zhivago*: Lara and Tonja', *Slavic and East European Journal*, vol. 34, no. 3 (1990), pp. 322–31.
39. For further discussion, see Helena Goscilo, *Dehexing Sex: Russian Womanhood During and After Glasnost* (Ann Arbor: University of Michigan Press, 1996), pp. 144–45.
40. Gitta Hammarberg, *From the Idyll to the Novel: Karamzin's Sentimentalist Prose* (Cambridge: Cambridge University Press, 1991); Gitta Hammarberg, 'Poor Liza, Poor Erast, Lucky Narrator', *Slavic and East European Journal*, vol. 31, no. 3 (Fall 1987), pp. 305–21.
41. Andrew, *Women in Russian Literature*, pp. 22–26.
42. J. S. Garrard, 'Poor Erast, or Point of View in Karamzin', in J. L. Black (ed.), *Essays on Karamzin: Russian Man-of-Letters, Political Thinker, Historian, 1766-1826* (The Hague: Mouton, 1975), pp. 40–55.
43. Caryl Emerson, 'Tatiana', in Hoisington, *A Plot of Her Own*, p. 12.
44. See, for example, V. Belinskii, 'Evgenii Onegin: stat'ia deviataia', in *Polnoe sobranie sochinenii*, 13 vols (Moscow: Akademiia Nauk SSSR, 1953–1959), vol. 7, pp. 480–500; Dostoevsky's Pushkin Speech of 8 June 1880, published in his *Dnevnik pisatelia* (August 1880).
45. Discussed in Virginia Woolf, 'Professions for Women', in *The Death of the Moth and Other Essays* (London: Hogarth Press, 1942), pp. 236–38; Alexander Welsh, *The City of Dickens* (Oxford: Clarendon Press, 1971), pp. 164–95.
46. This phrase refers to the first Mrs Rochester in Charlotte Brontë's *Jane Eyre*, who has been interpreted by feminist critics as a symbol of the darker side of the Victorian woman's nature, particularly her repressed passion and sexuality: see Gilbert and Gubar, *Madwoman in the Attic*. On Russian versions of these stereotypes, see Rosalind Marsh, 'Introduction', in *Gender and Russian Literature*, pp. 12–13.

47. See, for example, Graham Roberts, 'Poor Liza: the sexual politics of *Elizaveta Bam*', in Marsh, *Gender and Russian Literature*, pp. 244–62.
48. On the masochistic aspect of literary representations of women doing the laundry or ironing, see Bassein, *Women and Death*, p. 162.
49. D. H. Lawrence, cited in Jacobus, *Women Writing and Writing about Women*, p.13; see also Shoshana Felman, 'Rereading Femininity', *Yale French Studies*, no. 62 (1981), pp. 19–21.
50. Zinaida is described as 'bewitching and imperious' (I. S. Turgenev, *Polnoe sobranie sochinenii i pisem*, 28 vols (Moscow-Leningrad: Akademiia Nauk SSSR, 1960–8), vol. 9, p. 11 'she smiled mysteriously and cunningly' (p. 26); 'she again smiled enigmatically' (p. 27).
51. On the traditional association of female sexuality with evil, and men's fear of women, see H. R. Hays, *The Dangerous Sex: The Myth of Feminine Evil* (London: Methuen, 1966); W. Lederer, *The Fear of Women* (New York: Harcourt Brace Jovanovich, 1968).
52. On the association of women with hysteria, see Barbara Ehrenreich and Deirdre English, *Complaints and Disorders: The Sexual Politics of Sickness* (Old Westbury: The Feminist Press, 1973); Shoshana Felman, 'Women and Madness: the Critical Phallacy', *Diacritics*, no. 5 (Winter 1975), pp. 2–10; Elaine Showalter, *The Female Malady: Women, Madness and English Culture* (London: Virago, 1987).
53. Virginia Woolf, *Collected Essays*, vol. 1 (London: Hogarth Press, 1966), p. 204.
54. Ann Douglas, *The Feminization of American Culture* (New York: Knopf, 1977), p. 12.
55. On a similar theme in English literature, see Elaine Showalter, 'Towards a Feminist Poetics', in Jacobus, *Women Writing and Writing about Women*, p. 31.
56. Barbara T. Gates, *Victorian Suicide: Mad Crimes and Sad Histories* (Princeton: Princeton University Press, 1988), pp. 125–50. She also suggests (p. 98) that many Victorian men wanted to believe that 'redundant women [i.e., unmarried women] had no place to go but toward death'.
57. On this common association, see Bassein, *Women and Death*; for a striking Russian articulation of the relationship, see Iurii Lotman, 'The Origin of Plot in the Light of Typology', trans. Julian Graffy, *Poetics Today*, vol. 1, nos 1–2 (Autumn 1979), pp. 161–84.
58. Hélène Cixous, 'The Laugh of the Medusa', transl. Keith Cohen and Paula Cohen, in Elaine Marks and Isabelle de Courtivron (eds), *New French Feminisms: an anthology* (Brighton: Harvester, 1981), p. 255.
59. Nina Auerbach, *Woman and the Demon: The Life of a Victorian Myth* (Cambridge, MA: Harvard University Press, 1982); this view is applied to the nineteenth-century Russian novel in Rosenshield, 'Afterword', pp. 119–21. Although I dispute this interpretation, I accept Auerbach's view that nineteenth-century literary images had the power to bestow a significance and magic on women, allowing them to transcend their domestic confinement.
60. De Lauretis, *Alice Doesn't*, p. 111.
61. Laura Mulvey, 'Visual Pleasure and Narrative Cinema', *Screen*, vol. 16, no. 3 (Autumn 1975), p. 14.
62. Some emancipated Russian women objected to the portrayal of Natasha in the 'Epilogue' of *War and Peace*: see Mar'ia Tsebrikova (under the pseudonym 'Nikolaeva'), 'Nashi babushki', *Otechestvennye zapiski*, no. 6 (1868); for Inessa Armand's objection to the demeaning concept of the *samka*, see R. C. Elwood, *Inessa Armand, Revolutionary and Feminist* (Cambridge: Cambridge University Press, 1992), p. 17. Some modern critics regard the 'Epilogue' as more ambiguous, suggesting that Tolstoy implicitly condemns Pierre for sinking to Natasha's domestic level, but in my view, Tolstoy did not see Natasha's fate as anything other than

laudable (although he possibly felt some nostalgia for the 'lost fire' of youth in her eyes).
63. Rosenshield, 'Afterword', pp. 121-27.
64. Harriet Murav, 'Reading Woman in Dostoevsky', in Hoisington, *A Plot of her Own*, pp. 44-57.
65. F. M. Dostoevskii, *Polnoe sobranie sochinenii*, 30 vols (Leningrad: Nauka, 1972-90), vol. 23, pp. 145-46.
66. Fyodor Dostoevsky, *A Writer's Diary*, transl. and annotated by Kenneth Lantz, introduction by Gary Saul Morson (Evanston: Northwestern University Press, 1993), pp. 650-53.
67. Research suggests that the majority of women accused of witchcraft in medieval Europe were women over the age of forty, mostly widows or single women: see Norman Cohn, *Europe's Inner Demons* (London: Sussex University Press, 1975), p. 248. Erich Neuman, *The Great Mother: An Analysis of the Archetype*, transl. Ralph Manheim (Princeton: Princeton University Press, 1955), pp. 65-66 refers to the 'witch character of the negative mother', who is seen as possessive, aggressive, terrifying in her ability to manipulate and ensnare.
68. Daniel Rancour-Laferrière, *The Slave-Soul of Russia* (New York: New York University Press, 1995), pp. 137-58; Joanna Hubbs, *Mother Russia: the Feminine Myth in Russian Culture* (Bloomington: Indiana University Press, 1993), pp. 36-51.
69. Elizabeth Klosty Beaujour, 'The Uses of Witches in Fedin and Bulgakov', in Hoisington, *A Plot of her Own*, p. 76.
70. Another famous description of woman as a combination of Muse and domestic servant is the portrayal of Lara and Zhivago's last stay in Varykino (Pasternak, *Doktor Zhivago*, Chapter 14: Section 8).
71. M. G. Davidovich, 'Zhenskii portret u russkikh romantikov pervoi poloviny XIX veka', in A. I. Beletskii (ed.), *Russkii romantizm* (Leningrad, 1978), p. 67; discussed in Heldt, *Terrible Perfection*, p. 162, n. 8, who argues that 'it would be difficult to find a case of authorial indifference to female portraiture in all of Russian realism'.
72. Ol'ga Demidova, 'Russian Women Writers of the Nineteenth Century', in Marsh, *Gender and Russian Literature*, pp. 100-101. Russian works influenced by *Jane Eyre* included Apollinariia Suslova's *Svoei dorogoi* (Her Own Way, 1864), Iuliia Zhadovskaia's *Zhenskaia istoriia* (*A Woman's Story*, 1861), and Lidiia Kamskaia's *Moia sud'ba* (*My Fate*, 1863).
73. Tatyana Mamonova (ed.), *Women and Russia: Feminist Writings from the Soviet Union* (Oxford: Blackwell, 1984), p. xx.
74. See Helena Goscilo, 'Monsters Monomaniacal, Marital and Medical: Tat'iana Tolstaia's Regenerative use of Gender Stereotypes', in Jane Costlow, Stephanie Sandler and Judith Vowles (eds), *Sexuality and the Body in Russian Culture* (Stanford, CA: Stanford University Press, 1993), pp. 205-10.
75. Nina Baym, *Women's Fiction*, p. xi. One particularly vicious representation of a single woman is Odoevsky's eponymous Princess Mimi.
76. I would argue, however, that Varen'ka is not as important to Tolstoy's view of women, and that the whole 'mushroom-picking episode' in which Koznyshev fails to propose to her (6: 4-5) does not unfold as unambiguously according to her choice as Amy Mandelker suggests in *Framing 'Anna Karenina'*, pp. 169-78. Varen'ka feels that it would be the 'height of bliss' to marry Koznyshev, and she is 'faint with joy and fear' at the thought of his proposal (although her mixed feelings after the event do include a 'sense of relief'). It is interesting that Gareth Jones, 'Tolstoy', conference paper to the BASEES Nineteenth-Century Literature Study Group, Bristol, July 1996, interpreted Varen'ka as a Sentimentalist heroine, rather than a proto-feminist.

77. V. Belinskii, 'Russkie povesti M. Zhukovoi', in his *Polnoe sobranie sochinenii*, vol. 5, p. 117.
78. Maia Ganina, 'Tol'ko odna noch"', in *Povest' o zhenshchine: povesti, rasskazy, ocherki* (Moscow: Sovremennik, 1973), pp. 173-83; 'Mariia', 'Zolotoe odinochestvo', 'Uslysh' svoi chas', in *Izbrannoe* (Moscow: Khudozhestvennaia literatura, 1983), pp. 188-204, 369-401, 443-532.
79. See Natasha Kolchevska's chapter, this volume; I.Ratushinskaya, *Grey is the Colour of Hope*, trans. A. Kojevnikov (New York: Knopf, 1988).
80. See, for example, Elena Tarasova, 'Ne pomniashchaia zla' and Svetlana Vasilenko, 'Shamara', in Larisa Vaneeva (ed.), *Ne pomniashchaia zla* (Moscow: Moskovskii rabochii, 1990); Iuliia Voznesenskaia's *Zhenskii dekameron*, and many stories by Liudmila Petrushevskaia.
81. Costlow, '"Oh-là-là" and "No-no-no"', p. 137, n. 13 suggests that Kukshina was based on one particular woman, Evgeniia Petrovna Kittara, whom Turgenev met through the Ukrainian woman writer Marko Vovchok. However, Turgenev was also personally acquainted with George Sand, who smoked and wore men's clothes, and, although Patrick Waddington, *Turgenev and George Sand: an Improbable Entente* (Basingstoke: Macmillan, 1981) suggests that he greatly admired her, her close friendship with his beloved Pauline Garcia (Viardot) (Jeanette H. Foster, *Sex Variant Women in Literature: A Historical and Quantitative Survey* [London: Frederick Muller, 1958], p. 121) may have contributed to his somewhat jaundiced view of the 'new woman'.
82. For further discussion, see Straus, *Dostoevsky and the Woman Question*, pp. 146-54.
83. Thea Margaret Durfee, '*Cement* and *How the Steel was Tempered*: Variations on the New Soviet Woman', in Hoisington, *A Plot of Her Own*, pp. 89-101.
84. Fyodor Gladkov, *Cement*, trans. A. S. Arthur and C. Ashleigh (1929: repr., Evanston: Northwestern University Press, 1994), p. 27.
85. For further discussion of the utopian nature of 'sisterhood', see Helena Michie, *Sororophobia. Differences among Women in Literature and Culture* (Oxford and New York: Oxford University Press, 1992), p. 8.
86. On the frequent depiction of the rape or murder of bourgeois women in literature of the 1920s as 'a metaphor for class subjugation', see Catriona Kelly, *A History of Russian Women's Writing, 1820-1992* (Oxford: Clarendon Press, 1994), pp. 240-41.
87. Durfee, '*Cement* and *How the Steel was Tempered*', p. 98; Lynne Attwood, 'Rationality vs. romanticism: representations of women in the Stalinist press', unpublished conference paper (Birmingham, July 1996). It is possible that such stereotypes, descended from medieval hagiography, represented a male backlash against the greater assertiveness of some women in Stalinist society: on assertive female Stakhanovites, see Mary Buckley, 'Why be a shock worker or a Stakhanovite?', in Marsh, *Women in Russia and Ukraine*, pp. 199-213. On the requirement for women's 'modesty' in other cultures, see Dale Spender, *Women of Ideas and What Men Have Done to Them* (London: Routledge, 1982), p. 41.
88. On the image of the mother, see Kelly, *History of Russian Women's Writing*, p. 4.
89. V.Belinskii, 'Sochineniia Zeneidy R–voi', *Polnoe sobranie sochinenii*, vol. 7, p. 662.
90. Carolyn Heilbrun, *Reinventing Womanhood* (London: Victor Gollancz, 1979), p.16.
91. Adrienne Rich, *Of Woman Born: motherhood as experience and institution* (London: Virago, 1977), p. 225 refers to mother-daughter relationships as 'the great unwritten story'.
92. For further discussion, see Joe Andrew, 'Mothers and Daughters in Russian Literature in the First Half of the Nineteenth Century', *Slavonic and East European Review*, vol. 73, no. 1 (January 1995), pp. 37-60. For an example of a supportive mother-daughter relationship, see Ol'ga Freidenberg's diary, reproduced in

Elliot Mossman (ed.), *The Correspondence of Boris Pasternak and Olga Freidenberg, 1910-1954* (New York: Harcourt Brace Jovanovich, 1982).

93. See, in particular, the work of Nancy Chodorow, Nancy Friday, Susan Suleiman, Sue Miller, Luce Irigaray, Alice Walker, Adrienne Rich and Audre Lorde. For an interesting nineteenth-century exception to this rule, see Catriona Kelly, 'The First-Person "Other": Sof'ia Soboleva's 1863 Story "Pros and Cons" ("I pro, i contra")', *Slavonic and East European Review*, vol. 73, no. 1 (January 1995), pp. 61–81.
94. Nancy Chodorow, *The Reproduction of Mothering: Psychoanalysis and the Sociology of Gender* (Berkeley: University of California Press, 1978), p. 40.
95. For a discussion of male bonding in Pushkin's *Prisoner of the Caucasus,* Odoevsky's *New Year* (1837) and Gogol"s *Taras Bul'ba* (1835; revised 1842), see Andrew, *Narrative and Desire*, pp. 21, 51–55, 216. Male friendship is also a prominent theme in Pushkin's *Evgenii Onegin*, Lermontov's *Hero of Our Time*, Tolstoy's *War and Peace*, Babel"s *Red Cavalry* (1928), and much Soviet 'war prose'.
96. Elaine Showalter, *A Literature of their Own: British Women Novelists from Charlotte Brontë to Doris Lessing* (London: Virago, 1978), p. 117.
97. Claire Johnston (ed.), *Notes on Women's Cinema* (London: SEFT, 1974), pp. 28–29.
98. This paragraph is indebted to Nina Baym's ironic characterisation of the patriarchal nature of nineteenth-century American literature in *Women's Fiction*, pp. xiv–xv.
99. V. Belinskii, 'Povesti Mar'i Zhukovoi', *Polnoe sobranie sochinenii*, vol. 4, pp. 110–18, cf. Belinskii, 'Sochineniia Zeneidy R–voi', vol. 7, pp. 648–78.
100. Linda Edmondson, 'Women's Emancipation and Theories of Sexual Difference in Russia, 1850–1917', in Marianne Liljeström, Eila Mäntysaari, and Arja Rosenholm (eds), *Gender Restructuring in Russian Studies,* Slavica Tamperensia, no. 2 (Tampere, Finland: University of Tampere, 1993), pp. 39–52.
101. For further discussion, see John Mersereau, Jr., *Russian Romantic Fiction* (Ann Arbor: Ardis, 1983), Chapter 24; Andrew, 'A Crocodile in Flannel', pp. 23–25.
102. For Turgenev's use of Evgeniia Tur's 'Antonina', see Turgenev's 'Plemiannitsa' (1852), discussed in Jane Costlow, 'Speaking the Sorrow of Women: Turgenev's "Neschastnaia" and Evgeniia Tur's "Antonina"', *Slavic Review*, vol. 50 (1991), no. 2, pp. 328–35 (esp. p. 331); for his criticism of women's writing, see Turgenev, 'Plemiannitsa', *Polnoe sobranie sochinenii i pis'ma*, vol. 5, pp. 368–86 (esp. p. 374).
103. Victor Terras, *The Young Dostoevsky, 1846–1849. A Critical Study* (The Hague: Mouton, 1969), p. 54. There were, of course, numerous far cruder attacks on women writers: one of the most vicious was N. N. Verevkin, ['Rakhmannyi'], 'Zhenshchina-pisatel'nitsa', *Biblioteka dlia chteniia*, vol. 23 (1837), no. 1, part 1, pp. 19–134.
104. Otto Weininger, *Geschlecht und Charakter* (Vienna and Leipzig: W. Braumüller, 1903); translated in Roszak, *Masculine/Feminine*, p. 89.
105. Leon Trotsky, *Literature and Revolution*, trans. Rose Strunsky (Ann Arbor: University of Michigan Press, 1968), p. 41; Marsh, *Gender and Russian Literature*, p. 15.
106. Victor Erofeyev, 'Introduction: Russia's Fleurs du Mal', in *The Penguin Book of New Russian Writing* (Harmondsworth: Penguin, 1995), p. xxiv.
107. See Lynne Attwood, 'Sex and the Cinema', in Igor Kon and James Riordan, *Sex and Russian Society* (Bloomington: Indiana University Press, 1993), pp. 64–88.
108. Abram Terts (Andrei Siniavskii), *Mysli vrasplokh* (New York: I. G. Rauzen, 1966), p. 79.
109. See Pushkin's conventional advice to his wife in his letters 851, 918, 919, 947, in A. S. Pushkin, *Polnoe sobranie sochinenii*, 17 vols (Moscow and Leningrad: Akademiia Nauk SSSR, 1937–1959), vol. 15; discussed in Catriona Kelly, 'Educating Tatiana:

Manners, Motherhood and Moral Education (*Vospitanie*), 1760–1840', unpublished conference paper (Birmingham, July 1996), pp. 10–12. On Pushkin's praise of women, see his *Roslavlev* (1836), in vol. 8, part 1, p. 156; for his statement in a letter of 1825 to Raevsky that 'women have no character, they have passions in their youth, that is why it is so easy to portray them', see vol. 13, p. 197.

110. John Mersereau, Jr., *Mikhail Lermontov* (Carbondale: Southern Illinois University Press, 1962), pp. 5–14.
111. Simon Karlinsky, *The Sexual Labyrinth of Nikolai Gogol* (Chicago and London: University of Chicago Press, 1992)
112. Leonard Schapiro, *Turgenev: his life and times* (Oxford: Oxford University Press, 1978); Frank Friedeberg Seeley, *Turgenev: a reading of his fiction* (Cambridge: Cambridge University Press, 1991), Chapter 1.
113. Discussed in Geir Kjetsaa, *Fyodor Dostoyevsky: A Writer's Life*, trans. Siri Hystvedt and David McDuff (London: Macmillan, 1987), pp. 325–31; Straus, *Dostoevsky and the Woman Question*, pp. 5–6.
114. Dostoevsky, cited in Kjetsaa, *Fyodor Dostoyevsky*, p. 327.
115. One recent work is William L. Shirer, *Love and Hatred* (London: Aurum, 1994).
116. See Amy Mandelker, *Framing Anna Karenina*, p. 4. For a catalogue of Tolstoy's misogynistic views, see Ruth Crego Benson, *Women in Tolstoy: the Ideal and the Erotic* (Urbana: University of Illinois Press, 1977).
117. Donald Rayfield, 'Discrediting and trivialising Chekhov: archival compromat', paper at BASEES conference, Cambridge (April 1997).
118. Shoshana Felman, 'Rereading Femininity', *Yale French Studies*, 62 (1981), p. 21; cited in de Lauretis, *Alice Doesn't*, p. 111.
119. Adrienne Rich, 'Notes toward a Politics of Location', in *Blood, Bread and Poetry: Selected Prose, 1979–1985* (New York: Norton, 1986), p. 216.
120. Rosenshield, 'Afterword', p. 119 cites the authority of Carolina de Maegd-Soëp, *The Emancipation of Women in Russian Literature and Society* (Ghent: Ghent State University, 1978), pp. 95–110, who takes an uncritical view of nineteenth-century male writers' and critics' disparaging remarks about women writers.
121. N. Shelgunov, 'Zhenskoe bezdushie', *Delo*, no. 9 (1870), pp. 1–34 (esp. p. 11).
122. Arja Rosenholm, 'The "woman question" of the 1860s, and the ambiguity of the "learned woman"', in Marsh, *Gender and Russian Literature*, pp. 112–28; Arja Rosenholm, 'Khvoshchinskaia, Nadezhda Dmitrieva', in Marina Ledkovsky, Charlotte Rosenthal and Mary Zirin (eds), *A Dictionary of Russian Women Writers* (Westport, CT: Greenwood Press, 1994), pp. 286–88.
123. See the chapters by Katharine Hodgson on Ol'ga Berggol'ts, Adele Barker on Grekova, Julie Curtis on Voznesenskaia and Monika Katz on Petrushevskaia in this volume. Many women's writings of the Brezhnev era remained unpublished until glasnost.
124. On women's unconscious internalisation of sexist attitudes and desires, see Toril Moi, *Sexual/Textual Politics: Feminist Literary Theory* (London and New York: Routledge, 1985), p. 92; Cora Kaplan, 'Radical feminism and literature: rethinking Millett's *Sexual Politics*', *Red Letters*, no. 9 (1979), p.10; Carolyn Heilbrun, *Reinventing Womanhood*, p.29. This tendency was also acknowledged by Simone de Beauvoir, who commented that women 'still dream through the dreams of men': *The Second Sex* (Harmondsworth: Penguin, 1986), p. 132.
125. Judith Fetterley, *The Resisting Reader: A Feminist Approach to American Fiction* (Bloomington, IN: Indiana University Press, 1978), p. xx.
126. For further discussion, see Marsh, *Gender and Russian Literature*, pp. 14–17. Women writers in other cultures have expressed a similar view: for example, Mary McCarthy and Margaret Drabble, whose views are challenged in Heilbrun, *Reinventing Womanhood*, pp. 28–29.

127. The few works published in Russia which accept the value and autonomy of women's literature include Larisa Vaneeva, *Ne pomniashchaia zla* (Moscow: Moskovskii rabochii, 1990); Elena Trofimova (ed.), *Chego khochet zhenshchina* (Moscow: Linor, 1993).
128. For further discussion, see Jane T. Costlow, Stephanie Sandler and Judith Vowles, 'Introduction', in Costlow, Sandler and Vowles (eds), *Sexuality and the Body in Russian Culture* (Stanford: Stanford University Press, 1993), pp. 29–34; Helena Goscilo, 'Speaking Bodies', in Goscilo (ed.), *Fruits of her Plume: Essays on Contemporary Russian Women's Culture* (Armonk, NY: M. E. Sharpe, 1993), pp. 135–63.
129. See, for example, A. Shchegolev, 'Lozhnaia zhenshchina', *Leningradskii Universitet*, 16 March, 23 March, and 13 April 1990.
130. For a translation of critical articles, see Helena Goscilo (ed.), *Skirted Issues: The Discreteness and Indiscretions of Russian Women's Prose*, Russian Studies in Literature (Spring 1992).
131. Tat'iana Kravchenko, 'Ne tak strashen chert', *Literaturnaia gazeta*, 17 May 1995, p. 4.
132. See, for example, Tat'iana Sotnikova, 'Razkryvat' prestupleniia protiv lichnosti meshaet kadrovyi vopros', *Segodnia*, 17 Jan. 1996, p. 6; Tat'iana Bateneva, 'Deti riska', *Izvestiia*, 14 Aug. 1996 p. 5.
133. Rosenshield, 'Afterword', p. 119; de Maegd-Soëp, *Emancipation of Women*, pp. 242–43; for Tolstoy's comment of 1901 on Turgenev's influence in shaping the new Russian woman, see Turgenev, *Polnoe sobranie sochinenii*, vol. 8, p. 522.
134. Costlow, 'Speaking the Sorrow of Women'.
135. Demidova, 'Russian women writers', pp. 96–101.
136. This approach is recommended to women readers by Carolyn Heilbrun in *Reinventing Womanhood*, p. 140, and in her *Towards a Recognition of Androgyny*.
137. On this point in Anglophone literature, see Olsen, 'The Fiction of Fiction', p. 117.
138. For one example of the prescriptive approach, see Cheri Register, 'American Feminist Literary Criticism: A Bibliographical Introduction', in Josephine Donovan (ed.), *Feminist Literary Criticism* (Lexington: University of Kentucky Press, 1975), pp. 2, 19.
139. See, for example, R. Warhol and Diane Price Herndl (eds), *Feminisms* (New Brunswick, NJ: Rutgers University Press, 1991); Marks and Courtivron, *New French Feminisms*. Equally, there is a contemporary focus on 'masculinities': see R. W. Connell, *Masculinities* (Oxford: Polity Press, 1995).
140. Annette Kolodny, 'Dancing through the Minefield', *Feminist Studies*, vol. 6, no. 1 (Spring 1980), p. 19; see also Sydney Janet Kaplan, 'Varieties of Feminist Criticism', in Gayle Greene and Coppélia Kahn, *Making a Difference: feminist literary criticism* (New York: Methuen, 1985), pp. 37–58.
141. Elaine Showalter (ed.), *The New Feminist Criticism: Essays on Women, Literature, and Theory* (London: Virago, 1985), p. 107.
142. Cornillon, *Images of Women in Fiction*, p. ix.

Chapter 2

READING THE TEXTS – REREADING OURSELVES

Adele Barker

The fact that those of us in the Slavic field spend a good deal of time in transit between western critical theory and Russian texts has led me over the years to reflect on how I use the one to elucidate the other. Like many western critics of Russian literature, I am constantly searching for those often elusive intersections between the theory I employ and the literary texts I read. Sometimes the spaces that separate western theoretical models and Russian texts seem more intriguing than the closure which theory longs to effect. The fact that I have found the points of intersection frequently to be elusive has been all to the good, in that it has forced me to rethink, and in some cases to redefine, some of the critical categories that have shaped so much of my thinking in the wake of postmodernism, feminism, and cultural studies. What follows are my thoughts on some of the ways in which western critical theory and Russian texts in general, and Russian women's writing in particular, have intersected in my reading, each enriching yet often problematising the other in new and unexpected ways. Often in using the critical methodologies at my disposal, I find myself engaging in a dialogue with the methodologies themselves rather than selectively employing them as ways of speaking about a literary text. For me this dialogue has concerned itself with what happens when text and theory intersect, each acting upon the other, and indeed raising questions about the other, in ways that hold both to the test.

There are moments when, I must confess, I frankly despair of finding those intersections I implicitly long for between various postmodernisms and the Russian text. Reading the prison memoirs of Evgeniia Ginzburg, who languished for eighteen years in Stalin's Gulag, or even Lidiia Chukovskaia's *Sof'ia Petrovna*, a novel about a typist in a Leningrad publishing house, whose descent into madness comes to reflect the madness of the Stalinist regime itself, I cannot help wondering what place postmodern literary theories, with their debunking of the notion of a single all-embracing truth and their fixation on representations, have in works whose sole purpose was to exhume and bear witness to the truth of the Stalinist past. Postmodernism has brought with it the concept of multiple and fluid identities within cultures, within texts, and even within our own positioning as critics vis-à-vis the texts we study. Our job, in the words of one critic, has been to engage with a text 'in order to construe meanings rather than discover truth'.[1] Indeed, for many postmodern critics the notion of text, no less in literature than in life, has come to be regarded as material infinitely fluid, infinitely open to a 'plurality of possible meanings' occasioned in turn by race, gender, ethnicity, and our own personal concerns.[2]

How then does this kind of critical approach stand up to a body of literature whose sole function was to lay bare the truth about Stalin's Russia? Lidiia Chukovskaia once said that it was her desire to tell 'the true history' of Soviet life under Stalin.[3] Ironically, that truth was often couched within the pages of fiction rather than history in Soviet Russia, a fact which turned narrative into a form of indictment. The point is that for many Soviet writers of this century, the power of the word was invested with something very nearly sacred, as it became for the writer a weapon every bit as powerful as that used by the state against them (witness Solzhenitsyn's now famous dictum that the writer in Russia is like a second government). The very fact that the word itself possessed the capacity potentially to change reality is suggested by the proclamation with which Solzhenitsyn concluded his Nobel Lecture: 'One word of truth shall outweigh the whole world'.[4]

Even as we look, however, at what seems to be an enormous incongruity between western theory and Russian text, it is perhaps important to remember that not all contemporary theory is as eager to dismiss the idea of text as historical testament as do postmodern critics. There has been much debate among literary scholars in the West over what exactly the relationship is between postmodernism, feminism, and cultural studies, and indeed over whether feminist or cultural studies theory is even postmodern. Indeed, not all feminist theorists or cultural studies theorists care to align themselves with postmodernism, which rejects the very historical specificity within which much of cultural studies and, indeed, feminism, is grounded.

The relationship between the word and the reality it strove to depict brings much of Soviet literature into direct conflict with postmodern theories of language, indebted largely to Derrida and Lacan. At the risk of oversimplification, for Derrida meaning is no longer constituted as an unproblematic relationship between language and its referent, but rather is constructed as a play of signifiers in which the subject is constantly striving to find its place. Derrida questioned whether we could ever find notions of truth or meaning in the classical sense of the term, since he construed meaning, or the signified, as a constantly changing unstable product of words or signifiers.[5] Derrida's notion that we construct reality through language is reflected in Lacan, for whom the speaker or the 'I' is always attempting but never quite succeeding in articulating itself, because it is striving to do so through the Other, or the symbolic order, whose very essence implies the impossibility of the merger between language and its referent.[6] To carry the point one step further, if postmodern theories of language see text and the language in which it is written as inseparable from one another and ultimately self-referential, and if language is at best only part of a symbolic order referring to an endless stream of signifiers, then how can these theories mediate the experience of Russian writers for whom there would be real moral questions involved in the application of these linguistic theories to their attempts to tell the truth about the Stalin years? And finally, how can I morally as a critic reduce the phenomenon of Stalinism to mere 'text' upon which language works?

There is yet another area in which I think we need to be very careful in the application of western critical theory to Russian texts, notably to those penned by women. Since 1977, when Elaine Showalter published *A Literature of Their Own: British Women Novelists from Brontë to Lessing*, and two years later, when Sandra Gilbert and Susan Gubar completed their groundbreaking work *The Madwoman in the Attic*, feminist critics have frequently taken up the term 'palimpsestic', which Gilbert and Gubar use to refer to works 'whose surface designs conceal or obscure deeper, less accessible (and less socially acceptable) levels of meaning'.[7] Gilbert and Gubar make the point that nineteenth-century Anglophone western writers from Jane Austen to Mary Shelley, Emily Brontë, and Emily Dickinson were writing works that appeared to conform to, yet simultaneously subverted, patriarchal literary tradition, forming in Patricia Meyer Spacks's words 'subterranean challenges' to the patriarchal conventions to which the writers on the surface seemed to ascribe.[8]

How does this concept of palimpsestic writing apply to Russian women writers? The answer is that it applies very differently depending on the century and on the political winds of the day. While Russian women writers of the nineteenth century such as Evgeniia Tur, Evdokiia Rostopchina, and Nadezhda Khvoshchinskaia were forced to write palimpsestically, primarily because the censorship apparatus under Nicholas I precluded any direct expression of the *zhenskii vopros* (woman question),[9] the application of the concept of palimpsestic writing to the twentieth-century Russian literary canon is made more problematic by the fact that men as well as women were forced to resort to such subterfuge or to abandon it altogether, since one's very survival was frequently dependent on conforming to Party ideology and avoiding any explicit or implicit stance that might be construed as subverting the party line. While writers under Stalin often used a series of markers in their text to refer obliquely to those moments which lay outside official ideology,[10] the consequences of writing the kind of double-voiced or palimpsestic novels that Gilbert, Gubar, and Showalter refer to were obviously much more serious than simply the risk of not having one's voice heard. While there were occasional relaxations in the strictures imposed by the Party, allowing writers such as Vera Panova, for example, to make sporadic literary forays into a more private world away from the *kollektiv*, the overall effect that the Stalinist state exerted on the creation of palimpsestic texts was a muting one.[11] While one might argue that women's writing, because it, like all writing, is a gendered activity, will inevitably be palimpsestic as long as women are writing within a patriarchal system, one must also ask what effect totalitarian regimes have on the construction and expression of gender, as well as on the double-voiced quality of a literary text. In other words: when many writers, men as well as women, are forced to write palimpsestically, is there any difference between men's and women's double-voicedness?

The fact that so much of Stalinist literature was prescriptive, making it uncommonly difficult to produce the sort of double-voiced texts I discussed above, has also made us reluctant to explore beneath the surface of many post-Stalinist literary texts where one finds a greater dialogue between the author and the social and political system. Thus, for example, many of the literary works written by I. Grekova (the pen name of Elena Sergeevna Ventsel') suggest the possibilities of reading post-Stalinist works palimpsestically, partially because Grekova, like many others who began writing during the early 1960s, was attempting to write simultaneously within and outside the system. Mathematician-turned-writer when she was already in her forties, Grekova has been passed over by feminist critics because of what has been seen as too close an alliance on her part with the male scientific establishment in Soviet Russia. But I also think that part of our reluctance to engage with some of the non-dissident women's writing that emerged after Stalin's death in the 1960s stems from the fact that our own experience with Stalinist prescriptive literature has inured us to the potentially disruptive quality of a work written from within the system. As a case in point, Grekova's short story 'Damskii master' ('Ladies' Hairdresser', 1963) illustrates precisely the kind of double-voiced writing that Gilbert and Gubar are exploring in *The Madwoman in the Attic*, albeit with different political overtones.

The story explores the relationship between a middle-aged mathematician, Kovaleva, and a young hairdresser named Vitaly. The plot gravitates between Kovaleva's attempts to balance work and family and the fate of the young male hairdresser who, despite his best intentions to advance in his profession independently of the system, ends up capitulating to it by giving up hairdressing in favour of metal working. This story of the relationship between the hairdresser and this middle-aged mathematician contains a second text, one that implicitly interrogates the ideological underpinnings of a system that discourages and even suffocates true talent. In the unspoken spaces within the story, Grekova takes on the issue of the artist's place in official Soviet society. She suggests strongly through the character of the young hairdresser Vitaly that to practise art officially in her country is to capitulate to a system that would ultimately choke the creative life out of its artists, whether hairdresser, mathematician, or writer. It is in the recesses of this tale that the subtext intersects with the implicit gender concerns of the author (I say 'implicit' because Grekova has repeatedly denied the label 'woman writer' and argues strongly that writing should be a non-gendered activity.)[12] Issues of gender are germane, however, to her argument in that the system itself has ensured and perpetuated deeply embedded gender codes in Russian and Soviet society. There is a moment in the text when Kovaleva looks up at the mirror after a tortuous five hours of having her hair cut and permed. As she looks into the mirror, what she sees astonishes her:

> Well, well, well! So that's a permanent wave... A shining, vital mass of dark hair, with a lustrous, submerged network of fine white threads. It looked more like an expensive fur than a head of hair, a big, fancy hat that lay almost weightlessly on my head. And the little, curving lock that fell onto the left side of my brow as if by chance, as if the wind had just tousled my hair...
> 'Are you satisfied?', Vitaly asked.
> 'It's fantastic! You're a real artist!'[13]

Issues of gender and art are conflated in this scene as Kovaleva looks up and sees the new (re)vitalised image of herself, made over by

Vitaly, the male artist. Perhaps the moment would not be as symbolic as it is had Kovaleva not been led into the beauty parlour in the first place by memories of her father who always felt that having a haircut would help him get down to business. '*Ostrigus' i nachnu*' ('I'll get a haircut and get down to business'), she remembers him saying. It is always the image of the male from whom Kovaleva takes her cue, first from the father, then more and more gradually from Vitaly himself, as he first redoes her hair, then later provides the much needed critique of Kovaleva's handling of the social evening at the institute.

But what is Grekova suggesting about the relationship between art and gender in this work? Is she, in fact, implying that for herself, as for Kovaleva, the source of the creative act is male? Indisputably, Kovaleva identifies with Vitaly, as does Grekova. His image is meant to suggest Kovaleva's, and by extension Grekova's, own bifurcated selves. He is the self that is marginalised, the one that stands outside the system and is not quite sure that it wants the entrance ticket into it. In this sense he comes to embody a feature of Kovaleva who, as an artist in her own right, demands the same kind of freedom from constraints as does Vitaly in order to fashion numbers into art. He is that part of her that is all too much a part of the system and yet wants out, that part of her that gravitates to peripheral figures such as Vitaly, that part that is attracted to, yet fearful of, the anarchy represented by the games with the rabbits at the students' social evening. And he embodies within himself what is essential to Grekova's understanding of her own art, namely that to practise that art officially, to take it up full-time, is to capitulate to a system that would ultimately choke the creative life out of its artists, whether hairdresser, mathematician, or writer.

But is Vitaly merely the male artist who works his creativity upon various female heads of hair? Grekova's examination of gender and art is more complicated than this fossilised image, for she is constantly experimenting through the characters of Vitaly and Kovaleva with transgressing gender boundaries. Vitaly is not merely the male artist after whom Grekova and Kovaleva fashion themselves. If Kovaleva is created by Vitaly in front of the mirror, so too is she capable of her own creative act, as she pours over her mathematical problems, revelling in the joy of solution. If Kovaleva is creator as well as created, she is also an androgynous figure, at once both 'male' in her work at the institute and female in her persistent mothering of her own staff. Into the figure of Kovaleva, Grekova injects a note of the quasi-erotic as she looks at her secretary Galia, eyeing her 'big blue, enamelled eyes, slim little waist, the bulging calves on her firm legs' (p 58), and in a self-reflexive note comments on one of the girls at the dance, 'I like girls who dance with each other. You can rely on them' (p. 71).

On almost every level Grekova is engaged in breaking down procrustean gender stereotypes, not only in the relationship between Kovaleva and Vitaly but in her protagonist's response to the female world of which she is and is not a part. She flees from her role as homemaker only to take refuge in that traditional bastion of femaleness, the beauty parlour. Yet there too she feels estranged, shrinking under the glances of the women who spy the English book in her net bag, intimidated, as always, by the company of women.

There are no neat answers to the dilemmas which Grekova's female protagonist, and by extension, Grekova herself, must face over issues of women's split selves. For much as Kovaleva wrestles with these issues and with her two worlds, it is her ability to cross those borders, to break down the ideological underpinnings of the system which include notions of appropriate male and female behaviour in her society, that sets her free from the political and gender constraints of her own system, even as she continues to work within it.[14]

Obviously, not all women writers from Stalin's time until the end of the 1960s wrote works that were as radically and as potentially deconstructive of Soviet society as did Grekova. While Grekova's story was written during the period of relative relaxation under Khrushchev, those who wrote during the Stalin era were obviously forced to write differently. The stances that Grekova took were simply not available to writers from the 1930s to the early 1950s. Given the strict yet constantly changing parameters within which they worked, many writers simply chose to write for the drawer (Frida Vigdorova, for example, never published her travel notes which she wrote while working as a journalist because of censorship constraints). Others, ostensibly conforming to the doctrines of socialist realism, wrote more politically acceptable works reflecting party ideology. However, the highly prescriptive nature of the canons of socialist realism and of some of the works produced under its influence has determined and indeed deterred us from critical engagement with mainstream Soviet texts written after Stalin's death during times of relative political liberalisation.

My own personal view is that the very nature of Soviet reality in this century has put at least some of our critical views, namely postmodern theories of representation, on very shaky ground. However, as the example of Grekova suggests, there are other moments in which critical theory, in this case feminist theory, has enabled us to exhume the subtext of a work which implicitly subverts many of the political and gender codes of the early post-Stalin years.

There are other areas too in which critical theory and the reality of Soviet literary life have each benefited from their tenuous encounters with each other, specifically in reference to questions of dominant versus marginalised cultures.[15] Having its origins in post-colonialist theory, in writings by and about the subaltern, and in feminist literary theory, the term 'marginalisation' is a politically loaded one, referring to those voices and groups of people that have been silenced and written out of texts by the dominant cultures in a given society. Within this field western critics have explored the privileging of certain kinds of writing over others, certain cultures and certain voices over others, in order to see how entire groups, or entire genres have been excluded from the literary as well as from the historical process. The danger of interpreting the terms 'dominant' and 'marginalised' too literally, however, is that it causes us as critics to act as if those binary oppositions between centre and margin were in fact just that, whereas the two often maintain in both historical and literary discourse a much more complex, often nuanced relationship.

What I want to explore in the next few pages is the particular way in which the study of centre and margin has been configured in Russian and Soviet studies and how that structure has influenced much contemporary critical theory in the West. Long before work on the theory of dominant and marginalised cultures began to make an impact on western critical theory, those of us in Soviet studies were forced by the nature of the society we were studying to work within these binary oppositions between centre and periphery, official versus non-official culture. For most of this century, the reality of Soviet politics created for us structures which shaped our approach to the political, economic, and cultural life of that country. Notions of centre versus periphery, official versus non-official, and the moral tags associated with each, came to dominate our thinking and to create the parameters within which we wrote and thought. What we discovered, however, is that the relationship between centre and margin, high and low culture, was infinitely more complex than its definition in official ideology, and moreover, that the structures created by Soviet political and cultural life failed to tell the whole story about the relationship between official and non-official literary life in the Soviet Union. For example, while political and economic power as well as various forms of social control had their source in the central party authority, literary and cultural life, lived on the edges, was in and of itself an alternate source of power, though many would deny the ability of that marginalised culture to wield effective power. Moreover, the literature that was part of that periphery created, in the words of one contemporary critic, the moral consciousness of an entire generation of thinkers and writers long before the works they were reading were allowed to be published in Russia.[16] If official literature reflected and created a nexus of power, of perks and sinecures from the centre, it was precisely the location of some texts on the fringes of acceptability, or more frequently, in a place of total unacceptability, that defined their centrality for us in the West.[17] It is in fact true to say that the degree of influence the texts of Pasternak, Solzhenitsyn, Tsvetaeva, Akhmatova and others have had over our literary imagination and our social consciousness was directly proportional to the distance they occupied from the centre of Soviet power. This power emanating from the margins of Soviet society, while not overtly political, had important political repercussions and suggested within this context the uneasy and potentially explosive relationship between centre and margin of Soviet culture.

We were also forced early on to deal with notions of élitist versus popular culture, although in truth we defined those notions somewhat differently than do practitioners of cultural studies today. The notion of élitist versus popular culture in the West is largely a function of class hierarchy and of a consumer society. As defined by most western critics, élitist or high culture is primarily that of the educated minority who are conversant with the canons which make up the western cultural tradition. Interestingly enough, it is often the élitist culture which determines what shall fall into the category of popular culture, and in that sense its influence on the culture of the masses elides the traditional boundary separating high from low culture. Popular culture on the other hand is that cultural product not necessarily conceptualised by but most definitely consumed by the masses. In contemporary theory popular culture usually implies those products that are part of mass or commercial culture, be they television, video or popular fiction – in short, what Frederic Jameson refers to as the 'degraded' landscape of schlock and kitsch.[18]

The distinction between élitist and popular culture has traditionally taken a very different turn in the Soviet Union, partially because, officially at least, from the 1930s on, Party ideologues made little distinction between the two. I emphasise the word 'officially' because the gulf separating the élite from the masses was very real, though unstated. Beginning in the Bolshevik era, one encountered a high culture made up of the party élite and the Party ideologues who fashioned a culture designed for the masses.[19] I am connecting official with élitist culture here primarily because that official culture was the brainchild of the Party ideologues who laboriously created the ideology behind the production of Soviet popular culture, from film and literature to sporting events for the masses. Soviet society of the 1930s was a structure in which popular culture reflected an ideology designed by the élite for the masses, or *narod*, creating for them a culture accessible *to* them and designed to be consumed *by* them. In this sense the Soviet experience for the greater part of this century reinforced Harold Bloom's definition of the western canon as always reflecting the taste of the ruling élite, within which the muse became an élitist one.[20] Essentially, in order to reinforce power and strengthen the ideological basis of their society, the party élite created a culture which obfuscated and in some sense perpetuated the gulf between them and the masses below.

Here we encounter one of the potential discrepancies between western theory and Soviet reality, for it remains debatable to what degree this élitist/official culture was actually consumed by the masses. Surely it was to some extent, but while there was not a profit but rather an ideological motive involved on the part of the producers, the product, namely Soviet kitsch or socialist realism, was often rejected by the very group for which it was designated. While one can argue, as Boris Groys does, that marketing conditions ruled out the possibility that the ideology would not be bought, I think the opposite can also be argued, namely that although ideology guaranteed that the culture would be bought, it was not entirely clear that it was consumed as its planners hoped it would be.[21]

There are other areas as well in which western definitions of what constitutes popular and élitist culture break down on Russian soil, namely in terms of how the notion of the popular was understood during Soviet times. Essentially, the notion of popular culture was a much more complex one than its definition within the western idiom. On the one hand, it included the traditional, prerevolutionary culture of the rural people. Or, conversely, it could denote the culture of the urban masses influenced by industrialisation, or finally that sub-culture of individual groups who had their own songs, dances, theatre, and other artistic pursuits in Soviet Russia.[22]

Much of the important work on the relationship between the élite and the masses, work which has had a significant impact on western critical theory, was first done by Bakhtin, who explored and exploded the traditional binary opposition between élitist and popular culture. Bakhtin's work on Rabelais (*Rabelais and His World*, translated into English in 1968)[23] has been much cited, partly because it celebrates the notion of the carnivalesque as a transgressive phenomenon capable of undermining and overturning established orders and hierarchies on the part of the population at large. Although Bakhtin's study deals with the Middle Ages and the Renaissance, it must also be remembered that he wrote it during Stalin's time and was denied his *doktorat* on the basis of the ideas he set forth in it.[24] Although, on the whole, medievalists and Renaissance historians and literary critics had an easier time under Stalin than those working in more contemporary fields, in that they tended to be less affected by the scourge of ideology, readers of Bakhtin's argument could not help but be struck by the implicit parallels he draws between possibilities for subversion in Rabelais's time and in his own. While there has been much debate over his interpretation of the carnivalesque, some critics preferring to see it as a containing rather than a liberating force,[25] one of the important outcomes of his work was that he saw through those rigid hierarchical lines dividing the élite from the masses and initiated a line of inquiry that has increasingly led western critics to look beyond the oppositional moments within these hierarchies to construct a vision of a society as seen from below.

Bakhtin's work stands as an important moment in the interrelations between western critical theory and Russian texts in this century, because his work illustrates just one of the ways in which western critical theory has been influenced both by Russian critical thought as well as by Russian social and political experience from this century. In this case, Bakhtin's work suggested new ways to view traditional divisions between the centre and the margin of a given culture. Exported abroad, many of his original views have been interrogated and honed on western soil, only to be reintroduced back into Russia as we revisit the sites of official and non-official life on the pages of contemporary theory.

The dialogue between centre and margin discussed above has made itself felt in the study of Russian women's writing, precisely because for centuries women's literary endeavours were consigned to the margins of Russian, and then Soviet literary life.[26] Influenced powerfully by western feminist theory, which initially led critics to refocus attention on marginalised voices, scholars in the Russian field have been engaged in the recovery of the lost literature of Russia's eighteenth- and nineteenth-century women writers, literature written by authors who had to fight for publication and recognition by a male-dominated literary establishment.[27] Even in the twentieth century, despite the advances that women initially made with the advent of socialism, women's entrance ticket into literary life was still contingent upon their ability both to toe the party line and to write apparently non-gendered works. Writing thus became an acceptably gendered activity just as long as one wrote 'as a man'. Thus for critics studying twentieth-century Russian and Soviet women's writing, issues of marginalisation in women's literature revolved less around the necessity to recover lost texts than around the desire to make explicit the gendered concerns of women writers who themselves were outcasts or pariahs from the dominant literary establishment: Tsvetaeva, who was ostracised by both the émigré community abroad and official literary circles at home; Akhmatova, who was spared by Stalin but lived as a virtual outcast in her own country; and more recently, and somewhat differently, Liudmila Petrushevskaia, who throughout her literary career has been the target of criticism for having nothing uplifting to say to her readers. Often, ironically, this process of exclusion has been made more problematic by the vehement rejection of the label 'woman writer' by Russian women writers themselves, a rejection that has not been very different from that voiced by U.S. women writers of the past thirty years who have shared Mary McCarthy's loathing of 'this WW [woman writer] business with drapery and décor'.[28]

While the focus on the literature of the margins has aided critics substantially in rewriting the history of Russian literature by incorporating woman's voices into it, our tendency as critics to work within such polarities as centre versus margin, official versus non-official has led us to privilege certain voices over others. The fact that recent critical theory has simply fed into an already well-ingrained tendency among those of us in Soviet studies to validate non-official or marginalised literature has raised some problematic issues, for me at least. Desiring to give critical recognition to voices once silenced, and caught up in notions that the only Soviet literature worth reading was that which emanated from its unofficial ranks, we have tended, I think, to ignore some of the more officially sanctioned women writers who wrote during difficult times and attempted to negotiate the canons of socialist realism and Stalinism from within rather than from the periphery. Members of this group include, for example, Galina Nikolaeva (1911–1963) and Vera Panova (1905–1973), women who attempted to create spaces within the official literature for dialogue with the system from within its ranks. To many of us in the West, the very fact that these writers were published during the Stalin era has led us to view them as part of the official culture and thus to devalue much of what they had to say. Ironically, with the demise of the Soviet Union and its censorship apparatus, what was once an official culture has now itself been officially marginalised. However, it has carried into those margins the stigma of its own 'officialness', where it continues to remain relatively unstudied by western critics. Let me suggest some of the possible ways in which I think western critical theory can open new avenues through which we can look at these texts.

The impact that cultural studies has had on contemporary critical theory has led us to legitimise the study of popular culture, from film, pulp fiction and MTV to rollerblading – in short, cultural products that were formerly considered too low-brow to merit serious scholarly attention. While the claim can be made that this is not high art and therefore not worthy of serious scholarly study, what the study of popular culture has brought with it is the articulation of new and very interesting questions about the factors which drive culture and politics, questions regarding the relationship between culture, the market, and ideology, and what these questions suggest about our role as both producers and consumers of culture.[29] Cultural studies has already made its mark on the study of Soviet and Russian society, in that it has legitimised areas that were formerly regarded as either too low-brow or too much a part of official Soviet life to merit much interest. Suddenly the phenomena of the Soviet communal apartment, the bath-house, or Stalinist movie themes have become the subject of some very interesting work which raises questions regarding the relationship between official and non-official life and the boundaries separating the two.[30]

The application of cultural rather than purely literary theory to Russian women's texts in the Stalin and post-Stalin era can enrich our study of these texts substantially, in so far as it enables us to lift these texts out of the purely literary domain into one in which they can be seen as cultural documents, which speak to issues of how gender identity, the public and private personas, and cultural mythologies were constructed or played out under Stalin. In a sense, the very structure of Soviet society and the kind of literature it produced have already forced us into looking at these texts outside the purely literary arena, politicising them and seeing them as extra-literary phenomena.[31] I think a return to seeing them as cultural artefacts is important, because it allows us access to the interplay between ideology, the construction of national, cultural and gender identity, and the consumption of ideology in ways which a purely literary approach does not. Moreover, these are all issues which, perhaps because of their very complexity and because of the degree to which they were unconsciously imbibed by those who seemingly resisted them, still reverberate powerfully in current post-Soviet women's writing.[32]

The preceding comments can only begin to suggest the complexity of the intersections between what Russian writers write and the texts we critique. One of the biggest challenges ahead for us as critics is that the very structures that determined the shape of Russian literary life for most of this century – official versus non-official and centre versus margin – have evaporated with the demise of the Soviet Union and the literary canons that were part of its political life. Though the relationship between that centre and margin was constantly changing, the structure itself was one of the paradigms which determined for critics in the West who merited study and who did not. Without that topography, which set official off from non-official, acceptable from unacceptable, centre from margin, we are having to revise the maps of contemporary Russian culture. In some sense, what lies before us is not very different from the tasks that face Russian writers themselves. For they, too, are now learning to redefine themselves and their work outside the traditional framework, which simultaneously limited them yet created the boundaries within which they named themselves. It is finally in that area of rethinking, redefining and realigning those traditional margins that defined our work as critics and writers in both countries where we are able to find the common ground that has eluded us for much of this century.

Notes

1. Blanche H. Gelfant, *Cross-Cultural Reckonings: A Triptych of Russian, American, and Canadian Texts* (Cambridge: Cambridge University Press, 1995), p. 12.
2. Frederic Jameson in his *Postmodernism, or The Cultural Logic of Late Capitalism* (Durham, NC: Duke University Press, 1991) argues that one of the characteristics of the postmodern is that neither the historian nor the novelist can set out to represent the historical past. Instead, they can only 'represent their own ideas and stereotypes about that past', since the real world remains for ever out of reach (p. 25). If one applies this same idea to the construction of personality, there is in the postmodern no longer one complete self but a multitude of fragmented selves which, like the reality the artist strives to depict, is forever out of reach (pp. 14–15). Not all feminist theory, particularly American and Afro-American, would agree with Jameson's dismissal of the historical past. This is the crux of the debate between 'essentialism' and anti-'essentialism', revived and discussed by Diana Fuss in her book *Essentially Speaking: Feminism, Nature, and Difference* (New York: Routledge, 1989).
3. Lydia Chukovskaya, *Sofia Petrovna*, trans. Aline Worth, 1967; reprint (Evanston, IL: Northwestern University Press, 1988), p. 112.
4. Alexander Solzhenitsyn, 'Nobel Lecture', trans. Alexis Klimoff, in John Dunlop et al. (eds), *Solzhenitsyn in Exile: Critical Essays and Documentary Materials* (Stanford: Hoover Institution, 1985), p. 497.
5. See Terry Eagleton's explanation of Derrida and language in *Literary Theory: An Introduction* (Minneapolis: University of Minnesota Press, 1983), pp. 142ff. See also Jonathan Culler, *On Deconstruction: Theory and Criticism after Structuralism* (Ithaca: Cornell University Press, 1982).
6. See Jacques Lacan, *Ecrits: A Selection*, trans. Alan Sheridan (New York: W. W. Norton, 1977). Excellent discussions and explanations of Lacan's linguistic theories can also be found in Rosalind Coward and John Ellis, *Language and Materialism: Developments in Semiology and the Theory of the Subject* (London: Routledge, 1977), Chaps 6–7. See also Slavoj Zizek, *Looking Awry: An Introduction to Jacques Lacan through Popular Culture* (Cambridge: MIT Press, 1991), as well as his *The Sublime Object of Ideology* (London: Verso, 1989).
7. The word 'palimpsest' originally referred to a piece of parchment or other writing material from which the writing has been erased to make room for another text. See particularly Chapters 4 and 5 of Showalter's *A Literature of Their Own* (Princeton: Princeton University Press, 1977). Gilbert and Gubar use the term to refer to the numerous ways in which nineteenth-century women novelists were able to tell their own stories, despite tremendous pressure to re-enact the plots designed for them by male writers. One of the ways they did so was through the

image of the madwoman who becomes in these novels the author's double, 'an image of her own anxiety and rage' (p. 78). Sandra M. Gilbert and Susan Gubar, *The Madwoman in the Attic: The Woman Writer and the Nineteenth-Century Literary Imagination* (New Haven: Yale University Press, 1979), pp. 73ff.
8. Quoted in Gilbert and Gubar, *The Madwoman in the Attic*, p.75.
9. For example, Rostopchina's poem 'Nasil'nyi brak' was seen by some as a critique of Russia's subjugation of Poland. Tur's novella *Antonina* (1851) reads like a society tale, but actually deals with the position of women during her time. Similarly, Khvoshchinskaia's novella *Pansionerka* (1860) deals with the position of women in Russia and the choices available to them in the declining political situation of the day. I am grateful to my colleague Jehanne Gheith for supplying this information.
10. Vera Dunham notes the use by Stalinist writers of the conversation in the corridor of a train between two people late at night, a marker that was often used to suggest not only the personal but the possibility for dissent from official Stalinist ideology. Talk given at Yale University, summer 1987.
11. Panova's novel *Rabochii poselok* (*The Factory*), written in 1947, came under attack by the conservative literary establishment for its overly personal tone and its concentration on the individuals working in the factory, despite the fact that she had that same year received a Stalin Prize for her novel *Sputniki* (*The Train*). Similarly, immediately after Stalin's death Panova's *Vremena goda* (*Span of the Year*, 1953) was attacked by critics for its 'extreme pessimism and naturalism'. See V. Nazarenko, 'Ideinost' i masterstvo', *Zvezda*, no. 11 (1954), pp. 181–91.
12. See I. Grekova's introduction to *Soviet Women Writing: Fifteen Short Stories* (New York: Abbeville Press, 1990), pp. 9–14, which states that there are 'no grounds for dividing literature on a sex-basis... We can talk of "good" or "bad" literature, but not of "male" and "female" literature', p. 11.
13. I. Grekova, 'Ladies' Hairdresser', trans. Brain Oles, in Susan Hardy Aiken, Adele Marie Barker, Maya Koreneva, and Ekaterina Stetsenko, *Dialogues/Dialogi: Literary and Cultural Exchanges between (ex) Soviet and American Women* (Durham: Duke University Press, 1994), p. 55. Page references in the text are to this edition.
14. For an analysis of gender and politics in Grekova's 'Damskii master', see Susan Hardy Aiken, 'Stages of Dissent: Olsen, Grekova, and the Politics of Creativity', in Aiken, Barker, Koreneva, and Stetsenko, *Dialogues*, pp. 120–40.
15. For a cogent introduction to how cultural studies has come to be aligned with the study of marginalised discourses, see Simon During, 'Introduction', in *The Cultural Studies Reader* (London: Routledge, 1993), pp. 1–25. See also Homi K. Bhabha, *Nation and Narration* (London: Routledge, 1990), and G. C. Spivak, 'Can the Subaltern Speak?', in C. Nelson and L. Grossberg (eds), *Marxism and the Interpretation of Culture* (Urbana, IL: University of Illinois Press, 1988, pp. 217–313.
16. Lev Annensky made this point in a talk given at Yale University in the summer of 1987.
17. The Russian critic Dmitry Urnov has long argued that the West has failed to assess accurately the state of Soviet letters in this century because of our tendency to overvalue those works that were marginalised in their own country. He makes a similar point in a recent article on the new alternative prose which is currently enjoying great popularity, but which he finds unreadable. See 'Plokhaia proza', *Literaturnaia gazeta*, 1989, no. 6, p. 4.
18. Jameson, *Postmodernism*, p. 2.
19. Boris Groys makes the point in his *The Total Art of Stalinism: Avant-Garde, Aesthetic Dictatorship, and Beyond*, trans. Charles Rougle (Princeton: Princeton University Press, 1992), that socialist realism was, in fact, the product of an élite who had 'assimilated the experience of the avant-garde' which had nothing in common with the actual tastes of the masses, or *narod*. Further, he argues that socialist real-

ism bridged the gap between élitism and kitsch by making what he terms 'visual kitsch' the vehicle of élitist ideas (pp. 9–11). In regard to the term 'élitist', the Russian critic Lev Annensky argues that there has always been an élite in Russia and that it has always been distinct from the intelligentsia. Annensky sees the distinction between the two in the fact that the Russian intelligentsia has been an oppositional force to the government and has been characterised less by its practical expertise than by its ability to conceptualise and deal with abstract spiritual issues. What he sees in contemporary Russia is the crowding out of the intelligentsia by the élite. See Lev Annenskii, 'Vytesnenie intelligentsii', in N. I. Azhgikhina (comp.), *Novaia volna: Russkaia kul'tura i subkul'tury na rubezhe 80-90-x. godov* (Moscow: Moskovskii rabochii, 1994), pp. 19–24).

20. Harold Bloom, *The Western Canon: The Books and School of the Ages* (London: Macmillan), p. 34. Bloom similarly maintains that 'literary criticism, as an art, always was and always will be an élitist phenomenon', p. 17.
21. See Groys, *The Total Art of Stalinism*, p. 11.
22. Régine Robin discusses the difficulty of defining popular culture in her article 'Stalinism and Popular Culture', in Hans Gunther (ed.), *The Culture of the Stalin Period* (London: Macmillan, 1990), pp. 15–40.
23. Mikhail Bakhtin, *Tvorchestvo Fransua Rable i narodnaia kul'tura srednevekov'ia i Renessansa* (Moscow: Khudozhestvennaia literatura, 1965); republished as Mikhail Bakhtin, *Rabelais and His World*, trans. Helene Iswolsky (Bloomington: Indiana University Press, 1984).
24. For a more complete discussion of the history of Bakhtin's work on Rabelais, see M. M. Bakhtin, *The Dialogic Imagination: Four Essays*, ed. Michael Holquist, trans. Caryl Emerson and Michael Holquist (Austin: University of Texas Press, 1981), p. xxv, and Holquist's Prologue to Bakhtin's *Rabelais and his World*, pp. xiii–xxiii.
25. See in particular Terry Eagleton, *Walter Benjamin: Towards a Revolutionary Criticism* (London: Verso, 1981), in which he challenges Bakhtin's notions of carnival as undermining authority. Instead, he suggests, carnival is a licensed affair, in his words, a 'popular blow-off' which is essentially ineffectual as a revolutionary work of art (p. 148). See also Peter Stallybrass and Allon White, *The Politics and Poetics of Transgression* (Ithaca, NY: Cornell University Press, 1986), which goes beyond the debate over whether carnival is transgressive or conservative to examine from the point of view of political anthropology how the structure of carnival operates within a larger social context.
26. Like the anthologies of American literature, those of Russian and Soviet writing in both English and Russian have slighted women writers. For example, no women appeared among the thirteen authors included in Carl Proffer (ed.), *From Karamzin to Bunin: An Anthology of Russian Short Stories* (Bloomington: Indiana University Press, 1969), nor among the seven in Carl and Ellendea Proffer (eds), *Contemporary Russian Prose* (Ann Arbor: Ardis, 1982). Even in Kuleshov (ed.), *Povesti o liubvi* (Minsk: Vysshaia shkola, 1988), a two-volume collection of stories on love, in which one might expect more than a cursory glance to be paid to women writers, the editor seemingly assumed that not one woman had anything to say on the subject.
27. Particular work in this area has been done by Catriona Kelly, in her *A History of Russian Women's Writing, 1820–1992* (Oxford: Clarendon Press, 1994) and her accompanying *Anthology of Russian Women's Writing 1777–1992* (Oxford: Oxford University Press, 1994). See also her chapter on 'Sappho, Corinna, and Niobe: Genres and Personae in Russian Women's Writing, 1760–1820', in Adele Barker and Jehanne Gheith (eds), *A History of Russian Women's Writing* (Cambridge University Press, forthcoming). Major work on Russian women's nineteenth-century prose tradition is also being done by Jehanne Gheith, who is at work on a manuscript on women prose writers of the nineteenth century. See also Mary Zirin,

'Women's Prose Fiction in the Age of Realism', in Toby W. Clyman and Diana Greene (eds), *Women Writers in Russian Literature* (Westport, CT: Praeger, 1994), pp. 77–94, and Jane Costlow, 'Speaking the Sorrow of Women: Turgenev's "Neschastnaia" and Evgeniia Tur's "Antonina"', *Slavic Review*, vol. 50, no. 2 (Summer 1991), pp. 328–35. See also Marina Ledkovsky, Charlotte Rosenthal, and Mary Zirin (eds), *Dictionary of Russian Women Writers* (Westport, CT: Greenwood Press, 1994), which includes much previously unpublished information on Russia's eighteenth- and nineteenth-century women writers. Russian scholars have also begun to recover many of their own prerevolutionary women writers. See particularly V.V. Uchenova (comp.), *Dacha na Petergofskoi doroge* (Moscow: Sovremennik, 1986), *Svidanie* (Moscow: Sovremennik, 1987); *Tol'ko chas* (Moscow: Sovremennik, 1988); and *Tsaritsy muz: russkie poetessy XIX-nachala XX vv.* (Moscow: Sovremennik, 1989).

28. Elizabeth Sifton, interview with Mary McCarthy in George Plimpton (ed.), *Women Writers at Work:The Paris Review Interviews* (New York: Viking, 1989), pp. 189–90.

29. Frederic Jameson makes the point that aesthetic production today has become part of commodity production in general (*Postmodernism*, p. 4). One of the important essays on the link between culture and the consumer economy is Theodor Adorno and Max Horkheimer, 'The Culture Industry: Enlightenment as Mass Deception', reprint in During, *The Cultural Studies Reader*, pp.30–43.

30. See Svetlana Boym's *Common Places: Mythologies of Everyday Life in Russia* (Cambridge, MA: Harvard University Press, 1994), in which she identifies some of the cultural myths which dominated the written and unwritten laws of everyday life. Boym argues quite rightly that the combination of official ideology which devalued the everyday, as well as the historic and heroic conception of Russian culture as messianic, combined to exclude any serious study of everyday life from Russian scholarship (pp. 40 ff.). More and more work is being done on Russian and Soviet popular culture. In addition to Richard Stites' book *Russian Popular Culture: Entertainment and Society since 1900* (Cambridge: Cambridge University Press, 1992), which tracks the popular culture scene through the late 1980s, see also Nancy Condee (ed.), *Soviet Hieroglyphics: Visual Culture in Late Twentieth-Century Russia* (Bloomington: Indiana University Press, 1995), as well as her essay 'The Second Fantasy Mother, or, All Baths are Women's Baths', in Helena Goscilo and Beth Holmgren (eds), *Russia, Women, Culture* (Bloomington: Indiana University Press, 1996), pp. 3–30. See also Adele Barker and David Ramet (eds), *Contemporary Russian Popular Culture* (Durham: Duke University Press, forthcoming).

31. The approach taken by Katerina Clark in *The Soviet Novel: History as Ritual* (Bloomington: University of Chicago Press, 1981), who approaches the Soviet novel as at once an historical, anthropological, and only thirdly as a literary artefact, already prefiguring the kind of approach cultural studies theorists take now. The work does not deal specifically, however, with women writers or women's issues.

32. Petrushevskaia, in particular, returns both explicitly and implicitly to Stalinist issues in her works. A story such as 'Novye Robinzony' ('The New Family Robinson'), first published in *Novyi mir*, no. 8 (1989); trans. by G. Bird in Oleg Chukhontsev (ed.), *Dissonant Voices: The New Russian Fiction* (London: Harvill, 1991), pp. 414–24, is a more obvious throwback to Stalinist times. Petrushevskaia creates a scenario, ostensibly located at the end of the twentieth century but more than vaguely reminiscent of the Stalin period, of a family retreating deeper and deeper into the woods to escape their real or imaginary persecutors who hover invisibly yet as a real presence behind the scenes. While the Stalinist theme is not always this explicit in her fictions, the construction of the female persona in such works as 'Svoi krug' ('Our Crowd') and *Vremia noch'* (*The Time: Night*) is a miasma of fictional stereotypes from the Russian masters and the complex and often contradictory gender stereotyping that has been inflicted upon Russian women for the greater part of this century.

Part Two

WOMEN AND RUSSIAN CULTURE: FROM THE NINETEENTH CENTURY TO THE REVOLUTION

Chapter 3

THE BENEVOLENT MATRIARCH IN ELENA GAN AND MAR'IA ZHUKOVA

Joe Andrew

In her *History of Russian Women's Writing*, Catriona Kelly[1] remarks that the 'most memorable character' in Mar'ia Zhukova's *Vechera na Karpovke* (*Evenings by the Karpovka*, 1837; 1838)[2] is 'Natal'ia Dmitrievna [Shemilova] herself'. In distinguishing the organiser of the stories which make up the cycle in this way Kelly goes on to say: 'For once, a female survivor of the eighteenth century is portrayed as a benevolent matriarch, rather than as a terrifying virago.'

It is the purpose of this chapter to investigate some of the implications of these remarks. My main focus will be the depiction of female elders[3] and mothers in Zhukova's work (concentrating on *Dacha na petergofskoi doroge* [The Dacha on the Peterhof Road, 1845],[4] as well as *Vechera*). I will also seek to place this depiction in several different contexts, by offering a brief survey of the usual portrait of older ('post-sexual') women in the fiction of the period, before examining some of the theoretical issues involved in talking about 'women writing about women' (or 'gynocritics'). I will also seek to assess Zhukova's approach by way of a general contrast with other writers of the period, especially Elena Gan's treatment of older female characters (particularly the mother).[5]

Elsewhere in her work Kelly discusses some of the 'terrifying viragos' who have their roots in the eighteenth century. She has in mind the grotesque countess of Pushkin's *Pikovaia dama* (*The Queen of Spades*, 1863), amongst others, and it is undoubtedly the case that the typical image of older women in male-authored fiction during the development of Russian realism (and, of course, later as well) is generally negative. Indeed, one might well wish to start with an actual eighteenth-century example, namely, Prostakova in Fonvizin's play *Nedorosl'* (*The Minor*, 1780), a woman who is ultimately deprived of her usurped power in the sententious ending of the play.[6] Instances of denigration of the older female abound throughout the period in which Zhukova and Gan were active. Gogol', whom elsewhere I have dubbed 'The Russian Malleus Maleficarum',[7] is only the most outlandish instance. Perhaps his treatment of such characters as Ivan Shpon'ka's 'auntie' (to which I will return), the unnamed wife of Taras Bul'ba, or various unnamed women in the *Peterburgskie povesti* (*St Petersburg Stories*, 1842) and elsewhere may be attributed to his individual psychology,[8] but he is far from unique. Dictates of space preclude extensive treatment of this matter, but here I would merely note such instances as the mother in Turgenev (*Nakanune* [*On the Eve*, 1860]), *Pervaia liubov'* [*First Love*, 1860] and other works),[9] Odoevsky's grotesque Princess Mimi, or Dostoevsky's travesty mother (also unnamed) in *Netochka Nezvanova* (1849).[10] By and large, male authors of this period express various forms of matrophobia or a more general dread in the face of the mature female.[11] (It should be said that Chernyshevsky's treatment of Maria Alekseevna, the mother of the heroine Vera Pavlovna in *Chto delat'?* [*What Is To Be Done?*, 1863],[12] is an honourable exception, while Tolstoy's version of the mother is a more ambiguous case).

In reverse, the narrative focus is typically the 'sleeping beauty' motif. By this I mean that the plot typically (and, indeed, typologically) centres on versions of the *turgenevskaia devushka* (Turgenevan maiden) whose *fons et origo* is Pushkin's Tat'iana. Most prose works of the period have a *young* heroine whose story is based on love, which may or may not culminate in marriage. (And this is, of course, not a unique feature of Russian literature, as the case of Jane Austen amongst hundreds of others illustrates). The link between 'romance' and 'novel' remains very clear, and the double meaning of *roman* is revealing. Again, Tolstoy and Chernyshevsky are the exceptions which prove the rule: Chernyshevsky parodies this plot from the outset of his novel,[13] while Tolstoy breaches the same etiquette, as Eikhenbaum has noted, in his early work, *Semeinoe schast'e* (*Family Happiness*, 1859): 'Marriage is the starting point of the plot, rather than the dénouement (as it ordinarily is in love stories).'[14]

It is interesting to examine these tendencies in the major female prose writers of the period, especially Gan and Zhukova. In order to avoid charges of 'essentialism' (do they write 'as women'?), I will make a brief digression to explore the subject of 'gynocritics'. This term was coined (or rather *adapted*) by Elaine Showalter. Her definition is worth rehearsing at length:

> The second type of feminist criticism is concerned with *woman as writer* [Showalter's emphasis] – with woman as the producer of textual meaning, with the history, themes, genres and structures of literature by women. Its subjects include the psychodynamics of female creativity; linguistics and the problem of a female language; the trajectory of the individual or collective literary career; literary history; and, of course, studies of particular writers and works.[15]

Although Showalter's approach has been the subject of sharp criticism (especially by those more impressed by French feminists than by their Anglo-Saxon sisters),[16] it still has, I believe, much to teach us. As K.K. Ruthven, for example, has noted, it can assist us in the task of 'defining the specificity of women's writing'.[17] Or, as Sue Spaull has commented more recently, such criticism has as its aim 'to seek out a feminine aesthetic, or "essence" which differentiates women's writing from men's'.[18]

Now, it should be stated at the outset that such approaches are indeed a minefield where essentialist bombs lie hidden. Yet, while being aware of such dangers, it is, I think, possible to approach Gan, Zhukova, and other women writers of the period within the framework of gynocritics, and come up with some interesting findings. My main conclusions will refer to two main areas which could be summarised as the 'valorisation of the maternal', and 'giving women a voice'. Before exploring these aspects, however, I will briefly address the debt owed by women writers of this period to the male norm.

In terms of plots, it should be said at once that women prose writers of the period also, predominantly, orientated themselves around the 'sleeping beauty' story. That is, the ironic words of Chernyshevsky's narrator could well be applied to works by women too: 'The content of the tale is love, the main character, a woman.' In almost all of Gan's fictions, with the notable exception of *Naprasnyi dar* (A Futile Gift, 1842), the engine of the plot is the yearning of a young woman for love. (*Ideal* [*The Ideal*, 1837], *Medal'on* [The Locket], and *Sud sveta* [*Society's Judgement*, 1840] all centre on this theme, even if, in all instances, there is no happy outcome). Zhukova's work is more varied, perhaps, but the content of her tales is also love, more often than not. We see this especially in the majority of the constituent parts of *Vechera*, while *Dacha* shares the earlier work's concentration on the loves of young women.[19] Other women writers of the period were no more adventurous in this regard, as can be seen, for example, in Nadezhda Durova's *Sernyi kliuch* (*The Sulphur Spring*, 1839), Avdot'ia Panaeva's *Stepnaia baryshnia* (*The Young Lady of the Steppes*, 1855), or Nadezhda Sokhanskaia's *Posle obeda v gostiakh* (*A Conversation After Dinner*, 1858). These three works are all very different from each other, and are all quite different from the 'society tale' which was the major genre for both Gan and Zhukova, but in all three the main plot line centres on the love and, in two cases, the marriageability of the heroine.[20]

All this said, however, there are two clear tendencies which differentiate all these women writers, as already indicated. The main body of the ensuing discussions will look first at older women characters in the works of Gan and other women writers, and then in Zhukova's fiction, before exploring the way in which these two writers in particular give women a voice.

In the case of Gan, we see several instances of the 'valorisation of the maternal'. For Gan, this is more specifically the depiction of the childhood and education of the heroine at the knee of a now-dead *mother* as a lost, Edenic moment.[21] We see this from her first published work, *Ideal* (1837), onwards. In this work one woman stands apart from the mass who oppress the heroine, Ol'ga, and Gan establishes what is to be a vital, recurrent point of reference. When Ol'ga and her childhood friend (and confidante) Vera meet after six years apart, the narrator offers a brief glimpse of their shared childhood. They had been brought up by Ol'ga's mother, 'an intelligent, almost learned woman ... something of a free-thinker'. She herself had read all the French thinkers (presumably of the eighteenth-century Enlightenment), and had not only encouraged the two girls to read as widely as possible, but had also inculcated in them a sense of 'nobility' and 'self-sacrifice'. Moreover, she 'considered the immutable conditions of the everyday life of women as inventions, suitable only for the crowd'.[22]

A number of issues arise. The two girls have grown up in an exclusively feminine world, close to the mother. The maternal presence remains a lasting symbol of peace, purity and refuge, while the mother–daughter relationship is established as the *most* valorised and is rarely to be challenged. The maternal is certainly not repressed, nor denigrated, as in much of male-authored literature.

These motifs recur in *Medal'on* (1839),[23] where again, for the childhood scenes of the two heroines, we enter an all-female h(e)aven of remote, simple peace and tranquillity, where the two contrastive sisters are brought up by their grandmother. All the details echo the Sentimentalist tradition (we are again in the eighteenth century), which is treated positively, as it is elsewhere in Gan (although generally not in Zhukova). We hear of the 'old woman' and that 'the serious and slightly sad expression of her face would take on a shade of inexpressible tenderness; in her eyes, dimmed by time and tears, shone a reverential love'.[24] It is a place where, again, the absence of men is specifically commented upon and whose eighteenth-century qualities are marked even by the 'calling name' of their estate, 'Otradnoe' ('Joy'). As before, and as later too, the all-female community, organised around a strong maternal figure, suggests the ideal social structure, one that is indeed heavenly perfection: 'At that time their dwelling represented the image of earthly paradise'.[25] In both these stories, to be sure, problems arise when this Eden is abandoned. The feminine enclave and the maternal must be forsaken, and the loss is immense. Nevertheless, it is significant that the final scenes of *Medal'on* mark a return home, which acts as the locus for a partial recovery and reconciliation on the part of the tragic heroine/victim, Olimpiia.

Sud sveta provides a very similar etiology for the tragic heroine and, equally, a strong valorisation of the (lost) maternal. Like her predecessors, the heroine, Zenaida,[26] had grown up secluded from the world ('society'), nurtured by the all-powerful love of her mother:

> O! what love! ... If I tell you that she was our nurse, nanny, instructor, our angel of blessing on earth, then even so I will not express that infinite, selfless, all-sacrificing attachment with which she made our childhood happy.[27]

The maternal presence, the presexual world, is again recalled as a haven of paradise on earth. As before, however, the idyll is set in the past and has been lost and, as before, once maternal succour is removed, the girl is catapulted into the world where she will meet predatory males and vicious women. In this sense, Gan's treatment of the maternal is, in the end, ambiguous. There is no doubt that the daughter-mother relationship is one without equal, but is also one which has almost always been lost and one which is insufficient to prepare the daughter for the loss of the ideal, or for society's judgement.[28]

If in Gan the mother represents an ultimately powerless retreat against the world, then in Zhukova the maternal is treated positively, but also as a force for acculturation to accepted values. What Barbara Engel says about Russian society applies precisely to Zhukova's work:

> For the most part, close mother-daughter ties operated conservatively, because they facilitated a girl's adaptation to her appropriate social role and ensured that she successfully passed from her father's authority into her husband's – the mother acting as a kind of unwitting agent for a male-dominated society.[29]

We see this positive treatment of the conservative mother from the first story of *Vechera* ('Inok' [The Monk, 1837]) onwards. (It is significant that it is precisely in this story that we are introduced to the theme of 'patriarchal power' which is to run like a red thread through the work.)[30]

In 'Inok' the role of maternal presences, it should be said, is peripheral to the main action, which concerns the brutal slaying of an innocent wife (Aniuta) by her obsessively jealous husband (who then becomes the eponymous hero). In the introductory sections, however, we meet her mother-in-law, Agrafena Pavlovna, who is presented as an idyllic representative of traditional feminine values. Agrafena closely resembles Pulkheriia in Gogol''s 'Starosvetskie pomeshchiki' ('Old-World Landowners', 1835),[31] without any of the sickening, cloying sentimentality of her close contemporary. The reader is informed:

> A plump, red face and a happy smile were the signs of her character. She cooked some food whenever the fancy took her, ate to her heart's content, slept, fed her children and produced some great ones![32]

Another important detail is her delight in her daughter-in-law ('what's more, Aniuta's a good 'un! It's like as if we had a white swan living with us').[33] This close 'mother-daughter' relationship echoes the bond between Natal'ia Dmitrievna and her ward Liubinka which has already been established in the 'Preliminaries' to the cycle, and we will see a number of similar patterns later in completely different contexts. And this is precisely the point. Zhukova certainly should be considered an 'essentialist', in that for her, feminine nature remains the same everywhere. Kelly sees this as a proto-feminist point:

> By assembling a collection of narratives which represent women in various, rather disparate settings, she is able to argue that dissatisfaction is not unique to the narrow set of women represented in the 'society tale': very similar problems are faced by women from different historical periods, and from different social backgrounds.[34]

Natal'ia Dmitrievna puts it rather differently (and so, I think, would Zhukova herself): 'A woman's nature never betrays her, *even in old age*' [my italics: J.A.].[35]

Whichever argument one pursues, it is certainly the case that in nearly all the stories of *Vechera* we see a valorisation of the maternal and/or sections 'in praise of older women'.[36] In the next story, 'Baron Reikhman', we have a brief illustration of this last point, in the depiction of Lidiia Ezerskaia's mother, who is quite explicitly past her first flush of youth. But denigration is absent from this sketch: her advancing years are delicately touched upon: we are introduced to 'Ezerskaia, a fairly weighty lady ... of those years when every morning carries off a new beauty and bestows in return new, alas! artificial roses'.[37] Similarly, her relationship with Lidiia is shown to be amicable and mutually supportive.

It is in the life and tragedy of the central heroine Baroness Reikhman, however, that we see the main treatment of the maternal theme in this story. The opening line of the story itself is significant in this regard: '"How lovely you are, mamma!" said a four-year-old, red-cheeked boy' (p. 40). Thus speaks Coco, the young son of the Baroness. From the very outset, therefore, we see her *as a mother,* and it will be, as in *Anna Karenina,* one of her greatest 'sins' that she is prepared to abandon her *son.* Indeed, when her liaison with Levin is under way, Coco is locked away in the nursery so that they may be *à deux.* At the end, her worst punishment is that she is deprived of Coco. Equally significant is the fact that Levin reminds her precisely of her *maternal* (rather than *wifely*) duties as he begins to reconsider his position. And it is Levin, indeed, who delivers the 'essentialist' *sententia* of this story: 'Woman is created solely for the family; the area of activity beyond it is alien to her' (p. 60).

The logic of the plot (especially the punishment of the Baroness) suggests that Zhukova would not dissent from this view, and it gradually emerges that the 'rights and wrongs' of motherhood are one of the central preoccupations of the cycle. In a later story ('Provintsialka' [The Provincial Girl, 1847]), the narrator of this particular tale offers an expectedly essentialist (indeed, biologistic) explanation of the strengths of mother-daughter relations. He remarks that 'I have always been more affected by friendship between a father and daughter than between mother and daughter.' This is because it is much easier for mothers and daughters:

> Being of the same sex, a mother and daughter are friendly without any effort on either side; a mother only has to recall her own youth to understand her daughter's heart (p. 210).

We see this closeness, again, in Zhukova's earlier tale, 'Medal'on' ('The Locket', 1837), where the mothers of both heroines play precisely the role that Barbara Engel has delineated. As we have also seen, a critical motif in Gan is the paradisiacal girlhood of the heroine, who, nurtured by a perfect mother, becomes and remains the emblem of all that is good and holy, although in nearly every case the mother has died before the story proper begins. In Zhukova's tale this pattern is replicated in the biographical background to Mariia's story. However, whereas the idealistic education of Gan's heroines at their mother's knees leaves them ill-prepared for the harshness of 'patriarchal power', Mariia, 'from her earliest years' had been taught a bitter lesson: 'My plain one, you are not pretty, my plain one; there is nothing for you to do in the world; you will be a nun' (p. 86).[38] Mariia learns this lesson, and, more generally, her mother had been everything to her, the symbol of all that was finest: 'the heart of her mother replaced the universe for her; in it she lived like a queen ... It [her mother's heart] surrounded her with an entire world of the magic of maternal love' (p. 87). But also, as in Gan, this nurturing presence has been lost. It is significant, however, that the grave of her mother twice becomes a refuge for the daughter.

The mother of the other heroine, Sof'ia, is still alive and plays a crucial role in teaching this daughter to be dutiful.[39] We see them together in two critical scenes. The first of these is when Sof'ia is read a *pouchenie*, a religious word conveying both 'lesson' and 'sermon', warning her to abandon any interest in the lowly doctor, Vel'sky: 'You should not think about him; your father would never forgive you such an inclination: his prejudices are known to you' (p. 83). Here (and later) Princess Z. plays a dual role. Certainly, there is real intimacy and affection ('friendship') between mother and daughter, yet the mother's essential role is, as Engel has noted, to impart the lessons of society, of 'patriarchal power'. She later instructs Sof'ia as to the value and rewards of a match made according to mutual self-interest. This is what hers had been, and Sof'ia will learn this second lesson well: 'So, Sof'ia, God will reward you for your obedience; filial love never goes unrewarded' (p. 106). Sof'ia is, indeed, delighted with the arranged marriage and, as before, emphasis is placed on the real bond between mother and daughter (Vel'sky espies the Princess 'holding Sof'ia in her arms') (p. 106). At the same time, however, we must remember that the older woman is the one who perpetuates the conditions which restrain the natural inclinations of a woman's heart. The older woman is clearly important in Zhukova, as someone with real power and authority, but this authority is used in the interests of the 'prejudices' of the fathers, real or metaphorical. As in nearly all these stories, the logic of the plot is reinforced by an essentialist *dictum* (again from the privileged narrator): 'to love with self-abnegation is the lot of a woman' (p. 101).

It is in a later work by Zhukova, however (*Dacha na petergofskoi doroge*, written when Zhukova herself was over forty), that we see the strongest and most important treatment of older women, in the character of Elena Pavlovna (and others). Indeed, one of the characteristic features of both this story and Zhukova's 'The Locket' is the relative unimportance of male characters in the diegetic world. Whether in high-society St Petersburg or the provincial town in which the mad, tragic heroine Zoia is raised, nearly all the significant characters are female and men are acted upon rather than acting.

Prince Evgeny is organised by his mother, cousins and aunts, especially the heroic Elena Pavlovna; Mary, the other half of the diadic, contrastive heroines, has almost only female associates, while Zoia too is brought up by female elders. In terms of the central plot dynamics (Evgeny's hunt for a bride and ultimate marriage to a woman who thereby becomes Princess Mary), the action is always propelled by women, especially Elena Pavlovna. *Prima facie*, Zhukova presents a world that is matriarchal in structure and essence. Even more significant, both for the purposes of this chapter and in the broader context of the development of Russian literature, is the prominent part played specifically by positively depicted older women. Zoia is effectively brought up by Vera Iakovlevna who, although she partially and inadvertently colludes in her ward's seduction, is presented as a positive type. (In the light of recent British history it is interesting to note the author's commentary: 'Vera Iakovlevna was the most stubborn Tory, and, were she in England, would straight off have been made the leader of the party' [p. 286].) In turn, when they move to the provincial town to find Zoia a sensible match, we are introduced to Avdot'ia Vasil'evna, the hub of the town's life, shown 'unusual respect', at least in part because she 'was a remarkably intelligent woman' (p. 287).

Prima inter pares is Elena Pavlovna, aunt to Prince Evgeny, who in certain respects could be regarded as the moral centre of the work, its true heroine. She is introduced in the very first pages, and remains a dominant presence, and the prime mover of the plot. It is she who takes particular interest in her favourite nephew and his fortunes, and in turn, in the biographical background to her character, is presented as the model of a woman who has married for rational reasons and has not lived to regret it. She goes out of her way to ensure that her nephew will follow the same path and, once Mary has been selected, makes all the necessary arrangements. In these introductory sections, more than once she is termed 'an excellent woman' (without irony, in my view). When we later return to the main plot, it is once again Elena Pavlovna, still an 'excellent woman', who, in scenes of epic comedy, keeps the arrangements moving along, despite a sleepless night and a dreadful migraine. In the end, despite all obstacles, she has her way, and Mary begins the process of becoming the sort of woman Elena Pavlovna herself is. In this sense, she is the role model for the younger woman.

There are a number of other points that need to be made regarding this 'benevolent matriarch'. One could argue that the whole story can be read as a subtle parable against the 'patriarchal power' with which Zhukova seems to collude elsewhere. That is, the world *appears* to be organised for the 'prejudices' of men like Prince

Evgeny, whereas, in reality this tough female elder organises everything. In this respect she could be regarded as a humanised version of Shpon'ka's *tetushka* ('auntie'), which is precisely what Evgeny calls her (p. 255). As she puts it herself: 'I am prepared to forgive you everything, as long as you are obedient to me' (p. 255). Shpon'ka is terrified and emasculated by the 'terrifying virago' who is his relative.[40] Evgeny is merely organised.

Elena Pavlovna and her provincial equivalents organise the fictional world in another way, in that their values are clearly presented as the moral centre of the work. For once, it might be said, the Law of the *Mother* is operative. We see this most tellingly in the discussion held between Avdot'ia Vasil'evna, Vera Iakovlevna and another of Evgeny's aunts concerning contemporary morals and attitudes. Vera laments the passing of the old ways: nowadays there is 'A different education, everything foreign; whereas in our time it was simple. We didn't know corsets, or mazurkas; but for all that we were a bit stronger' (p. 303).

The tone of the scene is deliberately rather comical, but a very serious point is being made. To paraphrase these remarks, the reader of *Dacha* is being told that, if she reads the likes of Byron, dances long, complicated (and foreign) dances with strange men (and so on), a young woman is liable to fall in love with unsuitable strangers. Moreover, all the traditions of society which have made Elena Pavlovna 'an excellent woman' and which kept morals 'strong' will be threatened.

Elena Pavlovna, however, could be said to organise the fictional world in yet another, even more crucial sense. As already noted, she makes things happen, finds a fiancée, makes sure Evgeny is obedient to her will, and so on. In other words, *her* desire dictates the narrative flow. Put otherwise, without her and her wishes, *there would have been no narrative*. She is the prime narrative agent and, in the diegetic present at least, is seen nearly everywhere. That is, we should see her as a kind of *disguised author*.

Elena Pavlovna's 'authorship' is significant in yet another way, given that another of the projects of many of the women writers of the period was to 'give women a voice'. I shall return to this aspect of Zhukova (and Natal'ia Dmitrievna) in a moment, but first I would like to return briefly to Gan, who was certainly most concerned with exploring the problems, anxieties – and benefits – of female authorship[41] (as well as offering brief discussions of this aspect of the work of Durova and Sokhanskaia). This is especially true of Gan's last, unfinished work, *Naprasnyi dar*, but can be seen as a central theme throughout her major fiction. From the very first pages she published in 1837 (*Ideal*), she had placed the difficulties encountered by the outstanding woman at the centre of her fiction. With increasing insistence she had defined this theme more precisely as the problem of the *creative* woman. At the same time, she had privileged the woman *as writer* by ending several of her tales with the woman's story told by a woman – Ol'ga's letter which concludes *Ideal*, Sof'ia's telling of her sister's tale which forms the latter half of *Medal'on*, Zenaida's lengthy letter/confession which forms the last part of *Sud sveta*. And then she concluded her own life with the tragic story of Aniuta the poet. In the case of Durova's *Sernyi kliuch* the situation is less dramatic, in that we merely have a female *story-teller*, although the relative novelty of this at this stage in the development of Russian prose should not be minimised. Sokhanskaia's story, *Posle obeda v gostiakh*, is an altogether more striking instance of giving women a voice. The primary narrator is an unnamed woman, while the main story-teller, Liubov' Arkhipovna, not only recounts the history of her *own* trials and tribulations, but also peppers it with examples of the often moving, folk-inspired laments and other songs which she has composed. On the basis of the work of Zhukova, Gan, Sokhanskaia and Durova – whose famous memoirs should also be borne in mind – we can indeed conclude that it was clearly part of the project of Russian women writers to find a distinctively female *voice*.

All of these 'writers' are, however, *young* women. Gan and the others do not seek to present a more mature version of this personage, but this is precisely what Zhukova does, both in the 'disguised authorship' of Elena Pavlovna and, more explicitly, in Natal'ia Dmitrievna, the organiser and lead narrator of *Vechera na Karpovke*.[42] It is with a discussion of her character and role and other aspects of the work that this chapter will conclude.

The first point to be noted is that, at the outset, and at the end, this work of fiction is produced (in a number of senses) by women. Although the majority of the tales will have male narrators, it is a series of female characters who set the scene and establish the tone and themes.[43] Obviously, the name on the title page is female: to this we need to add immediately the unnamed, but grammatically marked female narrator of the framing introductory material, who is also the compiler/publisher of the work. The actual organiser and instigator of the 'original stories' which are here 'reproduced' in writing is Natal'ia Dmitrievna Shemilova, a woman of about sixty.[44] At once, at least implicitly, a polemical point is made. Women, even elderly semi-invalid women, can contribute to the development of Russian literature. (Indeed, as Aplin has noted,[45] the fictitious company who gather at Natal'ia Dmitrievna's eponymous summer house debate the state of Russian literature before setting out consciously to add to its riches.) In this context it is of no small significance that it is precisely the elderly woman – as opposed to any of the men – who initiates the literary evenings. Equally, we should not ignore the fact that she is also the narrator of the lead story, putting aside her knitting to do so! This detail too is deeply polemicised, recalling as it does the origin of text(iles).[46] And this implicit domestication (and *ipso facto*, feminisation) of literature continues as Natal'ia Dmitrievna introduces us to the world in which 'Inok' is set. She has learned the story at second hand from yet another female contributor to literature, an eighteen-year-old peasant woman.[47] (The only reason she had encountered the woman at all is because she had had to spend the night in her carriage rather than in the spider-filled post-house. The allegedly traditionally 'feminine' arachnophobia[48] is ironised, but also used to good advantage.) Similarly, and in one of the neat framing devices with which the cycle is rounded off, the last story ('Poslednii vecher' [The Final Evening]) is based on a woman telling her own tragic tale. From beginning to end, that is, *Vechera* develops the implicit polemical point that women have at least an equal contribution to make to literature.

Equally important is the character of Natal'ia Dmitrievna, who is, indeed, presented as 'a benevolent matriarch'. This valorisation of the older woman is highly significant in itself. It is doubly important, however, in that it is her voice which establishes the *dominanta* for the whole work. On the second page of the work, as soon as she mentions her, the narrator at once emphasises her purpose by regaling the reader with a fifteen-line sentence detailing the physical and moral charms of her friend. All goes to stress her essential humanity. She is

> ... of small stature, with clear blue eyes, pale and white like the old woman in Greuze's paintings, always wearing a white tulle cap, from under which her silvery hair could be seen ... always cheerful and welcoming, she seemed to me one of those few women who, on leaving the stage of high society where they glittered in their youth, take with them the pleasing address of society ladies, a heap of memories.[49]

This sentence reads to me almost as a literary manifesto: there *is* interest in a post-menopausal woman![50]

Her essential goodness is also manifested in her relations with her entourage,[51] described simply as 'a small circle of friends'. This warmth is especially important in her relationship with her doctor, Ivan Karlovich, which prompts a paean to friendship amongst the elderly. In turn we should also note the genuine love and affection between her and her niece/ward Liubinka. This intimacy is important in two regards. Firstly, it sets the pattern which is to follow (and which I have already discussed) of close 'mother-daughter' links. Secondly, yet another polemical point is made, in that the ward in Russian literature of the period is all too often the hapless victim of a tyrannical, older *female* guardian. (Pushkin's *The Queen of Spades* is the most famous, but by no means the only example: see *inter alia* Odoevsky's *Katia, or The Story of a Young Ward* (1834) or Herzen's slightly later *Kto vinovat? (Who Is To Blame?*, 1846). Significantly, it should also be noted that the [female] guardian-ward relationship is treated with positive warmth in Zhukova's *Samopozhertvovanie* (Self-Sacrifice), as well as in Durova's *Sernyi kliuch*, although this 'ethnic sketch' is set in an altogether different world from that of the 'society tale' in which the guardian-ward syndrome is most commonly portrayed).

Natal'ia Dmitrievna is, then, established in these opening pages as a woman of the old school, who has surrounded herself with a few close friends and relatives, who then proceed to tell summer tales, sometimes chilling, sometimes tragic, but nearly always with unhappy endings. This contrast (between frame and centre) is deliberately made, in that the 'benevolent matriarchy' established in this introduction acts as the first of several domestic interiors which serve as enclaves or safe havens against the storm of passions (often masculine in causation) which buffet the participants in the narrative world created by *Vechera*. The very positive approach to life (a very marked contrast to, say, Gogolian gloom), which is adopted towards and by Natal'ia Dmitrievna reinforces the overall significance of the introductory sections. The benevolence of a grandmother[52] provides security as well as entertainment.

Unlike other frame narrators of the 1830s, such as Rudy Panko and Belkin (the narrators of Pushkin's *Povesti Belkina* [*Tales of Belkin*, 1830] and Gogol''s *Vechera na khutore bliz Dikan'ki* [*Evenings on a Farm near Dikanka*, 1831; 1832]), Natal'ia Dmitrievna does not disappear from view once the cycle begins. Rather, she remains a dominant figure, reappearing in the interstices between stories as well as playing a prominent part at the very end. Her significance is especially important in the opening story, 'Inok'. Not only does she narrate it but, in fact, about one third of the story is taken up with explanatory prologues which, *en passant*, provide a second, vivid and this time self-uttered (*skaz*) portrait of Natal'ia, as well as giving a fair bit of biographical information about her. This life-story also acts as a critical tone-setting moment, in that she has grown up in a remote rural province, in the heart of *rus/Rus* ('the country/old Russia').[53] Equally, she identifies herself closely with religion and spiritual values. Both of these motifs (the rural and the holy), and, indeed, their interconnections, will play important roles in many of the later stories, especially 'The Locket'. To generalise from all this, we may say that Natal'ia Dmitrievna, the benevolent matriarch, as we see her both in old age and in an earlier incarnation, establishes many of the dominant themes, values and motifs of the work as a whole, which thereby becomes a kind of literary embodiment of her. In other words, *Vechera*, taken in its entirety, espouses the world-view of, and represents, in a sense *is*, a benevolent matriarchy.

It is, therefore, of considerable significance that Zhukova chooses to reintroduce Natal'ia Dmitrievna Shemilova at the cycle's conclusion, in two different ways. Firstly she plays a minor part in the diegesis of 'Poslednii vecher' as the 'angel-woman' (p. 262) who had shown philanthropic concern for the heroine-narrator of the tale, and then as the presiding genius, not only of the cycle's ending, but of the declaration of love between Vel'sky and Liubinka. She has thus held the whole work together: she began as the organiser of the evenings, then acted as first narrator and, therein, as the setter of themes and of moral tone. Now she concludes the work as the organiser of matrimony. Catriona Kelly has argued that 'There is considerable irony in the cementing of a marriage by a series of tales in general so remarkably pessimistic about the likely success of matrimony.'[54] I would see it differently. Zhukova has, it seems to me, deliberately ended on the note of 'all's well that ends well'. Indeed, the fact that we are presented with an ending suitable for a Romantic Comedy is made explicit – by, appropriately, Natal'ia Dmitrievna: 'I have allowed myself a small comedy' (p. 266), she declares, as she blesses the union, before pronouncing the final, summarising speech of the whole work, which would not, indeed, have been out of keeping in Shakespeare. Natal'ia Dmitrievna, undoubtedly 'the collection's most memorable character',[55] fuses art and life in her own benevolent image.

Mar'ia Zhukova, along with her younger contemporary, Elena Gan, as well as other women writers of the period, has established the older woman as a worthy subject for literary creation, and the female writer has ascended the stage of Russian letters. As Catriona Kelly notes: 'Zhukova's career was a turning point in the history of Russian women's writing',[56] and this, her first work, announces her as a deeply self-conscious contributor to the development of Russian literature as a whole.

Notes

1. See Catriona Kelly, *A History of Russian Women's Writing, 1820–1992* (Oxford: Clarendon Press, 1994), p. 90.
2. All forthcoming references to this work or its constituent parts will be to the following edition: M. S. Zhukova, *Vechera na Karpovke*, ed. R. V. Iezuitova (Moscow: Sovetskaia Rossiia, 1986). All translations from this and other works will be my

own. (Ed.: extracts from Zhukova's *Evenings by the Karpovka* are translated in Joe Andrew (ed.), *Russian Women's Shorter Fiction: An Anthology 1835-1860* [Oxford: Oxford University Press, 1996], pp. 122-81.)
3. 'Elders' has recently become the standard form of reference to persons in Britain above the age of sixty. I use the term not in this precise way but to refer to women who are mothers, or are merely significantly older than the normal run of heroines (16-21).
4. All references to Gan's *Dacha na petergofskoi doroge* will be to the following edition: V. Uchenova (ed.), *Dacha na petergofskoi doroge: proza russkikh pisatel'nits pervoi poloviny XIX veka* (Moscow: Sovremennik, 1986), pp. 245-322.
5. For an extended discussion of the mother figure in Russian literature of this period, see my 'Mothers and Daughters in Russian Literature in the First Half of the Nineteenth Century', *Slavonic and East European Review*, vol. 73, no. 1 (January 1995), pp. 37-60. I would particularly mention as a very useful background resource Adrienne Rich's *Of Woman Born. Motherhood as Experience and Institution* (London: Virago, 1977).
6. For a discussion of this, see Joe Andrew, *Women in Russian Literature, 1780-1863* (London: Macmillan, 1988), pp. 12-18, especially pp. 16-18.
7. See ibid., pp. 79-111.
8. For an excellent and highly relevant discussion of these problems, see Simon Karlinsky, *The Sexual Labyrinth of Nikolai Gogol* (Cambridge, MA: Harvard University Press, 1976).
9. For discussions of these works, see Andrew, *Women in Russian Literature*, pp. 145-54 and 122-35.
10. For discussions of these works, see Joe Andrew, *Narrative and Desire in Russian Literature, 1822-1849: The Feminine and the Masculine* (London: Macmillan, 1993), pp. 55-68 and pp. 214-26.
11. For an extended discussion of matrophobia in Russian and other cultures, see Andrew, *Narrative and Desire,* and Rich, *Of Woman Born*. One illustration of the etiology of this phenomenon will suffice in the present context: 'Woman to primitive man is ... at once weak and magical, oppressed, yet feared. She is charged with powers of childbearing denied to man, powers only half-understood ... forces that all over the world seem to fill him with terror'. From Jane Harrison, *Themis: A Study of the Social Origins of Greek Religion,* quoted in Rich, *Of Woman Born,* p. 84.
12. See Andrew, *Women in Russian Literature,* pp. 155-80, especially pp. 161-62.
13. See ibid., p. 156.
14. See B. M. Eikhenbaum, 'On Tolstoy's Crises', in Ralph E. Matlaw (ed.), *Tolstoy. A Collection of Critical Essays* (Eaglewood Cliffs, NJ: Prentice-Hall, 1967), pp. 52-55 (p. 53). Tolstoy's comments on those who conform to traditional plots were characteristically forthright: 'those who finish their novels with a wedding, as if that were so good that there is no reason to write any further – they all babble sheer nonsense' (quoted ibid.).
15. See Elaine Showalter, 'Towards a Feminist Poetics' in Mary Jacobus (ed.), *Women Writing and Writing About Women* (London: Croom Helm, 1979), pp. 22-41 (p. 25).
16. See, in particular, Toril Moi, *Sexual/Textual Politics. Feminist Literary Theory* (London and New York: Methuen, 1985), especially pp. 75-80.
17. K.K. Ruthven, *Feminist Literary Studies. An Introduction* (Cambridge: Cambridge University Press, 1984), p. 93.
18. See Sue Spaull, 'Gynocriticism', in Sara Mills, Lynne Pearce, Sue Spaull, Elaine Millard (eds), *Feminist Readings/Feminists Reading* (Hemel Hempstead: Harvester Wheatsheaf, 1989), pp. 83-121 (p. 84).

19. A partial exception to this tendency is to be found in Zhukova's *Samopozhertvovanie* (1840). Although love is certainly at the centre of the story, the heroine Liza forsakes a marriage of convenience to pursue a career as a *pension* teacher. For discussions of this story, see Kelly, *A History of Russian Women's Writing*, pp. 66, 83.
20. For translations of these three stories and further information, see Joe Andrew, *Russian Women's Shorter Fiction*, pp. 272–300, 319–97, 398–459. An excellent introductory resource for all the writers referred to in the present chapter is, of course, Marina Ledkovsky, Charlotte Rosenthal and Mary Zirin (eds), *Dictionary of Russian Women Writers* (Westport, CT: Greenwood, 1994).
21. For a discussion of these relationships in Russian society of the time, see Barbara Alpern Engel, *Mothers and Daughters: Women of the Intelligentsia in Nineteenth-Century Russia* (Cambridge: Cambridge University Press, 1983). A comment by Ekaterina Iunge, the daughter of a successful society woman, conveys the situation well: 'Mother's life was no longer separate from mine: we were always together. I rejoiced in the change in our relations, and my love for her became a kind of idolatry' (quoted ibid., p.13).
22. See 'Ideal', in V.I. Sakharov (ed.), *Russkaia romanticheskaia povest'* (Moscow, 1980), pp. 435–80 (p. 442). (Ed.: English translation in Andrew, *Russian Women's Shorter Fiction*, pp. 1–49.)
23. See 'Medal'on', in E.A. Gan, *Polnoe sobranie sochinenii* (St Petersburg, 1905), ed. N.F. Mertz, pp. 210–99.
24. Ibid., p. 260.
25. Ibid., p. 263.
26. It should, of course, be noted that Gan's pseudonym was Zenaida R–va.
27. See Gan's 'Sud sveta', in Uchenova, *Dacha na Petergofskoi doroge*, pp. 147–212 (p. 198). (Ed.: English translation in Andrew, *Russian Women's Shorter Fiction*, pp. 50–121.)
28. We encounter a variation on the theme of the all-female enclave headed by a matriarch in Nadezhda Sokhanskaia's *A Conversation After Dinner*. The heroine Liubov' Arkhipovna had grown up in a very different world from the cultured haven inhabited by Gan's heroines. The mother is also a much more ambivalent figure, not averse to beating her stubborn daughter into accepting an (initially) unloved husband. Liubov''s main emotional sustenance is from her sisters (as well as her singing), but in the end she is reconciled both to her husband, and to her mother. The overall view of this powerful story is that the mother, for all her failings, does her best for her daughter. In this sense, her function is closer to that delineated by Barbara Engel (see note 29), and illustrated in the work of Zhukova. All this said, we should also note that Liubov''s *all-female* girlhood environment represents, as in the case of Gan, a fondly remembered oasis.
29. See Engel, *Mothers and Daughters*, p.13. Elaine Showalter's interpretation of a similar practice is rather more acerbic: 'the feminine heroine grows up in a world without female solidarity, where women in fact police each other on behalf of patriarchal tyranny'. See Elaine Showalter, *A Literature of their Own: from Charlotte Brontë to Doris Lessing*, revised edition (London: Virago, 1982), p. 117. (The reference is to *Jane Eyre*.)
30. See Zhukova, *Vechera*, p. 21. For a discussion of this theme in Zhukova more generally, see Andrew, *Narrative and Desire*, pp. 139–83.
31. For a discussion of this work, see Andrew, *Women in Russian Literature*, pp. 86–101, and Karlinsky, *The Sexual Labyrinth of Nikolai Gogol*, pp. 62–67.
32. Zhukova, *Vechera*, p. 23.
33. Ibid. This use of traditional folk motifs for characterisation of the heroine will be supremely important in *A Conversation After Dinner*.

34. Zhukova, *Vechera*, p. 89. Hugh Aplin makes another, related point with admirable clarity: 'The central belief underlying Zhukova's depiction of society is that human nature is everywhere essentially the same, and it is human nature in all its variety that determines the basic features of human social life'. See Hugh Anthony Aplin, 'M. S. Zhukova and E. A. Gan. Women Writers and Female Protagonists, 1837–1843' (unpublished Ph.D. thesis, University of East Anglia, 1988), p. 107.
35. Zhukova, *Vechera*, p. 24.
36. Equally, we see a generally very positive view of the elderly mother in two other works of the period already referred to, namely, Zhukova's *Self-Sacrifice* and Panaeva's *The Young Lady of the Steppes*.
37. Zhukova, *Vechera*, p. 53, subsequent references in text to this edition.
38. Liubov' Arkhipovna's mother in 'A Conversation After Dinner' plays an equally 'frank' role vis-à-vis her daughter.
39. Again a comparison with *A Conversation After Dinner* is relevant, although, as already noted, the heroine's mother resorts to altogether more brutal means to make her daughter dutiful. In reverse, the mother, and father, of the heroine of *The Young Lady of the Steppes* allow the daughter Feklusha to have her own way in the choice of suitor.
40. For a discussion of this, see Andrew, *Women in Russian Literature,* pp. 81–85.
41. For a discussion of this, see Andrew, *Narrative and Desire,* pp. 85–138, especially pp. 131–38.
42. In *Self-Sacrifice* Zhukova follows the general trends of her peers. As in *A Conversation After Dinner* the frame narrator is a woman, who then recounts the story of the main heroine, Liza, who had told her own story to this unnamed narrator. Liza is certainly young: we do not know the age of the frame narrator, but her image is that of a young woman of society.
43. See Aplin, 'M.S. Zhukova and E.A. Gan', pp. 102–4, and Kelly, *A History of Russian Women's Writing*, pp. 79–80 for interesting discussions of the place of *Vechera* in the development of Russian literature.
44. It should be remembered how advanced an age this was at the time. Even in a more developed country like Britain, female life-expectancy was still only fifty-two in 1900. (I am indebted to Barbara Andrew for this information). A reverse tendency should also be noted. It was the habit of male writers in this period to refer to any woman beyond about forty as *starushka*. However 'affectionate' this diminutive may or may not be, it seems a patronising piece of ageism to the present writer. (For a discussion of this tendency, see Andrew, *Narrative and Desire*).
45. Andrew, *Narrative and Desire*, pp. 102–3.
46. For an excellent discussion of this, see Susan Bassnett, 'Textuality/Sexuality', in *Essays in Poetics*, vol. 9, no. 1 (1984), pp. 1–15. Amongst many other interesting observations, Bassnett notes the following:

> Mary Daly in *Gyn/Ecology* notes that the Latin *texere* (to weave) is the origin and root of both *text* and *textile* and adds: '"Texts" are the kingdom of males; they are the realm of the reified word, of condensed spirit. In patriarchal tradition, sewing and spinning are for girls; books are for boys.' (p. 10)

47. Aplin, 'M.S. Zhukova and E.A. Gan', pp. 104–5 notes the problem of authenticity involved in this encounter (or rather in the verbatim recollection of it), while remarking that it was a common problem in the literature of the period. (A famous instance, which Aplin cites, is the recollection of a song by Maksim Maksimych in Lermontov's 'Bela'.)
48. Whether this is covert play on the Arachne myth is debatable – though not impossible.

49. Zhukova, *Vechera*, p. 6.
50. For an excellent discussion of this topic, see Germaine Greer, *The Change: Women, Ageing and The Menopause* (Harmondsworth: Penguin, 1992). (I am grateful to Barbara Andrew for drawing my attention to this work.)
51. Kelly, *A History of Russian Women's Writing*, p. 90 makes the same point slightly differently: 'Natalya Dmitrievna ... is financially and socially independent, enjoys friendships of intellectual equality with male companions'.
52. Kelly observes that 'a benevolent grandmother organises story-telling to keep the family amused': ibid., p. 90.
53. This pun is used as the epigraph for Chapter 2 of Pushkin's *Evgenii Onegin*.
54. Kelly, *A History of Russian Women's Writing*, p. 90.
55. Ibid.
56. Ibid., p. 91. For a slightly more conservative assessment of her standing, see Aplin's entry in Ledkovsky, Rosenthal and Zirin, *Dictionary of Russian Women Writers*, pp. 747–51.

Chapter 4

MID-NINETEENTH-CENTURY DOMESTIC IDEOLOGY IN RUSSIA

Diana Greene

During the nineteenth century, domestic ideology held that middle-class women (or 'ladies') belonged in the home, where they were to be 'wives and mothers, to nurture and maintain their families, to provide religious example and inspiration, and to affect the world around them by exercising private moral influence', in short, to exhibit the qualities of 'piety, purity, submissiveness, and domesticity'.[1]

Both western and Russian women's historians have treated mid-nineteenth-century domestic ideology as a western phenomenon. Domestic ideology was first identified, described, and analysed by U.S. historians.[2] While their terminology and dates vary slightly, these historians all explain the phenomenon as having its roots in specifically nineteenth-century U.S. factors of history, economics (industrialisation), politics, demographics and culture.[3] The more recent and more general studies of nineteenth-century domestic ideology in Germany, France, and Britain connect it with bourgeois values.[4] Almost all historians see domestic ideology as a response to industrialisation which established a 'public' sphere of factory and office for men and a 'private' sphere of unpaid support functions in the home for middle-class women.[5]

Russian women's historians have not written very much or very consistently about mid-nineteenth-century Russian domestic ideology, perhaps because of the absence in Russia at that time of a strong middle class and significant industrialisation.[6] Nonetheless, a survey of Russian 'thick' (literary monthly) journals and children's magazines of the 1840s[7] indicates that the Russian periodic press was energetically promulgating domestic ideology.

In this chapter I will suggest some possible explanations for the presence of domestic ideology in Russia: diffusion, underlying parallels in the treatment of women, and a pan-European women's history. As I will show, Russian domestic ideology was extremely similar in content to the U.S. version (which has been studied in the most detail). In significance and effect, however, Russian and U.S. domestic ideology were very different, for reasons to be considered.

Domestic ideology may have entered Russia from Germany, via the *instituty,* or upper-class girls' boarding schools. Smolny, the first such *institut,* established by Catherine the Great in 1764, had originally reflected her French Enlightenment ideas concerning the education of women by including in the plan of study architecture, poetry writing, history, geography and physics, as well as such domestic arts as sewing and knitting. The next two empresses to administer the *instituty,* however, Mariia Fedorovna (1759–1828) and Aleksandra Fedorovna (1798–1860) – who were also German princesses like Catherine – appear to have been affected by the rising tide of German domestic ideology which they applied to the *institut* curriculum. A regulation in 1827 mandated that *instituty* teach only 'the law of God, essential studies [*neobkhodimye nauki*], useful handiwork, and home economics [*domashnee khoziaistvo*]'. In 1828 physical education was dropped from the curriculum, and by the middle of the century the twelve-year course established by Catherine had been reduced to six.[8] The prestige of the *instituty* – and the social prominence of its graduates – would have guaranteed the spread of the domestic ideology taught there.

A second channel of diffusion – and one that suggests the cross-European nature of the phenomenon – was the translation into Russian of English, French, and German conduct books promulgating domestic ideology, books which were then reviewed in the periodic press. For example, *Responsibilities of the Married Woman* was a Russian translation of a French translation of an English original by the famous conduct book writer, Sarah Ellis (1799–1872); *Advice to Young Ladies and Girls Concerning the Conservation of Beauty, the Preservation of Health, How to Dress, and Education* was a Russian translation and abridgement of an anonymous French original. Reviews of these books appeared in *Sovremennik, Otechestvennye zapiski,* and *Biblioteka dlia chteniia.* French and English conduct books even appeared in translation in two Russian children's magazines.[9]

In general, most of the reviewers commented favourably on the conduct books except for Vissarion Belinsky (1811–1848), Russia's most important literary and social critic. Belinsky, who clearly found the etiquette books, marriage manuals, and beauty guides which spread domestic ideology degrading and oppressive to women, seemed to make a point of reviewing such books in order to criticise the treatment of women in society. In his review of *Responsibilities of the Married Woman* he writes that were the book not so illiterately written, he would recommend it 'to our readers, not as a book of moral admonition, but as a curious system by which one can trace the sad story of women, often condemned – alas, not by Mrs. Ellis alone – to an entire life of deprivation, self-sacrifice, moral humiliation'.[10] Belinsky's views, however, did not make such books less prevalent in the periodic press.

But why would domestic ideology be accepted so readily from abroad? The answer may lie in the similar status in Russia and the West of the objects of domestic ideology: upper- and middle-class married women. For Russian non-serf women there was virtually no way to survive outside of marriage except to remain dependent on relatives or to enter a convent; there were few, if any, opportunities for them to earn money, and women inherited considerably less than their male siblings.[11] But within marriage, too, Russian women were at a considerable disadvantage. The law required a woman to live with her husband – whose permission she required to work, go to school, or travel – 'in unlimited obedience' (*v neogranichennom poslushanii*), while condoning a husband's corporal punishment of his wife 'short of severe bodily injury'. Even if a severely assaulted woman managed to get her husband convicted of the crime, the law would still require her to live with him when he returned from prison or exile. She could not obtain a legal separation on the grounds of abuse, since Russian Orthodox canon law, which regulated marriage law, did not recognise legal separations. And abuse, no matter how severe, never constituted grounds for divorce or annulment, which in any case were virtually impossible to obtain. (In cases of life-threatening abuse, occasionally the government stepped in and granted a woman a separate residence permit 'on special directives from the emperor'.)[12] Russian women were thought to have an advantage over women in the West because they could own property and in theory legally possessed their dowries. In fact, however, neither women's upbringing, nor the law, nor custom, nor the Church gave them any means of enforcing those rights.[13]

The constraints imposed on Russian married women, however, did not differ significantly from those imposed on married women in

Germany, Britain, the United States and France. In Germany under the influential Prussian civil code, *Das Allegemeines Landrecht*, an unmarried women remained the permanent ward of her father, and a married woman the permanent ward of her husband, who until the 1860s could take her to the police station to be beaten. Although divorce was available, and alimony for the wife possible if the husband alone was guilty, the husband retained custody of the children and of all marital property regardless of circumstances.[14]

In Britain and the United States (which followed British marriage law closely) a married woman was a *feme covert,* civilly dead with no legal existence or control over her person, property, earnings or children. In England, ecclesiastic courts granted women separations from abusive husbands, but without the right to their own property or earnings, which still belonged to their husbands until 1870; divorces were granted by special acts of parliament at the rate of less than two per year before 1857. In some of the United States the situation was better for women. During the 1840s four states passed very partial married women's property laws, and divorce was possible in some states.[15]

In France, women lived under the Napoleonic Code (1804), which despite many changes in regimes, remained in force until the end of the nineteenth century. French women were considered 'eternal minors', with no legal rights over their persons, property or children. Although a husband was not legally empowered to punish his wife, he could use the police to force her to live with him, and could kill her with impunity if he caught her in adultery (women were not given the same licence to kill their husbands). Under the 'community of goods' all marital property was administered by the husband during his lifetime and by a trustee thereafter. Divorce, first legalised by the French Revolutionary government, was abolished under the Restoration of Church and Monarchy (1816) and only reintroduced in 1884. Legal separations were available on grounds greatly favouring men, who continued to administer the 'community of goods'.[16]

In all of these countries women (married or single) rarely controlled their own property; in none of these countries could married women control their fertility, obtain custody of their children or control their children's property in case of a separation.[17] In none did a woman have freedom of movement (that is, the right to a separate domicile), freedom from unreasonable search and seizure, or freedom from confinement against her will (her person belonged to her husband or father, whose permission she had to obtain to work or travel). In all of these countries a husband could legally beat (or kill) and rape his wife. It is not surprising, then, that women's separate and unequal legal position in Russia as well as the West was reflected in an ideology which relegated them to a separate and unequal sphere.

Besides the subordinate position of women, a third, underlying factor may account for the presence of domestic ideology in Russia: Russia's participation in a larger, ongoing controversy concerning women's social role. Susan Groag Bell and Karen Offen have argued convincingly that since the Enlightenment, a cross-European debate has been taking place 'over women, their relationship to the family, and their claims to freedom', a debate that includes both Russia and the West. Not surprisingly, this debate has been accompanied by parallel events and movements in the women's history of many countries, as shown in several comparative studies.[18]

In particular, three periods of cross-European women's history throw light on the causes and results of domestic ideology. In the first period, the late eighteenth century, a few social philosophers in various countries started applying to women French Enlightenment ideas about the rights of man, resulting in a widespread discussion of women's status in society. Participants in this discussion included Theodor Gottlieb von Hippel (1741–1796) in Prussia, author of *Uber die bürgerliche Verbesserung der Weiber* (*On Improving the Status of Women*, 1792), Olympe de Gouges (1748–1793) in France, author of the *Déclaration des droits de la femme et de la citoyenne* (1791), Mikhail Nikolaevich Makarov (1789–1847) in Russia, advocate of higher education for women, Mary Wollstonecraft (1759–1797) in Britain, author of *A Vindication of the Rights of Women* (1792), and Abigail Adams (1744–1818) in the United States, who asked her husband, John, during the Second Continental Congress of 1776 to 'remember the ladies' in the future U.S. law code. During this period it became possible for a few upper- and middle-class women to participate in intellectual life, for example the influential political writer and novelist Mme de Staël (1766–1817) in France, the Bluestockings in England, and the writers and publishers Friederike Helene Unger (1751–1813) and Sophie von La Roche (1731–1807) in Germany. In Russia, intellectual women became fashionable. Catherine the Great herself wrote plays, memoirs and satire, as did many other Russian women. At the beginning of Alexander I's reign journals proliferated for upper-class women (*Zhurnal dlia milykh* [1804], *Damskii zhurnal* [1806, 1823–1833], *Aglaia* [1808–1810, 1812], *Kabinet Aspazii* [1815]), which occasionally encouraged women to educate themselves or to write. This is not to suggest that most Enlightenment thinkers meant their ideas on individual rights to be applied to women; Rousseau, for example, in his influential treatise on education, *Emile* (1762), wrote that

> Woman is made to please and be subjugated ... Thus the whole education of women ought to relate to men. To please men, to be useful to them, to make herself loved and honoured by them, to raise them when young, to care for them when grown, to counsel them, to console them, to make their lives agreeable and sweet – these are the duties of women at all times and they ought to be taught from childhood.[19]

In the second period, during the beginning and middle of the nineteenth century, there was a widespread sentimental and romantic reaction to Enlightenment ideas and the French Revolution throughout Europe. Women were encouraged to withdraw from public life as the few opportunities that had opened for them disappeared. In Russia, Paul, who during his brief reign (1796–1801) reversed as many of his mother's policies as possible, barred women from succeeding to the throne in the future. While under Alexander I (1801–1825) the Enlightenment debate concerning women's role briefly resumed, the feeling grew that women belonged in the home, a feeling fuelled by the Sentimentalism of such writers as Karamzin (*Bednaia Liza*, 1792) and Zhukovsky.[20] In any case, there could be no further talk of higher education or intellectual fulfilment for women during the Napoleonic invasion; anything French, including French Enlightenment ideas of equality, became unpopular. After the Napoleonic Wars, mysticism and political reaction characterised the remainder of Alexander I's reign, and Nicholas I, who admired and emulated Prussian militarism, was no more interested in expanding the rights of women than those of any other oppressed and potentially rebellious group in Russia.

Attempting to limit women to the private sphere, however, created its own reaction. By the first third of the nineteenth century a third period of pan-European women's history had started. Women's rights organisations arose to restore women to the public sphere by securing for them higher education, financial independence, political and legal rights. Historians have documented the many interrelations and mutual influences of women's rights activists in various countries.[21] Such women's movements included the French Saint Simonist women in the 1830s, the French Revolutionary feminists of 1848, the Vormarz women in 1840s Germany, the U.S. women's movement starting with the Seneca Falls Convention in 1848, the married women's property reform movement in 1850s Britain, and the Russian women's movement of the late 1850s and 1860s.[22]

In this cross-European context, then, let us now turn to specific examples of Russian domestic ideology. Along with the above-mentioned reviews of European conduct books, Russian thick journals often published expressions of Russian domestic ideology, which, like the U.S. version, exhorted women to be 'pious, pure, submissive and domestic'. The following examples, have, however, have been chosen from contemporary Russian children's magazines because these, in order to socialise young readers, presented standards of boys' and girls' behaviour with particular clarity and explicitness. In story after story, little girls who behave with insufficient piety, purity, submissiveness or domesticity are horribly punished. The young female reader defied domestic ideology at her peril.

Piety

A comparison of two children's magazines, one for girls (*Zvezdochka*, 1842–1849) and one for boys (*Biblioteka dlia vospitaniia*, 1843–1846), would suggest that piety was an exclusively female concern.[23] No prayers appear at all in the boys' magazine, *Biblioteka dlia vospitaniia*. In the girls' magazine, *Zvezdochka*, however, we find prayers not only in Russian, but also in English, French, and German, as well as stories with such titles as 'Rasskaz o dobrykh detiakh' ('A Story About Good Children'), 'Dobraia devochka' ('The Good Little Girl'), 'Dobraia teten'ka' ('The Good Little Aunt'), and 'O tom kak malen'kie deti dolzhny ponimat' molitby gospodniu' ('How Little Children Should Understand Praying to God').[24] No such stories appear in the boys' *Biblioteka dlia vospitaniia*. Here not only do piety, and even Christianity, receive little attention, but we find a series of articles on Greek mythology and Ancient Eastern gods and goddesses (1843, 1–2: II), subjects absent from *Zvezdochka*.

In one case in *Zvezdochka* biographical facts are actually distorted in order to create an example of piety for girls. A biography of Jacqueline Pascal (1625–1661), sister of Blaise Pascal, correctly recounts that at age thirteen she rescued her father from exile by writing a poem to Richelieu, and at age fifteen she won a poetry award. After that, we are told, 'Jacqueline no longer concerned herself with poetry. Her mind was serious by nature and turned to more important subjects. Following the advice of her famous father, she removed herself completely from the world while still in the flower of her youth and became a nun in the Abbey of Port Royal des Champs where she died at age thirty-six.'[25]

In fact, according to the *Larousse Grand Dictionnaire Universel* (XII: 348–49), Pascal's father and brother strenuously opposed her becoming a nun. Nonetheless, the *Zvezdochka* version of Pascal's life presents its readers with an embodiment of female piety, a quality that apparently consists of not writing (a theme that appears in several stories), obeying one's male relatives, taking the veil, and dying young.

Purity

As nineteenth-century society polarised women into pure and impure – respected and not respectable – it was vital that girls learn the importance of purity early on. To be pure meant that a girl or woman knew nothing of sex or of the power she possessed to attract males, experienced no sexual feelings outside marriage, and fewer sexual feelings than her husband within marriage. An article that appeared in *Literaturnaia gazeta* (1840) by a Nichipor Kulesh entitled 'What If I Had a Daughter' rhapsodically describes girls' training in purity:

> Until the age of fifteen my daughter would have grown up under the sole influence of her gentle, virtuous mother. She would have heard only those things which accorded with her age and understanding, and which would perfect her moral education ... *She* would not know that passions exist in the world and that they are hidden in embryonic form in herself ... She would be imbued with religion which would serve throughout her life as her guide, comforter, as a goal of her life, and as a bright thought in the face of death. Her mother's solicitude would develop her youthful heart – a heart protected against premature gusts of passion – and put into it that gentleness of character, that tender view of the world, that infinite condescension, which make women so fascinating.[26]

'Vanity', or a girl's exploration of her power to attract males, represented a major threat to her purity, and therefore justified draconian countermeasures. In 'Liden'ka', a cautionary tale which appeared in *Zvezdochka* in 1842, the unfortunate heroine, who appears to be around six, commits the crime of painting her cheeks with water colours to make herself more beautiful. Until she can learn that 'good nature and affection in all relations deserve much more respect than rouge and fancy dresses', her parents completely ignore her and forbid her sisters to play with her, a withdrawal of love that is described in painful detail. At the end of the story the chastened Liden'ka hopes her parents will forgive her:

> In fact they would often say, 'We cannot completely forget that one of our girls added an adult stupidity to a children's mistakes. But we will *try* to forget this to the extent that she will try to *correct herself*...'. But she herself never completely forgot what had happened to her, and for a long time afterwards, even after all her friends had stopped reproaching her, whenever they looked at her more seriously than usual, each time she would think involuntarily, 'Oh! They were probably remembering my rouged cheeks!'.[27]

No mention of purity (or vanity) appears in the boys' *Biblioteka dlia vospitaniia*.

Submissiveness

While all children were expected to be submissive to (that is, controlled by) adults, boys and girls were subject to different kinds of control, as can be seen from a translation of a French conduct book for children which appeared in *Zvezdochka*. Little boys only had to submit to physical control; they were not to fidget. Little girls, who, it was assumed, would not fidget, were expected to be psychologically and emotionally submissive as well:

> She [the little girl] must always be modest, simple, quiet and affectionate to everyone. This must be expressed in her face, in all her movements and her words. A well-brought-up young girl has in her something resembling the Angels and therefore it is fitting for her to constantly remember that this resemblance demands of her extraordinary sweetness, goodness, affection and pleasantness in her disposition and in all her actions and words.[28]

In 'Schastlivye deti' ('The Happy Children'), a story which appeared in *Zvezdochka*, young readers are introduced to three paragons, Mashen'ka, Liuben'ka, and Vanechka, who are happy because they are submissive:

> You will have already guessed, dear friends, that such sweet children had no idea what it meant to be disobedient. It was only necessary to ask them to sing or play or dance or read a book or recite a fable from memory and they would do it as well as they could, and if you only knew how willingly, and with what a sweet air.[29]

A girl's submissiveness might be undermined by intellectual interests. Her exploration of her intellectual powers – like her exploration of her sexual power – was considered 'vanity' and dealt with sternly. In a story which appeared in *Zvezdochka*, 'Perepiski sestry s bratom' ('Correspondence Between a Sister and Brother'), a girl who merely expresses the wish to write is portrayed as a threat to the social order who must immediately be made to submit to rightful male authority.

When thirteen-year-old Masha, in a letter to her seventeen-year-old brother, mentions that she 'would like very much to be a [woman] writer [*pisatel'nitsa*]', he replies with shock, outrage, and threats of abandonment:

> 'A writer! Do you understand all the importance of this word, little girl? Of course not! It must be that you want to be a writer ... only so people will talk about you, that friends and strangers will praise you, perhaps even publish something of your works ... Yes, believe me, my dear Masha, that any little girl who already want to see her little trivialities in print deserves to be punished... Don't be surprised that I speak to you so mercilessly. I

am sure that you don't have that stupid desire yet. . .If you don't agree with me, but feel an irresistible desire to write for people to read you when you are still such a young girl, then it is better not to send me your letters'.

Masha's mother, too, is properly chastised by her son for letting Masha get so out of hand. In her last letter Masha tells her brother that she has renounced her '*insolent literary schemes*' (*derzkie literaturnye zatei*) and is 'even afraid of the name, [woman] writer'. In the final letter her brother congratulates her on these changes.[30]

Domesticity

Many of the stories in *Zvezdochka* warn girls against failings that might interfere with domesticity. Carelessness, although never mentioned in the boys' magazine, constitutes a fatal flaw for girls.[31] In 'Prekrasnaia kukla Avrora, ili neberezhlivaia devochka' ('The Beautiful Doll Named Dawn, or the Careless Girl'), the heroine leaves her new doll with eyes that open and shut near the stove, and half the face melts. When her mother tells her that the doll cannot be repaired because it was the only one of its kind sent from London, the girl keeps the doll as a perpetual psychological hair shirt, saying, 'Let the sight of you, poor Dawn, for ever teach me carefulness.' The story ends, 'Every day she thought how bad it was to be careless and this thought helped her correct her fault and make of herself the most tidy and careful girl.'[32]

As these and many other stories show, girls were coerced to accept domestic ideology through guilt, shame, humiliation, and threatened loss of parental love (which for children is a matter of survival). Yet paradoxically, in Russia, as in the United States, domesticity was generally assumed to be an inborn trait in women. Even the progressive *Sovremennik* expressed this view in an article supporting better education for women (on the grounds that it would make them better wives and mothers). The author notes that since the 'natural women's sphere' includes 'love of order', women are better qualified than men to manage domestic matters, household expenses, and take those 'small precautionary measures which men's more independent minds often reject'.[33]

Domestic Ideology in Russia and the United States

While the content of domestic ideology in the United States and Russia was similar, its significance and effects were very different, as we would expect in two countries with such different histories and institutions. In the United States, the 'Great Awakening' of evangelical religion which started in 1795 allowed American women (with the encouragement of their ministers) to speak in public, write for and edit moral reform magazines, form moral and missionary societies, and circulate and sign petitions. These activities, which U.S. historians believe fuelled the feelings of moral superiority and even self-righteousness that characterised the ideology in the United States, also trained women in social activism. In addition, in the United States even poor working women could aspire to 'ladyhood', making domestic ideology a more 'democratic' or widespread phenomenon. Finally, during the 1840s a vigorous popular press spread domestic ideology through an impressive number of women's magazines (forty-three, not including moral reform and abolitionist periodicals), many edited or written by women, as well as through conduct books, while women's fiction presented poor but virtuous heroines using domestic ideology to achieve independence and social empowerment.[34]

That is, many U.S. women attempted to use the idea of women's separate sphere and moral superiority to empower themselves. Even Sarah Josepha Hale, editor of *Godey's Ladies Book* – the most famous of the magazines supporting domestic ideology – in 1837 urged the passage of a married women's property law by citing women's moral superiority and their need to have more influence over their husbands and children. However, as Ann Douglas writes, 'genuine success was hardly possible' for American women who pursued 'partially feminist goals by largely anti-feminist means.'[35] Ladies could hardly win autonomy through an ideology that made them dependent on a husband for economic resources, class privilege, social position, self-definition, self-esteem, and the meaning of their lives, which gave them no protection from spousal abuse, which barred them from political power and any serious creative expression, and which effectively divided them from their natural allies, women of other classes and races who faced many of the same constraints.

In 1848 another more radical group of women used the political, organisational, and public-speaking experience they had gained in reform movements (revival, temperance, abolition) to organise the first women's rights convention at Seneca Falls. There, American women claimed for themselves the same 'inalienable rights' claimed by American men in the *Declaration of Independence*.[36]

In Russia conditions were very different. Women's religious activism – which focused on the creation of women's communities – offered women not engagement with society, but rather refuge and autonomy. Social mobility for women was virtually impossible. Moreover, Russia at this time stagnated under Nicholas's 'censorship terror'; except for fashion journals there were no periodicals for women.

In contrast to U.S. writers of women's fiction, the Russian women writers who dealt with *polozhenie zhenshchiny* (upper-class women's position in society) – Nadezhda Durova, Elena Gan, Mar'ia Zhukova, Avdotiia Panaeva, Karolina Pavlova – offered their readers few happy endings; they certainly were in no position to mobilise an active constituency of women. In contrast to the woman-run Seneca Falls Conference, the first Russian women's movement, which arose in the late 1850s, was publicised and theorised by men, such as Nekrasov, Chernyshevsky, Herzen, Druzhinin, Pirogov, and Mikhailov. On the positive side, radical Russian men, unlike most American men, could sympathise with women's domestic oppression because of their own political oppression. On the negative side, however, they interested themselves in 'the woman question' only as part of the larger revolutionary issue. The oppression of serfs by upper-class men and women interested them far more than the oppression of serf women by serf men or the oppression of upper-class women by upper-class men.[37]

Although domestic ideology is considered a nineteenth-century phenomenon, it was not newly created by industrialisation or capitalism: its roots in western culture extend back at least to the Greeks, who divided men's sphere, the *polis*, from women's, the *oikos* (household). Writing at the dawn of industrialisation, Rousseau for one was aware of this legacy; in *Emile* he approvingly describes the confinement of married women in ancient Sparta: 'Shut up in their houses, they limited their cares to their households and their families. Such is the way of life that nature and reason prescribe for the fair sex.' In ancient Rome women lived under a lifelong legal male 'guardianship', a condition which, as we have seen, existed at least through the first half of the nineteenth century in the law codes of England, France, Germany, the United States and Russia. In the Judaeo-Christian tradition we also find roots of domestic ideology, especially in two biblical passages cited repeatedly during the nineteenth century, *Proverbs* 31:10–31 (the description of the virtuous woman) and St Paul: 'But I suffer not a woman to teach, nor to usurp authority over the man, but to be in silence' (*Timothy* 2:11–12). None of these sources, however, accounts for the mid-nineteenth-century outpouring of domestic ideology throughout Europe, Russia and the United States in conduct books, etiquette books, children's literature, novels, and the popular press.[38]

Several historians have pointed out that at this time large numbers of unmarried lower-class women first began to earn their own wages in industry and domestic service, which gave them at least some financial independence. It seems likely, as Linda Edmondson writes, that domestic ideology was the 'anxious reassertion of a previously unchallenged assumption in the face of unprecedented social and economic change rather than ... the creation of a new norm'. Certainly, in American conduct books we see authors trying to keep middle-class women in the home and out of the public sphere, using what Sarah Newcomb calls the 'rhetorics of religion, nature, and pragmatism': 'God demands you to conform to your role, nature proves God's gender differences are right ... and it is very expedient and useful to do so.' In *The Young Lady's Aid to Usefulness and Happiness*, for example, Jason Whitman urges all Christian women never to speak in public because Jesus would not want them to leave their 'appropriate spheres of duty'. In *The American Lady* Charles Butler writes that a girl 'who take[s] to scribble ... should be carefully instructed that merely to exercise [her talents] as instruments for the acquisition of fame and the promotion of pleasure is subversive of her delicacy as a woman and contrary to the spirit of a Christian'. In *How to be a Lady: A Book for Girls Containing Useful Hints on the Formation of Character*, Harvey Newcomb instructs girls to anticipate the wants of others, be tidy and quiet, and to cultivate submission, advice that he does not offer boys in his companion book, *How to Be a Man: A Book for Boys Containing Useful Hints on the Formation of Character*.[39]

Despite the fact that many historians consider industrialisation – and single working-class women's greater economic independence – the most important factors in the development of European and U.S. nineteenth-century domestic ideology, it is not entirely surprising that an unindustrialised Russia also embraced domestic ideology. As we have seen, Russia shared with Europe many background factors that contributed to domestic ideology: legal constraints on women, participation in the cross-European debate on the position of women in society, cultural and religious traditions that viewed women as 'other', as well as a Europeanised court, intelligentsia and periodic press all very interested in European events and trends. On the other hand, as we have seen, domestic ideology had a very different significance in the United States – where large numbers of politically active middle-class women attempted to use it to empower themselves – and in Russia, where the fewer upper-class women affected by it generally remained isolated from each other. Such differences in western and Russian women's history may account for twentieth-century differences in the women's movement in Russia and the West.

Notes

Most of this paper was researched under an IREX GS-YF grant to (then) Leningrad and an NEH Travel to Collections Grant to the University of Illinois at Champaign-Urbana. I am very grateful to Rhonda Clark, Rochelle Ruthchild, and Ann Healy for their knowledgeable and most useful suggestions.

1. Nancy Cott, *The Bonds of Womanhood: "Woman's Sphere" in New England 1780–1835* (New Haven: Yale University Press, 1977), p. 8; Barbara Welter, *Dimity Convictions* (Athens: Ohio University Press, 1976), p. 21.

    Domestic ideology did not apply to 'non-ladies'. Excluded in the United States were all African-American women, native American women, pioneer women, immigrant women, poor women. See Mary Beth Norton, 'The Paradox of "Women's Sphere"', in Carol Ruth Berkin and Mary Beth Norton (eds), *Women of America* (Boston: Houghton Mifflin, 1979), pp. 139–49; Erlene Stetson, 'Studying Slavery: Some Literary and Pedagogical Considerations on the Black Female Slave', in Gloria T. Hull et al. (eds), *All the Women are White, All the Blacks are Men, But Some of Us are Brave* (Old Westbury: Feminist Press, 1982), pp. 61–84; Alice Kessler-Harris, *Out to Work: A History of Wage-Earning Women in the U.S.* (New York: Oxford University Press, 1982); Daniel Sutherland, *Americans and Their Servants* (Baton Rouge: Louisiana State University Press, 1981).

2. Barbara Welter, 'The Cult of True Womanhood 1820-1860', *American Quarterly* (1966), pp. 151–74, also in Barbara Welter, *Dimity Convictions*, pp. 21–41; Gerda Lerner, 'The Lady and the Mill Girl', *Midcontinent American Studies Journal*, vol. 4, no. 1 (Spring 1969), pp. 5–15; Cott, *The Bonds of Womanhood*; Ann Douglas [Wood], *The Feminization of American Culture* (New York: Knopf, 1977); Norton, 'The Paradox of "Women's Sphere"', pp. 139–49; Mary Ryan, 'The Empire of the Mother: American Writing About Domesticity 1830-60', *Woman and History*, nos 2-3 (Summer/Fall 1982).

3. The terms used by historians, and the periods referred to, include Welter: 'the cult of true womanhood', 1820–1860; Cott and Ryan: 'the cult of domesticity', 1780–1835, and 1830-60 respectively; Douglas: 'the feminization of America', 1820–1875. I use the broader term 'domestic ideology'.

    An example of a specifically U.S. factor is the Age of Jackson (1829–1837) which, by empowering working men relative to middle-class women, led women to look for compensating power in a sphere of their own. Edward Pessen, 'The Working Men's Party Revisited', in Frank Gutell (ed.), *Essays on Jacksonian America* (New York: Holt, Rinehart and Winston, 1970), pp. 177–92; Alice Rossi, *The Feminist Papers* (New York: Bantam, 1973), pp. 271–72.

4. Germany: Karin Hausin, 'Family and Role Division: the Polarization of Sexual Stereotypes in the Nineteenth Century – An Aspect of the Dissociation of Work and Family Life', in Richard Evans and W.R. Lee (eds), *The German Family: Essays on the Social History of the Family in Nineteenth- and Twentieth-Century Germany* (London: Croom Helm, 1981), p. 53; Ruth Dawson, '"And This Shield is Called – Self Reliance": Emerging Feminist Consciousness in the Late Eighteenth Century', in Ruth-Ellen Joeres and Mary Jo Maynes (eds), *German Women in the Eighteenth and Nineteenth Centuries: A Social and Literary History* (Bloomington: Indiana University Press, 1986), p. 157.

    France: Claire Goldberg Moses, *French Feminism in the Nineteenth Century*. (Albany: SUNY Press, 1984), pp. 6, 14, 18. Linda Clark, *Schooling the Daughters of Marianne: Textbooks and the Socializing of Girls in Modern French Primary Schools* (Albany: State University of New York Press, 1984), pp. 8–9.

    Britain: Mary Poovey, *The Proper Lady and the Woman Writer: Ideology as Style in the Works of Mary Wollstonecraft, Mary Shelley, and Jane Austen* (Chicago: University of Chicago Press, 1984), pp. 6, 8, 19; Nancy Armstrong, 'The Rise of the Domestic Woman', in Nancy Armstrong and Leonard Tennenhouse (eds), *The Ideology of Conduct: Essays on Literature and the History of Sexuality* (New York: Methuen, 1987), pp. 96–141.

5. Working-class women carried the 'double burden' of work in both the public and private spheres. See Theresa McBride, 'The Long Road Home: Women's Work

and Industrialization', in Renate Bridenthal and Claudia Koonz (eds), *Becoming Visible: Women in European History* (Boston: Houghton Mifflin, 1977), pp. 282-95.

6. Richard Stites does not mention domestic ideology, although he discusses the Romantic 'idealization of the Russian woman as the embodiment of Virtue and Maternity': *The Women's Liberation Movement in Russia* (Princeton: Princeton University Press, 1978), pp. 15-16. Barbara Engel writes that Russia, which unlike Europe, lacked a bourgeoisie, 'never developed a comparable ideology of domesticity', but later posits a 'Russian version of the cult of domesticity' created by 'rebels' (Passek, Panaeva, Pavlova, etc.): *Mothers and Daughters* (New York: Cambridge University Press, 1983), pp. 6, 27-42; Linda Edmondson discusses domestic ideology in industrialised European countries but not in Russia: *Feminism in Russia, 1900-17* (Stanford: Stanford University Press, 1984), p. 6.

See Richard Pipes, 'The Missing Bourgeoisie', in *Russia Under the Old Regime* (New York: Charles Scribner's Sons, 1974), pp. 191-220. Reginald E. Zelnik writes that industrialisation did not take hold in Russia until the 1890s: 'The Peasant and the Factory', in Wayne S. Vucinich (ed.), *The Peasant in Nineteenth-Century Russia* (Stanford: Stanford University Press, 1968), pp. 173, 179.

7. *Biblioteka dlia chteniia, Finskii vestnik, Literaturnaia gazeta, Moskvitianin, Otechestvennye zapiski, Sovremennik, Syn otechestva, Zvezdochka, Biblioteka dlia vospitaniia.*

Because four major thick journals were established during the 1840s – *Otechestvennye zapiski* (1839), *Literaturnaia gazeta* (1840), *Moskvitianin* (1841), and Nekrasov and Panaev's *Sovremennik* (1846) – as well as two children's magazines, *Zvezdochka* (1842) and *Biblioteka dlia vospitaniia* (1843), this is a convenient decade for observing the presence of domestic ideology in the Russian periodic press. Richard Wortman shows, however, that Russian empresses were expected to model motherhood, if not domesticity, from the reign of Nicholas I (1825): 'The Russian Empress as Mother', in David Ransel (ed.), *The Family in Imperial Russia: New Lines of Historical Research* (Urbana: University of Illinois Press, 1978), pp. 60-74. I suggest that the new emphasis on the empress as mother was part of the same anti-Enlightenment reaction to women in the public sphere that also fostered domestic ideology (as discussed below).

8. E. Likhacheva, *Materialy dlia istorii zhenskogo obrazovaniia v Rossii (1086-1856)* (St Petersburg, 1988), vol. 1, p. 108; vol. 3, pp. 3, 7, 62-63. In 1828 there were eleven *instituty* in Russia, and by 1855, twenty-four more. Richard Wortman, 'The Russian Empress as Mother', pp. 60 ff.; Engel, *Mothers and Daughters*, p. 24; Christine Johanson, *Women's Struggle for Higher Education in Russia 1855-1900* (Kingston: McGill-Queen's University Press, 1987), p. 108, n. 4.

9. Conduct books, according to Sarah Newcomb, 'attempt to formulate for the youthful reader a code of ethical behavior that delineates approved gender roles': 'Wise and Foolish Virgins: "Usable Fiction" and the Early American Conduct Tradition', *Early American Literature*, vol. 25, no. 2 (1990), p. 140. For conduct books as the basis of domestic ideology, see Sarah Newcomb, *Learning to Behave: A Guide to American Conduct Books Before 1900* (Westport: Greenwood, 1994), p. 6, and Nancy Armstrong and Leonard Tennenhouse, 'The Literature of Conduct, the Conduct of Literature, and the Politics of Desire: An Introduction', in Armstrong and Tennenhouse, *The Ideology of Conduct,* pp. 1-24.

Translations of European conduct books: G-zha Ellis, *Obiazannosti zamuzhnei zhenshchiny i polozhenie eia v obshchestve (s frantsuzskogo perevod Gustava Briune v dvukh chastiakh)* (St Petersburg 1848), reviewed in *Sovremennik*, no. 2 (1849), pp. 142-47 and no. 5, p. 55, and *Otechestvennye zapiski*, no. 2 (1849), p. 117. This was probably an adaptation of Ellis's *The Wives of England* (1843). On Ellis, see Paul Schlueter and June Schlueter (eds), *An Encyclopedia of British Women Writers* (London: Garland Publishing, 1988), pp. 156-57. *Sovety molodym damam i devitsam kasatel'no sokhraneniia krasoty, sberezheniia zdorov'ia, umen'ia odevat'sia i obrazovaniia* (St Petersburg, 1848), translated from the French by M. R–va ('Vstuplenie', p. 8), reviewed in *Biblioteka dlia chteniia*, no. 2 (1848), p. 37, *Sovremennik*, no. 1 (1848), 'Mody', pp. 6–8, and *Otechestvennye zapiski*, no.1 (1848), pp. 56–57, and nos. 3–4, p. 104; Zhozefina Lebassiu, *Blagovospitannoe ditia, ili kak dozhno sebia vesti (s frantsuzskogo)* (St Petersburg, 1847), reviewed in *Sovremennik*, no. 2 (1848), p. 137; *Prizvanie zhenshchiny (s angliiskogo)* (St Petersburg, 1840), reviewed in *Otechestvennye zapiski*, no. 1 (1840), p. 14.

'Sovety malen'kim detiam', a translation from the French children's magazine *Le Bon Génie*, appeared in the Russian children's magazine, *Zvezdochka*, no. 6 (1844); 'Prakticheskoe vospitanie' (*Practical Education*, 1798) by the English writer Maria Edgeworth (1767–1849) and her didactic father, Richard Edgeworth, appeared in the children's magazine, *Biblioteka dlia vospitaniia* (1843–1844). On Edgeworth, see Schlueter and Schlueter, *Encyclopedia of British Women Writers*, p. 150.

10. *Sovremennik*, no. 2 (1849), p. 143. All translations are mine unless otherwise stated.

11. Under the 1835 *Svod zakonov* (legal code) a sister inherited 1/14 of her brother's share of immovable (real) property and 1/8 of her brother's share of movable property. Aleksei Vasil'evich Kunitsyn, *O pravakh nasledovaniia lits zhenskogo pola* (Kharkov, 1844), p. 9. Michelle Marrese, however, argues that in some cases daughters were given a larger share of immovable and movable property than was prescribed by law: 'Noblewomen and Provincial Economic Life in Eighteenth-Century Russia', conference paper (AAASS National Convention, 1995).

12. *Zhenskoe pravo: Svod uzakonenii i postanovlenii otnosiashchikhsia do zhenskogo pola s raz"iasneniem statei svoda zakonov po resheniiam kassatsionnogo departamenta pravitel'stvuiushchego senata* (St Petersburg, 1873), p. 108. The commentary states, 'It is the unconditional duty of spouses to live together' (p. 108); Laura Engelstein, *The Keys to Happiness: Sex and the Search for Modernity in Fin-de-Siecle Russia* (Ithaca: Cornell University Press, 1992), p. 32; William Wagner, *Marriage, Property and Law in Late Imperial Russia* (Oxford: Clarendon Press, 1994), p. 65. For marriage law concerning those of other religions living in Russia, see Engelstein, *The Keys to Happiness*, p. 28; Gregory Freeze, 'Bringing Order to the Russian Family: Marriage and Divorce in Imperial Russia, 1760–1860', *Journal of Modern History*, vol. 62, no. 4 (December 1990), p. 744. Freeze writes that in the nineteenth century the Russian Orthodox Church 'virtually eliminated the legal possibility of terminating a marriage ...', granting between 1836 and 1860 a yearly average of 33 annulments and 58 divorces for the entire Russian empire (pp. 711, 743, 724, 733); Robin Bisha, 'The Promise of Patriarchy: Marriage in Eighteenth-Century Russia' (unpublished Ph.D. dissertation, Indiana University, 1993), p. 90. Bisha points out that noblewomen often were much younger than their husbands, another factor that made such marriages less than equal (pp. 96, 99). See also Freeze, 'Bringing Order to the Russian Family', p. 744.

13. Stites, *The Women's Liberation Movement*, p. 7; I.A. Malinovskii, *Lektsii po istorii russkogo prava* (Rostov, 1918), p. 411; Linda Edmondson, *Feminism in Russia*, p. 11; Bisha, *The Promise of Patriarchy*, pp. 90, 125–55.

Of course, not every Russian wife was a victim of abuse; at least some Russian women must even have managed to dominate their husbands through sheer force of personality. The nervousness of some men about marriage can be inferred from 'humorous' articles such as 'Poleznye sovety novobrachnomu' ('Useful Advice for New Husbands') in the collection *Skalozub i peresmeshnik. Sobranie veselykh rasskazov, satiricheskikh ocherkov iz peterburgskoi zhizni*, compiled by G. K. (1847), pp. 248–54, which includes such useful recommendations as:

'Don't wear a nightcap in front of your wife', 'Don't tell your mistress intimate things about your wife' – and the popularity of Gogol''s works about reluctant grooms, 'Ivan Fedorovich Shpon'ka and his Auntie' (1832) and *Marriage* (1842).

14. Richard Evans, *The Feminist Movement in Germany 1894–1933* (London: Sage, 1976), pp. 12–13; Priscilla Robertson, *An Experience of Women: Pattern and Change in Nineteenth-Century Europe* (Philadelphia: Temple University Press, 1982), p. 162.

15. Norma Basch, *In the Eyes of the Law: Women, Marriage and Property in 19th Century New York* (Ithaca: Cornell University Press, 1982), pp. 16–17. (Separate courts of chancery, available only to the rich, administered antenuptial contracts and trusts to allow some married women to keep control of their property: Basch, p. 21). On separated British wives, see Caroline Norton, *English Laws for Women in the Nineteenth Century* (London, 1854); Robertson, *An Experience of Women*, p. 246.

    On the United States, see Basch, *In the Eyes of the Law*, p. 26. In New England, courts granted absolute divorces; at the other extreme, South Carolina (except for a period of ten years under Reconstruction) granted no divorces on any grounds whatsoever until 1949. See Nelson Blake, *The Road to Reno: A History of Divorce in the United States* (New York: Macmillan, 1962).

16. Paul de Lauribar, *Le Code de L'éternelle mineure (Philosophie du droit féminin)*, (Paris: Librairie Plon, 1922), pp. 176, 186, 218, 243, 317–18; Robertson, *An Experience of Women*, pp. 277–78. As in England, there was a legal loophole (the 'dotal regime') for wealthy families who wanted to safeguard a daughter's property from her husband (subject, of course, to her desire and ability to maintain ownership): ibid., p. 278.

17. France was the only country in Europe during the nineteenth century where married couples regularly practised birth control, possibly because Napoleon's abolition of primogeniture made it necessary to limit the number of children in order to preserve family inheritances. Here too, however, the husband controlled all aspects of marital sexuality and family planning. See Angus McLaren, 'Doctor in the House: Medicine and Private Morality in France, 1800–1850', *French Historical Studies*, vol. 10, no. 3 (1978), pp. 39–54; Robertson, *An Experience of Women*, pp. 16, 47, 193.

18. Susan Groag Bell and Karen M. Offen, *Women, the Family, and Freedom* (Stanford: Stanford University Press, 1983), vol. 1, p. v. See, for example, Edward Shorter, 'Female Emancipation, Birth Control and Fertility in European History', *American Historical Review*, vol. 78, no. 3 (June 1973), pp. 605–40; Bridenthal and Koonz, *Becoming Visible*; Eleanor Riemer and John Fout, *European Women: A Documentary History: 1789–1945* (New York: Schocken Books, 1980); Robertson, *An Experience of Women;* John Fout, 'An English-Language Bibliography on European and American Women's History', in John Fout (ed.), *German Women in the Nineteenth Century* (New York: Holmes and Meier, 1984), pp. 368–423.

19. On von Hippel, see Ruth Dawson, 'And This Shield is Called – Self Reliance', pp. 157–60; on Makarov, see Serafim Serafimovich Shashkov, *Istoriia russkoi zhenshchiny* (St Petersburg, 1879), pp. 234–37; on Abigail Adams, see Rossi, *The Feminist Papers*, pp. 7–15; on Mme de Staël, see Eva Sartori and Dorothy Zimmerman (eds), *French Women Writers: A Bio-Bibliographic Source Book* (New York: Greenwood, 1991), pp. 463–72; Sylvia Myers, 'Learning, Virtue, and the Term "Bluestocking"', *Studies in Eighteenth Century Culture*, vol. 15 (1986), pp. 279–88; Jeannine Blackwell, 'Bildungsroman mit Dame: The Heroine in the German "Bildungsroman" from 1770 to 1900' (unpublished Ph.D. dissertation, Indiana University, 1982); Engel, *Mothers and Daughters*, p. 206, n. 32. N.M. Lisovskii, *Russkaia periodicheskaia pechat' 1703–1900* (Petrograd: 1915), pp. 8–17. Jean-Jacques Rousseau, *Emile, or On Education*, intro., transl. and notes by Allan Bloom

(New York: Basic Books, 1979), pp. 358, 365. For the effects of Rousseau's ideas about women on Enlightenment and Romantic thinking, see Sheila Rowbotham, *Women, Resistance and Revolution: a History of Women and Revolution in the Modern World* (New York: Vintage, 1974), p. 38; for the influence of Rousseau and *Emile* in Russia see Andrew Wachtel, *The Battle for Childhood: The Creation of a Russian Myth* (Stanford: Stanford University Press, 1990), pp. 38, 71.

20. Bell and Offen, *Women, the Family, and Freedom*, vol. 1, pp. 133–34. Shashkov, *Istoriia russkoi zhenshchiny*, p. 232. On the closing of opportunities for women in France, see Robertson, *An Experience of Women*, pp. 326–28; in the United States, see Gerda Lerner, 'The Lady and the Mill Girl', *Midcontinent American Studies Journal*, vol. 4, no. 1 (Spring 1969), pp. 5–15; Linda Kerber, *Women of the Republic* (Chapel Hill: University of North Carolina Press, 1980), p. 283.

21. For example, Edmondson, *Feminism in Russia*, pp. 1–3, 5–6, 8; Bell and Offen, *Women, the Family, and Freedom*, pp. 5–6; Richard Evans, *The Feminists: Women's Emancipation Movements in Europe, American and Australia, 1840–1920* (New York: Barnes and Noble, 1977); Fout, 'An English-Language Bibliography on European and American Women's History', pp. 368–423.

22. Claire Moses, 'Saint-Simonian Men/Saint-Simonian Women: The Transformation of Feminist Thought in 1830s France', *Journal of Modern History*, vol. 54, no. 2 (June 1982), pp. 240–67; Leon Abensour, *Le féminisme sous le règne de Louis-Philippe et en 1848* (Paris: Plon, 1913); Renate Mohrmann, 'Reading Habits of Women in the Vormarz', in Fout, *German Women in the Nineteenth Century*, pp. 104–17; Lia Secci, 'German Women Writers of the Revolution of 1848', in ibid., pp. 151–71; Rossi, *Feminist Papers*; Lee Holcombe, *Wives and Property: Reform of the Married Women's Property Law in Nineteenth Century England* (Toronto: University of Toronto Press, 1983); Stites, *The Women's Liberation Movement in Russia*.

23. *Zvezdochka* (1842–1863), for children up to age fourteen, was dedicated to 'the noble girls of the Institutes of her Imperial Majesty', and published in St Petersburg by Aleksandra Ishimova (1804–1881). On Ishimova, see Marina Ledkovsky, Charlotte Rosenthal, and Mary Zirin (eds), *Dictionary of Russian Women Writers*, pp. 262–63. Contributors included Iakov Grot, Petr Pletnev, and V. F. Odoevsky. *Biblioteka dlia vospitaniia* was intended for nine to thirteen year-old boys (no. 1 [1844], p. vii) and published in Moscow by Avgust Semen (1783–1862). On Semen, the well-known French typographer and publisher, see R. N. Kleimenova, *Knizhnaia Moskva pervoi poloviny XIX veka* (Moscow: Nauka, 1991), pp. 47, 107–10, 126–27. Contributors included T. N. Granovsky, S. P. Shevyrev, and A.S. Khomiakov. A.G. Dement'ev, *Russkaia periodicheskaia pechat' (1702–1894)* (Moscow: 1969), pp. 302, 306–7. Both *Zvezdochka* and *Biblioteka dlia vospitaniia* received excellent reviews in *Sovremennik*, vol. 26 (1842), pp. 24–27 and *Otechestvennye zapiski*, nos. 1–2 (1843), p. 72, respectively.

24. Prayers: *Zvezdochka*, no. 10 (1842), otdelenie (part) II, p. 13; no. 4 (1844), II, pp. 114–15; no. 5 (1844), II, pp. 25–31 and 43–44; no. 6 (1844), II, pp. 45–50. Stories: no. 9 (1842), I, pp. 168–70; no. 11 (1842), II, pp. 25–35; no. 5 (1843), II, pp. 28–56; no. 2 (1844), II, pp. 14–15.

25. *Zvezdochka*, no. 1 (1844), p. 256.

26. Nichipor Kulesh, 'Chto esli b u menia byla doch',' *Literaturnaia gazeta*, no. 8 (27 Jan. 1840), pp. 171–72. Italics are in text.

27. *Zvezdochka*, no. 5 (1842), II, pp. 44, 47. Italics are in text.

28. 'Sovety malen'kim detiam', *Zvezdochka*, no. 6 (1844), II, p. 59.

29. *Zvezdochka*, no. 10 (1842), II, pp. 18–19.

30. *Zvezdochka* (1845), chast' (part) IV (Oct.), pp. 43–44, 101, 102, 103. Italics are in text. Masha's brother may also be horrified because here, as in other texts of the time, women's writing is implicitly equated with 'sexual display', and women

writers with prostitutes. See Catriona Kelly, *A History of Russian Women's Writing, 1820-1992* (Oxford: Clarendon Press, 1994), p. 75; Catherine Gallagher, 'George Eliot and Daniel Deronda: The Prostitute and the Jewish Question', in Ruth Yeazell (ed.), *Sex, Politics and Science in the Nineteenth-Century Novel* (Baltimore: Johns Hopkins University Press, 1986), pp. 39-62.

31. 'Carefulness is more necessary for girls than for boys', M. Edzhevort [Maria Edgeworth], 'Prakticheskoe vospitanie' ('A Practical Upbringing'), *Biblioteka dlia vospitaniia* (1844), I, p. 256.
32. *Zvezdochka*, no. 1 (1844), II, pp. 16-17.
33. D. Matskevich, 'Zametki o zhenshchinakh' ('Notes About Women'), *Sovremennik*, vol. 20, no. 3 (March 1850), part VI, p. 55. Between 1840 and 1850 only three children's magazines were founded in Russia but at least forty were founded in the United States: see N.M. Lisovskii, *Russkaia periodicheskaia pechat' 1703-1900* (Petrograd, 1915); R. Gordon Kelly, 'Selected Bibliography of Children's Periodicals', in Kelly (ed.), *Children's Periodicals of the U.S.* (Westport: Greenwood, 1984), pp. 554-55. Most of these U.S. children's magazines were directed primarily at boys, but also included domestic ideology. For example, one series of stories which ran in the very popular *Parley's Magazine* in 1844, urged boys to treat their sisters with respect, but reminded girls 'in the present state of society, it is at least advisable, that however a woman's mind be cultivated, she should still consider the domestic circle as her peculiar sphere and be more anxious to contribute to the comfort of all around her than dispute for prizes in the public schools': 'Stories Called Facts to Correct Fancies No. 2', *Parley's Magazine* (1844), p. 43. On *Parley's*, see Kelly, *Children's Periodicals*, pp. 345-56.
34. Rossi, *The Feminist Papers* (New York: Bantam, 1973), pp. 254-58; Jane Rendall, *The Origins of Modern Feminism* (New York: Schocken Books, 1984), pp. 73-82. Susan Kennedy, *If All We Did Was to Weep at Home: A History of White Working-Class Women in America* (Bloomington: Indiana University Press, 1979), p. 18; Bertha-Monica Stearns, 'Reform Periodicals and Female Reformers, 1830-60', *American Historical Review*, vol. 37, no. 4 (July 1932), pp. 678-99; Caroline Garnsey, 'Ladies' Magazines to 1850: The Beginnings of an Industry', *New York Public Library Bulletin*, vol. 58 (1954), pp. 83, 88; Nina Baym, *Women's Fiction* (Ithaca: Cornell University Press, 1978), pp. 18, 22, 50.
35. Basch, *In the Eyes of the Law*, p. 120; Ann Douglas [Wood], *The Feminization of American Culture* (New York: Knopf, 1971), p. 45.
36. Rossi, *The Feminist Papers*, pp. 274-81, 415-18. American feminism, however, too often excluded women of 'other' classes and races.
37. On Russian women's religious activism, see Brenda Meehan-Waters, 'Popular Piety, Local Initiative and the Founding of Women's Religious Communities in Russia, 1764-1907', *St Vladimir's Theological Quarterly*, vol. 30, no. 2 (1986), pp. 117-42; Brenda Meehan-Waters, 'To Save Oneself: Russian Peasant Women and the Development of Women's Religious Communities in Prerevolutionary Russia', in Beatrice Farnsworth and Lynne Viola (eds), *Russian Peasant Women* (New York: Oxford University Press, 1992), pp. 121-33; Brenda Meehan-Waters, *Holy Women of Russia* (San Francisco: Harper, 1993).

On Russian censorship and the censorship terror, see Charles Ruud, *Fighting Words: Imperial Censorship and the Russian Press 1804-1906* (Toronto: University of Toronto Press, 1982) and Marianna Tax Choldin, *A Fence Around the Empire: Russian Censorship of Western Ideas under the Tsars* (Durham: Duke University Press, 1985). The last of the early nineteenth-century Russian women's journals, *Damskii zhurnal*, closed in 1833: see Barbara Heldt, *Terrible Perfection: Women and Russian Literature* (Bloomington: Indiana University Press, 1987); Kelly, *A History of Russian Women's Writing*. On the varying views about women held by Pirogov,

Mikhailov, Chernyshevsky and others, see Richard Stites, *The Women's Liberation Movement in Russia*.

38. John Evans, *War, Women and Children in Ancient Rome* (New York: Routledge, 1991), p. 112; Euripides: 'For silence and modesty are the best ornaments of a woman and to remain quietly within the home', *Children of Heracles* (430 BC), lines 173-74; Rousseau, *Emile*, p. 366; Eva Cantarella, *Pandora's Daughters: The Role and Status of Women in Greek and Roman Antiquity* (Baltimore: Johns Hopkins University Press, 1981), pp. 113, 121; for the connection between domestic ideology and novels see Newcomb, 'Wise and Foolish Virgins', and Armstrong and Tennenhouse, 'The Literature of Conduct, the Conduct of Literature', pp. 2-3, 11, 14-15, 22.

39. Edmondson, *Feminism in Russia, 1900-17*, p. 7; also Lerner, 'The Lady and the Mill Girl', pp. 12-13 and Norton, 'The Paradox of Women's Sphere', pp. 141, 146; Newcomb, *Learning to Behave*, p. xii. Jason Whitman, *The Young Lady's Aid to Usefulness and Happiness* (Portland: S.H. Colesworthy, 1839), pp. 206-53 (p. 215); Charles Butler, *The American Lady* (Philadelphia: Hagan and Thompson, 1836), pp. 159, 162; Harvey Newcomb, *How to be a Lady: A Book for Girls Containing Useful Hints on the Formation of Character* (Boston: Gould, Kendall and Lincoln, 1847), pp. 39, 54, 89, 95, 125; Harvey Newcomb, *How to Be a Man: A Book for Boys Containing Useful Hints on the Formation of Character* (Boston: Gould, Kendall and Lincoln, 1847).

Chapter 5

CRITICISM AND JOURNALISM AT THE TURN OF THE CENTURY ON THE WORK OF RUSSIAN WOMEN WRITERS

Irina Kazakova

Perestroika in the Soviet Union exposed numerous problems which had ostensibly not existed before. One of these topical issues was the 'woman question' – although to this day Russian society has not fully acknowledged that this should be regarded as one of the most vital contemporary problems. Whereas in the West women's issues have never left the pages of the press, and a huge amount of research has been devoted to this subject, in Russia people were told that the woman question had been solved, and any consideration of it through the prism of Russian culture provoked nothing but bewilderment. Russian society is only just beginning to become accustomed to such concepts as 'women's culture', 'women's literature', 'women's themes'. And when we say these words, it feels as if we are stepping across an abyss dividing us from the time when they were commonplace.

The women's movement in Russia was exceptionally wide-ranging, and from the middle of the nineteenth century the intellectual life of Russian society not only reflected the themes and forms of emancipation, but also developed under the influence of the events of the women's movement. Literature and the women's movement

Translated by Rosalind Marsh

were interrelated. In interpreting these processes, Russian literary criticism and journalism made many discoveries which not only reflected the socio-political issues espoused by the contemporary women's movement, but also raised universal questions relevant for all time: women and the world, women and culture, women and creativity. Nowadays, although we cannot agree with all the conclusions and observations contained in these works of criticism, an exploration of them is still of considerable interest.

The end of the nineteenth century marked the beginning of a new phase in the history of the women's movement in Russia. The number of women's societies and organisations increased. Women's rights were extended; it became possible to obtain secondary and higher education, to work, and attain economic independence through work. In 1897 there were already six million women living on their own salaries. One of the most popular and accessible professions for women was literature: women worked extensively in the editorial offices of various journals and newspapers. Critics immediately commented on this: 'There have never been so many women in Russian literature as now. A woman writer with a reputation, a woman who translates or writes for a newspaper, is far from being a rarity in Russian society.'[1]

At the same time, critics drew attention to the changing role of the woman writer: K.F. Golovin emphasised that she had begun to 'occupy a more prominent place than ever, not only in terms of quantity, but also of quality'.[2] One feature of this period was that the content of women's writing expanded, transcending the confines of purely 'feminine themes': as N. Nadezhdin observed, 'The woman writer has responded to all the prevailing trends in life and literature, and reflected in her work all the most important moods of the moment'.[3]

All these trends enabled critics to devote great attention to women's writing, to interpret it as a distinctive phenomenon in literary life, and to define its place and role in the contemporary literary process. In their analysis of women's writing, critics, irrespective of their ideological stance, unanimously interpreted it as a progressive aspect of social and literary life. S.I. Ponomarev, for example, in his book *Nashi pisatel'nitsy* (Our Women Writers, 1891), emphasised that women's writing needs to be encouraged, as 'a society becomes truly civilised and human only through the contribution of women'. Nevertheless, a fairly widespread view in many works of criticism which regarded the actual fact of women's writing in positive terms was that 'nature imparts the spark of talent to women', but never 'endows them with genius'.[4]

Women writers were criticised for their lack of any capacity for independent thought, which was regarded as an indispensable condition for creativity. This led to the conclusion that no woman writer would ever be able to make any new contribution to literature, but would only repeat ideas which were already in existence. The intellectual inadequacy of women writers was usually contrasted with women's ability to 'be guided by a moral instinct' and their 'intuitive faith'.[5] For that reason, the subject of women's literature was defined as the representation of feelings and emotional experiences, a narrowness of theme which, in the critics' opinion, considerably impoverished its content.

When demonstrating the weakness of women's literature, critics compared it with the best examples of so-called 'masculine' literature, and analysed its specific and distinctive features as defects. But if in M. Protopopov's article 'Zhenskoe tvorchestvo' (Women's Writing, 1891) the influence of biology on literature is only implicit ('if a woman, as a moral being, is characterised by some typical and specific features, then, of course, these features must have a powerful effect on all her intellectual activity, including literature'), in the following years works appeared which traced a more direct relationship between biological sex and creativity.

This is true first and foremost of Otto Weininger's book *Sex and Character* (1903; translated into Russian in 1909), which exerted a significant influence on his contemporaries.[6] According to Weininger, woman is by her very nature anonymous, she cannot be a genius, and creative individuality is alien to her. These ideas were developed in N.Ia. Abramovich's *Zhenshchina i mir muzhskoi kul'tury* (Woman and the World of Masculine Culture, 1913), in which the author, analysing the works of women writers, comes to the conclusion that 'women's creativity is actually absent, it does not exist as a manifestation of the human spirit, as an original, innate identity', and that 'women's participation in the intellectual life of the world is insignificant'.[7]

Only a few works, written mainly by women, expressed the idea that it is precisely the specificity and distinctiveness of women's writing that give it its greatest value. This view was argued in Elena Koltonovskaia's book *Zhenskie siluety* (Women's Silhouettes, 1912), which also follows Otto Weininger's idea that in every human being a masculine and a feminine principle are present in different combinations. Koltonovskaia argues that 'woman participates in the creation of human culture, in intellectual work, not with her basic feminine elements, but with her secondary, masculine ones'. But, as distinct from Weininger and his disciples, who did not acknowledge the value of women's writing at all, Koltonovskaia not only recognises its worth, but also speaks of its 'original, clearly defined features'.[8]

The view that the specific, characteristic features of women's writing constitute its particular value was also expressed by Laura Margol'm in her *Kniga o zhenshchine* (Book about Woman, 1895), which emphasised that 'Woman, as the most subjective of all creatures on earth, can only give us herself, fragments of her own soul, and this is her most valuable contribution to literature.'[9]

Contrary to critics' wishes, many women writers did not claim to raise any significant social, philosophical or political problems in their works, but quite consciously focused their attention on the complex world of the female soul. The well-known writer Ol'ga Shapir stressed in her manifesto that her 'valuable contribution' to literature could only be the fact that she 'spoke on behalf of women', 'without imitating the male pen'. She defended the right to exist of a distinctive literature in which 'the authentic voice of women's definitions of life' could be heard, while recognising that this would give critics a pretext to attach to her works the 'ironic label of lady's fiction'.[10] Similar views were also expressed by other women writers: Mariia Krestovskaia, for example, identified a necessary condition for her literary work as 'the courage to analyse myself truthfully'.[11]

Critics correctly pointed out that it was not until the end of the nineteenth century that the tendency to express their identity, to make it the subject of their literary research, had become a characteristic feature of women's literature. This was demonstrated by women writers' refusal to adopt male pseudonyms, their predilection for the genre of the story in the form of a diary or letters, and the use of first-person narration focusing on the inner world of the heroine. It was for that reason that Laura Mar'golm wrote that earlier women's literature had been 'anonymous writing', that is, 'imitation of male models in form and content'. But now, Margol'm emphasised, a new period of women's writing had begun, in which women writers were starting to depict 'the essence of women's nature'. The same view was expressed by the socialist feminist Aleksandra Kollontai in her article 'Novaia zhenshchina' (The New Woman, 1913): 'from the time when women writers began to speak in their own words about their own women's issues, their works ... have possessed a special value and significance'.[12]

A similar point of view was expressed by M. Rubinshtein in his article 'Zhenskii vopros kak problema kul'tury' (The Woman Question as a Cultural Problem, 1911), which acknowledged the service Weininger had performed in analysing the woman question not only as a social and political problem, but also as a cultural and philosophical one. Starting from the question Weininger asked about women's ability to serve the culture of the spirit, the author argued that such service bears no relation to genius, but presupposes the presence of 'something individual, personal, particular, unrepeatable'. Inasmuch as a woman, as a human being, possesses individuality, 'without her there would be unbridgeable gaps in writing as a whole'.[13]

It was not only the works of women writers, but also the actual personality of the creative woman which began to interest critics. Elena Koltonovskaia devoted a great deal of attention to this question in her book *Zhenskie siluety*. She argued that the creative woman is dependent on her inner world, with which she is in constant conflict, and that this conflict 'colours women's writing and invests it with a special hue of inherent tragedy'.[14]

The tragedy inherent in women's writing was also noted by Margol'm in her *Kniga o zhenshchine*. She considered that a talented woman can never find total satisfaction in her vocation or her art, because her heart remains untouched by them, and human beings can only be happy when all sides of their personality can be freely expressed. Margol'm called contemporary women's striving for emancipation a pernicious error, because such women had rejected their essence. In her opinion, outstanding creative women were 'sick with an incurable disease ... a split between the behest of their reason and the profound essence of women's nature'. For that reason, many of them had become 'victims of this tragic conflict'.[15]

Such an interpretation of the essence of the creative principle in women did not accord with contemporary views on the woman question and the women's movement. For example, A. Kovrov, the critic of the journal *Russkoe bogatstvo,* claimed that Margol'm 'is an exception in the entire world of women's writing, and in opposition to the whole world of women in general'.[16] Indeed, her book provoked a storm of angry protest from many women writers. M.N. Azimirova (Maran), for example, in her book *Zhenshchina i ee sud'i* (Woman and her Judges, 1896), rejected Margol'm's theory, accusing the author of an 'insulting trick' worthy only of 'misogynists'.[17]

Thus, despite these disputes about the essence of women's creativity and women's place in literature, critics unanimously affirmed that women writers had brought to literature their own special themes, their way of seeing the world, 'their feminine nature'. Critics singled out as a specific feature of women's literature an interest in women's inner life, in self-analysis and the complex nuances of human relationships. But perhaps the most characteristic feature which critics identified was the depiction of the so-called 'new woman'. Despite the fact that interest in the woman question had found reflection in the works of many writers of that time, notably A. Amfitcatrov, P. Boborykin, I. Potapenko, and the writers of the *Znanie* publishing association (1898–1913), critics pointed in particular to the service which women writers had performed in creating this image. N. Nadezhdin commented: 'It is only women writers who show us this image...they draw her out of the narrow confines of the personal life into the arena of social action'. An article written in 1907 by the feminist economist Mariia Pokrovskaia was devoted to an analysis of the 'new female types' in the works of Sof'ia Kovalevskaia and Ol'ga Shapir.[18] The critics A. Skabichevsky, K. Golovin, M. Protopopov and L. Gizhitskaia all wrote about the 'new heroine';[19] and a whole series of critical works were devoted to the 'new woman' portrayed by Anastasiia Verbitskaia.[20]

Aleksandra Kollontai, examining this theme in her article 'The New Woman', wrote: 'Literature of the last ten to fifteen years, the most recent writers and particularly women writers, can no longer avoid this emerging type, and cannot fail to portray her in the pages of their new works'. On the basis of quite a large number of literary works, she defined the 'new women' as 'heroines with independent needs from life, who affirm their individuality and protest against the enslavement of the human being in the state, the family and society'.[21]

At the same time, critics suggested that many authors depicted the 'new woman' through external signs only, but that her psychology remained the same as that of the woman of the past, for whom love and personal happiness were the principal values in life. P. Kogan, for example, in an article on the image of women intellectuals in the stories of Anastasiia Krandievskaia, reproached the writer's heroines for 'not taking a single step in the direction of "inner liberation" from the power of men' and 'from the power of feeling'. The critic points out: 'The more we read Mrs Krandievskaia's collection, the sadder and more hopeless are the conclusions to be drawn about contemporary woman, the more clearly do her total intellectual inadequacy and dependence on man come to the fore'.[22]

The heroines of another writer, Vera Mikulich (Lidiia Veselitskaia), were rebuked in a similar vein. The critic of the journal *Russkoe bogatstvo* writes with pity and scorn about the author's depiction of spiritually rich, morally pure women who by virtue of their emotional subtlety are unable to 'win' happiness for themselves, and are capable only of bearing suffering with dignity. For him these are 'weak, powerless women ... who are incapable either of defending themselves from misfortune, of attaining happiness, or even of retaining a lover's affection'. He thinks that 'their inner flabbiness, their spiritual feebleness, is only too evident'.[23]

Thus, critics at the turn of the century identified the basic themes, questions and images characteristic of women's prose, and its social significance. It was more difficult to analyse the original artistic vision of the world, the common aesthetic qualities inherent in the works of women writers. The critic who succeeded in doing this in the most interesting way was Koltonovskaia in her collection *Zhenskie siluety*. She was one of the first to comprehend and convey the specific nature of women's view of the world and its reflection in the content and style of women's writing.

In her analysis of women writers, Koltonovskaia passes judgement on their talent, using the concepts of 'masculine', 'feminine', and 'universally human' principles in art. In her view, V. Mikulich 'not only fails to conceal her feminine individuality and feminine sympathies, but does nothing but embody this feminine nature of hers'. It is precisely this 'narrow, specifically feminine world' that the critic regards as Mikulich's main virtue as a writer. Referring to Mariia Krestovskaia's writing, the critic comments that she is a 'typical woman writer', that is, 'she concentrated on women's problems with a purely womanly sincerity', but at the same time, she lacks the 'feminine narrowness, limitations and tendentiousness typical of high-principled feminists'. On the other hand, Koltonovskaia thinks that Ekaterina Letkova's work contains no 'subjective lyricism, no rich emotionality' – the characteristic features of women's literature – and that she 'does not concentrate on female psychology'. In Valentina Dmitrieva's work, the critic perceives 'an inadequate expression of woman's nature'. Koltonovskaia was able to distinguish clearly which particular features of women writers' style could be ascribed to a lack of skill and talent, and which were a result of the specific nature of female individuality. She was able to define the characteristic features of women's writing as, in the first instance, an interest in female psychology and the world of feelings, subjectivity of interpretation, emotionality and lyricism, and the ability to analyse emotions.

Russian criticism and journalism at the turn of the century approached the works of women writers, women's literature, as a single whole, as a particular type of literature and a distinctive phenomenon in the literary process. It was acknowledged that women's writing possessed its own typical features, its own specific character, that women writers could express both a universally human, and their own, feminine view of the world, which was valuable because of its distinctive nature. Critics at the turn of the century identified the themes and problems which women writers addressed most closely. The first attempts were made to define the specific features of women writers' artistic vision of the world.

After the revolution of 1917, when women gained equal legal, political and economic rights with men, it was considered that 'the woman question' no longer existed in Russia, and that a division of writers on the basis of sex was typical only of foreign critics, who had been greatly influenced by the women's movement. Western literature experienced a feminist boom in the 1970s, which not only gave rise to an entire distinctive field of women's literature and feminist literature, but also to so-called feminist criticism. Foreign criticism and literary scholarship have been very successful in elaborating many theoretical questions in this area.

In Russia, particularly in recent years, a whole galaxy of talented women writers has emerged; and the right of such concepts as 'women's literature' and 'women's prose' to exist has come to be affirmed and fought for once again. It is said more and more frequently on the pages of contemporary newspapers and journals that the 'woman question' in Russia has not been solved, and that for a long time the very idea of 'the feminine' did not seem to exist at all. It is therefore a particularly opportune moment to turn to forgotten Russian sources for an analysis of this question.

Notes

Full publication details for references have been supplied wherever possible.
1. V. Chuiko, 'Sovremennye zhenshchiny-pisatel'nitsy', *Nabliudatel'*, no. 4 (1889), pp. 44–47.
2. K.F. Golovin, *Russkii roman i russkoe obshchestvo* (St Petersburg, 1897).
3. N. Nadezhdin, 'Zhenshchiny v izobrazhenii sovremennykh russkikh zhenshchin-pisatel'nits', *Novyi mir*, no. 92 (1902), p. 290.
4. S.I. Ponomarev, *Nashi pisatel'nitsy* (St Petersburg, 1891).
5. M. Protopopov, 'Zhenskoe tvorchestvo', *Russkaia mysl'*, nos. 1, 2, 4 (1891).
6. Otto Weininger, *Geschlecht und Charakter* (Vienna and Leipzig: W.Braumüller, 1903).
7. N.Ia. Abramovich, *Zhenshchina i mir muzhskoi kul'tury* (Moscow, 1913).
8. E. Koltonovskaia, 'Zhenskoe (Vmesto predisloviia)', in her *Zhenskie siluety* (St Petersburg, 1912), pp. v–xiii (p. viii).
9. L. Margol'm, *Kniga o zhenshchine*, transl. from German (Kiev and Khar'kov, 1895), p. 110.
10. O. Shapir, in F.F. Fidler (comp.), *Pervye literaturnye shagi. Avtobiografii* (Moscow, 1911), pp. 46–55.
11. M. Krestovskaia, 'Zhenskaia zhizn'. Povest' v pis'makh', *Severnyi vestnik*, nos. 11–12 (1894), no. 1 (1895), and *Mir bozhii*, nos. 2–4 (1903).
12. A. Kollontai, 'Novaia zhenshchina', *Sovremennyi mir*, no. 9 (1913), pp. 151–85 (p. 166, note 8).
13. M. Rubinstein, 'Zhenskii vopros kak problema kul'tury', *Vestnik vospitaniia*, no. 6 (1911), pp. 120–40.
14. Koltonovskaia, *Zhenskie siluety*, p. xiii.
15. Margol'm, *Kniga o zhenshchine*, p. 110.
16. A. Kovrov, 'Zhenskii vopros. Vesti iz Germanii', *Russkoe bogatstvo*, no. 19 (1896), p. 96.
17. M.N. Azimirova (Maran), *Zhenshchina i ee sud'i* (St Petersburg, 1896), p. 8.
18. M. Pokrovskaia, 'Novye zhenskie tipy v proizvedeniiakh russkikh pisatel'nits', *Zhenskii vestnik*, no. 11 (1907), pp. 270–2.
19. See, for example, A. Skabichevskii, 'Zhenskii vopros s tochki zreniia bul'varnogo publitsista', in *Sochineniia. Kriticheskie etiudy*, 2nd edition (St Petersburg, 1890); A. Gizhitskaia, 'Novaia zhenshchina v literature', *Mir bozhii*, no. 1 (1897).

20. See, for example, V. Chimishliiskii, *Zhenskie tipy v proizvedeniiakh A.Verbitskoi* (St Petersburg, 1904).
21. Kollontai, 'Novaia zhenshchina', pp. 152–53.
22. P. Kogan, 'Iz zhizni i literatury: intelligentnaia zhenshchina v rasskazakh g-zhi A. Krandievskoi', *Obrazovanie*, no. 2 (1902), pp. 31–8.
23. 'Novye knigi', *Russkoe bogatstvo*, no. 12 (1898).

Chapter 6

ACTRESSES, AUDIENCE AND FASHION IN THE SILVER AGE: A CRISIS OF COSTUME

Catherine Schuler

Speaking before the First Russian Women's Congress in 1908, Isabella Grinevskaia proclaimed to the assembled representatives of Russian feminism that the apogee of the actress had been achieved in their own era.[1] Although Grinevskaia's declaration was, perhaps, excessively optimistic and slightly hyperbolic, her sense of a sea-change in the status of Russian actresses was generally well-founded. It was also belated. When Grinevskaia spoke before the Women's Congress, the ascendancy of the Russian actress had not only been achieved, but was already in decline. The period alluded to by Grinevskaia, which includes, but is not limited to, the Silver Age, extends from approximately 1870 to 1910. During this time, unprecedented numbers of women sought employment in the theatre, starring actresses dominated the Russian stage in St Petersburg, Moscow and the provinces, and actress-managers became familiar figures in the theatrical landscape.

Facilitated by the ever-increasing power of the mass-circulation press, the public preoccupation with actresses and 'women's themes' during this period was stimulated by increased westernisation, with its concomitant subversion of traditional gender ideology and hierarchy, and by the Russian women's movement. Because the effects of westernisation on Russian actresses were multiple and complex, a comprehensive treatment is beyond the scope of the present chapter.[2] For that reason, I have chosen to concentrate on one of the most intriguing and, from the standpoint of gender ideology, most noxious effects of westernisation on Russian actresses: the escalating demand for high fashion and the economic and moral consequences of this trend for women in the theatre.

During the final decades of the nineteenth century, when Russia was in the throes of a *krizis teatra* (theatre crisis),[3] relations among various factions in the theatre community were distinguished by ideological discord and partisan squabbling. If members of this community could agree on little else, however, most acknowledged that the unprecedented demand for fashionable clothing on stage had precipitated a 'crisis of costuming', which threatened the interests, prosperity and continued progress of Russian theatre. Although complaints about the general oppression of women in the theatre were often suppressed or dismissed, even opponents of women's rights conceded that the consequences of the costume crisis were particularly serious for actresses.

Although actresses have long borne the obligation to dress fashionably both on and off stage, at the end of the nineteenth century the obsession with fashion reached pathological proportions. Entrepreneurs, directors, and even actresses themselves helped to stimulate and feed the seemingly insatiable appetite of audiences in St Petersburg, Moscow and the provinces for elaborate, fashionable, outrageous and excessively expensive costuming. From the perspective of gender ideology, two factors had a particularly powerful impact on the growing appetite of audiences and members of the increasingly commercially inclined theatre community for elaborate western (especially Parisian) fashions: the introduction into Russia of western feminism and the popularity of western touring stars.

Among the many crises that rocked Russia at the end of the century, the crisis of gender identity precipitated by the women's movement was simultaneously the most elusive and global. The *zhenskii vopros* (woman question) in Russia was multi-faceted, and the barrage of articles, feuilletons, and books published about it during the period focused on several related issues, including the proper role of women in public and private spheres, the role of biology and environment in the subordination of women, problems of deviant sexuality and prostitution, and proper relations between the sexes. Liberals, who tended to accept Enlightenment arguments about egalitarianism, supported expanded educational and employment opportunities for women. Endeavouring to counteract the alien ideology of sexual equality that threatened to undermine family and state, conservatives combed through the misogynist wisdom of the ages for evidence to support their contention that women were innately inferior and destined by nature to be subordinate and submissive to men.[4] An important ideological 'side-effect' of the gender war that was sparked off between feminists and their detractors was the destabilisation of conventional *zhenstvennost'* (femininity), a phenomenon that had tremendous resonance in the theatre.

Balancing precariously along the shifting ideological fault lines of post-emancipation Russia, the theatre was simultaneously a harbinger of change and a buttress of tradition. Challenges to hegemonic sex/gender ideology were reflected in both the content of the drama and in its realisation in performance, but because any expression of political dissent was subject to severe censorship, the relationship between Russian feminism and the theatre was largely indirect. The suffrage theatres and women's collectives that flourished alongside the British and American feminist movements were absent from Russia, and little specifically feminist dramaturgy was produced. Although many of the concerns expressed by actresses about conditions of employment in their profession echoed general concerns of the feminist movement, few dared to espouse feminism publicly. Nonetheless, Russian feminism was important to the theatre for the questions it raised about the role of women in society, questions which stimulated the production of a tremendous amount of book, periodical, and newspaper literature. And because theatre was an increasingly powerful – albeit strictly regulated – tool of social control, the controversy over sex/gender ideology was often enacted within its walls.

It was the debate between feminists and their critics over *zhenskaia priroda* ('women's nature') that destabilised *zhenstvennost'* as a fixed term of cultural discourse, and it is the conceptual instability of the term that helps to explain the public fascination with actresses during the period. In a culture seeking to reconcile competing sex/gender ideologies, actresses bore the weight of excessive symbolic signification. For that reason, their off-stage lives – romances, sexual escapades, political sympathies, and tastes in clothing, home furnishings, food, and other personal items – were as intriguing to audiences as their onstage performances. In 'Private Parts and Public Places', Juliet Blair argued that actresses as a generic category of women are unique because they have socially sanctioned access to the public space.[5] This was particularly true in pre-revolutionary Russia. The debate over *zhenstvennost'* focused public attention on actresses largely because in Russia they were the most visible, concrete embodiments of particular gender qualities and ideals. In a culture that still demanded silence, obedience, and invisibility from its women, actresses became highly visible representatives of, and concrete points of reference for, both the preservation of old and the construction of new paradigms of *zhenstvennost'*. The new paradigms tended to reflect a range of western values and images, while the old tended to reproduce ideals and concepts associated with a neo-slavophile sensibility.

In their search for alternatives, advocates of westernisation considered several exemplars, including the American 'New Woman', the Shavian 'unwomanly woman' (modelled on the expatriate Russian artist Mariia Bashkirtseva), and western starring actresses, especially Sarah Bernhardt and Eleonora Duse.[6] These international 'superstars', who attracted thousands of spectators when they toured Russia during the 1880s and 1890s, were particularly alluring, and provided Russians with contrasting models of *zhenstvennost'*.

Sarah Bernhardt made her Russian début in 1881 and, having discovered that substantial amounts of money could be earned in that country, returned several times. Bernhardt's influence on Russian actresses is indisputable, but she was a problematic figure for Russians because she embodied so many qualities inappropriate for – at least by conservative standards – a truly feminine woman. Bernhardt, a mistress of the public relations coup, who slept in a coffin, paraded around in the most outrageous Parisian fashions (including male attire), had multiple, well-publicised sexual liasons, owned her own theatre, enjoyed tremendous personal, professional, and financial autonomy, and who indulged in emotional excesses on-stage and off, simultaneously provided Russian women with an alternative – and apparently very attractive – model of *zhenstvennost'* and threw Russian critics into a fury.[7]

If Bernhardt's rebellious individualism, preference for the provocative and instinct for *reklama* (marketing) provoked ambivalence among critics, their response to Eleonora Duse was, in effect, universally enthusiastic. Admired for her modesty and subdued elegance, Duse's immense capacity for suffering and the apparent emotional authenticity of her mimesis resonated powerfully among Russian audiences. Aleksandr Kugel' wrote of Duse: 'In art, some raise the soul, others purify it. Duse belonged to the latter: through her suffering she purified our souls.'[8] The phrase *vechnaia zhenstvennost'* (eternal femininity), the ambiguity of which was heightened by its frequent application to a wide range of contrasting actresses, was often applied to Duse's characters. If Bernhardt's appeal was based on sensational commercial sexuality, Duse spoke to a higher ideal: the liberation of the human spirit. She was less disruptive than Bernhardt precisely because the qualities of *zhenstvennost'* she exhibited – modesty, restrained stylishness, strong maternal instinct, conjugal devotion, self-sacrifice, elevated idealism, and unambiguous heterosexuality – were simultaneously exotic and familiar in the Russian context.[9]

Although critical response to Bernhardt was equivocal, both actresses enjoyed unprecedented popularity with Russian spectators, many of whom not only eulogised the western stars at the expense of native actresses, but seemed to derive special pleasure from comparing the Russians unfavourably with their western competitors.[10] It is hardly surprising, then, that Bernhardt and Duse, who inspired considerable envy and emulation, became the standards against which many critics measured native actresses and by which actresses measured themselves. In their rush to compete for the hearts, minds and roubles of Russian spectators, Russian actresses hurried to copy external marks of gender manifested by their western rivals, the most accessible of which was clothing.[11]

By the late 1880s, an actress's wardrobe had become the principal determinant of professional advancement. Although a minority of actresses resisted western trends, most succumbed to the mounting pressure to conform to western fashion ideals. A continuum existed during the period. Actresses like Polina Strepetova, who categorically rejected western trends in clothing and drama, were located at one end of the continuum; actresses like Lidiia Iavorskaia, who flaunted the most outrageous Parisian fashions and was entirely identified with western drama, were at the other. Positioned along the continuum were moderates like Vera Kommissarzhevskaia (the 'Russian Duse'), whose understated, western-influenced elegance was distinguished by just the right touch of national identity.

Mariia Gavrilovna Savina, the *grande dame* of the Aleksandrinsky Theatre, was the first to exploit the public's appetite for western fashions effectively. During the 1870s, critics and spectators responded enthusiastically to her western-influenced ingénues.[12] In the 1880s, assisted by Viktor Krylov, the author of wildly popular adaptations of French society drama, she made a successful transition into the type upon which her fame still rests: the unsympathetic *svetskaia dama* (fashionable lady). Savina's extraordinary ability to market personal style and fashionable clothing engendered frequent comparisons to Bernhardt. But in contrast to an actress like Iavorskaia, whose emulation of the French star reached pathological proportions, Savina sounded the depths of her audience's taste for Parisian decadence, recognised that although real, it was not limitless, and adapted her appearance and demeanour accordingly.

Nonetheless, Mariia Gavrilovna understood that an 'adequate' wardrobe was not sufficient; high fashion and multiple costume changes drew the St Petersburg *beau-monde* into the theatre. Supported financially by the tremendous resources of the Imperial Aleksandrinsky theatre, she spent unprecedented sums of money on costuming; in time, productions featuring Savina became pretexts for elegant displays of new gowns.[13] Although she frequently complained of being reduced to a 'fashionable attraction' by Aleksandrinsky directors and 'bloated' spectators who came to the theatre to 'digest dinner' while watching her parade her wardrobe,[14] Savina was instrumental in stimulating an appetite for Parisian fashions that eventually permeated Russian theatre at all levels.

The effects of this trend were simultaneously positive and pernicious. On the positive side, increased concern for fashionable clothing helped to improve the collective relationship between actresses and female spectators. Historically, actresses, who were classified in the public imagination with prostitutes, thieves and other unsavoury denizens of the demi-monde, were debarred from polite society.[15] Class barriers between Savina and her female audience broke down precisely because women in the audience began to see characters and situations with which they could identify. With respect to costumes and manners, Krylov's Russian adaptations of French society drama required Savina to imitate current fashion; thus she reflected an image back to women in the audience that the higher ranks had already achieved and the lower aspired to imitate. These were the women they wanted, or imagined themselves, to be: witty, attractive to men and always beautifully dressed.

Although a tiny minority of starring actresses in private commercial and imperial theatres profited from the trend toward ever more elaborate, excessively expensive costumes, many more were severely disadvantaged. As rapacious entrepreneurs, directors and male spectators found ways to turn the trend to their own advantage, women in both imperial and private theatres in the capitals and provinces paid the price.

The costume crisis touched theatres all over Russia, but its moral and economic consequences were particularly pernicious in private provincial theatres. Speaking in 1897 before the First All-Russian Congress of Representatives of the Stage, Iuliia Tarlovskaia-Rastorgueva, a Russian actress working in Poland, addressed the situation of women in the theatre directly. Arguing that conditions of employment and quality of life for actresses had changed markedly for the worse over the past thirty years, Tarlovskaia asked the assembled representatives of Russian theatre whether any woman could prosper as an actress without risking her honour, respectability, and individuality.[16] Conditions continued to deteriorate to the point that, fourteen years later, an anonymous critic called the position of women on the stage 'tragic' and declared that equality between women and men in the theatre was a dangerous myth: 'Although there is plenty of interest in actresses', this commentator wrote, 'there is no respect for women.'[17]

Throughout the period, prostitution and sexual patronage were identified by critics and concerned theatre workers as two of the most persistent and pestiferous problems facing the theatre community.[18] Although changes in audience composition after the Emancipation may have exacerbated the situation,[19] most contemporary commentators agreed that the twin plagues of prostitution and patronage issued from a single source: excessive wardrobe demands. Mariia Velizary, a moderately successful character actress who travelled the provincial circuit during the late 1880s and 1890s, understood the significance for actresses of a suitable wardrobe. When the theatre in which she worked went bankrupt, Velizary was forced to pawn her entire personal stock of costumes. 'This was', she wrote in her memoir, 'an absolute disaster for an actress, because how could you have a career without a wardrobe? What is an actress without costumes? She is a beggar; her route to the stage is cut off.'[20]

Although the 'wardrobe crisis' affected both actresses and actors, the burden on women was far greater. Actors were contractually obligated to supply their own costumes for plays requiring contemporary dress, but the theatre paid for historical costumes (a practice which discouraged productions of historical plays). Actresses, on the other hand, were required to supply both contemporary and historical costumes, including head-dresses.[21] According to one contemporary commentator, previously this arrangement had not been especially onerous, because an actress's wardrobe had consisted of three dresses: one for historical dramas and two for contemporary plays.[22] In an article for the *Ezhegodnik imperatorskikh teatrov* (Yearbook of the Imperial Theatres), N.S. Vasil'eva, who performed and taught for many years at the Aleksandrinsky Theatre, observed that before the 1880s, an actress who owned a white muslin dress for ingénue roles and a black velvet for heroines was adequately prepared to join a company.[23] Until very late in the century, few provincial theatres had the resources to stage historically accurate productions, so historical costuming was conceived in terms of four broad categories: Greek, French, Spanish, and boyar.[24] These conventions apparently satisfied consumers of theatrical art until the 1880s and 1890s, when the Meiningen tours stimulated an antiquarian craze,[25] and touring stars like Bernhardt and Duse created a vogue for extravagant costuming in the capital cities. Having learned from their western competitors that audiences would pay good money to see a fashion extravaganza, imperial actresses began to imitate them. The vicious circle was complete when the native stars, many of whom toured the provinces during the summers with their magnificent wardrobes, stimulated an appetite for extravagant costuming among provincial spectators and entrepreneurs.

As their wardrobe expenditures were subsidised by the Imperial theatres, starring actresses like Savina could afford multiple elegant costumes for each production. Few of their less privileged colleagues had the private resources to provide spectators with fashion extravaganzas. When Grinevskaia spoke before the Women's Congress in 1908, she claimed that even though salaries for actors and actresses were roughly equivalent, actresses spent up to two-thirds of their salary on costumes.[26] This expenditure was not caprice but a condition of their employment. Playwrights, entrepreneurs, and directors defended themselves from charges of exploitation by claiming that they were simply responding to public pressure. Crying that they simply could not afford to hire actresses who did not own substantial wardrobes, entrepreneurs increasingly placed a higher value on fashionable clothing than on talent, preferring a well-dressed actress to one with authentic ability and experience. This alarming trend provoked one witty fellow to observe that if he were to dress up a mannequin in fine clothing and send it to the Theatre Bureau during Lent, it would leave with a contract for six hundred roubles a month.[27]

Grinevskaia argued that the tendency of avaricious entrepreneurs and directors to pander to the low and often capricious taste of provincial spectators for vapid amusement was a principal cause of the costume crisis. The public wanted spectacle but entrepreneurs, who were too mean to pay for the necessary scenery and costumes out of their own pockets, refused to produce the historical dramas and spectacle melodramas that would satisfy the audience's appetite for elaborate sets and costumes. Instead, they transformed contemporary domestic plays into extravaganzas by requiring actresses to make multiple costume changes for even the simplest salon dramas.[28] One critic of excessive costuming told of his experience with a play, the action of which required a very modest environment. Unfortunately, the playwright had included a 'ball' scene. Given the milieu established by the text, this 'ball' should have been little more than a small party thrown by a civil servant for friends and family. Not satisfied with such modest surroundings, however, the director and entrepreneur decided to enhance the spectacle by requiring the leading actress to purchase an entirely new wardrobe for the scene. Protesting that she already had a perfectly acceptable ball gown, the actress resisted their demands. But because she had already worn the existing gown more than once, they forced her to buy a new one.[29]

The author also noted with a touch of irony that if spectators demanded new sets for each production, entrepreneurs and directors would categorically refuse to pander to public taste because the money for these items would come out of their own pockets. Instead, the producers of provincial theatre preferred to 'decorate their own often wretched productions at the expense of women's honour, soul and body'.[30] He added that actresses bore the entire burden of costuming. Actors, who could get by with the same frock coat for every production, often looked as wretched as the scenery and were largely exempt from excessive expenditures for costumes.[31] According to Grinevskaia, entrepreneurs and directors who preferred actresses with wardrobes to actresses with talent, not only encouraged moral depravity among theatre workers, but also fostered the current level of mediocrity on the Russian stage.[32]

Demands on actresses for sexual favours were certainly not new at the end of the nineteenth century. The only novelty was the connection established by contemporary commentators between excessive demands for elaborate costumes and the growing problem with prostitution and sexual patronage. For most provincial actresses, the economic equation was simple: entrepreneurs demanded elegant wardrobes, actresses needed money in order to buy them, but their salaries were not sufficient. In an article entitled 'Actresses and Wardrobe', N.I. Aberdukh suggested that the obligation to own a fine wardrobe discouraged virtuous behaviour among actresses.[33] In the same article, A. Mursky told of a young actress who, in spite of her best intentions, could not avoid the necessity to 'sell her body' when she was forced by an unscrupulous entrepreneur to buy a boyar's costume, a ball dress, and a fashionable hat on a salary of twenty-five roubles a month.[34]

With the notable exception of starring and first-level actresses, salaries were generally too low to cover expenses; for that reason, many actresses resorted to sexual patronage and prostitution to cover necessary expenditures on wardrobe. Provincial actresses' average monthly salaries ranged from thirty to fifty roubles for walk-ons (*vykhodnaia*) to between three and four hundred for particular types (*na amplua*).[35] Although these salaries may seem attractive when compared to the remuneration for typical low-level government jobs, teaching positions, and skilled crafts,[36] critics of existing conditions argued that the hidden costs of life in the theatre left actresses with little discretionary income. N.F. Arbenin pointed out that a discrepancy often existed between an actress's reported and real salary.[37] Because the regular theatre season lasted only six months, the average monthly salary must be reduced by half in order to obtain an accurate picture of economic reality.[38] In addition, the peripatetic existence of a typical provincial actress required more substantial expenditures for hotels, meals in restaurants, and travel expenses than the settled lives of teachers and government employees.

A leading actress receiving a salary of four hundred roubles a month during the regular season could, if she lived modestly, spare between two and three hundred roubles for costumes. Actresses who received smaller salaries could hardly afford to sew one or two new dresses each season and remake the old ones in accordance with current fashion. After paying travel and living expenses, walk-on and second-level actresses had not a copeck to spare for costumes.[39] Considering that in 1897 an average historical costume cost between seventy and one hundred roubles, few actresses could afford substantial, and at the same time elegant, wardrobes.[40] And because entrepreneurs and directors demanded such wardrobes, most actresses were compelled to engage on some level in commercial sex. As one observer noted, if women had no thought of prostitution before going on stage, necessity compelled them to become acquainted with 'the life' once they joined a theatre.[41] An article on actresses and prostitution published in 1909 relates the story of a director who complained that after he took the trouble to introduce a particular actress (or insolent woman, as he called her) to a wealthy merchant, she later had the nerve to come crawling to him for a salary.[42] In an anonymous appeal to entrepreneurs, one actress complained that when she protested against the entirely inadequate salary of thirty roubles a month offered to her by a provincial entrepreneur, he told her that she must 'arrange something' with one of the wealthy men loitering around the theatre.[43]

Although many imperial actresses received substantial wardrobe subsidies, even they were not exempt from the financial pressures related to costuming. Mariia Savina's wardrobe expenditures, which have already been cited, were not extraordinary. According to Grinevskaia, the amount of money another Aleksandrinsky actress, Vera Michurina-Samoilova, spent in one year on costumes was sufficient to support ten middle-class families in relative comfort.[44]

Although most observers agreed that rapacious entrepreneurs and predatory directors created, perpetuated, and profited from this abusive system, several saw the problem differently. In 1897, for example, an anonymous critic argued on the pages of *Teatr i iskusstvo* (Theatre and Art) that actresses themselves were to blame for the existing state of affairs, because they insisted upon dressing in the most elegant contemporary fashions regardless of the requirements of the play itself. By his account, in the past actors had resigned themselves to wearing whatever suited the character, even though it did not enhance their personal appeal. But if a director suggested to a contemporary actress that she should wear a historically authentic costume for the sake of the play, her reply would invariably be: 'Is it pretty?'. Unlike their male colleagues, actresses, driven by personal vanity alone, were exclusively concerned with pleasing and impressing the 'various princes and Petr Ivanyches' sitting in the first row.

Even the most secure actress would, he claimed, play Marguerite sitting in her prison cell dressed in a white cashmere peignoir.[45]

In 1909, N.I. Aberdukh tried to persuade the readers of *Rampa i akter* (Footlights and the Actor) that drama schools were to blame. Arguing that they encouraged 'cruel competition' among young women and reinforced unhealthy 'marketing' practices, Aberdukh called upon these institutions to reconsider their pedagogical methods. He also suggested that, attracted by romantic fantasies of luxury and comfort, too many young women fled to the stage not because they loved art, but in order to escape violent, unhappy, poverty-stricken family situations. The theatre would not solve the problems of prostitution and sexual patronage, Aberdukh insisted, until financially secure, well-educated, morally irreproachable women from the upper classes began pursuing careers in the theatre.[46] When such allegedly exemplary women did begin to appear on stage, however, they were also deemed unsatisfactory. In 1911, two years after Aberdukh called for greater refinement among actresses, N.S. Vasil'eva complained of the appalling mediocrity of the current crop of actresses, a group consisting primarily of neurasthenics in search of 'experience, emotion, and transformation'. These *damy* (ladies), most of whom had little talent and were concerned exclusively with *vneshnost'* (outward appearance), came to the stage because they simply had nothing else to occupy their time.[47]

At the end of the period, during the war years, a new perspective emerged as critics like N. Smirnova simultaneously apologised for, and censured actresses. Arguing that since it was a requirement of their profession, actresses should not be blamed for their vanity and excessive stylishness, she nonetheless encouraged them to set an example for others: as leaders of fashion, they started the trend toward excessive fashionability and now, when Russian soldiers were dying and patriotic civilians starving, they had, according to Smirnova, a moral responsibility to reverse the trend.[48]

That wardrobe was the most pressing issue for many actresses is clear from the protocol of the First All-Russian Congress of Representatives of the Stage. Although many challenged the accuracy of Tarlovskaia's general assessment of actresses' degraded status, even her critics agreed that the burden of increasingly elaborate production values fell primarily on actresses and that excessive elegance on stage had to be curbed.[49] But what could be done?

In an ineffectual attempt to address the problem, members of the Congress proposed to change rule seventy-three of the standard contract so that it read: 'Actresses receiving between fifty and seventy-five roubles a month must have at least four dresses, including a ball gown and a visiting dress, even if they are inexpensive. Those receiving less than fifty roubles are not obliged to purchase a ball dress, but may obtain one from the theatre's wardrobe.'[50] Well-intentioned though it might have been, this entirely inadequate proposal, which did little to change existing conditions, suggests that Russian actresses had little authority within the very institutions and organisations charged with protecting their interests. Because issues peculiar to actresses were largely ignored by both the Congress and the Russian Theatre Society which organised it, their situation continued to deteriorate: after 1900 the chorus of complaints about excessive demands for elegant costumes grew louder, and instances of professional prostitution and sexual extortion were documented more frequently.

Notes

1. I.N. Grinevskaia, 'Zhenshchina na stsene', *Biblioteka teatra i iskusstva*, no. 6 (1909), pp. 3–24. Grinevskaia gave an abbreviated version of this article at the Women's Congress, which was published in 1908 with the rest of the papers.
2. Interested readers can refer to my more comprehensive study, Catherine Schuler, *Women in Russian Theatre: The Actress in the Silver Age* (London: Routledge, 1997).
3. In its narrowest sense, the *krizis teatra*, which was covered widely in books and journals, refers specifically to the conflict that arose between partisans of *bytovoi* and *uslovnyi* theatre. *Bytovoi* refers to domestic drama produced in a recognisably realistic setting. *Uslovnyi* is best translated as 'conventional' (in the sense of theatre that makes deliberate use of theatrical conventions). During the Silver Age, the term was associated primarily with Symbolism, decadence, and other abstract movements.
    This 'crisis' was not the sole source of dissension in the theatre community. The rise of the omnipotent Wagnerian director, increased commercialism, obsolete production practices, the degraded condition of provincial theatre and general social unrest were among the other factors that destabilised Russian theatre during this period. The literature on these crises is manifold. Interested readers should see, among other sources, *Trudy 1-ogo vserossiiskogo s"ezda stsenicheskikh deiatelei* (St Petersburg: n.p., 1898); A.R. Kugel', 'Rezhisser', in *Utverzhedenie teatra* (Leningrad, Izdatel'stvo zhurnala *Teatr i iskusstvo*, n.d.), pp. 41–59. In 1908, the editors of *Teatr i iskusstvo* published a three-part series entitled 'Krizis teatra' (see nos. 17, 18, and 20). Much of the debate over the relative merits of *bytovyi* and *uslovnyi* theatre was in response to two books published during the period. One, *Kniga o novom teatre* (A Book About the New Theatre), included essays by advocates of symbolism; the other, *Krizis teatra* (The Crisis of Theatre), included essays by the opposition. Chekhov's *Chaika* (*The Seagull*, 1896) also offers useful insights into the conflicts within the theatre community at the end of the century.
4. Many sources in English and Russian are available on this subject. Among others, see Linda Edmondson, *Feminism in Russia* (Stanford, CA: Stanford University Press, 1984); Laura Engelstein, *The Keys to Happiness: Sex and the Search for Modernity in Fin-de-Siècle Russia* (Ithaca, NY: Cornell University Press, 1992); Barbara

Evans Clements, Barbara Alpern Engel, and Christine D. Worobec (eds), *Russia's Women: Accommodation, Resistance, Transformation* (Berkeley, CA: University of California Press, 1991); Barbara Alpern Engel, *Mothers and Daughters of the Intelligentsia in Nineteenth Century Russia* (Cambridge: Cambridge University Press, 1983); *Trudy 1-ogo vserossiiskogo zhenskogo s"ezda pri russkom zhenskom obshchestve v S.-Peterburge* (St Petersburg: n.p., 1909); I. Astaf'ev, 'Psikhicheskii mir zhenshchiny: ego osobennosti, prevoskhodstva i nedostatki', *Russkii vestnik*, no. 12 (1881) part II, pp. 591–640; 'Zhenstvennost' i sinie chulki', in *O zhenshchinakh: mysli starye i novye* (St Peterburg: n.p., 1886). For an extensive bibliography of primary literature on the woman question in Russia, see 'Ukazatel' literatury zhenskogo voprosa na russkom iazyke', *Severnyi vestnik*, no. 7 (1887), pp. 1–33 and no. 8, pp. 34–56.

5. Juliet Blair, 'Private Parts in Public Places: The Case of Actresses', in Shirley Ardener (ed.), *Women and Space: Ground Rules and Social Maps* (Oxford: Berg, 1993), p. 206.

6. For information on Bashkirtseva's influence, see Charlotte Rosenthal, 'The Silver Age: highpoint for women?', in Linda Edmondson (ed.), *Women and Society in Russia and the Soviet Union* (Cambridge: Cambridge University Press, 1992), p. 32. Russians were introduced to the American 'New Woman' by articles like 'Pis'mo iz Ameriki', which appeared as a series in *Severnyi vestnik* in 1896. One particularly interesting instalment (no. 2, part II, pp. 49–57) offers a rather unrealistic picture of the American 'New Woman'. Apparently the author of the letters was persuaded that American women had achieved 'absolute equality' with men in regard to education. From the author's point of view, the American 'New Woman's' objective was to obtain 'independence, emancipation from men in all regards'. In the article, much attention was devoted to dress reform and to women who wore bloomers and rode bicycles.

6. For a sampling of critical response to Bernhardt, see Em. Beskin, 'Koroleva zhesta', *Rampa*, no. 16 (1908), pp. 246–48; V. Khabkin, 'Sarah divine', *Rampa*, no. 1 (1909), p. 2; Aleksandr Kugel', 'Sara Bernar', in *Teatral'nye portrety* (Leningrad: Iskusstvo, 1967), pp. 322–23.

Even today, Sarah Bernhardt remains an enigmatic figure for western historians, who cannot agree on the nature of her influence in Russia. Laurence Senelick agrees with Chekhov and Bernhardt's other Russian detractors that it was baneful; Arthur Gold and Robert Fizdale are more sympathetic and emphasise Bernhardt's enormous influence on other actresses, including her chief rival, Eleonora Duse. See Laurence Senelick, 'Chekhov's Response to Bernhardt', in Eric Salmon (ed.), *Bernhardt and the Theatre of Her Time* (Westport, CT: Greenwood, 1984), pp. 165–81; Arthur Gold and Robert Fizdale, *The Divine Sarah* (New York: Vintage Books, 1992).

7. Aleksandr Kugel', 'Eleonora Duse', in *Teatral'nye portrety*, p. 311.

8. For contemporaneous reactions to Duse, see Aleksandr Kugel', 'Eleonora Duse', in *Teatral'nye portrety*, pp. 307–18; 'Eleonora Duse', *Severnyi vestnik*, no. 8 (1891), part II, pp. 117–35; 'Sovremennaia zhenshchina na stsene', *Teatral* (1897), nos. 105, 106, 108, 109, 110, and 114; Ivan Ivanov, 'Eleonora Duse', *Artist*, no. 19 (1891), pp. 136–48; A. Shvyrev, 'Eleonora Duse', in *Znamenitye aktery i aktrisy* (St Petersburg: n.p., 1902), pp. 263–74; E.Koltonovskaia, *Zhenskie siluety* (St Petersburg, 1912), pp. 151–77.

9. See, for example, A. Volynskii, 'Kritika', *Severnyi vestnik*, no.12 (1896), part II, pp. 53–66. Volynsky wrote that after seeing Bernhardt and Duse (he especially admired Bernhardt), it was painful to sit through a production with woefully second-rate Russian performers. He admits of several exceptions – Mariia Savina, Mariia Ermolova, and Glikeriia Fedotova – but for the most part Russian performers of both sexes were a sorry lot.

I do not intend to suggest, however, that all critics and spectators shared Volynsky's preference for western actresses. Nationalism, which was on the rise throughout much of the period, turned support for Russian performers into an issue of patriotism. Some actresses (Polina Strepetova, for example) enjoyed enthusiastic support precisely because they resisted western trends.

10. Actress/novelist Mariia Krestovskaia's parable of theatrical life, *Lelia* (1885) offers an instructive example of the semiotics of costume during this period. In this story, an innocent young woman with a bit of natural talent for acting is lured away from hearth, husband and child after being infected by the theatre 'disease'. The first concrete sign of her corruption is that she returns home wearing 'long red gloves à la Sarah Bernhardt'. Mariia Krestovskaia, 'Lelia', in *Vne zhizni i ugolki teatral'nogo mirka* (St Peterburg: A.S. Suvorin, 1889), p. 334.

11. M.G. Svetaeva, *M.G. Savina* (Moscow: Iskusstvo, 1988); Aleksandr Kugel', 'Teatral'nye zametki', *Teatr i iskusstvo*, no. 1 (1904), p. 15. According to Svetaeva, Savina was the first Russian actress to play western-style ingénues. Although Kugel' agreed, he did not believe ingénues in the western sense existed in Russian theatre. 'Strictly speaking', he wrote, '[the ingénue] is not characteristic of Russian national theatre'.

12. Savina regularly received a substantial wardrobe subsidy in addition to her yearly salary of 12,000 roubles. At the height of her popularity, she claimed to have spent 7,000 roubles a year on costumes. See, 'Neizdannye vospominaniia M.G. Savinoi', in *Teatral'noe nasledstvo* (Moscow: Iskusstvo, 1956), p. 519.

13. *M.G. Savina i A. Koni: perepiska, 1883–1915* (Leningrad-Moscow: Iskusstvo, 1938), pp. 17, 41. An article that appeared in *Severnyi vestnik* clarifies the difference between Savina and Iavorskaia with respect to personal style and fashionableness. Savina, beloved by all, was coquettish and self-assured. Her wardrobe, although elegant, was never overstated and always appropriate to the role. Iavorskaia, on the other hand, was 'fantastical and capricious'. Her costumes were chosen not on the basis of suitability for the character, but because they were the most expensive examples of the latest Parisian fashions. See, A. Volynskii, 'Literaturnye zametki: Peterburgskie teatry', *Severnyi vestnik*, no. 8–9 (1898), p. 167.

14. Russia was certainly not unique in this regard. The low status of actresses was characteristic of European theatre and probably originated with the female mimes of Greek and Roman antiquity.

15. 'Doklad Iulii Vasil'evnoi Tarlovskoi-Rastorguevoi', *Trudy 1-ogo vserossiiskogo s"ezda stsenicheskikh deiatelei* (St Petersburg: n.p., 1898), pp. 32–33.

16. 'Krizis teatra', *Rampa i zhizn'*, no. 24 (1911), p. 4.

17. Although professional prostitution was not unknown in the theatre community, critics probably exaggerated the number of professional prostitutes masquerading as actresses. Sexual patronage was, however, widespread, and few actresses could survive financially without it, especially in the provinces.

18. S. Svetlov, 'Aktery i zhizn'', *Teatr i iskusstvo*, no. 29 (1904), pp. 536–37. Svetlov argued that the abolition of serfdom created a new class of spectators, which forced entrepreneurs constantly to seek novelty in order to satisfy the rather debased tastes of this new public.

19. Mariia Velizarii, *Put' provintsial'noi aktrisy* (Leningrad: Iskusstvo, 1938), pp. 110–12.

20. A.N. Voznesenskii, 'Stsenicheskii dogovor', *Studia*, no. 11 (1911), p. 5.

21. 'Doklad N.F. Arbenina', *Trudy 1-ogo vserossiiskogo s"ezda stsenicheskikh deiatelei*, p. 137.

22. N.S. Vasil'eva, 'Kak voznikli dramaticheskie kursy', *Ezhegodnik imperatorskikh teatrov* (1911), vypusk (issue) V, p. 2. Although Arbenin's and Vasil'eva's accounts do not correspond exactly, it is clear that costume demands were more reasonable in the past.

23. Nikolai Karabanov, 'Teatr v provintsii', *Studia*, no. 24 (1912), p. 2.
24. The Russian tours of the Meiningen Theatre had tremendous influence on Russian directors. The company was headed by Georg II, Duke of Saxe-Meiningen, whose fame as the first modern director rests in part on his attention to historical accuracy and detail.
25. Grinevskaia, 'Zhenshchina na stsene', p. 13.
26. 'Zhenshchina na stsene', *Teatral'naia Rossia*, no. 17 (1905), p. 290.
27. Grinevskaia, 'Zhenshchina na stsene', pp. 14–15.
28. 'Kak oni stali prostitutkami', *Rampa i akter*, no. 25 (1909), pp. 408–9.
29. Ibid., p. 409.
30. Ibid.; Grinevskaia, 'Zhenshchina na stsene', p. 14.
31. Grinevskaia, 'Zhenshchina na stsene', p. 15.
32. N.I. Aberdukh, 'Artisty i tualety', *Rampa i akter*, no. 27 (1909), p. 439.
33. Ibid., p. 440.
34. 'Kak oni stali prostitutkami', p. 407; 'Doklad N.F. Arbenina', p. 135. Arbenin suggests that leading men and women received between three and six hundred roubles a month. In rare instances, an actor or actress could earn as much as eight hundred roubles, but the average salary was four hundred. It is worth noting that starring actresses like Savina could earn more than 35,000 roubles in a good year.
35. For a survey of women's salaries in a variety of occupations, see P.N. Arian (ed.), *Pervyi zhenskii kalendar'* (St Peterburg: n.p., 1903), pp. 470–83. According to Arian's statics, women rarely earned more than one hundred roubles a month. Most earned less than fifty.
36. 'Doklad N.F. Arbenina', p. 135. The discrepancy between reported and actual salary affected both actresses and actors.
37. Ibid., and S. Svetlov, 'S akterskogo rynka', *Teatr i iskusstvo*, no. 9 (1904), p. 189. Arbenin also argued that summer salaries were so low that they should not even be considered. He put the total salary for a summer season at five hundred roubles. Svetlov placed the average summer salary at between seventy-five and one hundred roubles a month, or about three hundred for the summer season.
38. 'Kak oni stali prostitutkami', p. 408.
39. 'Doklad N.F. Arbenina', p. 136.
40. 'Kak oni stali prostitutkami', pp. 407–8.
41. Ibid., p. 409.
42. Aktrisa, 'Pis'mo k antrepreneru', *Rampa i zhizn'*, no. 20 (1915), p. 11.
43. Grinevskaia, 'Zhenshchina na stsene', p. 14.
44. 'Nechto o stsenicheskoi vneshnosti nashikh artistok', *Teatr i iskusstvo*, no. 4 (1897), pp. 74–75. The author is surely correct in suggesting that personal vanity was a factor, but actresses had to be pragmatic. If they insisted on flattering gowns, it was in large part a response to audience taste. Because critics wrote primarily about actresses, it is virtually impossible to assess whether the author's remarks about actors reflect gender bias, or whether actors really were more modest and cooperative in this respect.
45. Aberdukh, 'Artisty i tualety', p. 439.
46. Vasil'eva, 'Kak vozníkli dramaticheskie kursy', p. 11.
47. N. Smirnova, 'O roskoshi i mode', *Rampa i zhizn'*, no. 18 (1916), p. 4.
48. 'Protokol', *Trudy 1-ogo vserossiiskogo s"ezdu stsenicheskikh deiatelei*, p. 116.
49. Ibid., pp. 163–64.

Part Three

WOMEN WRITERS FROM THE REVOLUTION TO THE PRESENT

Chapter 7

THE ART OF SUGGESTING MORE: AKHMATOVA AND THE DIAPHORIC MANNER

Sheelagh Graham

> Depths should be concealed in the surface.
> (Hugo von Hofmannsthal)

'Diaphor' has to do with what Mallarmé called 'cancelling the word "like" from the dictionary'. The word appears to have been first used in the sense in which I shall use it in this chapter by Philip Wheelwright in his book *Metaphor and Reality* (1971),[1] to describe the way poetry, and particularly – though not exclusively – modernist poetry, can create new meanings by juxtaposing apparently unrelated material; he opposes this device to what he calls epiphor, the extension of meaning through comparison (that is, metaphor as it is traditionally understood).

What engendered this essay, however, was not Wheelwright's analysis of the diaphoric, but an article by the American scholar Jeanne Kammer.[2] Seizing on Wheelwright's word, she first expands on his implication that diaphor is favoured by modern poets: where earlier poets, especially the Romantics, made statements via metaphor, the moderns prefer suggestion, presentation rather than statement, oblique expression that corresponds to the scepticism and uncertainty basic to the modern temper. Kammer goes on to argue that the flowering of poetry by women in the modern period is not coincidental with the move to obliquity and fragmentation in modern art; the way women think and therefore write, Kammer suggests, suits the modern taste for the reticent, tentative, undogmatic; for art that declines to make assertions, approaching its goals by circuitous routes, leaping over gaps in logic. Thus women's poetry has found a readership among both sexes in our age.

Kammer's article provides a refutation (if any were needed) of those reproaches levelled at Akhmatova by contemporary male critics, including Nikolai Gumilev (her first husband), about the lack of connection between constituent parts in Akhmatova's early lyrics. As a (sympathetic) reviewer, Boris Eikhenbaum, put it, 'Her words do not merge into one another; they merely adjoin one another, like the pieces of a mosaic design.'[3] Kammer suggests that 'the diaphoric mode, for women, may reflect an internal division and fragmentation, private experience opposed to the public one of men', so that for her the effect of, say, T.S. Eliot's 'Sweeney among the nightingales', with its accumulation of disconnected images, suggests 'a condition of the collective modern temper', whereas the effect of Emily Dickinson's 'After Great Pain' is of a group of images and associations pointing inwards to a single 'interior nerve centre'.

A possible explanation for this poetic device of simply setting down, presenting unrelated fragments, Kammer goes on to say, may be found in 'the myriad domestic and social occupations culturally assigned to women that involve the visual ordering of random elements'. Mary Ellmann makes similar points: she considers an important aspect of modern writing to be 'the shift from significance to insignificance', and that women, having been confined for centuries in what she calls 'the underlife', are at home with the insignificant and take readily to making art out of it.[4]

Two lines from a poem in the cycle 'Tainy remesla' ('Craft Secrets', 1936-1960) may be interpreted as Akhmatova's typically oblique endorsement of the diaphoric mode:

По мне, в стихах всё быть должно некстати,
Не так, как у людей.[5]

(For me, everything in poetry should be not what you expect,/ Not as people think it should be.)

This could refer to her method of placing unconnected things side by side, in a small space, with the poet inviting the reader to ponder the unspoken, the enigmatic gaps between what is expressed. This enigmatic quality (the subtext discerned by the alert reader) combines with the laconicism and formal simplicity of her poems – the concreteness of her limited poetic vocabulary, the shortness of the sentences, the simplicity of the connectives, or indeed the absence of connectives – to set up a satisfying tension.

Let us consider some examples of Akhmatova's diaphoric manner, bearing in mind Jeanne Kammer's commentary on Philip Wheelwright's use of that word: '[Diaphor] is rooted in the associational properties of the subconscious mind, its movement is not necessarily linear and does not require syntactic support... [It is] configuration rather than statement.'

The first example is taken from one of Akhmatova's most famous early poems, 'Menia pokinul v novolun'e':

> Пусть страшен путь мой, пусть опасен,
> Ещё страшнее путь тоски ...
> Как мой китайский зонтик красен,
> Натёрты белом башмачки!
>
> 1911 (*BP: 55*)

(My path may be terrible, dangerous,/ More terrible still is the path of yearning.../ How red is my Chinese parasol,/ My slippers chalkwhitened!)

This sets the pattern for many stanzas in her early work: pairs of lines detached from each other by a full stop or ellipses or, more rarely, the conjunction '*i*' (and). The last two lines in the example above were chosen by Gumilev as the epigraph to his poem of 1912 'Ukrotitel' zverei'; presumably they struck Gumilev, in their concreteness and strong visual impact, as an exemplar of the Acmeism he was propagating so enthusiastically at that time. But more striking is the lack of obvious or stated connection between the two halves of the stanza, though the superficial connection is clear if we remember the mask the poet assumes in this lyric, that of a tightrope walker (probably a metaphor for the need to tread warily in relations with the opposite sex). But what is the deeper link?

Krishna Rayan, who also sees the oblique – or, as he prefers to call it, suggestion – as 'the prevailing mode of modern poetry', points out that there can be no suggestion without suppression or omission.[6] In other words, absences create presences, the reader fills in the gaps, understands the discontinuities and silences. Whether s/he does so as the author would wish depends, of course, on the degree to which the reader corresponds, in Gumilev's phrase, to *chitatel'-drug*, the ideal reader.

The reader understands too that in a lyric poem there is no such thing as irrelevant detail that might be excised in the way an editor scores out superfluous words in prose copy. The Chinese parasol and whitened slippers are 'significant', what Eliot called 'objective correlatives', pointing mutely to some intense emotion or abstraction or revelation the author chooses not to name, as occurs, for instance, in those Japanese lyrics called Haiku and the very short poems by writers such as Akhmatova's contemporary Ezra Pound who were influenced by and imitated oriental forms. Consider the following example of Haiku, 'the art of expressing much and suggesting more in the fewest possible words', as the *Encyclopaedia Britannica* defines it, through the precise placing of what Pound called 'the luminous detail'; it features another oriental umbrella:

On an umbrella a patter of raindrops;
But it enters next door;
The evening darkens.[7]

Returning to 'Menia pokinul v novolun'e', one could argue that in this poem the transition from first to second couplet in the stanza quoted is not abrupt, that there is no discontinuity if one goes along with Zhirmunsky's description of Akhmatova's early lyrics as 'fragments of a novella'. (He is following in the footsteps of Mandel'shtam, who considered that the origin of Akhmatova's poetry lay in the nineteenth-century novel.) In that case the second pair of lines could be taken as a way of rendering the heroine's psychological portrait: the tightrope walker is trying to suppress her fear by focusing attention on external details (more precisely, details of her own appearance, a sign of female insecurity being the tendency to be aware of herself only as reflected in others' eyes). No such explanation, however, accounts for the lack of connection between the sentences in the following stanzas:

На кустах зацветает крыжовник,
И везут кирпичи за оградой.
Кто ты: брат мой или любовник,
Я не помню, и помнить не надо.

1911 (*BP:* 13)

(The gooseberry bushes are in bloom,/ On the other side of the fence someone is carting bricks./ Whether you are my brother or my lover,/ I don't remember, and there's no need to.)

Мне с тобою пьяным весело –
Смысла нет в твоих рассказах.
Осень ранняя развесила
Флаги жёлтые па вязах.

1911 (*BP:* 20)

(I enjoy it when you're drunk – / Your stories make no sense./ Early autumn has hung out / Yellow flags on the elm trees.)

Commenting once on 'the apparent irrelevance and unrelatedness of things', Eliot wrote:

> When a poet's mind is perfectly equipped for work, it is consistently amalgamating disparate experiences; the ordinary man's experience is chaotic, irregular, fragmentary. The latter falls in love, or reads Spinoza, and these two experiences have nothing to do with each other, or with the noise of the typewriter or the smell of cooking; in the mind of the poet these experiences are already forming new wholes.[8]

What 'new wholes' are created in the first of the above-quoted stanzas? How is the sight of the gooseberry blossom and men carrying bricks related to the heroine's acute realisation of her quandary? Is it simply that she becomes suddenly aware of the uncertain nature of her relationship with the man at a particular time and place? Or is there another connection beyond that and beyond the essential fact of union by rhythm, rhyme and incantatory flow, in these juxtaposed sentences, answering the question, 'why', not 'what'?

Kammer would say that since virtually all of Akhmatova's poems have a female narrator-persona and the majority of her early poems are about love, then the space or silence between the two couplets may correspond to the enforced public silence of women in male-dominated societies, particulary the obligatory *pudeur*, the taboo that forbade a woman to express her sexuality. For women writers in the early twentieth century, as in the nineteenth, the impulse to compressed speech 'may derive in part from habits of privacy, camouflage and indirection ...; for the reclusive, emotionally vulnerable personality ... the ambiguity of saying and not saying' may be the only acceptable mode of communication. Hence the attraction, for women poets wary of the scorn of male critics, of the oblique mode ('Match me the Silver Reticence', as Emily Dickinson put it) and their consequent efflorescence in the modernist age.

Of course, preference for the cryptic, refusal to make statements or to elaborate comparisons is a feature of modern writing by both men and women. Nor is the mode unique to literature: silences are a feature of some avant-garde music, for instance. To quote Alice Jardine, 'Modernity seems to be about not knowing, about not being sure, about having no story to tell. It also seems to be about loss; loss of identity, loss of truth, legitimacy, knowledge, power – loss of control.'[9] Men are as aware of these negatives as women. Kammer, however, persuasively argues that the poet who is a woman is more likely for historical-cultural reasons to find that she is at home in the indirect mode. Such reasons would have been almost as powerful in Akhmatova's youth as they were in the first half of the nineteenth century when Evdokiia Rostopchina wrote the following lines, taken from her poem 'Kak dolzhny pisat' zhenshchiny' ('How women should write', 1840):

Да! женская душа должна в тени светиться,
Как в урне мраморной лампады скрытый луч,
Как в сумерки луна сквозь оболочку туч,
И, согревая жизнь, незримая теплиться.[10]

(Yes! a woman's heart should glow in the shade,/ Like concealed lamplight in a marble urn,/ Like the moon through cloudcover at dusk,/ And, as it warms life, flicker invisibly.)

The contrast between the metaphorical obviousness of Rostopchina's style and the enigmatic quality of Akhmatova's is striking. Consider the following Akhmatova stanza:

Столько просьб у любимой всегда!
У разлюбленной просьб не бывает.
Как я рада, что нынче вода
Под бесцветным ледком замирает.

1913 (*BP*: 71)

(How many favours a lover can ask!/ A woman no longer loved asks none./ How glad I am that the water now/ Lies still under a colourless film of ice.)

Admittedly, such is the impression of psychological truth in the first two lines (spoken with the same kind of authority as the opening sentence of *Anna Karenina*) that there may be a temptation to treat the next pair of lines metaphorically. But it would be banal to interpret the frozen water as somehow equated with a heart numbed by the realisation (here implied) that the *I* is no longer loved, or the heroine's gladness (line 3) as 'explained' by Nature's sympathy with her desolate condition. The adjective *bestsvetnyi* makes the ice too real for that, the colourlessness of ice being a fact the heroine simply notices, and assigns as much or as little importance to as love's ephemerality – which may or may not grieve her; it is simply a fact of life, like the freezing of water at a certain temperature. The reader apprehends intuitively and immediately the emotional-psychological complexity, maybe paradoxality, that exists in the space after the first full stop. It is the possibility of oscillating interpretations that makes Akhmatova's poetry feel modern, where so much by her contemporaries does not.

Speaking of Akhmatova's early love poems, Aleksandr Kushner said in an article of 1989:

Very often there is not a word about love in them; there is talk of anything but – flowers in the house, a pile of vegetables beside the vegetable plot, a pond and the carp that live in it – nevertheless we somehow realise that all this too is about love. Love presupposes a passionate, interested attention to the world, to life in all its manifestations; love sharpens the sight and makes the hearing acute ... These signs [*primety*] of Akhmatova's, these remarks casually dropped, are the result of such intense straining not of the sight so much as the heart [*dusha*] that in her later poetry they are encountered more and more rarely; she no longer had the strength for them.[11]

Kushner is right; the juxtaposition of lines of emotional import and apparently unconnected descriptions of objects in the material world are essentially a feature of Akhmatova's early work, indeed the poetry of a very limited period: 1911 to 1914. I have found only two examples of this simple juxtaposing in her later work, one dating from 1915 and one from 1921, with a doubtful example I shall refer to later dating from 1941.

One might expect diaphor to be a constant in a poet's work. Why is it not in Akhmatova's case? Kushner's explanation for the disappearance of what is considered a typical Akhmatova device from her later poetry is plausible. I would like to suggest two other reasons for the suddenness of its disappearance: literary fashion and Russian history.

The years 1911 to 1914 are the heyday of Acmeism. Diaphor (or, using Eliot's term, the objective correlative) employs the concrete or everyday detail, and for that reason it was an appropriate device for the Acmeists intent on deflating Symbolism. Acmeism's call to be true to the things of this world found no better response than Akhmatova's loving regard for what is, whether lichen on a stone, the smell of goosefoot (*lebedka*) weeded out of the flowerbeds, a red parasol, or the way ice cracks on a puddle as you step on it. 'The role of diaphor is to create presence', says Wheelwright. Akhmatova's poetry does that supremely well. If Acmeism succeeded in its task of refocusing attention on the word and what it denotes, it was thanks largely to the early poetry of Akhmatova. But then Acmeism was overtaken in the mad rush of twentieth-century modernism by other schools of poetry where the restrained, 'take it or leave it' quality of diaphor had no place.

As to history, it is surely no coincidence that Akhmatova's striking use of juxtaposition, her particular type of obliquity as instanced in the examples above virtually ended with the outbreak of war in 1914. I suggest that under the impact of that tragedy the device that helped make her a sensationally popular poet in pre-war Russia, linked as it was to both her and her readers' bourgeois or bourgeois-bohemian way of life (nightclubs, carriage rides, interiors with flowers and Sèvres china, gardens, lovers' rendezvous in parks decorated with classical sculptures, gloves, riding-crops, hats with feathers), came to seem frivolous or trivial as she realised that 'the real twentieth century' (*nastoiashchii dvadtsatyi vek*) had begun, and her prophetic soul told her it was going to be harsh and bitter.

Or perhaps she simply grew out of the rather obvious pattern of juxtaposed couplets, and her diaphoric mode developed into something closer to what her contemporaries in Anglo-American poetry, the Imagists, were trying to do, as described by Richard Aldington in 1914: 'We convey an emotion by presenting the object and the circumstances without comment ... We make the scene convey the emotion.'[12] This might be a description of a poem like Akhmatova's 1940 lyric entitled 'Pro stikhi' ('About poetry'):

Это – выжимки бессонниц,
Это – свеч кривых нагар,
Это – сотен белых звонниц
Первый утренний удар ...
Это – тёплый подоконник
Под черниговской луной,
Это – пчёлы, это – донник,
Это – пыль, и мрак, и зной.

(*BP*: 340)

(It is the husks of sleepless nights,/ It is the soot of crooked candles, / It is the first morning peal/ From hundreds of white bell-towers/ It is a warm window sill,/ Under the Chernigov moon,/ It is bees, it is scented clover,/ It is dusk and dark and heat.)

Whereas in Akhmatova's earlier poems the pronoun '*ty*' (you) or '*on*' (he) makes it clear that the cause of the emotion is the male partner, in 'Pro stikhi' only the title tells us what these various details evoke. If the title were omitted we would be at a loss to say what these unrelated things, singly or in accumulation, suggest.

Akhmatova's poetry continued to be cryptic, favouring the *mnogotochie* (ellipsis) noted by Gumilev as peculiarly appropriate to her manner, but the later poetry is cryptic more because of the extreme compression and what looks like indifference as to whether the reader understands or not. Consider this example:

Кто чего боится,
То с тем и случится, –
Ничего бояться не надо.
Эта песня пета,
Пета, да не эта,
А другая, тоже
На неё похожа ...
Боже!

1943 (*BP*: 459)

(Whatever you fear,/ Is what will happen to you , – / Fear nothing. / This song is sung, / Sung, but not this one,/ Another one, / Very like it / O God!)

On the rare occasion when Akhmatova in her later poetry employs the pattern of juxtaposed couplets common in earlier poems, it has a different cadence:

Жить – так на воле,
Умирать – так дома.
Волково поле,
Жёлтая солома.

1941 (*BP:* 539)

(If to live – then in freedom,/ If to die – then at home./ Volkovo field,/ Yellow straw.)

The contrast is due not only to the different rhythm of these *dol'niki* or to the powerful interchange of meaning in the rhyme words. The voice has changed. The brevity is no longer motivated by a woman's wish to protect herself from a predatory male or domineering husband. It is the voice of a human being battered by life but determined to endure. The words are uttered through clenched teeth.

Writers living in the Soviet Union in Stalin's time had to be cryptic. Akhmatova saw no escape, as she said in a poem dating from 1944, from 'strange lyrics where chasms yawn right and left' (*BP:* 552). However, Anna Akhmatova's sybilline quality was not something forced on her by conditions in Stalin's Russia. It was a necessity of her secretive nature. It was also peculiarly feminine, a means of self-defence. Akhmatova was a woman of the twentieth century, neither able nor willing to do what Rostopchina had done – internalise her slavery – but for temperamental reasons equally unable and unwilling to enter the public arena. In her later work she was at best able to take the stage as the actor does, disguised, putting on the mask of such heroines as Cleopatra, Boiarina Morozova (a seventeenth-century Old Believer who was arrested, tortured and finally starved to death for her faith), Antigone and others:

Мне с Морозовою класть поклоны,
С падчерицей Ирода плясать,
С дымом улетать с костра Дидоны,
Чтобы с Жанной на костёр опять.

1962 (*BP:* 480)

(I must bow low with Morozova,/ Dance with Herod's stepdaughter,/ Ascend with the smoke of Dido's pyre,/ Only to go into the flames again with Joan of Arc.)

The gender of the poet affects the poetic output. The voice may be neutral but it cannot be neuter. Gender may affect the themes and content of poetry and also the mode. The fact of Akhmatova's sex is one explanation of her preference for suggestion (diaphor) over statement (metaphor).

Notes

1. Philip Wheelwright, *Metaphor and Reality* (Bloomington and London: Indiana University Press, 1971).
2. Jeanne Kammer, 'The art of silence and the forms of women's poetry', in Sandra M. Gilbert and Susan Gubar (eds), *Shakespeare's Sisters: Feminist Essays on Women Poets* (Bloomington, IN and London: Indiana University Press, 1979), pp. 153–64.
3. B.M. Eikhenbaum, *O poezii* (Leningrad, 1969), p.8.
4. Mary Ellmann, *Thinking about Women* (London: Virago, 1979), p. 227.
5. Anna Akhmatova, *Stikhotvoreniia i poemy*, Biblioteka poeta (Leningrad: Sovetskii pisatel', 1976), no. 334. All further quotations from Akhmatova's poems will refer to this edition (*BP*, followed by the number of the poem). The poem from which these lines were taken was written in 1940, the year in which she was at last able to publish a selection of her lyrics under the title *Iz shesti knig*, adding a diaphorically tending epigraph that she had first used in her earliest book, *Vecher* (1912), as though recognising in these two lines from the French poet André Theuriet a reflection of her own manner: 'La fleur des vignes pousse / Et j'ai vingt ans ce soir.'
6. Krishna Rayan, *Suggestion and Statement in Poetry* (London: Athlone Press, 1972), pp. 2–3.
7. R.H. Blyth, *Haiku* (Tokyo: The Hokuseido Press, and Heian International, South San Francisco, 1981–1982), vol. 4, p. 1184.
8. Quoted in Wheelwright, *Metaphor and Reality*, pp. 82–83.
9. Alice Jardine, 'Opaque texts and transparent contexts: the political difference of Julia Kristeva', in Nancy K. Miller (ed.), *The Poetics of Gender* (New York: Columbia University Press, 1986), pp. 96-116 (p. 100).
10. Quoted in Viktor Afanas'ev, *Svobodnoi muzy prinoshen'e. Literaturnye portrety. Stat'i* (Moscow: Sovremennik, 1988), p. 408.
11. Aleksandr Kushner, 'Poeticheskoe vospriiatie mira', *Literaturnaia gazeta*, 21 June 1989, p. 3.
12. Quoted in Louis Menand, *Discovering Modernism: T.S.Eliot and his context* (New York and Oxford: Oxford University Press, 1987), p. 135.

Chapter 8

UNDER AN UNWOMANLY STAR: WAR IN THE WRITING OF OL'GA BERGGOL'TS

Katharine Hodgson

Ol'ga Berggol'ts (1910–1975) is best known as the poet of the nine-hundred-day siege of Leningrad during the Second World War. Most of this time she spent in the city making frequent radio broadcasts which brought her immense popularity. The war transformed her from a relatively unknown poet into a symbol of the city's resistance, the 'Voice of Leningrad', the 'Muse of the blockade'.[1] At the end of the war she wrote a poem reflecting on the way her wartime experiences had changed her. 'Stikhi o sebe' ('About Myself') begins:

И вот в послевоенной тишине
к себе прислушалась наедине.
[…]
Какое сердце стало у меня,
сама не знаю – лучше или хуже:
не отогреть у мирного огня,
не остудить на самой лютой стуже.

И в чёрный час зажжённые войною
затем, чтобы не гаснуть, не стихать,
неженские созвездья надо мною,
неженский ямб в черствеющих стихах …[2]

(And now in the silence after the war/ I have listened to myself in private.// […] I cannot tell whether my heart / has become better or worse:/ it cannot be warmed by a peaceful fire,/ or chilled in the fiercest frost.// And, kindled by war in a dark hour,/ thereafter never to be extinguished or die down,/ is the unwomanly constellation above me,/ the unwomanly iamb in my bristling verses...)

The war, Berggol'ts appears to be suggesting, has deprived her of qualities she considers to be feminine, such as gentleness and emotional responsiveness, but endowed her and her writing with 'masculine' severity, even harshness. However, while most of what Berggol'ts wrote during the war portrays women living under siege, the question of war's effect on them *as* women is not explicitly raised until much later, in contrast with the wartime poetry of some women who served at the front, which does consider the effects, both liberating and traumatic, of their assumption of traditionally masculine roles.[3] By making the distinction between the warlike masculine and the pacific feminine in 'About Myself', Berggol'ts aligns herself with an enduring tradition which defines war as an essentially male activity, even in an age when, as in the Leningrad siege, civilians can be as much on the front line as any soldier, and when, as in the Soviet Army, women serve at the front alongside men.

Literary representations of war have tended to focus on the experiences of men fighting at the front. Civilians and, particularly, women appear only in peripheral roles which emphasise their perceived position as man's Other, the essentially un-warlike counterpart of the belligerent male. Jean Bethke Elshtain has noted the tendency towards portraying men and women in wartime as 'beings who have complementary needs and exemplify gender-specific virtues', regardless of the extent to which this actually corresponds to reality.[4] War, it can be argued, puts men and women back in their proper places.[5] In the twentieth century women have, however, taken on wartime roles which have brought them out of their traditional occupations. Sandra Gilbert has noted women's sense of being liberated into a world of action during the First World War, finding excitement and fulfilment where they had previously experienced only powerlessness. Conversely, men immobilised in trench warfare experienced an unaccustomed lack of power and freedom of movement.[6] Discussions of women writing about war make the point that women feel themselves to be out of place, therefore represent themselves in terms of unchallenging female stereotypes which marginalise and efface them. Women, as Susan Schweik puts it, are categorised as peripheral; war is the place where women are not.[7] It has been suggested that women writing about war have internalised their marginalisation to the extent of repressing the authentic voice of their own experience.[8] All of these points will be discussed in relation to Berggol'ts's writing.

As a Soviet poet of the Second World War, Berggol'ts is unusual simply because she was a woman.[9] Though the idea of writing as a 'woman poet' was alien to Soviet culture – citizenship came before anything else, and the 'woman question' had supposedly been resolved by early economic and social changes after 1917 – the concept of the war poet in the Soviet canon as elsewhere is almost exclusively male. The fact that Berggol'ts is both a war poet and a woman has led some critics to ask how a fragile woman could have become Leningrad's symbolic soldier-poet.[10] It could be said in reply that it would have been even more surprising had a man taken on that role, given the preconceptions about gender roles which permeate Soviet wartime poetry. As will be shown below, the fact that Berggol'ts was a woman was by no means coincidental to her wartime success. I shall then consider to what extent Berggol'ts felt that women's wartime achievements had been too dearly bought.

Any discussion of Ol'ga Berggol'ts as a woman war poet has to be based on an understanding of the situation of women in the Soviet Union. According to Elshtain, women in wartime are portrayed as 'civic beings' responding not just to family demands, but to social claims as well.[11] Soviet women were, however, expected to satisfy these dual demands in peacetime. Perhaps this might suggest that Soviet society perceived itself to be, if not actually at war, then constantly preparing for war.[12] Elsewhere after the 1914–1918 war women had been expected to return to the domestic sphere from their brief spell as 'temporary citizens'.[13] Yet while Soviet culture gave prominence to the female worker and political activist, it also projected another image of woman as unenlightened, caught up in private and domestic matters, and therefore unable to play a full role in society. Private life, and, by implication, traditional female concerns, were dismissed as being of little relevance unless they could be integrated into the new social structure, and even then woman's social responsibilities were expected to take precedence over her family.

The status of Soviet women political activists as figures of moral authority did not rely solely on changes wrought by revolution, but derived partly from Russian tradition. The rehabilitation of traditional values which took place during the 1930s repealed legislation on abortion and divorce. It also revived patriotic sentiment, reclaiming past male leaders such as Ivan the Terrible and Peter the Great, but also the concept of Mother Russia, a female embodiment of the nation. There is evidence that early Russian culture valued feminine strength and wisdom.[14] The warrior-heroes of traditional verse epics do battle with, and are sometimes defeated by, warrior-maidens, while the much later 'superfluous men' of nineteenth-century novels behold with awe the instinctive moral sense of their female counterparts.[15] Given the combination of Russian tradition and the Soviet call to women as civic beings, it is not surprising that the outbreak of war in 1941 brought young women as well as men rushing to serve in the armed forces. Many demanded that they be allowed to go and fight instead of taking on more traditional female roles; women were involved in all aspects of the Soviet war effort, though their achievements were often insufficiently acknowledged.[16]

That Berggol'ts became the poet who was able to give voice most convincingly to the trials of life under siege in Leningrad owed a good deal to traditional perceptions of woman as a touchstone of moral values, as well as to the more recent view of woman as activist and citizen. The war Berggol'ts recorded, however, had little in common with the one she had expected, where women saw men off to the front for a brief, victorious battle.[17] During the siege of Leningrad, conditions obliterated distinctions between front and rear, soldiers and civilians. All were within range of enemy artillery, and all, with the exception of a few officials at party headquarters, were starving.[18] The sphere generally associated with women – the provision of food and home comforts, and the raising of children – was practically wiped out in a city under daily shell-fire, whose inhabitants were, for a time, living in cold, dark flats on a bread ration of 125 grammes a day. The soldiers around the city were, for the most part, fighting a static war, powerless to change the situation.

Much of Berggol'ts's wartime poetry equates civilians and soldiers:

И каждый, защищавший Ленинград,
вложивший руку в пламенные раны,
не просто горожанин, а солдат,
по мужеству подобный ветерану[19]

(And each one who has defended Leningrad,/ who has placed a hand in its blazing wounds,/ is not simply a city-dweller, but a soldier,/ equal in courage to any veteran).

From equating soldiers and civilians it is not such a great step to valuing the achievements and experiences of female non-combatants with those of male combatants. Are the women Berggol'ts portrays, then, no longer on the margins of the literary representation of war, or are they represented solely in terms of 'acceptable' gender roles as 'selfless, nurturing, subordinate servers and observers'?[20] There is no question that some of the Leningrad women Berggol'ts portrays fulfil precisely that kind of role, as does the poet herself, offering sympathy and encouragement to her audience.[21] Others, however, are depicted as monumental, heroic figures, in terms more commonly associated with male soldiers. Conditions in Leningrad left little room for men to be portrayed in a conventionally warlike role. Indeed, Berggol'ts suggests that the height of heroism for a Leningrad soldier is the gift of his last crust of bread to hungry children.[22] In general, contemporary Soviet war poetry evokes a soldier's heroic qualities by focusing on the moment of his death in battle, which occurs instantly, without pain or fear. At this moment he commonly appears to be transformed into a statue, motionless, existing outside time as a monument to his own heroism.[23] Female soldiers were often portrayed by male poets with emphasis on their spiritual, feminine qualities rather than on their military, masculine actions; clearly most authors found the portrayal of women in aggressive roles unacceptable, or feared that fighting women risked losing their femininity.[24] Curiously enough, Berggol'ts's attempts at a conventional portrayal of male military heroism were few and relatively unsuccessful.[25] She was, however, much more successful in using existing stereotypes to convey the qualities required to survive the Leningrad blockade, where the real drama was an internal drama of endurance rather than a brief blaze of glory which led to peaceful immortality. To portray the unspectacular heroism of women under siege, Berggol'ts adopted the statue image usually applied to the triumphant soldier, and combined it with details from the everyday world of the Leningrad housewife. In a poem written in December 1941 she imagines a statue of her neighbour going out to collect her bread ration under shell-fire:

А тебе – да ведь тебе ж поставят
памятник на площади большой.
Нержавеющей, бессмертной сталью
облик твой запечатлят простой.

Вот такой же: исхудавшей, смелой,
в наскоро повязанном платке,
вот такой, когда под артобстрелом
ты идёшь с кошёлкою в руке.[26]

(And you will be commemorated/ in a monument set up on a great square./ Incorruptible, immortal steel/ will preserve your simple figure.// Just as you are now: thin, courageous,/ in a hastily tied headscarf,/ just as you are when you go out under artillery fire/ with your purse in your hand.)

The obvious discrepancy between the conventionally heroic and the mundane produces, rather than a comic effect, a sense of just how much effort was required to bridge that gap. The actions that Berggol'ts's heroines perform are unspectacular in themselves. They fetch water, bread and firewood, take the dead for burial. Far from being presented as insignificant 'women's work', however, these everyday acts are transformed into heroic acts, and the women who perform them are elevated to symbols of suffering and endurance. The bread and firewood they carry take on meanings clearly linked with Christian imagery. A description of a woman clutching part of a wooden cross, studded with nails, which she has taken from a cemetery for firewood, evokes the Leningraders' daily road to Calvary:

> Вот женщина стоит с доской в объятьях;
> угрюмо сомкнуты её уста,
> доска в гвоздьях – как будто часть распятья,
> большой обломок русского креста.[27]

(There a woman is standing with a plank of wood in her arms;/ her lips are grimly pressed together,/ the plank has nails in it – like part of a crucifix,/ a large piece broken off from a Russian cross.)

Berggol'ts describes women carrying on with the ordinary business of living in a situation which demanded they show the same courage and self-sacrifice expected of front-line soldiers. In foregrounding the spiritual aspects of the struggle for survival Berggol'ts recasts the war in terms which privilege women, already perceived as the embodiment of a culture's moral values, a reflection of the archetypal Mother Russia. Men are, indeed, largely absent in her wartime poetry. Those that do appear are frequently portrayed as dead or dying, while women suffer but refuse to succumb. It is true that women were physically better adapted to survive starvation, and that many of the early deaths from hunger in Leningrad were among men. Yet it is difficult to catch even a hint of female triumphalism in her work. The women Berggol'ts portrays, herself included, are prey to weakness, doubts, despair. Unlike the women writing of their experiences in the 1914–1918 war, they feel no sense of liberation except, perhaps, the freedom that comes from confronting death.

Yet to judge from Berggol'ts's first poetic response to the war, it did bring liberation of another kind, a release from the nightmare of mass arrests of the 1930s, together with a chance to offer wholehearted support for the state against real, rather than fictitious enemies.[28] Berggol'ts herself, an enthusiastic Communist, did not escape the purges. Her former husband, the poet Boris Kornilov, was arrested and shot, while she was excluded from the Party and the Writers' Union in 1937, reinstated in 1938, and arrested shortly afterwards. She was released from prison after several months.[29] The war certainly gave writers and editors greater freedom of expression for a time. Berggol'ts was able to be relatively honest about conditions in Leningrad, though this often meant struggles with the censors. It can be argued that Berggol'ts, being a woman, was given greater licence to speak of suffering and painful emotions. As the Leningrad poet Nikolai Tikhonov later wrote, in wartime it was only women writers who had the right to admit to fatigue and weakness.[30] This claim seems to be borne out by much of the poetry written by women during the war years, who appear to have had tacit permission to express emotions that might have been considered defeatist coming from a man.[31] It seems reasonable to suggest that to have had a male poet playing the role Berggol'ts took on would have risked emphasising the military impotence of the besieged city. Furthermore, as a woman Berggol'ts could be identified with the powerful image of Mother Russia, who both inspired spiritual fortitude in her sons and appealed to them for protection. This image precisely fitted Berggol'ts's wartime poetic persona, simultaneously intimate and authoritative.

The association between women and honesty relied to a certain extent on women's identification with the private sphere, which offered some asylum from the encroaching state, a space free from political slogans where more reliable truths might be found.[32] Berggol'ts's audience was grateful for her honesty and avoidance of false pathos, and responded to her intimate, conversational style with letters about their own blockade experience.[33] Although Berggol'ts recognised the importance of private experience, her work emphasises women's civic role in the blockade. Writing as she was within the confines of the official media and in the light of her own convictions, Berggol'ts maintained that her personal life was inextricably linked with the life of her society. Her poems published in wartime do give details of her own experience as a token of sincerity which justifies her role as spokeswoman for the whole city. From shared experience comes a shared faith in victory. This approach, however, threatens to marginalise individual experience, when the striving to fulfil a social role means that Berggol'ts sidelines, or attempts to sublimate her own emotions. 'Pamiati zashchitnikov' (In Memory of the Defenders) is a requiem for a young soldier, written at the request of his sister in 1944, but it begins and ends with the poet's acknowledgement of her failure to produce a requiem for her husband, who died in January 1942. A poem of 1945 addressed to her dead husband says that she finds it easier to mourn for strangers than for him.[34]

There is a certain amount of awkwardness in Berggol'ts's attempts to integrate private emotions with her public role. A poem of 1942 is a telling illustration of the gulf between the two, contrasting the confident reply she gives to a sentry on the street with her interior monologue. The certainty of the poet's identity collapses when she tries to find a sense of her private self, now that she has left her old, uninhabitable home and all its memories of her dead husband and children:

«Вот пропуск мой. Пожалуйста, проверьте.
Я здешняя, и этот город – мой.
У нас одно дыханье, дума, сердце ...
Я здешняя, товарищ постовой.»

Но я живу в квартире, где зимою
чужая чья-то вымерла семья.
Всё, что кругом, – накоплено не мною.
Всё – не моё, как будто б я – не я.[35]

('Here is my pass. Please, do check it. / I live here, and this is my city./ We share one breath, one thought, one heart .../ I live here, comrade sentry.'// ... But I live in a flat where this winter/ someone's family of strangers died./ Nothing around me was gathered together by me./ Nothing is mine, as though I am not myself ...)

The discrepancy between the poet's public and private self surfaces in sudden shifts of style, particularly in her longer poems, where one voice is marked by set phrases bordering on slogans, by conventional imagery and a proliferation of exclamation marks and capital letters: Man, Soldier, Worker. This contrasts sharply with a voice which is restrained, lyrical and uses material drawn from everyday life.[36] While the latter voice often dominates the beginning of a work to striking effect, it is the former, official voice which brings the poem to its conclusion. The presence of competing voices within women's war poetry is described by Laurie Smith as an 'internal, often subtextual struggle for voice', the presence of a repressed voice which threatens to erupt. Smith identifies this as a sign of woman struggling to escape from the male-centred representation of war which keeps women silent or fixed in supportive, nurturing, marginalised roles. The voice which is consistently marginalised in Berggol'ts's poetry articulates private experience which the civic role assigned to women threatens to subsume. As the lines just quoted show, Berggol'ts's private experience did conflict with her public persona. On most occasions the belief that social duties took precedence over personal concerns leads her to gloss over this conflict, presenting her civic statements as if they are more significant than private experience. Nevertheless, the most striking and effective lines of her blockade poems are intensely personal, and require no justification in terms of representing a shared experience.

One poem Berggol'ts wrote during the war does make a conspicuous attempt to indicate a gap between women's actual experiences and their representation by implicitly male artists. A Leningrad woman finds it hard to recognise herself in her own portrait, which shows no sign of her fear, exhaustion, grey hair or rough hands. The war, she argues, has left its indelible marks which the artist has chosen to ignore:

И не проходят даром эти дни,
Неистребим свинцовый их осадок:
Сама печаль, сама война глядит
Познавшими глазами ленинградок.

Зачем ты меня изобразил
Такой отважной и такой прекрасной,
Как женщина в расцвете лучших сил,
С улыбкой горделивою и ясной?

Но, не приняв суровых укоризн,
Художник скажет с гордостью, с отрадой:
– Затем, что ты – сама Любовь и Жизнь,
Бесстрашие и Слава Ленинграда![37]

(These days do not pass without leaving their mark,/ Their leaden traces are indelible:/ Sorrow itself, war itself look out/ from the knowing eyes of Leningrad women.// Why did you portray me/ looking so brave and so beautiful,/ a woman at the peak of health and strength,/ with a proud, bright smile?// But, despite her severe reproaches/ the artist happily and proudly replies:/ 'Because you are Love and Life itself,/ the Courage and Glory of Leningrad!')

The artist, admittedly, has the last word, but his platitudes do not compare favourably with the woman's honest account of herself. Berggol'ts avoids the common Soviet treatment of women during wartime, exemplified in the artist's speech, which concentrated on a thoroughly idealised portrayal of women buoyed up by their 'effortless' moral powers. Instead she draws attention to the strains, mental and physical, which the women of Leningrad could not escape. The effects of war are not limited to the men on the battlefield, and will not end when the battle does.

By far the most vivid illustration, however, of the way in which war affected women can be found in Berggol'ts's prose fragment of 1962, 'Blokadnaia bania' (The Blockade Bath-House). Berggol'ts turned to autobiographical prose in the 1950s, publishing her *Dnevnye zvezdy* (Daytime Stars) in 1959. A second volume was planned for which 'The Blockade Bath-House' was destined, but the book was never completed. The fragment recalls a visit to a Leningrad bath-house twenty years previously and describes the emaciated women she found there. Berggol'ts's piece finds an echo in the blockade memoirs of the writer Kornei Chukovsky, who recalls his sense of shock on encountering women in a bath-house in March 1942. It was not mixed bathing that shocked Chukovsky. During the blockade the segregation of the sexes was often abandoned as an incomprehensible prejudice; modesty seemed irrelevant in a world so far removed from its pre-war self. It was the sight of the women's skeletal bodies which frightened him even more than his own emaciation.[38] The female figure used in contemporary literature and art to symbolise Mother Russia, tradition and continuity, was represented as being untouched by the war. The bodies of real women, particularly in Leningrad, showed what the war had done to them.

Like Chukovsky, Ol'ga Berggol'ts was appalled by the women she saw in a bath-house in the spring of 1942. Her portrait is, as his could not be, also a self-portrait:

> Тёмные, обтянутые шершавой кожей тела женщин – нет, даже не женщин – на женщин они походить перестали – груди у них исчезли, животы ввалились, багровые и синие пятна цинги ползли по коже. У некоторых же животы были безобразно вспучены, – над тонкими ножками, – ножки без икр, где самая толстая часть – щиколотка.[39]

(The women's bodies were dark, with rough skin stretched tightly over them – no, they weren't even women– they had ceased to look like women – their breasts had vanished, their stomachs had caved in, crimson and dark blue patches of scurvy had crawled across their skin. Some of them had hideously bloated stomachs, – above their skinny legs, – legs without calves, the thickest part of which was the ankle.)

Such physical detail would have been considered gratuitously naturalistic by wartime Soviet standards. To the reader familiar with Berggol'ts's wartime poetry such emphasis on deformity is unexpected, and therefore a forceful reminder of the realities of the blockade. In her poetry Berggol'ts focuses on sparse details – a slice of bread, a flickering candle – which indicate a reality too well known to her original audience to need further amplification. Yet the physical detail in 'The Blockade Bath-House' is an expression of the evils of war: the women's disfigured bodies, says the author, are more terrible than the sight of soldiers' severed limbs. These women represent the ideal of human beauty, love and motherhood, all of which are profaned by war; war has made them, in effect, into non-women.

The bathers' reactions when confronted by one woman whose normal physical appearance conforms to that ideal are uniformly hostile. Berggol'ts describes her own feelings of revulsion at the sight of a healthy, well-nourished female body, something she perceived as a mockery of the other women's degradation, a reminder of a female identity that they have lost. To the starving women there can only be one explanation: the newcomer has stolen food from them and their children. For them the vision of ideal womanliness is associated with corruption. At the end of the episode Berggol'ts presents one more female figure who is in direct contrast to the entire repertoire of female images in Soviet war poetry. If war has turned the bathers into non-women, this creature verges on the non-human. She is no immaculate Mother Russia, but a hideous spider-like old woman, almost bald and with a bulging hernia, seen by the author as an embodiment of war who, like one of the Greek Fates, impassively devours her innocent victims. The nightmarish spectacle of the blockade bath-house shows women as the victims and the embodiment of war. The male experience of combat is explicitly marginalised, war itself is presented in a defamiliarised form which reveals its hideous cruelty.

The reader returning from 'The Blockade Bath-House' to Berggol'ts's wartime poetry is, perhaps, minded to look for a hidden polemic deploring the way in which war has divorced women from their feminine identities. The fact that her heroines are shown in terms more commonly used to portray male heroics is surely an attempt to express the real value of women's achievements which would otherwise risk being overlooked. Yet the adoption of the heroic statue image could also be read to mean that the civic role required of them meant the destructive imposition of masculine values. Furthermore, scattered across Berggol'ts's post-war writings are hints that it was not just the war which imposed masculine values on Soviet women while devaluing feminine qualities, but the regime itself. In one poem of the 1950s, the 'unwomanly star' of Mars blazes above a woman yoked to the plough. Her diary of 1949 records a visit to a village where she saw women taking the place of horses at the plough. The legacy of the war means that there are few men who are not invalids, but it is the system itself that forces the women to shoulder an enormous burden of work and social obligations, to the detriment of their private well-being.[40]

Although Berggol'ts did not publicly or explicitly express doubts about the way Soviet society had marginalised and devalued women's experiences, her vigorous defence of lyric poetry and particularly love poetry in the early 1950s is also a defence of a literary genre which had been rejected, like women's private concerns, because it was deemed to have no social significance. Her protest emerges most clearly in a poem of 1960, first published only thirty years later:

Неузнанные женские стихи.
Они начнутся с самой первой строчки,

С тоски о муже. О погибшей дочке.
Пускай они унылы и плохи,
Я не для вас пишу. Глубокой ночью.
Одна. Опухли веки – навсегда,
Пришло страшнейшее из одиночеств:
То одиночество напрасного труда.
И всё напрасно: юность и дерзанье,
Развёрнутая сила белых плеч,
Неразделимое с тобой страданье
Виденье мести – одинокий меч.⁴¹

(Unrecognised women's verses./ They begin from the very first line/ with sorrow for my husband. About my dead daughter./ No matter that they're depressing and bad,/ it's not you I'm writing for. In the deepest night./ Alone. My eyelids are swollen – for ever,/ the most terrible loneliness of all has begun:/ the loneliness of work done in vain./ And all was in vain: youth and daring,/ the unfurled strength of white shoulders,/ the suffering I did not share with you,/ the vision of vengeance – a lonely sword.)

Here, for once, Berggol'ts describes her sense of exclusion not as a prisoner or one subjected to political persecution, and not as a writer struggling to make her voice heard, but as a woman, whose deepest concerns are deemed to count for very little. In wartime Berggol'ts shows women as the central figures in the drama of the Leningrad siege, privileged by their exemplary moral status. Yet this centrality depends on their assuming the role of warring citizens. The cost of this role to women is something that emerges only gradually in Berggol'ts's writing. The personal cost of serving as the 'Voice of Leningrad' emerges in her last long poem of the war years, where the violent images in her address to the city confirm the high price exacted by her civic role, and her self-sacrificial acceptance of that price:

Неся избранье трудное своё,
из недр своей души
            я стих свой выдирала,
не пощадив живую ткань её ...
и ясно мне судьбы моей веленье:
своим стихом на много лет вперёд
я к твоему пригвождена виденью,
я вмерзла
        в твой неповторимый лёд.⁴²

(Bearing my difficult destiny,/ from the depths of my soul/ I tore out my verses,/ not sparing my soul's living flesh .../ And my fate's command is clear:/ for many years to come/ I shall be nailed to your vision by my verses,/ frozen in your inimitable ice.)

Notes

This chapter, and the conference paper on which it is based, were written in the course of a Postdoctoral Research Fellowship awarded by the British Academy.

1. See A. Rubashkin, 'Vspominaia blokadnuiu muzu', *Neva*, no. 1 (1980), pp. 193–94; 'Golos Leningrada', *Zvezda*, no. 1 (1969), pp. 133–47.
2. 'Stikhi o sebe', *Sobranie sochinenii*, 3 vols (Leningrad, 1988–1990), vol. 2, p. 88 (hereafter referred to by volume and page number only).
3. See the poetry of Galina Nikolaeva and Iuliia Drunina, both of whom served at the front in the medical corps. Their work is discussed in K.M. Hodgson, 'The Other Veterans: Soviet Women's Poetry of World War Two', in John and Carol Garrard (eds), *World War Two and the Soviet People* (Basingstoke: Macmillan, 1993), pp. 82–85.
4. Jean Bethke Elshtain, *Women and War* (Brighton: Harvester, 1987), p. 4.
5. Michelle Perrot, 'The New Eve and the Old Adam', in Margaret Randolph Higonnet, Jane Jensen et al. (eds), *Behind the Lines: Gender and the Two World Wars* (New Haven and London: Yale University Press, 1987), p. 60.
6. Sandra Gilbert, 'Soldier's Heart: Literary Men, Literary Women and the Great War', in Higonnet, *Behind the Lines*, pp. 197–227. See Jan Montefiore, *Feminism and Poetry*, 2nd edition (London, 1994), pp. 65–70, for a discussion of women's poetry of the 1914–1918 war, and Gilbert's treatment of it.
7. Susan Schweik, 'Writing War Poetry Like a Woman', *Critical Enquiry*, vol. 13, no. 3 (1987), p. 541.
8. Laurie Smith, 'The Subject Makes a Difference: Poetry by Women Veterans of the Vietnam War', *Journal of American Culture*, vol. 16, no. 3 (1993), pp. 74–75.
9. Other Russian women poets writing during the war include Anna Akhmatova, Margarita Aliger, Vera Inber, Galina Nikolaeva, Iuliia Drunina, Mariia Petrovykh, Polina Kaganova, Elena Ryvina, Kseniia Nekrasova, Liudmila Popova, Ekaterina Sheveleva, Elizaveta Poliakova.
10. See A. Pavlovskii, *Stikh i serdtse* (Leningrad, 1962), p. 34.
11. Elshtain, *Women and War*, p. 9.
12. See Evgenii Dobrenko, '"Stoi! Kto idet?". U istokov sovetskogo manikheistva', *Znamia*, no. 3 (1993), pp. 180–89, on the militarisation of Soviet culture.
13. See Sharon Ouditt, *Fighting Forces, Writing Women: Identity and Ideology in the First World War* (London and New York: Routledge, 1994), for a discussion of women as 'temporary citizens' during the First World War.
14. See Joanna Hubbs, *Mother Russia: the Feminine Myth in Russian Culture* (Bloomington and Indianapolis: Indiana University Press, 1988).
15. See Barbara Heldt, *Terrible Perfection: Women and Russian Literature* (Bloomington and Indianapolis: Indiana University Press, 1987), pp. 12–15.
16. See Svetlana Aleksievich, *U voiny ne zhenskoe litso* (Moscow, 1989); John Erickson, 'Soviet Women at War', in Garrard, *World War Two and the Soviet People*, pp. 50–76.
17. See, for example, her poems 'Ia pet' ne liubliu v predosennikh poliakh …', vol. 1, p. 50; 'Predchuvstvie', vol. 1, p. 138.
18. See Andrej Tschernow, 'Die Todesration: weisse Flecken im sowjetischen Bild der Blockade', in Antje Leetz (ed.) *Blockade Leningrad 1941–1944: Dokumente und Essays von Russen und Deutschen* (Hamburg: Rowohlt, 1992), pp.186–95.
19. 'Fevral'skii dnevnik', vol. 2, p. 37.
20. Laurie Smith, 'The Subject Makes a Difference', p. 24. The shared experience of war, it has been suggested, actually promotes nurturing behaviour in male soldiers, as well as neuroses hitherto associated only with women. See Elshtain, *Women and War*, pp. 206–9; Sandra Gilbert, 'Soldier's Heart', in Higonnet, *Behind*

the Lines, p. 223; Elaine Showalter, 'Rivers and Sassoon: The Inscription of Male Gender Anxieties', in ibid., pp. 62-65.
21. For example, 'V gospitale', vol. 2, pp. 13-14; 'Ia budu segodnia s toboi govorit' ...', vol. 2, pp. 21-22; 'Pesnia o zhene patriota', vol. 2, pp. 56-57.
22. See Berggol'ts, 'Armiia', vol. 2, p. 32.
23. For example, Pavel Shubin, 'Russkii soldat', *Izbrannoe* (Moscow, 1988), p. 292; Sergei Podelkov, 'Vysota', *Radi zhizni na zemle: stikhotvoreniia o Velikoi Otechestvennoi voine* (Moscow, 1975), p. 124; Anatolii Chivilikhin, 'Iz dnevnika', *Golos vremeni* (Moscow-Leningrad, 1964), p. 29; Boris Slutskii, 'Pamiatnik', *Izbrannoe* (Moscow, 1980), p. 9.
24. See Hodgson, 'The Other Veterans', pp. 80-82.
25. See the death of the commander in 'Leningradskaia poema', vol. 2, p. 45.
26. 'Razgovor s sosedkoi', vol. 2, p. 31.
27. 'Leningradskaia osen'', vol. 2, p. 51. The religious significance of this image is intensified when the author imagines the ashes from this plank, mixed with nails, placed in a future museum as a relic of the siege. Related imagery can be found in 'Leningradskaia poema', vol. 2, p. 43; 'Razgovor s sosedkoi', vol. 2, pp. 30-31.
28. See her first poem of the war, 'My predchuvstvovali polykhan'e ...', vol. 2, p. 7.
29. See L. Levin, *Takie byli vremena*, 2nd edition (Moscow, 1991), pp. 8--21, 41, 48-51. See also L. Chashchina, 'Put'' vozvrata: k 80-letiiu so dnia rozhdeniia Ol'gi Fedorovnoi Berggol'ts', *Leningradskaia panorama*, no. 5 (1990), pp. 24-25.
30. From a letter to Dmitrii Khrenkov, quoted in his book on Berggol'ts, *Ot serdtsa k serdtsu*, 2nd edition (Leningrad, 1982), p.138.
31. See Hodgson, 'The Other Veterans', p.79.
32. See Beth Holmgren, *Women's Works in Stalin's Time: On Lidiia Chukovskaia and Nadezhda Mandelstam* (Bloomington: Indiana University Press, 1993), p. 2.
33. 'Iz chitatel'skoi pochty', in G.Tsurikova and V.Kuz'michev (comps.), *Vspominaia Ol'gu Berggol'ts* (Leningrad, 1979), pp. 253-64; A.Rubashkin (comp.), 'Desiat' pisem: vmesto literaturnogo portreta', *Zvezda*, no. 5 (1970), pp. 173-80.
34. 'Pamiati zashchitnikov', vol. 2, pp. 68-73; 'Mne ne povedat' o svoei utrate...', vol. 2, p. 87.
35. 'Otryvok', vol. 2, p. 53.
36. 'Fevral'skii dnevnik', vol. 2, pp. 34-39, contains particularly clear examples of these contrasting voices.
37. 'Leningradke', vol. 2, p. 223.
38. Kornei Chukovskii, 'V osazhdennom Leningrade: otryvki iz starykh voennykh zapisok', in A.M. Beilin (comp.), *Riadom s geroiami* (Moscow-Leningrad, 1967), pp. 21-22. For other accounts, see Ales' Adamovich and Daniil Granin, *Blokadnaia kniga* (Moscow, 1991), pp. 403-4.
39. 'Blokadnaia bania', *Ogonek*, no. 19 (1990), p. 16.
40. See her poem 'Pervorossiisk', *Izbrannye proizvedeniia* (Leningrad, 1983), p. 485, and a fragment in her diary for 1949, 'Iz dnevnikov Ol'gi Berggol'ts', *Znamia*, no. 3 (1991), p. 170. For further discussion, see K.M. Hodgson, 'Kitezh and the Commune: Recurrent Themes in the Work of Ol'ga Berggol'ts', *Slavonic and East European Review*, vol. 74, no. 1 (January 1996), pp. 1-18.
41. 'Neuznannye zhenskie stikhi ...', *Ekho* (Moscow, 1990), p. 28.
42. 'Tvoi put'', vol. 2, p. 84.

Chapter 9

A DIFFICULT JOURNEY: EVGENIIA GINZBURG AND WOMEN'S WRITING OF CAMP MEMOIRS

Natasha Kolchevska

[I want] to reveal to the reader the heroine's spiritual evolution, the gradual transformation of a naive young communist idealist into someone who had tasted unforgettably the fruits of the tree of the knowledge of good and evil, a human being who amid all her setbacks and sufferings also had moments (however brief) of fresh insight in her search for truth. It is this cruel journey of the soul and not just the chronology of my sufferings that I want to bring home to the reader. (Evgeniia Ginzburg, *Whirlwind,* II: 423)[1]

A combination of spiritual autobiography, personal testimony, and *Bildungsroman,* Evgeniia Ginzburg's six-hundred page narrative, which ends with these words, is one of the best known and most widely read accounts of the Stalinist labour camps. Often mentioned in historical and literary surveys[2] and widely assigned to students of twentieth-century Russia, recently *Whirlwind* has attracted critical attention for its place in Russian cultural and social history and as a major work in the tradition of Russian women's autobiographical or memoir literature.[3] I will examine Ginzburg's account of her eighteen years of incarceration and exile in the Soviet Gulag of Kolyma, Magadan and other points in Russia's Far East as an example of women's autobiographical writing that lies within and outside the traditions of other autobiographical and memoir literature, and as a work that both internalises and creates a counter-discourse to the prevailing paradigms that shaped Ginzburg's own awakening to moral and literary consciousness.

Russian literature has never drawn strict distinctions between writers, philosophers, and socio-political activists. Much as it is a part of the literary process, what writers write and say has also been seen as part of larger social and historical processes. As the very different examples of Solzhenitsyn and Siniavsky illustrate, a hallmark of dissident writing during the Soviet period was the writer's use of his own experientially based history to challenge official history's claims to coherence and power.[4] Ginzburg's narrative falls within this important tradition, but no less significant is its rendition of counter-history from a feminine perspective, a perspective which, because it emphasises the interdependence, multiplicity, human solidarity and equally human complicity of that hell that was the Gulag, is a particularly telling human narrative of this defining Soviet experience.

While it stands squarely in the tradition of camp memoirs, both the psychological perceptions and the narrative strategies of *Whirlwind* reflect a woman's consciousness, in that the loci of memory and the means of rendering them have a pronounced gender inflection. The distinctions between autobiography and memoirs as practised by men and women, and the dangers of ignoring specifically feminine approaches to various types of life writing, have been widely discussed in recent literature.[5]

In particular, using developmental studies conducted by Nancy Chodorow and Carol Gilligan, numerous feminist critics have noted the relational focus and interdependence of women. Extending this to women writers, Sidonie Smith observes that 'males represent experiences of self, others, space, and time in individualistic, objective, and distant ways, while females represent experiences in relatively interpersonal, subjective and immediate ways'.[6] Elissa Gelfand, who has focused on narratives written from prison by French women, finds that 'women's attitude is not one of destructive hostility toward others, but is instead diffuse and sometimes self-depriving in proportion to the adversity they have met'.[7] Barbara Heldt, one of the few Slavists to incorporate considerations of gender into her discussion of Ginzburg's writings, compares her relational approach to Solzhenitsyn's heroic, self-confident one: 'Ginzburg, while describing the most abject inhumanities, also seeks and finds the human spirit: this is her "great aim", but it is performed rather than stated. Her continual forging of links with other human beings ... gave life to others and surviving strength to herself'.[8] The aim of this essay is to examine the strategies through which this relational, diffuse self is deployed in *Whirlwind* to give authority and conviction to the author's reconstruction of her experience.

Rather than relate a case history of one exemplary figure's trek through the Stalinist camps, to have, as it were, one speak *for* the many, *Whirlwind* is emphatically one woman speaking as one *of* the many. While Solzhenitsyn's Ivan Denisovich marshals all of his efforts to preserve the unitary self, Ginzburg's strategies are interwoven with, and indivisible from, her relations with the women and men who share her life in camp and exile. In one sense, she tells the story of a particular Soviet woman, defined by socio-economic, class, and personal boundaries: privileged and well-educated, a historian, educator and journalist, with all the connections that came with membership in a prominent Communist family, Ginzburg was among those women who consciously took advantage of the fruits of post-Revolutionary policies promoting women's social emancipation and intellectual equality. The obverse of those policies was a negation (for both men and women) of individuality and interiority: social, collective goals subsumed private life, and women were pushed into a social system that they had little hand in defining. By the 1930s, this was complicated by Stalin's contempt for women (whom he called 'herrings with ideas'[9]).

The relative singularity of Ginzburg's position, and of her implied superiority, however, is gradually transformed after her arrest, and *Whirlwind* quickly becomes the story of one distinguishable member of a collective, in this case the collective of tens of thousands of innocent women caught in the net of purges and repressions. I find that the distinction that Doris Sommer makes between the dominant tropes of traditional autobiography and of the Latin American testimonial is useful here:

> The singular [heroine] represents the plural not because [she] replaces or subsumes the group but because the speaker is a distinguishable part of the whole ... There is a fundamental difference ... between the metaphor of autobiography and heroic narrative in general, which assumes an identity by substituting one (superior) signifier for another (I for we, leader for follower, Christ for the faithful) and metonymy, a lateral identification through relationship, which acknowledges the possible differences among us as components of the whole.[10]

Put another way, the hierarchical arrangements of Ginzburg's pre-arrest life, in which she played the part of a naïve, conscientious acolyte entering the seemingly safe niche of sanctioned Soviet institutions – family, academic career, Party worker – are transformed into a series of lateral relationships that emphasise personal and communal interdependency as they preserve individual difference.

It is this shared experience, through which the author/heroine and her subjects create each other, which she narrates, speaking not *for* them, in the colonising voice of a master author, but as *one* of them.

After her arrest, as the earlier respected authority figures are replaced by figures of brute power and coercion with no moral or ideological force behind them, Ginzburg must rely on other models to sustain her. The implications of this change for her 'spiritual evolution' are dual. Faced with the gross illogicality of a system whose apparent aim is to arrest and annihilate those who a few years – even months – earlier had been its model citizens, the post-arrest Evgeniia is continually forced to go beyond the received wisdom of her mentors. Indeed, her strong belief in the superiority of logical thinking and the suppression of emotions, and her participation in the construction of meaning on a grand scale, give way to more intuitive forms of knowing. To cite one example, as the threat of arrest grows, her wise, peasant mother-in-law advises her to disappear into the countryside. With time, Evgeniia understands the wisdom of that warning, and her own political naïvety in ignoring it.

Repeatedly, the rational Communist Ginzburg's received knowledge is challenged, but rather than respond to these challenges abstractly, Ginzburg sifts her own and others' responses through a relational grid: she uses virtually every encounter to evaluate her own behaviour, and to examine the growth of a new consciousness, of a new identity that is truer to herself than was the old one. With her arrest comes the first awareness of herself as an independent consciousness: 'For the first time in my life', she reflects, 'I was faced by the problem of having to think things out for myself, of analysing circumstances independently and deciding my own line of conduct' (I, 74). Accustomed to seeking advice and guidance from fellow (male) Communists, after her arrest she turns first to a male prisoner in the adjacent cell for explanations of what is happening to her: 'All these anguished questions I put to Garei, ten years my senior in age and fifteen as a Party member. But his advice was not such that I could follow it, and it left me still more puzzled' (I, 74). Tellingly, while her communication with Garei is verbal (or rather, telegraphic, since they communicate, à la Vera Figner, by knocking out coded messages through their prison walls), Ginzburg's first indication of what is to follow in Stalin's purges of Communist Party members comes through the 'tragic story' of 'Comrade Pitkovskaia'. Her tale, which like Ginzburg's was of a life totally dedicated to the cause of the Party (selfless, hardworking, guilt-ridden over her husband's joining the opposition in 1927), ends in suicide after she loses her job as a result of her husband's arrest. While the message from both Garei and Pitkovskaia is the same – think for yourself – Pitkovskaia's is rendered mutely, symbolically: 'As I looked at the sad little grave, surmounted by neither cross nor star, I told myself: No, I won't do that. I shall put up a fight. They may kill me if they can – but I won't help them' (I: 19). The exemplary woman Communist's mode, involving total submission to the male-defined collective will, will not be Ginzburg's.

The narrator's voice in *Whirlwind* is personal and individualised, yet it is constantly engaged in a variety of dialogues with 'significant others'. While the Party demanded that these significant others be fellow Communists, and that non-Party members be treated with suspicion, Ginzburg's own experience, as it incorporates the full range of Soviet society, and of Russian culture,[11] reveals the inauthenticity of that system. Communication is more effective, significant and diverse in those later prison and exile experiences than it had been in her pre-arrest life. As the processes leading to her arrest take their toll, Ginzburg's conversations even with her husband become increasingly circumspect and unsatisfactory. In retrospect, Ginzburg sees the inauthenticity of her whole life prior to her arrest, an inauthenticity that grows with ironic momentum in the narrative's first chapters. The chapter entitled 'The year 1937 begins', which immediately precedes her expulsion from the Party, and is, metaphorically, the focal point of her pre-arrest life, consists of two incidents. The first is a tensely dramatic scene in which, after husband and wife quarrel yet again about the meaning of the mass arrests of Party members, and she physically and symbolically pulls away from him, Ginzburg irretrievably loses her gold watch in the snow:

> Our troubled faces, as we bent over the snowdrift and dug into it with our bare hands, seemed to foreshadow the misfortune that was almost upon us. The dreadful thing was that each of us knew exactly what the other was thinking: that we were only pretending to be upset by the loss of the watch and determined to find it. It wasn't the watch but our lives that were lost ... What could a quarrel between husband and wife matter now? We no longer had a part in life with its ordinary human relations. But this was only between the lines, as it were, and was unspoken even between ourselves. (I: 37)

This incident is followed directly by the family's last holiday together at a vacation home for the Party élite (a former estate of Prince Viazemsky, Ginzburg points out), during which 'a large number of "ruling class" children...divided all those around them into categories according to the make of their cars. Lincolns and Buicks rated high, Fords low'. The juxtaposition of these two charged scenes illustrates Ginzburg's navigation of two types of imagery: while the children's shallow view of people as extensions of their cars is primarily a social comment, losing her watch is part of a continuum of temporal and spatial imagery that forms one of the central matrices for the narrative.

The Russian and English language editions of Ginzburg's memoir signify two major matrices of narrative organisation. The Russian edition is subtitled, *Khronika vremen kul'ta lichnosti* (A Chronicle of the Times of the Cult of Personality), while the two volumes of the English edition omit any subtitle, presenting instead maps that trace Ginzburg's journey and the location of the major camps in the Soviet Far East. Each edition evokes a defining category in human experience – historical time and geographical space – which Mikhail Bakhtin has suggestively defined through his concept of the chronotope as 'the intrinsic connectedness of temporal and spatial relationships that are artistically expressed in literature', and 'the place where the knots of narrative are tied and untied'.[12] Several chronotopic motifs coexist in Ginzburg's narrative, including what Bakhtin has characterised as 'the adventure time of everyday life', in which the hero undergoes a metamorphosis and has 'individual responsibility, experiences guilt, and can therefore be punished and ultimately redeemed'.[13] However, this chronotope is limited by its separation of the individual's life from that of his society: '[The hero's life] is his own business, is unaffected by specific social forces or historical changes, and leaves no mark on society'.[14] A more modern chronotope, that of the *Bildungsroman*, or what Bakhtin called 'the novel of historical emergence', situates individual growth within historical and social forces: 'the hero emerges along with the world and he reflects the historical emergence of the world itself'.[15] By contrast with earlier chronotopes, this one involves greater interiority, creative initiative, historical or time consciousness, and 'social becomings'.

My purpose is less to elaborate on the applicability of these and other possible chronotopes to Ginzburg's narrative, however, than to address the gender inflection of space and time relationships, to explore the ways in which these are expressed differently through a woman's consciousness. Ginzburg's narrative offers an interesting negotiation of the commonplace that women's literature is preoccupied with domestic, confined space. In many ways, her tale focuses on what Claudine Herrmann has called 'the material continuity – of daily life and of the species'.[16] Although not through her own agency, Ginzburg is torn from that domestic space and propelled into a trajectory that continues through most of her adult life (time) across a space that is as vast geographically as the (ex-)Soviet Union itself. Paradoxically, while her freedom of movement is severely restricted by camp regimens, commandants' caprices, and Kolyma's unforgiving climate, the heroine's forced journey in *Whirlwind* (her 'cruel journey of the soul') is the spatial correlative and the *sine qua non* of her quest for spiritual self-discovery.

Ginzburg repeatedly domesticates space by carving up her road through life into tameable, personalised segments that conflate physical and social realms. Soon after her arrest the mass holding cell becomes a place of extended and shared sisterhood, as women with vastly different backgrounds share the physical and psychic space of their plights. Later, she nostalgically laments having to leave her isolation cell (which ironically, because of overcrowding, she shares with a cellmate): 'Could we not live just a little longer in our cell, in our very own solitary cell? We had left part of our lives in it; we had rejoiced in books and told stories of our childhood. How could we leave it all of a sudden like this?' (I: 266). Sometimes through self-agency, more often through 'luck', 'miracles', and 'the fantastic' (Ginzburg's words), she is transferred from the hostile and open space of the outdoors, where women are sent to fell centuries-old trees, to those familiar women's environments of the dairy farm, the kitchen, the hospital, the nursery and the school. At the dairy farm, 'the thought that I should be sleeping not on a plank bunk but in a completely separate cubbyhole of my own gave me back my dignity as a human being' (II: 50). Not for the first time, human relationships and humanised space converge here, and her reconstituted dignity is reinforced by an 'intense friendship' with another prisoner, Wilhelmina Rupert, a tally clerk at the farm. Once released to permanent exile in Magadan, improving her living quarters becomes a major preoccupation, and this quest converges with a close friendship with her oldest friend from prison and the camps, Iuliia, and the (re-)establishment of her family.[17]

Conversely, on those occasions when Ginzburg is forced to confront raw, untamed nature, she does so by accepting the power of her surroundings rather than attempting to test their limits, like the paradigmatic male hero of adventure and heroic tales (and of socialist realist fiction) would be expected to do. Not knowing whether she will live or die as, deathly ill, she is carried onshore after a horrendous month-long sea passage from the mainland, Ginzburg greets her fate with Buddhist-like acceptance:

> The sky began to glow with wonderful shades of mauve and lilac: my first Kolyma dawn was breaking. I felt, all of a sudden, a strange lightness and acceptance of my fate. True, this was a cruel and alien land. Neither my mother nor my sons would find the way to my grave. But all the same, it was part of mother earth – I had reached land, and need no longer fear the leaden, shark-infested waters of the Pacific Ocean. (I: 360)

Later, in a dramatic chapter redolent of Russian Romantic fiction, Ginzburg's awe and fear of Siberian nature, rather than a sense of conquest, come to the fore (II: 174–79). Thus, while not reversing the rhetoric of domesticity and continuity, she explores, appropriates and subtly alters it, expanding her own concepts of self and agency in the process.

As Ginzburg is wrenched out of the comfortable, but hierarchical, spaces of her previous life other kinds of physical and mental 'signifying spaces', to use Julia Kristeva's term,[18] now defined by women, supplant those 'masculine' ones. The result is a world with two categories of space: a *macrocosm* – the whole Gulag system, in which concepts of hierarchy, power, and domination rule, and the disposition of one group's space (the prisoners') is controlled by others,[19] and a *microcosm* – in which there is a respect for what Claudine Hermann calls 'an empty space...a [protective] distance'[20] for the mental and physical integrity of others. Ginzburg uses recurring images of serf or slave/master relationships to characterise the first category. The second category, that space of women prisoners' 'shared suffering and common shame' (II: 122) she represents through venues of common physical and psychological bonding: the holding cell, the transit train and ship, the various shared quarters in the camps. Later, when she is (provisionally) freed, the theme is repeated – first in the room she shares with Julia, then the apartment in a barracks she finds for her newly formed, fragile second family.

Like the post-arrest Ginzburg, this new family – which consists of her second husband, Anton Walter; an adopted daughter, Tonia; and later, her younger, surviving son, Vasily Aksenov (subsequently to become a famous writer) – has been created out of the pain and active resistance to the life-negating forces of the camps. Moreover, its existence is based on the heroine's having attained a higher level of consciousness through her search for a more authentic self. Significantly, her 'adoption' of each of her new family members involves a choice or a deed that is a defining moment in the change and continuity that define Ginzburg. Anton, a German Catholic, a homeopath, a healer – as Ginzburg learns to be during her imprisonment – and a gentle gossip who is wise like her ex-mother-in-law, is the antipode of the ideologically correct and humourless Pavel Aksenov. Typically, Ginzburg's first finding Tonia involves a certain element of luck, but her fight to adopt the little girl involves a challenge to make the system decide in favour of family and humanity. Significantly, when Ginzburg finally sees her sister again after a fourteen-year hiatus, she

> turned out to be a complete stranger. With all her ardent family love for me, her complete willingness to come to my aid in whatever way she could, she displayed an organic indifference to everything that was a matter of burning, consuming concern to me, all that for me and for all of *us* [Ginzburg's emphasis] mattered most for the rest of our days. (II: 410)

Blood ties cannot replace the shared experiences of the camps; again this is expressed not as her sister's rational decision but as an 'organic indifference', an inability to know with all of one's being the form and significance of those experiences. Ginzburg has moved from a perception of the world as, to quote Bakhtin again, 'a ready-made givenness' (*gotovaia dannost'*) to something created by human effort.[21]

In Ginzburg's woman-centred world, women's concerns, and specifically, concerns about the plights of their bodies and of their children, play a significant role. Thus, although probably not consciously, since she describes her journey as one of 'spiritual evolution', she engages in a dialogue with a masculine tradition that has valorised spiritual over physical experience, and the general over the individual. Even when she claims that the physical pain she and her fellow cellmates and Kolyma prisoners felt was 'inexpressible', she does not accept these assaults stoically or philosophically, but rather, expresses her fears and anxieties personally and vividly: 'If only [Zina] had known how little use I was to find for higher education and how much for physical endurance' (I: 134), Evgeniia comments when a fellow prisoner assures her that she will land on her feet because she is an intellectual.

As in male-authored camp literature, individual responses to the physical realities of the Gulag are a recurring theme. Ginzburg is acutely demoralised by the deterioration of her own body: at her first interrogation, El'shin, her most humane interrogator, comments on her attractiveness (I: 67), but not long after, following a protracted interrogation, she asks herself, 'Was this a conspiracy of all the demons in hell to turn me from a thirty-year-old woman into an old crone of a hundred?' (I: 93). It is not long before she, like Zina, her closest friend in the communal holding cell, becomes a 'bruised and swollen, classless, ageless, almost sexless ... groaning piece of flesh' (I: 126). When she is manhandled by a guard in her isolation cell, it is 'his paws on my breast' that unleash a physical resistance of which she had been previously incapable, and shortly thereafter, having been able to wash herself with a minute quantity of water, 'now I was once more a human being and not a grimy, hunted animal' (I: 218–19). Expressions of her palpable fear of conditions and illnesses range from cessation of menstruation to dysentery and breast cancer. However, here Ginzburg's concern about her own hurting body is often accompanied by an attempt to respond, through caring and nurturing, to the physical pain of others. Emulating the other-directedness of earlier perfect Russian heroines, Ginzburg is ever selfless: although she compares her own physical condition with that of other prisoners, expressing relief, for example, that she, unlike women prisoners interrogated after her, was not physically tortured, she is most impassioned about the physical condition of others. Thus, the common plights of women's bodies *embody* their relationships to one another, as they fight the 'melancholy of non-existence', the annihilation of body and therefore spirit, which the camps did all in their power to force on them.

Ironically, as the years in the Gulag contrive to rob her and other women of their femininity and sexuality, these become the very modes of individual and collective resistance. Remnants of 'feminine' clothing from their pre-arrest lives are joyfully shared, and become secret treasures to be hidden at all cost from the guards. Rare sensuous pleasures are deliciously remembered many years later. Sometimes, as when a doctor prescribes a hot, pine bath in a 'dazzling, white' tub, for the dysentery-ridden Evgeniia, her response is individual, purely sensory. More often, however, these are loci of mutual joy: taken in pairs from their isolation cells to the bath-house one last time before their journey east to Siberia, Ginzburg recalls the women's feelings of 'devotion and true love for one another' (I: 263–64). Freely chosen sexual pleasure (as opposed to the ever-present possibility of rapes by the 'common' prisoners and guards) is sought, even in the knowledge that it could only take place in 'hasty, perilous meetings in some sketchy shelter' (II: 13). Perhaps the best image of the pursuit of sex in the face of danger is the case of a love affair between a former ballerina and a former actor: 'there was always the fear of being caught, exposed to public shame, and assigned to a penal labour brigade, i.e., posted to some lethal spot; you might end up paying for your date with nothing less than your life' (II: 12), she concludes.[22] While Solzhenitsyn puts a love affair to similar use in *The First Circle*, Ginzburg's account achieves its particular poignancy because, while she is sympathetic to the man, she identifies with the woman, who is quickly robbed of her beauty, as she is robbed of her baby, dead before he is six months old. Even though, as Conquest reports, women 'on the whole seem to have survived [the camps] much better than men',[23] often they pay the higher emotional and physical price.

The mother/child matrix serves as a way of comprehending the world, as it enables Ginzburg to contextualise her own fate. Pondering her likely execution, she thinks, 'how could they possibly think of killing me for no reason at all – me, Mother's Genia [the familiar form of Evgeniia], Alesha's and Vasia's mother, by what right …' (I: 173). Later, some of the most poignant fears in Ginzburg's life revolve around the possible loss of her own motherhood:

> All these reasonable daytime fears were nothing compared with my dark, night-time forebodings, which were utterly irrational. Perhaps as a result

of someone's evil designs I was doomed to lose both my children. Alesha was no more ... and Vasia, the last spark of my now almost extinct life ... would simply disappear into thin air. And again, as during those sleepless nights at El'gen, I heard the formula of despair hammering in my ears. No one will ever call me Mother again. (II: 260-61)

In the single passage in *Whirlwind* in which Ginzburg, having learned of her mother's death, speaks of her, she does so by juxtaposing images of her courage and endurance with the illicit power and 'grotesque kingdom' of Stalin, whom she variously dubs the 'Georgian Serpent' and 'Great Slaughterer'. Here, the thread tying mother and daughter is not verbal, but visual: while all her mother's letters had been taken away from her, two photographs – of her mother as a schoolgirl and as an old woman – preserve the memory, and she is reincarnated through her daughter's words: 'she was a quite ordinary, uncelebrated mother. The mother of a prisoner. She had accomplished her silent, unconscious feat of endurance in the years when she was an aged widow without a home of her own' (II, 307). I am aware that Ginzburg's iconic cameo of her mother, which owes much to the nineteenth-century selfless and silent mothers of Russian prisoners and revolutionaries, may pose problems for the modern reader, yet I offer it as a way of understanding her underlying values, values that inform her subjectivity with a consciousness that is based on a biological and familial continuum.

Discourses on motherhood, on mother-child relations and on the different fates of children who shared, through no fault of their own, in their mothers' fates, serve a central function in Ginzburg's narrative. Motivated by a mother's anxiety and grief over separation from her own two sons (the older one, Alesha, dies during the siege of Leningrad), this discourse goes beyond concrete feelings about biological children to function as a heuristic model for human relations. Repeatedly, she remarks that speaking of their children is forbidden by the women prisoners themselves, and this prohibition makes the pain of their despair more palpable, their silenced grief and despair a common bond. Perhaps the most telling use of the mother-child relationship and of its tie to language and memory, is that of the prisoners' young children who populate the children's home in the El'gen camp where she was 'lucky' enough to work for a year. Volume Two opens with Ginzburg situating the home in terms of exterior and interior signifying spaces:

> The children's home was also part of the camp compound. It had its own guardhouse, its own gates, and its own barbed wire ... The very fact of being there restored to me the long-lost faculty of weeping. For more

than three years my eyes had smarted from tearless despair. But now, in July 1940, I sat on a low bench ... and cried. I cried without stopping ... Yes, this undoubtedly was a penal camp hut. But it smelled of warm semolina and wet pants. Someone's bizarre imagination had combined the trappings of the prison world with simple, human, and touchingly familiar things now so far out of reach that they seemed no more than a dream ...

[The children] aroused my atavistic instincts. I wanted to gather them all together and hug them tight so that nothing could hurt them. (II, 3)

The message of the children's home is dual: through her work in the home, Ginzburg's thread to her own motherhood is rewoven, but she also confronts the truth that these children, raised in the liminal space between men's and women's worlds, are scarred, different. Undernourished because their mother's milk is 'acidulous from ... grief' (the mothers were not allowed to stay with their daughters and sons), few of the children even know the word 'Mamma'. Most, even the four-year-olds, cannot talk: 'inarticulate howls, mimicry, and blows were the main means of communication'; and they eat 'like little convicts, hastily, with no thought for anything else'. Children such as these, even those who survive, will have no empathy with their parents' suffering or attempt to preserve their memory.

Nevertheless, this is not Ginzburg's last word on children and memory. Volume Two goes on to recount Ginzburg's creation of a second family, a hybrid, with her son Vasia's arrival in Magadan, of the earlier one and of that camp experience which shaped and transformed Ginzburg into the author of this narrative. By extracting one child, Tonia, from the children's home, that 'most satanic invention of all inventions' that the 'Georgian Serpent' could conjure and by imparting to her surviving biological son her own experiences of the Gulag she, like her own mother, never loses faith in the ability of children to understand the truth, and to preserve memory.[24] The connection that she makes between biological continuity and human memory, then, is twofold. First, both are interwoven facets of human survival: children, like texts, offer the best, most enduring hope for the human species. Secondly, as products of both cyclical (biological) and linear (cultural, historical) phenomena, children and texts are bridges that their (female) creators construct between the here and now and eternity or, to paraphrase Kristeva, 'between the singular and the ethical'.[25] Compassion and care move from the sphere of the individual, familial, and domestic to principles of justice in a cultural and historical context. In this sense, Ginzburg's text is another of her 'children', a child who, unlike Alesha, will survive to leave its mark on history.

Notes

1. All references in the text are to the two-volume English edition of Evgeniia Ginzburg's *Journey into the Whirlwind* (San Diego: Harcourt Brace Jovanovich, 1967) and *Within the Whirlwind* (San Diego: Harcourt Brace Jovanovich, 1981). The Russian version, *Krutoi marshrut*, was serialised in the Latvian journal *Daugava* in 1989 and published in Moscow by Sovetskii pisatel' in 1990. For the sake of brevity, when referring to the text I abbreviate the title as *Whirlwind*, followed by volume and page number
2. For discussions of Ginzburg's memoir, see Adele Barker's entry on Evgeniia Ginzburg in Marina Ledkovsky, Charlotte Rosenthal and Mary Zirin (eds), *Dictionary of Russian Women Writers* (Westport, CT: Greenwood, 1994), pp. 205–6; Edward J. Brown, *Russian Literature Since the Revolution* (Cambridge, MA: Harvard University Press, 1982), pp. 287–91; Olga Cooke, 'Evgeniia Ginzburg', in Neil Cornwell (ed.), *Reference Guide to Russian Writers* (London: Fitzroy Dearborn, 1998), pp. 320–22; Barbara Heldt, *Terrible Perfection* (Bloomington: Indiana University Press, 1987), pp. 153–56; Vol'fgang Kazak, *Entsiklopedicheskii slovar' russkoi literatury s 1917 goda* (London: Overseas Publications Interchange, 1988), pp. 212–13; Catriona Kelly, *A History of Russian Women's Writing, 1820–1992* (Oxford: Clarendon Press, 1994), pp. 367–68; and Marshall Shatz, 'Soviet Society and the Purges of the Thirties in the Mirror of Memoir Literature', *Canadian-American Slavic Studies*, vol. 2, no. 2 (1973), pp. 250–61.
3. For a fascinating analysis of Ginzburg's memoir in terms of cultural codes, see Nadya Peterson, 'Dirty Women: Cultural Connotations of Cleanliness in Soviet Russia', in Helena Goscilo and Beth Holmgren (eds), *Russia, Women, Culture* (Bloomington: Indiana University Press, 1996), pp. 180–97, *passim*. For a discussion of Ginzburg and autobiographical writing by Russian women, see Beth Holmgren, 'For the Good of the Cause: Russian Women's Autobiography in the Twentieth Century', in Toby W. Clyman and Diana Greene (eds), *Women Writers in Russian Literature* (Westport, CT: Praeger, 1994), pp. 131–34.
4. For more on the challenge that first-person narratives present to official history, see Donald Fanger, 'Conflicting Imperatives in the Model of the Russian Writer: The Case of Tertz/Sinyavsky', in Gary Saul Morson (ed.), *Literature and History: Theoretical Problems and Russian Case Studies* (Stanford: Stanford University Press, 1986), pp. 112–13, and Jane Gary Harris, 'Diversity of Discourse: Autobiographical Statements in Theory and Practice', in Jane Gary Harris (ed.), *Autobiographical Statements in Twentieth-Century Russian Literature* (Princeton: Princeton University Press, 1990), p. 4.
5. The literature on women's autobiography has grown quite extensive. The texts that I have used for my discussion include: Shari Benstock, 'Authorizing the Autobiographical', and Susan Stanford Friedman, 'Women's Autobiographical Selves: Theory and Practice', both in Shari Benstock (ed.), *The Private Self: Theory and Practice of Women's Autobiographical Writings* (Chapel Hill: University of North Carolina Press, 1988), pp. 10-33 and 34-62; Nancy Chodorow, *Feminism and Psychoanalytic Theory* (New Haven: Yale University Press, 1989); Leigh Gilmore, *Autobiographics: A Feminist Theory of Women's Self-Representation* (Ithaca: Cornell University Press, 1994), pp. 16-64; Françoise Lionnet, *Autobiographical Voices: Race, Gender, Self-Portraiture* (Ithaca: Cornell University Press, 1989); and Sidonie Smith, *A Poetics of Women's Autobiography: Marginality and the Fictions of Self-Representation* (Bloomington: Indiana University Press, 1987).
6. Smith, *A Poetics of Women's Autobiography*, p. 13.
7. Elissa Gelfand, *Imagination in Confinement: Women's Writings from French Prisons* (Ithaca: Cornell University Press, 1983), p. 125.

8. Barbara Heldt, *Terrible Perfection*, p. 153, remarks:

> How different [Ginzburg's] attitude toward the meaning of her own life from that of Solzhenitsyn, who incarnates ultimate male autobiographical certainty:
>
> [as he interprets it] I have done many things in my life that conflicted with the great aims I had set myself – and something has always set me on the true path again. I have become so used to this, come to rely on it so much, that the only task I need set myself is to interpret as clearly and as quickly as I can each major event in my life. (Alexander Solzhenitsyn, *The Oak and the Calf*, transl. Harry Willetts [New York: Harper and Row, 1980], p.111.)

9. See Rosalind Marsh, 'The birth, death, and rebirth of feminist writing in Russia', in Helena Forsås-Scott (ed.), *Textual Liberation: European Feminist Writing in the Twentieth Century* (London: Routledge, 1991), p. 149.
10. Doris Sommer, '"Not Just a Personal Story": Women's Testimonials and the Plural Self', in B. Brodzki and C. Schenk (eds), *Life/Lines: Theorizing Women's Autobiography* (Ithaca, NY: Cornell University Press, 1988), p. 108. The basic distinction that Warren and Wellek make between these two tropes is also germane: 'metonymy and metaphor may be the characterizing structures of two poetic types – poetry of association by contiguity, and poetry of association by comparison', in R. Warren and A. Wellek, *Theory of Literature*, 2nd edition (Chicago: University of Chicago Press, 1956), pp. 184–85. Ginzburg's narrative, focusing as it does on the female prisoners' interrelatedness and lateral identification (at least with political prisoners, if not with common criminals) uses metonymy as its basic structure, while, paradoxically, the comparison of Ivan Denisovich's seemingly trivial, everyday actions with those of his campmates, singles out and heroicises him.
11. Ginzburg's references to Russian and European culture, and her incorporation of female historical figures into her narrative, give it an intertextuality and resonance that space does not allow me to explore here. Like the bonds of sisterhood, motherhood and childhood that I do discuss later, these references are manifold and wide-ranging.
12. Mikhail Bakhtin, 'Forms of Time and of the Chronotope in the Novel', in M. Holquist (ed.), *The Dialogic Imagination: Four Essays by M. M. Bakhtin* (Austin: University of Texas Press, 1990), p. 387.
13. In Katerina Clark and Michael Holquist, *Mikhail Bakhtin* (Cambridge, MA: Harvard University Press, 1984). As Clark and Holquist observe:

> The time aspect of this chronotope type is thus characterised by a sudden change that leaves its trace in the further life of the individual. It is a time of biographical crisis, threshold moments. The corresponding space of this chronotype is characterized by the fusion [as Bakhtin writes] of 'the course of an individual's life (at its major turning points) with his actual progress through space or his road – i.e. his wanderings ... Space becomes more concrete and saturated with a time that is more substantial'. (pp. 283–84).

14. Gary Saul Morson and Caryl Emerson, *Mikhail Bakhtin: Creation of a Prosaics* (Stanford: Stanford University Press, 1990), p. 387.
15. Ibid., p. 411.
16. Claudine Herrmann, 'Les coordonées féminines: espace et temps', translated in Elaine Marks and Isabelle de Courtivron (eds), *The New French Feminisms* (Amherst: University of Massachusetts Press, 1980), p. 172.
17. Kelly, *A History of Russian Women's Writing*, p. 368, and Holmgren, 'For the Good of the Cause', pp. 132–33, both mention the revalorisation of domestic space and everyday human values in recent women's literature, including prison camp memoirs. Holmgren writes:

> As their political goals become more generalized and focused on the issue of human rights [women memoirists] both reflect and help facilitate the movement of post-Stalin Soviet soci-

ety away from public life ... to the private sphere, personal attachments, and individual fulfillment. ... They revalue the domestic sphere – that prison-house for earlier generations of female revolutionaries – as a locus of material pleasure, moral value, and freedom. Their quest, however, signalled no simple retreat into domesticity; after all, once safe at home, they committed the oppositional act of writing their memoirs.

18. Julia Kristeva, 'Women's Time', in Toril Moi (ed.), *The Kristeva Reader* (Oxford: Blackwell, 1986), p. 209.
19. Herrmann, 'Les coordonées féminines', characterises this category as 'a space of conquest and expansion, *full* space', p. 169.
20. Ibid., p. 115.
21. Morson and Emerson, *Mikhail Bakhtin*, p. 489, n. 11.
22. Robert Conquest, *The Great Terror: A Reassessment* (New York: Oxford University Press, 1990), p. 315. In one of his few comments on sexuality in the labour camps, Conquest notes that 'all accounts agree that even the debilitating work and diet did not damp down [women's] sexual feelings, as it did in the case of men': ibid. He also mentions the frequent mass rapes of women political prisoners by female criminal prisoners or *urkas*.

    Ginzburg often drops behind the veil of Soviet-style *pudeur*, and avoids any discussions of sex. The story of her courtship with Anton Walter makes no mention of any nascent sexual feelings, and in the one chapter in which she focuses on the difficulties of sex and love among prisoners, she omits the doings of the criminal prisoners: 'The professional criminals are beyond the bounds of humanity. I have no desire to describe their orgies, although I had much to put up with as an involuntary witness' (II: 12). Ginzburg includes one passage (II: 42) in which a female prisoner, in exchange for bread, consents to oral sex with a peasant. The passage focuses on the psychological consequences for the woman, and abstains from any graphic detail.
23. In an interview project with camp survivors, Irina Shcherbakova concludes that women constituted about two-thirds of camp survivors, indicating a much higher survival rate (into the 1960s and 1970s) than was the case for men. See I. Shcherbakova, 'The Gulag in Memory', in *The International Yearbook of Oral History and Life Stories* (New York: Oxford University Press, 1992), p. 103. Note also Ekaterina Breshkovskaia's comment that among late nineteenth-century revolutionaries, 'women ... were far less likely than men to become ill, go mad, or die, because the women took far better care of each other': quoted in Barbara Engel, *Mothers and Daughters: Women of the Intelligentsia in Nineteenth Century Russia* (Cambridge: Cambridge University Press, 1983), p. 202.
24. As Ginzburg prepares to write her memoir, she first outlines her ideas to Vasia: 'he was my first listener', she tells us. Vasily Aksenov's novel *Ozhog* (1980) covers some of the same terrain as does his mother's memoir, but is written from the next generation's viewpoint. See David Lowe, 'E. Ginzburg's *Krutoj marshrut* and V. Aksenov's *Ožog*: The Magadan Connection', in *Slavic and East European Journal*, vol. 27, no. 2 (1983), pp. 200–10.
25. Julia Kristeva, 'A New Type of Intellectual: The Dissident', in *The Kristeva Reader*, p. 296. Also see Martha Nussbaum, 'Perceptive Equilibrium: Literary Theory and Ethical Theory', in R.Cohen (ed.), *The Future of Literary Theory* (New York: Routledge, 1989), pp. 58–85, *passim*.

Chapter 10

WOMEN MEMOIRISTS ON PASTERNAK

Neil Cornwell

The memoir form has assumed considerable importance in twentieth-century Russian literature, due not only to the prurient delights of gossip and anecdotage but also to its vital documentary role as witness in the preservation of memory. At the same time, the memoir form invariably stems from unreliable narration, attitudinal bias and unverifiable factuality. Nevertheless, memoirs have been seized upon as powerful records of the minutiae of otherwise unrecorded or vanished particulars of fascinating lives or events. Due to well-known cultural and political circumstances, as well as to considerations of privacy or discretion, these accounts were frequently written *dlia iashchika* (for the drawer) and only published years, sometimes decades, later and often posthumously. Appearing first among dissident circles or in the West, and subsequently achieving home publication under perestroika, many such documents now occupy a place alongside the main artistic literary works of the century and have achieved the status of major texts in their own right.

In a century in which women's writing in Russia has assumed major importance and gained great recognition, it is not surprising that many, if not the majority, of leading memoirists have been women. It might also be said that the memoir form, given the role of most Russian women for most of the century, is a form which has been particularly conducive to female exploitation. Beyond that, women's memoirs in Russia this century arguably fall into two types, or sub-genres. One would be the personal account of life and struggle in this strife-torn epoch (such as Evgeniia Ginzburg's *Into the Whirlwind*) and/or a particular professional milieu within this overall situation (perhaps Lidiia Ginzburg best fits this category). Secondly, and no doubt also including a strong element of content of the first type, we have those memoirs which ostensibly centre around a famous man (often a husband or lover): here the memoirs of Nadezhda Mandel'shtam are the most celebrated example. Equally interesting, at least, is the probably smaller sub-category of women on women (Lidiia Chukovskaia's bulky recollections of Akhmatova being perhaps the best known instance). Concentrating in this chapter on texts which primarily fall into the second category (that is, 'woman on man'), I will focus on the case of Pasternak, who attracted the attention of a considerable number of women memoirists and correspondents, including Chukovskaia (ostensibly through the prism of Akhmatova), Zoia Maslenikova and Ariadna Efron; earlier, Marina Tsvetaeva and Ol'ga Freidenberg; and later, the westerners: Jacqueline de Proyart and Renate Schweitzer. The main texts, though, both as examples of the independent genre of reminiscences and as sources for Pasternak studies, must be the memoirs of Ol'ga Ivinskaia and of Zinaida Pasternak. Ol'ga, often dubbed Pasternak's 'mistress', was his close friend, literary collaborator and sexual partner out of wedlock from 1946 until his death in 1960.[1] Zinaida was Pasternak's second wife: his married partner and the mother of one of his sons as well as of two by her first marriage, his companion from 1932 until his death and his general housekeeper.

The first point to make about these two women is to stress the personal tragedies that both lived through outside their relations with Pasternak. Ol'ga Ivinskaia had lost two husbands before she met her 'god' and 'magician', Pasternak (the first committed suicide and the second died, leaving her with two young children). A son of Zinaida Pasternak's by her first marriage died in 1945 of a lingering disease. Both women were of, or closely connected with, the cultural intelligentsia: Ol'ga more on the literary side (she worked at the journal *Novyi mir* and later became a translator), and Zinaida with the world of music. Both women subsequently underwent periods of crisis directly or indirectly related to their relationship with Pasternak and his complex path through the cultural-political controversies of the Stalin period and the 'thaw' of the 1950s, not least the 'Pasternak' or *Zhivago* affair itself.[2]

First to be printed were the Ivinskaia memoirs, published in Paris in 1978, having been completed in first draft in 1972.[3] As the subtitle *Gody s Borisom Pasternakom (My Years with Boris Pasternak)* indicates, Ol'ga's narrative basically runs from their first meeting in the *Novyi mir* offices in 1946 to the painful account of her being denied access to him (in her capacity as unofficial spouse) throughout his last illness. It also includes more problematic areas, such as her version of what he had told her of his previous life and career, as well as more personal ones: in particular the harrowing details of her prison and camp experiences from 1949 to 1953, when, so she and Pasternak concluded, she was arrested as a surrogate for him. Pasternak himself later wrote of this:

> She was put in jail on my account, as the person considered by the secret police to be closest to me, and they hoped that by means of a gruelling interrogation and threats they could extract enough evidence from her to put me on trial. I owe my life and the fact that they did not touch me in these years to her heroism and endurance ...[4]

Ol'ga was pregnant at the time of her arrest and she underwent a horrifying miscarriage in prison. Later, at the height of the Nobel Prize crisis, they contemplated a suicide pact. After Pasternak's death, and, as she says, lacking the Pasternak name, she and her daughter Ira were sent to the camps on dubious charges of smuggling Pasternak royalties from Italy (home of the Feltrinelli publishing house, which first published *Doctor Zhivago* in 1957). Ol'ga herself writes in her Foreword:

> I am aware that any individual view of another person cannot be the whole truth. There are people who saw Pasternak in a different light. If they also write down their memories of him, I shall read with interest – and perhaps with pleasure – what they have to say about the Pasternak whom they knew. (Ivinskaia: xxxix)

It would be intriguing to know how much pleasure she may have derived from reading Zinaida's memoirs. According to Ol'ga (Ivinskaia: 58), Pasternak very much wanted a 'reconciliation' between her and Zinaida and hoped that his sister Lidiia might be the person to effect this. Such a thing was probably an impossibility, but in any case Lidiia only arrived in Moscow after Pasternak's death. The two women were fated to preserve their ardent rivalry which developed steadily from 1946 and reached its zenith over the last five years of Pasternak's life, when Zinaida ran the official 'big house' at Peredelkino, while Ol'ga presided over the alternative 'little house', within convenient walking distance. There was apparently talk of Pasternak abandoning the regime of 'the big house' in favour of its smaller variant, or even a separate life with Ol'ga at Tarusa, and there may have been attempts, but this never came to pass. At a number of times of crisis, such as Pasternak's enforced departure to Georgia at the time of Harold Macmillan's visit to Moscow and for the duration of Pasternak's final illness, it was Ol'ga who found herself excluded. Only on the day of Pasternak's funeral was she able to penetrate the big house and view the body: 'no one stopped me at the door' (Ivinskaia: 348).

There was, then, perhaps not surprisingly, no love lost between the two women. Ol'ga reports a mutual friend, Liusia Popova, 'imagining the look on Zinaida Nikolayevna's face when she heard' of his incipient love affair (Ivinskaia: 15). Of course, we cannot necessarily take Ol'ga's testimony, in this regard in particular, as wholly objective, but her version tells of Pasternak's unhappiness with 'his no longer young wife' (Zinaida was fifteen years older than Ol'ga and apparently aged rapidly in her forties; there is, too, considerable evidence that Pasternak rapidly lost sympathy with older women whom he had known when they were young). Nevertheless, he viewed her as a Little Red Riding Hood figure (*Krasnaia shapochka*), difficult to abandon, despite his alleged 'fear of her iron character and voice', the explanation for which being that 'she comes from the family of a gendarme colonel'; Pasternak, Ol'ga's version goes, discovered his 'mistake' in his first year of living with Zina; the person he had really liked was not her but Garrik (her first husband, the pianist Genrikh Neigaus) (Ivinskaia: 19–20).

His love for Ol'ga notwithstanding, Pasternak would tell her that he could not 'go through with all the horrors of leaving my family'. 'By this time', Ol'ga writes, 'Zinaida Nikolayevna had heard about me, and was also beginning to make his life a misery' (Ivinskaia: 25). By the time of Ol'ga's release from her first term in the camps in 1953, when the prospects of a union between them might have been brightest, Pasternak had suffered a heart attack, from which he felt (no doubt quite justifiably) that he owed his recovery to Zinaida. This led him to attempt – though not for long – a non-resumption of relations with Ol'ga, rather than a cementing of them. A disappointed Ol'ga refers at this point to 'the full flavour of his words – the mixture of candour, guileless charm, and undeniable heartlessness' (Ivinskaia: 26). While Ol'ga had been in prison, Pasternak had been called in to collect copies of his own works which he had given to Ol'ga and which had been confiscated upon her arrest; he later confessed, to her chagrin, that he had torn out the inscriptions he had written to her when he had brought the books home, for fear of Zina's reaction. Whatever else, Ol'ga's shrewdness at least is not in dispute; many of her judgments, of Pasternak as of others, carry a sharp ring of conviction, as in this comment encompassing Pasternak and his two official wives:

> He had no patience with amateurism – which is perhaps why he considered his first wife's painting as nothing more than an idle way of filling in time, and placed a much higher value on what he regarded as Zinaida Nikolayevna's sensible housekeeping talents, the loving care with which she looked after the garden. (Ivinskaia: 29)

Ol'ga perhaps had good professional reason to resent Zinaida's attempted prevention of the publication of her [Ol'ga's] translations of the Georgian poet Titian Tabidze alongside those of Pasternak (Ivinskaia: 34–50).

On a political level, Ol'ga implies that Zinaida was pro-Stalinist (though no doubt her attitudes could equally be seen as protective of her family). This comes out in Ol'ga's account of Pasternak's relations with Mandel'shtam and with Tsvetaeva. Regarding the former, according to Ol'ga, Zinaida 'loathed the Mandel'shtams and considered that they were compromising her "loyal" husband' (Ivinskaia: 68). In the case of Tsvetaeva, Ol'ga writes movingly, and with no trace of personal motivation, of Pasternak's deep affection for Marina and his feelings of guilt over her tragic fate. He blamed himself for not inviting Marina and her son to stay with him at Peredelkino instead of allowing their hasty evacuation in 1941, due 'partly to his own indecisiveness and partly because of the domestic situation at the Peredelkino house' (Ivinskaia: 180). With regard to what might have been a match of poets made in heaven, Marina is quoted (via her daughter Ariadna) as saying 'I could never live with Boris Leonidovich, but I want a son by him', so that 'he would live in him through me' and 'I could never live with him – because I love him too much'. Pasternak, for his part, on being told by Ol'ga, 'You should have married Marina then', replied vehemently: 'Olia, we could never have lived together – Marina combined every kind of female hysteria in concentrated form' (Ivinskaia: 182). Their meetings in Moscow, following their 'romance by letters' and Pasternak's indecisive advice to Marina in 1935 over returning to Russia, were a disappointment to both and Pasternak's own domestic circumstances had evolved and become yet further complicated. Pasternak was reluctant to compromise the 'kind of "Olympus" at the "big" house' that Zinaida had created for him; 'tormented by compassion and pangs of conscience' over his deteriorating relations with Zina 'he evidently decided that he must find some other solution for Marina, rather than impose her unwelcome presence on Zinaida Nikolayevna', this allegedly 'uncouth woman who had failed to respond to his love' (Ivinskaia: 186–88).

While the Ivinskaia memoirs provided probably the first solid evidence of Ol'ga as a prototype for Lara in *Doctor Zhivago*, Ol'ga herself admits that the novel's characters should rather be seen as 'composite images – Tonia having something of me and of Zinaida Nikolayevna, just as Lara would also have elements of both of us, and of somebody else as well,' nevertheless she affirms, 'there is more of Zinaida Nikolayevna in Tonia's character, and of me in Lara's' (Ivinskaia: 198–99).

A further striking element of the Ol'ga Ivinskaia memoirs is her stout defence of Pasternak against charges of spinelessness brought against him by Solzhenitsyn and his dissident supporters of a slightly later era. Referring to the private readings of extracts from *Doctor Zhivago* which began as early as the late 1940s, she writes: 'One must not forget that in those years Boris Leonidovich was not only the first, but perhaps the only professional writer in the Soviet Union to do something of this kind', whereas Solzhenitsyn, in his embroilments of the 1960s and early 1970s, 'was treading a path already opened up by Boris Leonidovich in very much more terrible times' (Ivinskaia: 269). The importance of the decision to ban *Doctor Zhivago* in 1956/1957, as of the decision to publish it taken under perestroika exactly thirty years later, was in each case a litmus test of the times, the significance of which it would be difficult to overestimate.

Zinaida Pasternak's memoirs were written, it seems, between 1962 and 1964; she died in 1966 and the surviving typescript was partially published in the Leningrad journal *Neva* in 1990.[5] A fuller version has now been published. They cover, as well as her Pasternak years, the period of her early life, that is to say the revolutionary and Civil War period. Most notably from this epoch we learn of a Lara-Komarovsky type of affair which she conducted with her cousin (their ages being about fifteen and forty-five respectively). However, unlike Lara in the novel, Zinaida in real life continued to hold this cousin in her affections; after his death a token from him reached Zinaida, causing not inconsiderable jealousy on the part of Pasternak. She subsequently thought that Pasternak had presented Komarovsky very negatively by comparison.[6]

Zinaida Eremeeva's first marriage was undertaken to look after Neigaus (Neihauz), the helpless pianist, and she recounts their travels together and his performances. We are given considerable detail on Neihauz and Valentin Asmus (a philosopher and logician who later became a close friend of Pasternak) and his wife, at the time when their paths first intersected with that of the Pasternaks in about 1931. This includes much fascinating and hitherto unknown or little known information; for instance it appears that at this time Irina Asmus was in love with Pasternak (ZP, 2: 131) and therefore jealous of Zinaida, who had first met Pasternak through the Asmuses.

It emerges from these memoirs that Zinaida (like the young Ol'ga, but distinct, it would seem, from the mature Ol'ga) did not really understand Pasternak's verse. Accordingly, Pasternak said he would write '*proshche*' (more simply) for her (ZP, 2: 131), leading to the reformed style of *Vtoroe rozhdenie* (*Second Birth*, 1932), which celebrates, among other things, his new life with Zinaida. Information is given on Pasternak's personality, on her relationships or involvements and those of others (though there are some omission marks in the text). The crisis of her affair with Pasternak is related, stressing the difficulties of the break-up of their respective marriages. We hear of Pasternak's feelings for Zhenia (his first wife): a mixture of lyricism and guilt. We are told too of Pasternak's apparent suicide attempt, by drinking iodine when the crisis was renewed after their trip to Georgia (ZP, 2: 136).

On a writers' trip to the Urals, Pasternak was appalled by the poverty and hunger there and the expectation that he would write 'positively'. This was followed by Pasternak's illness, his trip to Paris and subsequent collapse in Leningrad in 1935. We hear too of Pasternak's famous phone call from Stalin and the 'spontaneous' tone he was able to adopt (ZP, 2: 141). There are remarks on Mandel'shtam, whom (as Ivinskaia reports) Zinaida strongly disliked (ZP, 2: 140) and on the arrest of Pil'niak: Zinaida's reminiscences of the purges and her fears that Pasternak would fall victim to these.

Wartime brought a period of evacuation and separation. Zinaida worked with disadvantaged children in Chistopol', while Pasternak remained in Moscow for a time before joining her. Her sick son Adik was being treated for tuberculosis of the spine in Sverdlovsk. They were able to return to Moscow in June 1943, only to find both their residences has been ransacked during their absence. Adik was returned to a Moscow clinic in 1944 and, upon his death the following year, Pasternak treated Zinaida to the Iurii Zhivago philosophy that 'the dead continue living in the memory of their near ones'; however, this was of little consolation to Zinaida (ZP, 4: 129).

In the post-war period, Pasternak took up with Ol'ga Ivinskaia (though the timing and circumstances in Zinaida's account to do not exactly match other sources). 'In her looks, I liked her a lot', writes Zinaida, 'but her manner of conversing not at all; notwithstanding her coquettishness, there was something hysterical about her. She certainly flirted with Boria' (ZP, 4: 129). After the war, according to Zinaida, there occurred a time of 'general debauchery' in which many Soviet writers traded in their old wives for new models and the young girls went along with this, 'for the lack of marriageable men' (ZP, 4: 129-30). Allegedly, plenty of attention was paid to Pasternak in this period by such '*bezdel'nitsy*' (flibbertigibbets) whom Zinaida felt obliged to 'chase away with a stick' (ZP, 4: 130), to preserve Pasternak's peace and quiet while he wrote *Doctor Zhivago*.

Zinaida is at some pains to stress that Pasternak was not religious in any strict sense, and not a church-goer; if anything, he worshipped nature. There is no mention of any 'conversion'. Zinaida sees a distinct distance in this and other matters between Pasternak and Iurii Zhivago: Zhivago, as a figure, was no match for Pasternak.

As time goes on, Zinaida has to admit, 'a certain part of his life did not fall within my field of vision and therefore it is difficult to describe that time' (ZP, 4: 131). She also admits reproaching Pasternak for precipitating the *Zhivago* affair by passing a typescript to the Italians; furthermore, she reacted to news of the Nobel Prize with fears ultimately for his life. Any comments she makes on Ol'ga Ivinskaia, as expected, are far from favourable: Ol'ga is referred to as '*eta dama*' (that woman), and said to be full of lies and machinations; Pasternak was allegedly always trying to throw her off, but she would cling on by moral blackmail, and so on. During his last illness, Zinaida claims to have softened:

> Several times I asked whether he wouldn't like to see Ivinskaia and told him: it's all the same to me now, I can easily let her in to see you and fifty more such beauties. But he categorically refused, and I couldn't understand this. (ZP, 4: 136)

According to Ol'ga, his refusal to have her admitted was based on his continued vanity: his false teeth had been removed! Neither his death nor funeral were to bring any reconciliation: Zinaida claims to have needed protection as the body was being carried out, 'so that I wasn't pushed out of the way by Ivinskaia with her daughter and her girl-friends who were trying their hardest to shove their way forward' (ZP, 4: 137). The memoirs themselves, of course, perpetuate this flavour of eternal enmity.

With regard to other literary figures in this period, Zinaida accuses the Futurist poet Aleksei Kruchenykh of virtually pimping; the novelist Konstantin Fedin, First Secretary of the USSR Writers' Union from 1959 to 1971, is regarded as a betrayer and a general washout; whereas the poet Aleksei Surkov, First Secretary of the Writers' Union from 1953 to 1959, perhaps surprisingly, comes out not quite as badly as might be expected. As for Zinaida being pro-Stalinist, or at least pro-Soviet (of course, still no unusual thing in the early 1960s), apart from a more cautious and conciliatory tone throughout her text than that adopted by Ol'ga, the conclusive indicator is the words – however we may care to interpret them – that she would have liked to say, but did not, over Pasternak's grave: '*Proshchai, nastoiashchii bol'shoi kommunist, ty vsei svoei zhizn'iu dokazyval, chto dostoin etogo zvaniia*' (Farewell, you true great Communist, you proved with your whole life that you were worthy of that name) (ZP, 4: 137).

This is the undoubtedly valuable voice of Zinaida Pasternak: a strong character in her own right who had a moving and fascinating life. She enjoyed a musical temperament and some ability and she was an artistic wife and companion, first to a famous pianist and then to Russia's foremost poet. She had, like all too many of her generation, more than her share of tragedies and she finally found her own voice as a memoirist, in her late sixties, as Pasternak's widow. In this way she has given her side of the Pasternak story, as well as her own, and publication has finally enabled her, albeit posthumously, to counter her rival and enemy Ol'ga Ivinskaia. Which of them, if either, will have the last word is difficult to predict, but at least each has now had her say.

In sum, Zinaida Pasternak's memoirs, in terms of Pasternak studies, are an important biographical source, paralleling (and perhaps counterbalancing) those by Ol'ga Ivinskaia, and exceeding in interest those by, for instance, Aleksandr Gladkov (1973; English translation, 1977) and Aleksandr Pasternak (1983; English translation, 1984).[7] Zina's role as the (first, and perhaps even main) prototype of Lara in *Doctor Zhivago* is established by her account of her early life and first affair. She adds much to our knowledge of Pasternak's crisis (both personal and literary) of the early 1930s, including his suicide attempt; of people within the Pasternak circle then and later; of their trips to the Urals and Georgia; of Pasternak's own personality; and his illness of the mid-1930s that surrounded his stays in Paris and Leningrad. There is a yet further (earwitness) account of the famous 1934 phone call from Stalin, and there are interesting comments on Mandel'shtam and Pil'niak and, later, on Ivinskaia, Kruchenykh, Surkov and Fedin. Zhivago's philosophy of death proves identical to Pasternak's consoling words to Zinaida on the death of her son Adik; Zinaida sees a considerable difference between Pasternak himself and his character Zhivago; Pasternak is revealed as not religious in any strict sense (and not a church-goer, though he had an interest in its liturgy and imagery). These are all valuable insights. We get, too, Zinaida's version of the *Zhivago* affair and her view of Pasternak's relations with Ivinskaia. Zinaida's is a valuable voice which we might not now ever have expected to hear. In addition, her memoirs are the personal testimony of a woman of character and courage who suffered various tragedies and difficulties; she emerges not only as an interesting example of the Soviet literary wife but comes into her own as a woman of the Russian intelligentsia.

Notes

1. Editor's note: Ol'ga Ivinskaia's name came to the fore again in November 1996, when Pasternak's love letters to her were put on sale at Christie's in London, following her death in Moscow in 1995 at the age of 82. See Maggie O'Kane, 'Author's love letters to "heroine" of *Dr Zhivago* up for sale', *Guardian*, 5 November 1996, p. 9.
2. Editor's note: see Robert Conquest, *The Pasternak Affair: courage of genius; a documentary report* (Philadelphia: Lippincott, 1962).

3. Ol'ga Ivinskaia, *V plenu vremeni: gody s Borisom Pasternakom* (Paris: Fayard, 1978); Olga Ivinskaya, *A Captive of Time: My Years With Pasternak,* trans. by Max Hayward (London: Collins/Harvill, 1978; and Fontana/Collins, 1979). All further references in the text will be to the 1979 translation (Ivinskaia, followed by the page number).
4. Written in German, 1958; quoted from Olga Ivinskaya, *A Captive of Time* (1979), p. 117.
5. Z. Pasternak, 'Vospominaniia', *Neva* (1990), no. 2, pp. 130-46; no. 4, pp. 124-38. All further quotations in the text are taken from this publication (ZP, followed by volume and page number); translations are my own. These memoirs have been republished from the original typescript, with omissions, in E.V. Pasternak and M.I. Feinberg (eds), *Vospominaniia o Borise Pasternake* (Moscow: Slovo, 1993). Pasternak's letters to Zinaida have now also been published: *Pis'ma B.L. Pasternaka k zhene Z.N. Neigauz-Pasternak* (Moscow, 1993).
6. A recent essay concerned with Lara and Komarovsky notes the parallel with Zinaida Nikolaevna's biography, and indeed refers to Zinaida's displeasure at the way Pasternak reworked the relationship in question, in that 'he stripped her first love of its halo by representing her cousin, Nikolay, as a scoundrel and a cad in the form of Komarovskij': Brett Cooke, 'Mrs Komarovskij: Sexual Abuse in *Doktor Živago*', *Russian Language Journal*, vol. 48, no. 159-61 (1994), pp. 103-26 (p. 123, n. 6). Biographical and novelistic jealousies were evidently made to match.
7. (Editor's note: see Alexander Gladkov, *Meetings with Pasternak: a memoir* [London: Collins/Harvill, 1977]; Aleksandr Pasternak, *A Vanished Present: the Memoirs of Alexander Pasternak*, ed. and trans. Ann Pasternak Slater [Oxford: Oxford University Press, 1984]). Other recently published memoirs and correspondence on or concerning Pasternak include: L. Chukovskaia, *Zapiski ob Anne Akhmatovoi*, 2 vols. (Paris: YMCA Press, 1976, 1980); L. Chukovskaia, *The Akhmatova Journals, Volume 1, 1938-41*, trans. by Milena Michalski and Sylva Rubashova (London: Harvill, 1994); N. Vil'mont, *O Borise Pasternake: Vospominaniia i mysli* (Moscow: Sovetskii pisatel', 1989); Z. Maslenikova, *Portret Borisa Pasternaka* (Moscow: Sovetskaia Rossiia, 1990); *Perepiska Borisa Pasternaka* (Moscow, 1990).

Chapter 11

IULIIA VOZNESENSKAIA: A FRAGMENTARY VISION

Julie Curtis

Most readers in the West are familiar with the name of Iuliia Voznesenskaia for two reasons.[1] The first is through her association with the brief flurry of feminist activity in Leningrad in 1979 and 1980 which led to the publication, together with Tat'iana Mamonova and others, of the almanac *Zhenshchina i Rossiia (Woman and Russia)*; almost at the same time, Voznesenskaia became identified with a specifically religious feminist group, the Mariia Club, which published a number of issues of a journal called *Mariia*. Voznesenskaia's reputation otherwise rests largely on her first novel, *Zhenskii dekameron (The Women's Decameron)*,[2] a cheerfully frank, occasionally bawdy account of the intimate lives of women in Russia, which at first glance seems to fit rather uneasily alongside the piety of the Mariia Club. Voznesenskaia has described herself since then as a 'women's writer' rather than a feminist, and it is this notion, peculiarly useful in a Russian context, which seems to unify her work. One of the functions of the present study is to illustrate just what Voznesenskaia means by this term.

Voznesenskaia was born in September 1940; her father was a Communist who held a senior post in the military and after the war served in East Germany, where Voznesenskaia spent some of her childhood (1945–1949). Although her parents were to some extent disillusioned by the repressions of the late 1940s, her father did not come to share Voznesenskaia's political convictions, which was why she was so delighted when he professed himself proud of the way she conducted herself at her trial in 1976. As a young woman, Voznesenskaia made at least one attempt to escape from the USSR. She first came into open conflict with the Soviet authorities in 1964 while a student at the Leningrad Institute of Theatre, Music and Cinema. A conviction for 'resistance to the authorities' (she was accused of assaulting a policeman) brought her studies to an end and she was sentenced to a year's corrective labour in a factory. In the 1970s she became a central figure in Leningrad's 'Second Culture' (or 'alternative culture', as she preferred to call it),[3] hosting poetry evenings and exhibitions of unofficial art in her flat, becoming involved in a variety of projects for largely *samizdat* publications, and often to be found doing the hard work of typing, taking minutes, or organising meetings which these projects entailed. For all the Bohemian style of life in the Second Culture, the undertakings with which she was associated were typically run in a very businesslike fashion, with records kept of all editorial meetings, archives preserved, and an absolute ban on alcohol at all artistic evenings. She also had two sons to look after (Andrei, born in 1960, and for some years now a member of the editorial board of the Russian émigré journal *Posev*, and Artur, born in 1964); however, she has also been described by her friend Konstantin Kuz'minsky as '*mat' poetov*' (mother to the poets) because of the way in which she nurtured the careers of so many poets while taking care of them in the most practical ways.[4] Those who know her have characterised her as a very lively, humorous and also loyal friend, slight of build but full of energy and zest for life. Her courage and integrity have evidently been buttressed throughout her adult life by her unswerving faith as a Christian. Finding herself in prison on her birthday, she tells us of the prayer she uttered: 'Lord, I thank You for this sense of my complete righteousness, the correctness of my path, and for the thirty-six years of my life, lived as You have commanded'.[5]

If anything, Voznesenskaia writes poetry more readily than prose. She started writing as a child, and during the late 1960s she completed, amongst other things, a long poem, 'Invasion', on the events in Czechoslovakia, which circulated in manuscript form. Her second, and in her opinion most successful, unpublished volume of verse, 'Kniga razluk' (The Book of Partings), was completed just before her arrest in December 1976, and reflects her sense of loss as an increasing number of her friends leave to go abroad:

Ты не первый. Иди. За пределами станешь пророком.
Только Боже избавь оглянуться за милым порогом:
соляные столбы вдоль дороги, как свечи на тризне.
Как они высоки, эти слёзы о бывшей отчизне![6]
('К Kuzmin'skomu', 16.4.1974)

(You are not the first. Leave. Beyond the frontiers you will become a prophet./ Only God help you if you look back over your beloved threshold:/ pillars of salt stand along the road, like candles at a funeral feast./ How tall they are, these tears for a lost homeland!)

She herself takes her poetry very seriously, while not overrating her talents, and this modest view of her abilities has largely been shared by reviewers. She is conscious, though, that as a woman, her attempts to be a poet arouse the antagonism of the men in her life: she writes to a lover, Iul' Rybakov, whom she appreciates not least because he does take her poetry seriously, that 'poetry is the one thing which other men and my husband struggled against with all their might. It's always the same: first of all people fall in love with the poetess, and then they try to turn her into a domestic idiot chained to the kitchen'.[7] For three years after her marriage she did not write a line. She has also written a cycle of fairy-tale poems, 'Skazki i istorii' (Fairy-tales and Stories), a reflection of a concern she has raised in recent years about the dearth in Russia of good literature for children and for adolescents.[8]

The mid-1970s marked a radicalisation of Voznesenskaia's political views as the Second Culture (which she distinguished – at least initially – from dissidence) came to suffer increasing persecution at the hands of the Soviet authorities and the KGB. It is characteristic that when, in 1976, she and her friends began to plan a volume of poetry by young and unpublished poets, their first step was to request the assistance and support of the Leningrad branch of the Writers' Union. This request, while clearly intended as a provocation, nevertheless suggests that she believed that the official channels and procedures ought to be available to all writers, and not just to paid-up members of a Union. No assistance was forthcoming, and the volume, 'Lepta' (An Offering) remained unpublished. Meanwhile, the KGB began to take an increasing interest in the activities of Voznesenskaia and her circle. A typical escapade in the summer of 1976 involved Voznesnenskaia, on the fifth day of a hunger-strike, shinning down a drainpipe from the third floor to escape house arrest and attend a protest exhibition she had devised: she and a number of artists had decided to go ahead and hold the exhibition despite a ban by the authorities, only they agreed amongst themselves that it would become a purely 'conceptual' event, and that the exhibits would be represented by 'a number of moving objects, some in uniform and some in civilian dress' – in other words, by the KGB themselves.[9]

In September 1976 Voznesenskaia and some of her friends were arrested in connection with the defacing that summer of a number of trams and public buildings in Leningrad (including the Peter and Paul Fortress) with large painted slogans which proclaimed, for example, that 'The Party is the enemy of the people'. During interrogations she conducted herself with great courage and wit, refusing absolutely to provide any evidence or cooperate in any way whatsoever. This earned her the rueful respect of at least some of her interrogators. Her friends, however, did cooperate with the investigation, a fact which initially troubled her until she realised that the two men – Iul' Rybakov and Oleg Volkov – had been pressurised into doing so on the grounds that if they agreed to play down the political nature of their activities and pretend they had just been engaging in vandalism then many others, including Voznesenskaia, would be released without further ado. Soon after coming out of prison, Voznesenskaia found herself in a strange, almost comic situation. On one and the same day, 28 November 1976, she simultaneously received summonses to OVIR, the department which issued visas for foreign travel, and to the prosecutor's office. She was told that mysterious 'friends' in Israel had issued an invitation to her to emigrate, and she was pressed to collect the appropriate documents for her departure as quickly as possible – if necessary, omitting those she could not quickly obtain. At the prosecutor's office, on the other hand, she was told that new charges were being pressed against her. It took considerable courage on her part, one feels, to turn down the opportunity to leave – something she had been contemplating for some time – in order to stay in Russia while her friends were being put on trial, even though this would mean almost certain imprisonment for herself. 'Where would I go at this moment, when my best friends are in their hands? Perhaps refusing freedom is the highest freedom'.[10] Shortly after she had refused the invitation to emigrate, on 21 December, she was arrested and put on trial for slandering the Soviet state.

On 29 and 30 December 1976, Voznesenskaia, who had by now embarked on a hunger-strike which was to last seven weeks in all (she abandoned it when her health seriously deteriorated) appeared in court. The accusations were based on a number of documents confiscated from her and others by the KGB. These included the single copy of her satirical journal *Krasnyi dissident* (The Red Dissident), the cover price of which was given as 'three years of exile with or without the right to receive parcels' (an underestimate, as it turned out); the project she and others had drafted in April 1976 for a second almanac of poetry to replace the 'Lepta' idea, entitled 'Mera vremeni' (A Measure of Time), which, amongst other things, charged the authorities with the fact that there was neither freedom of speech nor of the press in the USSR; her answers to a questionnaire circulated to a number of people in Leningrad as the basis for a book by a certain Igor' Siniavin; and the autobiography which she had typed under dictation for a friend, Gennady Trifonov. Trifonov was under investigation at the time for homosexual activities and apparently turned out to have had certain links with the KGB; to everyone's dismay, when Voznesenskaia was accused of having written the text of his memoirs herself, he failed to contradict the charge. Voznesenskaia, by contrast, behaved in exemplary dissident fashion during her trial, refusing to incriminate others. She conducted her own defence; during her closing speech she turned her back demonstratively on the judge and addressed her friends instead, insisting that she had written nothing but the truth and proclaiming the poet's right to freedom. She concluded by commenting ironically on the sentence passed on her, a 'humane' five years of internal exile in Vorkuta which supposedly took into account the fact that she was the mother of two children.

Voznesenskaia described some of her experiences on her journey into internal exile in February 1977 in her 'Letter from Novosibirsk', published in the almanac *Woman and Russia*, which detailed the sexual humiliations and violence suffered by women prisoners. On arrival in Vorkuta in 1977 she found the peculiar restricted freedom of internal exile unbearable, and when she heard that her younger son was unwell she managed to slip away and return to Leningrad. It was not long before she was caught and returned to Vorkuta, where she was retried at the end of June 1977. Her remaining four years of exile were commuted to a two-year sentence to labour camp, a change which Voznesenskaia actually welcomed with a sense of relief.

Voznesenskaia has documented her time in prison and in labour camp in a number of memoirs.[11] In some she records the harsh regime imposed upon the women in these institutions, while elsewhere she tells the story of her own personal experiences, interweaving them with anecdotes from the lives of the many other prisoners she encountered there; both the format of these memoirs, as well as the actual substance of some of the anecdotes, would seem to have suggested a form for the patchwork of stories of women's lives that makes up *The Women's Decameron*, written some years later. Voznesenskaia herself coped with the experience of prison by being determined to retain her dignity throughout – an example, perhaps, of the '*volia*' (inner freedom) which is an important theme of *Zvezda Chernobyl'* (*The Star Chernobyl'*, 1987). She took with her jeans and a sweater, but also a long, low-cut black dress which she wore on occasion to boost her morale; she decorated her cell with flowers if possible; she learned to use tooth-powder as well as oatmeal to make face-masks and look after her skin (she developed boils, scurvy and psoriasis during this time and her eyesight suffered badly); she kept up a routine of exercises; she insisted on addressing all the other prisoners with the polite '*vy*' (you) form; and she kept up her writing: 'I had only to express reality in verse for it to lose all its power over me'.[12] Voznesenskaia would set out specific times for her writing and insist that others observed them, after which she would be prepared to join in the general '*boltovnia*' (chatter). In the camp she helped to run poetry and literature classes as well as Bible readings, and there can be no doubt that her faith was vital to her during this period.

It is clear that it was her time in prison and in the labour camp which focused Voznesenskaia's attention on the lives of women in particular. Up until then, she seems to have had no particular interest in her own sex as a distinct group. In 1975 Tat'iana Mamonova had approached her with the idea of a women's almanac, but it took her experiences of imprisonment to make her feel that the situation of women required special attention. In her diary for 1975 and 1976 she was capable of making airy remarks about not really liking women, 'a decorative sex, but useless in practical terms', although elsewhere she could be equally scathing about Soviet men who, she felt, were so feeble and socially inadequate that they barely had the right to marry. She concludes: 'I'm a woman with rather old-fashioned views: my husband must offer support and protection to me everywhere and in all things.'[13] During her imprisonment, however, she had ample opportunity to observe the plight of women across the social spectrum, of whom she reckoned that only about fifteen per cent were real criminals. It is from prison that she wrote to a male friend, commenting that 'You men are swine for making the world as it is. We women would have made it cosier and happier, if we'd had our way: [...] your discoveries, your much-vaunted progress (with its prisons, camps, atom bombs, and heaven knows what other male entertainments) – all this comes from a hidden inferiority complex – you just can't give birth to a child, that's what it is!'.[14] Reflecting on the enormous harm done to women's physical and mental health in the camps, and the great damage suffered by their families and especially their children, she concludes that 'Two or three years for a man is not such a long sentence. But for a woman it is colossal. During this time, as a rule, her family falls apart, and the woman loses her home.'[15]

Obviously, on her return to Leningrad in 1979, Voznesenskaia found the new ferment of feminist ideas very sympathetic, and she participated in the publication of *Woman and Russia* in November 1979. But the radical western brand of feminist thought which had been embraced by Mamonova and her colleagues did not really correspond to her own convictions or attitudes to certain issues: like many Russian women, she appears to have found the lesbian activity she encountered in the camps very alien, for example, and reportedly has had rather mixed feelings about abortion.[16] By December 1979 she, Tat'iana Goricheva and others began to plan their own journal and they decided to set up their own group, the Mariia Club, which held several discussions of issues concerning women. She later stated that 'If the movement which grew up around the *Woman and Russia* almanac introduced new ideas to the democratic movement, then the Mariia Club above all represented a new democratic community in action.'[17] Based on a shared religious faith which held up Mary, Mother of God as a sacred ideal, their philosophy sought to counter the materialism and godlessness of Soviet society with feminine, rather than feminist, values such as sacrifice and unselfish love. The members of the Mariia Club believed that this feminine culture would represent a true democracy, unlike the false democracies of masculinity, for they concluded that 'democratism is in the profoundest sense a female quality'. The Mariia Club received support in a letter from one of Voznesenskaia's heroes, Aleksandr Solzhenitsyn, who considered their views to be very much at one with his own hopes for a revival of Russian Orthodox values.[18]

In 1980, in the run-up to the Moscow Olympics, Voznesenskaia was once again pressured to leave the Soviet Union. This time she was not confronted by the loss of her own liberty by the authorities, but with that of her elder son, Andrei. He was threatened with immediate drafting into the armed forces and service in Afghanistan, the invasion of which had already prompted Voznesenskaia to a written protest. This time Voznesenskaia, who had been considering emigration increasingly seriously, did not refuse and she left at five days' notice, on 11 May 1980. She settled in West Germany, where she worked for a human rights organisation and became involved in journalistic work for the journals *Posev* and *Grani*, writing articles on social affairs and literary matters relating to the Soviet Union. She divorced her first husband, Vladimir Okulov, in 1980 and in 1985 married Vladimir Kromas.

In 1986 Voznesenskaia's first novel, *The Women's Decameron*, was published in English and in Dutch, although it was not to appear in Russian for a further two years. This was perhaps out of a concern for the sensibilities of a Russian émigré community unused to such frankness in language and content relating to sexual matters – certainly their reactions to Eduard Limonov's graphic account of his heterosexual and homosexual activities in New York, *Eto ia, Edichka* (*It's Me, Eddie*, 1979), had been very negative. There might seem to be a paradox in that the first somewhat bawdy novel in modern Russian by a woman should have been written by a member of the Mariia Club, although there is, of course, no obvious reason to equate religious faith with prudishness. Boccaccio's own *Decameron* shares, indeed, some of its qualities with Voznesenskaia's text: it too has the overall effect of being bawdy but moral, for, as Boccaccio says, 'no story is so unseemly as to prevent anyone from telling it, provided it is told in seemly language'.[19] Boccaccio's work is equally one in which women figure as the principal protagonists and narrators, and indeed as the putative audience: women are the initiators of the idea of how they and their male friends should while away the time of the plague; it is women who for the most part select the themes of the stories they should tell each day, and of course they represent seven of the ten story-tellers.

The very structure of Voznesenskaia's *Women's Decameron* establishes it as a dialogue amongst the various heroines. The authorial voice introducing the various stories refrains on the whole from comment, while making quite clear its sceptical attitude to the Soviet regime. One of the ingenious features of the novel is the gradual process of characterisation which is achieved as each of the ten women present tells her story, which enables us to build up a picture of the personality and past history of each of the speakers. This is one of the fundamental differences between Voznesenskaia and Boccaccio, whose narratives all concern third parties, with characterisation confined to the framing material. Despite the static setting of Voznesenskaia's narrative, with the ten women confined to a ward, isolated from friends, relatives and the outside world, dramatic movement is achieved as the fates of two of the characters in particular, the down-and-out Zina and the much-abused and superficially sophisticated air-stewardess Al'bina are resolved – Zina's lover Igor' being traced for her by her new friends, while Al'bina is chivvied out of her scepticism, which masks in reality a lack of self-confidence, into accepting the affection of the father of her child. There is narrative development too, in the contributions of the engineer Natasha, who opens with the tale of her lost childhood love and concludes with the story of how she met him many years later. All the women in the ward are brought closer to one another, although not by their shared experience of quarantine and recent motherhood, which is scarcely alluded to. In this respect Voznesenskaia's novel is not entirely typical of the use of the hospital ward as a chronotope in so much writing by Russian women in the 1970s and 1980s, which broaches the previously taboo topics of gynaecology and the medical treatment of women.[20] Instead, the inmates are brought together by the discovery that as women their lives have far more in common than the differences in their lifestyles and social status might have suggested. The text, then, functions as a novel in its plot structure and characterisation, leading to a happy conclusion and a moral. It also serves a very important function as a documentary about women's lives and *byt* (humdrum existence), charting episodes good and bad which are never mentioned in official Soviet publications. It stands, indeed, as an heir to Baranskaia's 1965 story *Nedelia kak nedelia* (*A Week Like Any Other Week*) in that respect, and as a forerunner of the kind of oral history which came into vogue under glasnost with the work of people such as the Belarusian writer Svetlana Aleksievich (a close friend of Voznesenskaia's) in recording the experience of women and children during the Great Patriotic War. In its focus on the sexual relations between men and women (and occasionally between women and women), on living conditions and especially the shortage of decent housing, and on the prevalence of alcoholism and crime, *The Women's Decameron* entered waters virtually uncharted in Soviet literature at the time.

Voznesenskaia's own experiences are particularly reflected in the narrations of two of the women, Galina, with her experience of life in the camps and her religious faith ('Christianity has become a form of dissidence these days'[21]), and the theatre director, Emma, the initiator of the story-telling scheme; occasionally episodes from Voznesenskaia's life surface in the narrations of others. There are explicit references to her friend Konstantin Kuz'minsky and to his emigration, as well as to her own arrest and trial. The '*nomenklaturnaia dama*' (high-up Party lady) Valentina discovers that her prejudices against the drop-out Zina (a class for whom Voznesenskaia has particular respect)[22] and the dissident Galina are perhaps not that well-founded, and she has a few truths brought home to her about the realities of Soviet life and the particular burdens placed upon women. At the same time, she is revealed to be no less human than the other women, and they come to understand her better too: her stories of making love with her husband underneath a fallen poster of Khrushchev, or of averting a rape by accidentally wrapping the elastic of her mittens round her assailant's testicles are amongst the most hilarious in the volume. Exuberant wit characterises many of the narrations and is, indeed, one of the great merits of the work; instead of the prudery of much Soviet writing about sex, or the bleak grotesqueries of much of the *chernukha* (black writing) of recent years, Voznesenskaia has succeeded in overcoming what Catriona Kelly describes as the particular challenge for Russians of finding an appropriate language for writing about sex which is neither clinical nor obscene.[23]

One is left with an impression of the fortitude of these women who, although they have to put up with violence, sexual abuse, material hardship and the indifference of the Soviet authorities to the needs of families and children, nevertheless muddle through. Almost every narrative concerns some sort of difficulty involving cramped housing and broken families, and particularly children who are abandoned by their fathers. Despite all this, the women retain a certain romantic idealism about love and an innocence of heart which makes their various infidelities, for example, seem an irrelevance. Equally, these Leningrad women are aware of political repression and the gap between government rhetoric and reality, but for the most part they are not subversive: Valentina is by no means the only one in the ward who believes the official line on history and international affairs. The novel's conclusion, if any, is the modest one that although it is possible to live like this, and each of the women has found some sort of happiness, they would like to make things easier and more civilised in certain respects – a stoical attitude which reflects Voznesenskaia's view that many of the best things in Russian life are created and preserved by women: the will to make things better, to understand one's neighbours, and to enjoy life to the full.

Apart from her work for *Posev* and *Grani*, Voznesenskaia also worked extensively after 1985 for Radio Liberty, based in Munich. This put her in an ideal position to gather an enormously wide range of documentary materials from radio broadcasts and printed sources relating to the nuclear disaster at Chernobyl' in April 1986, which she then used to punctuate the chapters of her novel *The Star Chernobyl'* (1987). The effect of these sections is to chart the disinformation and the criminally inadequate and contradictory reporting of the disaster at the highest levels of government, and testifies to the fear and confusion which gripped the authorities in the face of a real threat to the health of the people, to political stability, and to international relations. The narrative itself highlights the shockingly uncaring attitude of the authorities in failing to plan the evacuation of the communities near Chernobyl' in such a way as to minimise distress to individuals. In Voznesenskaia's view, clearly, the disaster brought out the hollowness of the Gorbachev administration's claims to more open government and its cynicism with regard to the welfare of its citizens. In such a situation individuals were thrown back on their own resources, and once again in Voznesenskaia's writings women come to the fore and display the courage and determination necessary to salvage something from the tragedy.

The autobiographical heroine, Anna, is a former dissident who is living in West Germany at the time of the disaster; she makes a living by giving lectures on Russian literature and women poets in particular, and on the day the news breaks of the leak of nuclear contaminants she is on a lecture tour in Sweden and poised to become emotionally involved with a Swedish translator, Sven. He is working on the poems of Irina Ratushinskaia and other women poets, and reference is made in particular to one poem where the image of the 'plague' of Communism threatening the West acquires a further topical significance as an image of the cloud of radiation moving towards Europe.[24] The image also provides a coincidental link with the plague which forces Boccaccio's story-tellers into retreat. Anna has two sisters: the elder, Anastasiia, is a schoolteacher and Party member, somewhat reminiscent of Valentina in *The Women's Decameron*, who has sacrificed everything to bring up the other two after the deaths of their parents; the younger, Alena, is a pretty and impulsive girl who marries her sweetheart Ivanushka, an atomic scientist. He takes her off to live with him in a town called Chernobyl', where Alenushka gives birth to twin boys and is expecting again at the time of the disaster. The autobiographical nature of the text is underlined by Voznesenskaia, who gives the three sisters the patronymic and surname of her own mother, Ol'ga Nikolaevna Lebedeva, 'whose letters gave me comfort and support in the camp'.[25] The novel focuses initially on the helplessness of Anna, who breaks the ban Anastasiia had imposed on her seven years previously about contacting her sisters from the West, in order to alert Anastasiia to the disaster. But increasingly our sympathy and attention become fixed on Anastasiia, who during her desperate attempts to get information about Alena and her family loses all her illusions about the integrity of the Soviet authorities, hands in her Party card, and finally enters the contaminated zone itself. Having already learned of her brother-in-law's death, she eventually discovers that Alena is also dead, and we must presume that she herself perishes in the zone, if not from the effects of the radiation, then from stress combined with the serious heart condition from which she suffers.

Anna's story meanwhile concentrates on the loneliness and frustrations of exile, and follows her through her growing relationship with Sven. There are one or two cloying moments in the narrative; he is somewhat caricaturally naïve about the Soviet Union, for all his supposed talent and sensitivity as a translator. When the news reaches them of Anastasiia's disappearance into the contaminated zone, Anna resolves that their relationship must end and that she must cross the border back to the USSR to see what she can do. But Sven takes the decision out of her hands, recognising her impetuosity as well as her courage, and decides that they will get married and that he, not she, will then go to the Soviet Union to rescue her twin nephews, who have survived, but are seriously ill. Previously Anna and Sven had had a discussion about the difference between the notions of *svoboda* (freedom) and *volia* (inner freedom, free will, or freedom of action), contrasting, on the one hand, Anna's limited 'freedom' in the West and her inability to help her sisters, while Anastasiia in 'unfree' Russia does at least have the opportunity to act decisively. The novel picks up the point Voznesenskaia makes elsewhere that even the strong occasionally feel the need for a shoulder to lean on. In one letter to her lover she comments, 'Nobody guessed how arduous and unpleasant, how troublesome and difficult it was being a "strong woman". Thank you for giving me vulnerability'.[26] Like Christa Wolf's novel *Störfall (Accident)*, also written from the perspective of Germany in the immediate aftermath of the disaster,[27] *The Star Chernobyl'* presents the events at Chernobyl' and the scandal of the attempts to cover up the consequences as a largely masculine crime, that of the pursuit of scientific knowledge, combined with that of the pursuit of political power in the case of Voznesenskaia. The novel ends with an unanswered question posed by an American to a Russian, asking about the possibility of pursuing alternatives to atomic energy. The Apocalyptic message of the epigraph suggests that Voznesenskaia wishes us to consider the events at Chernobyl' as a dramatic warning of what is to come if mankind does not attempt to restore sanity to its undertakings.

In 1987, the same year as the publication in Russian of her two best known novels, Voznesenskaia also published in Germany and Holland a volume which came out in English under the title *Letters of Love*. This was a selection of letters written to and from labour camps, all of them, as she says, in some way talking about love, whether it be love for family, for friends, for poetry, for one's country or for God. 'Moreover, I have chosen from the whole pile only letters from women. Why? Not only because after the publication in the West of my *Women's Decameron* I need to justify my title of "women's writer", and not only because I do actually consider myself to be one.'[28] The authors of these letters are not identified, although some of them, including the whole of the third section, which is made up of letters to a lover (Iul' Rybakov) who is serving a sentence in another camp, are patently her own. In 1990 Voznesenskaia returned to Leningrad for the first time, where she celebrated her fiftieth birthday, and was reported then as saying that she hoped one day to return to live in Russia.

More recently, Voznesenskaia has written a series of four detective novels figuring a Munich-based aristocratic heroine, Countess Apraksina, who assists the German police in cases involving Soviet citizens or Russian émigrés. Apraksina was born in 1917, the birth year of the Soviet Union, and has every intention of outliving what she views as a corrupt and decrepit old creature. Two of the novels, *Rusalka v basseine* (Mermaid in a Swimming Pool), a story about illegal Russian immigrants in Germany, and *Liubimykh ubivaiut vse* (Everyone Kills the Ones They Love) appeared in 1994, published by Mosty in Moscow. In the latter story Apraksina unravels a murder case involving three Russians in a triangular relationship, drawing upon her knowledge of the properties of herbal teas and her insight into the details of the lives of Russians at home and in emigration. She is presented as a post-Soviet Miss Marple, whizzing around Munich in a red Volkswagen Beetle, tending her elegant garden in a pink track-suit or poring over her Macintosh to trace the identity of Russians resident in Germany. These works are relatively lightweight and clearly directed at a commercial market. As ever, the novels have autobiographical dimensions (Apraksina calls in at Radio Liberty, for example), and to that extent they would seem to invite us to share a sense of the settled identity Voznesenskaia has achieved for herself in the post-Communist environment of the new Germany.

When we survey Voznesenskaia's writings it is striking that almost all of them are in some sense fragmentary in character. To a certain extent this was a matter of necessity: in internal exile she declares that she has decided to record her Odyssey 'in the form of brief notes: this makes it easier to remember them and to conceal them, or smuggle them out to the outside world, or leave them for safekeeping with someone reliable'.[29] But diary entries, correspondence, short lyrics, the hundred stories which make up *The Women's Decameron*, autobiographical prose alternating with poems and accounts of individual episodes from other people's lives, journalistic articles and the snippets of documentary text which punctuate the narrative of *The Star Chernobyl'* – all of these reflect her instinct, and her gift, for combining small parts to create a kaleidoscopic whole. This mosaic of semi-documentary material which captures the reality of women's lives is characteristic of the closely focused and relatively small-scale scope of much women's writing in general and of Soviet women's writing in particular (Baranskaia, Tolstaia, Petrushevskaia), where the fabric of everyday and concrete existence is brought into literature to subversive effect in a literature and a culture where the problems of reality were for so long ignored.

Voznesenskaia's description of herself as a 'women's writer' is, then, an apt one, since it makes much more sense of her position than the label 'feminist', which has little clear significance in a Russian context.[30] If anything, her brief association with Mamonova's group has somewhat confused our picture of her. But her works demonstrate her commitment to providing a woman's vision of her world, and the assertion of that vision as one which often seems saner and more humane than those of men.[31] To put it crudely, it would appear from Voznesenskaia's works that if women had been running the Soviet Union, things would have been different and things would have been better. In both her major novels Voznesenskaia's heroines are placed in a situation (quarantine in a maternity hospital, and international disaster) where inequalities and differences in social class and political outlook are obliterated. Instead, what emerges is a sense of common humanity, a sisterly solidarity or at least a democratic spirit, which enables the women to make the best of their plight and defy adversity.

Notes

1. Voznesenskaia's work has received relatively little attention in scholarly studies; the principal sources of information relating to her life and her writings include documents assembled in K.K. Kuzminsky and G. Kovalev (eds), *Blue Lagoon Anthology of Modern Russian Poetry*, vol. 5B (Newtonville, MA: Oriental Research Partners, 1980–6); Jerzy Kolodziej, 'Iuliia Voznesenskaia's Women – With Love and Squalor', in Helena Goscilo (ed.), *Fruits of her Plume: Essays on Contemporary Russian Women's Culture* (Armonk, NY, and London: M.E.Sharpe, 1993), pp. 225–38; and the entry on Voznesenskaia by K. Henry in Marina Ledkovsky, Charlotte Rosenthal and Mary Zirin (eds), *Dictionary of Russian Women Writers* (Westport, CT: Greenwood, 1994), pp. 733–35.
2. *The Women's Decameron* is also sometimes known in Russian as *Damskii dekameron* – that is the title, for example, given on the copyright page of the 1986 English translation (London: Quartet), where it is suggested that the novel was first published as *Damskii dekameron* in 1985. The first known publication in Russian, however, seems to have been in 1987 under the title *Zhenskii dekameron* (Tel-Aviv: Zerkalo), perhaps to emphasise its feminist credentials (see the comments made by Catriona Kelly in *A History of Russian Women's Writing* [Oxford: Clarendon Press, 1994], p.2, in which she explains that the term *damskaia* is considered even more disparaging than the term *zhenskaia* when applied to prose and poetry). The novel was first published in Russia in 1992 (Moscow: Vernisazh).
3. *Mariia – Zhurnal rossiiskogo nezavisimogo zhenskogo religioznogo kluba 'Mariia'*, no. 1 (Leningrad/Frankfurt-on-Main, 1981), p. 18.
4. Kuzminsky and Kovalev, *Blue Lagoon*, p. 12.
5. Diary entry for 19 September 1976, published in Kuzminsky and Kovalev, *Blue Lagoon*, where the bulk of the text has no pagination.
6. Published in *Tret'ia volna*, no. 6 (1979), pp. 35–40.
7. Julia Voznesenskaya (ed. and comp.), *Letters of Love: Women Political Prisoners in Exile and the Camps* (London: Quartet, 1989), p. 85.
8. See, for example, Iu.Voznesenskaia, 'O detskom knizhnom golode i knige L.Borodina', *Posev*, no. 9 (1982), pp. 56–58.
9. The years from 1975 to 1977 are documented in considerable detail in Kuzminsky and Kovalev, *Blue Lagoon*.
10. Diary entry for 2 December 1976, Kuzminsky and Kovalev, *Blue Lagoon*, no pagination.

11. Iuliia Voznesenskaia, 'Letter from Novosibirsk', published in Tatyana Mamonova (ed.), *Woman and Russia* (London: Sheba, 1980), pp. 63-70; 'Zapiski iz rukava', continued as 'Romashka belaia', in *Poiski*, no. 1 (1979), pp. 149-206; no. 4 (1982), pp. 153-82; and no. 5-6 (1983), pp. 303-35; 'Zhenskii lager"', *Grani*, no. 117 (1980), pp. 204-31.
12. In 'Romashka belaia', *Poiski*, no. 5-6 (1983), p. 317.
13. Kuzminsky and Kovalev, *Blue Lagoon*, pp. 15 and 27.
14. Voznesenskaya, *Letters of Love*, p. 94.
15. Voznesenskaia, 'Zhenskii lager"', in *Grani*, no. 117 (1980), p. 228.
16. Tatyana Mamonova, *Russian Women's Studies: Essays on Sexism in Soviet Culture* (Oxford: Pergamon, 1989), p. 154.
17. *Mariia*, no. 1 (1981), p. 17.
18. *Mariia*, no. 1 (1981), p. 18; no. 2 (1982), p. 101.
19. Boccaccio, 'Author's Epilogue', *The Decameron* (Penguin: Harmondsworth, 1972), p. 829. For a more extensive discussion of the relationship between Boccaccio and Voznesenskaia's novel see W. Feinstein, 'Twentieth-century Feminist Responses to Boccaccio's Alibech Story', in *Romance Languages Annual*, no. 1 (1989), pp. 116-20 and Kolodziej, 'Iuliia Voznesenskaia's Women', pp. 225-28.
20. For discussions of the hospital setting as a major chronotope of Russian women's fiction see Kelly, *History of Russian Women's Writing*, pp. 366-67 and Helena Goscilo, 'Women's Space and Women's Place in Contemporary Russian Fiction', in Rosalind Marsh (ed.), *Gender and Russian Literature: New perspectives* (Cambridge: Cambridge University Press, 1996), pp. 326-47.
21. Voznesenskaia, *Zhenskii dekameron* (Tel-Aviv: Zerkalo, 1987), p. 258.
22. Iu.Voznesenskaia, 'Zhenskii lager"', *Grani*, no. 117 (1980), pp. 223-25; 'Eshche odin klass?', *Posev*, no. 3 (1983), pp. 31-34. Beth Holmgren sees this as typical of the way recent fictional experiments have explored 'unsanctioned female roles and perspectives (the heroine as social misfit and fantasist) and taboo topics (female sexuality)' in *Women's Works in Stalin's Time: On Lidiia Chukovskaia and Nadezhda Mandelstam* (Bloomington and Indianapolis: Indiana University Press, 1993), p. 173.
23. Kelly, *History of Russian Women's Writing*, p. 386.
24. Voznesenskaia, *Zvezda Chernobyl'* (New York: Liberty, 1987), p. 27.
25. Voznesenskaya, *Letters of Love*, dedication.
26. Voznesenskaya, *Letters of Love*, p. 79.
27. Christa Wolf, *Störfall: Nachrichten eines Tages* (1987), published in English as *Accident* (London: Virago, 1989).
28. Voznesenskaya, *Letters of Love*, p. 5.
29. Voznesenskaia, 'Zapiski iz rukava', *Poiski*, no. 1 (1979), p. 150.
30. For an illuminating discussion of the Russians' scorn for the notion of 'women's writing', see Kelly, *History of Russian Women's Writing*, pp. 352-53; it may be that in calling herself a 'women's writer' Voznesenskaia is placing herself in a rather different category.
31. For a discussion of the notion of a 'woman's vision', see Kolodziej, 'Iuliia Voznesenskaia's Women', pp. 231ff.; he in turn draws on the sociological evidence for such a phenomenon provided through interviews by C. Hansson and K. Liden, the editors of *Moscow Women*: (New York: Pantheon, 1983).

Chapter 12

THE OTHER WOMAN: CHARACTER PORTRAYAL AND THE NARRATIVE VOICE IN THE SHORT STORIES OF LIUDMILA PETRUSHEVSKAIA

Monika Katz

An initial unbiased reading of a short story by Liudmila Petrushevskaia inevitably leaves one feeling confused and somewhat perturbed. The ruthlessness of the characters, the cruelty of their actions, the hopelessness of the circumstances – one cannot help asking oneself what model of reality is being projected and with what intention.

The scholarly approach deals with intratextual structures, defines what the unbiased reader unconsciously senses and puts it into a broader literary, historical and social context. I have approached the texts from two angles: firstly, I examine the image of women, and secondly, the narrative voice. My goal is a classification of Liudmila Petrushevskaia's prose within the realm of *bytovaia literatura* (everyday literature). As will be shown, the author's originality lies in her representation of women and in the dethroning of the narrator as a moral authority.

Translated by Nina Draganić

Images of Women in Liudmila Petrushevskaia's Short Stories

It is striking that in Liudmila Petrushevskaia's prose and plays the majority of the main characters are women. Do her works thereby fall under the heading 'women's literature'? Unlike the author, who consistently rejects such a classification, I would like to answer this question affirmatively. I define women's literature as literature written by women and dealing with women and specifically female problems, as well as with the portrayal of women in literature and/or the role of women in society.

To this day the 'strong-woman motif'[1] dominates in Russian literature. In the nineteenth century, the authors of the great realistic novels created the strong woman as a complement to the *lishnii chelovek* (superfluous person), who was, in fact, actually a *lishnii muzhchina* (superfluous man). These strong women compensated for the weaknesses of the men, who, torn by inner conflicts, were constantly in search of their place in society. They embodied *tsel'nost'* (wholeness/integrity), which ranks highly up in the hierarchy of Russian social values. In the twentieth century, the strong woman served as a model for the positive heroines of socialist realism: full of self-sacrifice and devotion, they fulfilled their tasks in the family as mothers, wives and housewives, as well as in their careers. The traditional female interior was extended to embrace the workplace, women thus assuming important functions in the private as well as in the public sphere.

In her story *Nedelia kak nedelia* (*A Week like Any Other*, 1969), Natal'ia Baranskaia puts the following characteristic words into the mouth of the seventy-year-old figure Mar'ia Matveevna: 'You have to be proud to be a good mother, and a good production worker to boot. You are a true Soviet woman'.[2] The true Soviet woman, the positive heroine of socialist realism, was useful to society in two ways: as a mother and as a working woman, reproducing in the traditional interior sphere and productive in the public sphere, in this case equal to man as far as tasks, functions and duties were concerned.

In post-socialist realist literature – in village and *kolkhoz* prose, as well as in urban and everyday literature – this model underwent certain alterations, but was still retained as the basic pattern. In the early 1960s and 1970s, *bytovaia literatura* resisted the distortion of reality, the *lakirovka* (varnishing) of socialist realism, and pitted against it a claim to honesty and uprightness. The female characters no longer struggled devotedly for the realisation of higher idealistic goals, but rather they struggled with the difficulties of everyday Soviet life – overcrowded public transport, insufficient supplies of food and consumer goods, especially in the satellite towns around the capital cities – and they fought against time.

Ol'ga Nikolaevna, the heroine of Natal'ia Baranskaia's story in diary form, is one possible paradigm for the portrayal of women in everyday literature. Constantly in a hurry, she suffers because she cannot devote herself completely either to her job or to her family. But, like her co-workers, she believes that a renunciation of one of the two spheres – either the private (motherhood and family), or the public (participation in social life or a career) – would lead to an impoverishment of her life, and of women's lives in general. Mar'ia Matveevna is pitted against the younger women as a sort of archaic model. But a close analysis reveals that the basic desire has remained unaltered: although the times have changed, the constant factors for the successful self-realisation of women are still considered to be motherhood in combination with a career.

These constant factors are radically dismantled by Liudmila Petrushevskaia. In her prose, a career no longer serves as a means of self-realisation, despite the fact that most of her female characters belong to the cultured class and are members of the academic or technical intelligentsia. The collective at their place of work offers no support: in contrast with *Nedelia kak nedelia*, there is no communal solidarity. Nor does the family offer a place of refuge: if the women are not single, widowed or divorced, their husbands are burdensome appendages who do not even fulfil their family duties. They are left with only the children, for whom they bear the sole responsibility, a responsibility they take seriously. Their only purpose in life, love of their children, claims their full attention, but at the same time leads them into isolation.

'Strana' (Country)[3] deals specifically with the isolation in such a mother-child relationship. This sketch describes the daily routine of a mother who lives with her child in a one-bedroom apartment. In the lonely evenings she consoles herself with alcohol. The only happy time for her is at night, when, in her sleep, she can escape into a fantasy world, a world in which she and her little daughter, the narrator suggests, would be better off if they were never to return.

Liudmila Petrushevskaia avoids looking for causes as explanations. She does not enquire as to women's real identity and refuses to create a model. She merely describes a woman's relationship to her environment, and thereby stands in the tradition of Chekhov and Trifonov. The short story 'Svoi krug'[4] points out rather drastically the disturbed relationship between the individual and the group. Out of a multitude of achronological episodes, strung loosely together by means of association, the first person narrator paints a portrait of her friends and the relationships between them. The title 'Svoi krug'

('My Circle', meaning a circle of friends) stands in stark contrast to the facts described: the relations are anything but friendly. The narrator as protagonist plays the part of the *enfant terrible* in the group. Due to her sarcastic and cynical manner of holding up a mirror to her friends in a rather crude language, she evokes hatred but is nonetheless tolerated. As she discovers that she is suffering from a terminal illness, she provides primarily for the future of her seven-year-old son, Alesha. Since she does not believe in the humanity of her so-called friends and consequently knows that an appeal to their consciences would be in vain, she resolves to secure her son's future by means of a staged performance: in the presence of her friends and her divorced husband, Alesha's father, she beats her child viciously for only a minor offence. This brutal cruelty, from which the friends save the child, awakens in them the protective instinct of a rescuer towards the innocent victim of a fury. The heroine has calculated the reaction of her friends correctly: flattered egoism is more likely to lead to altruism than an appeal to friendship and compassion.

Her conduct is merely a response to the behaviour of her environment. The heroine is not an intrinsically evil character – she is simply part of an environment in which each individual egotistically seeks his own gain. The female protagonist in 'Strana' is rejected by her surroundings to the point that she herself resigns and withdraws. The protagonist in 'Svoi krug', on the other hand, realises the 'laws' of this microsociety and uses them to her own advantage. The self-characterisation at the beginning of the story – she describes herself as being a *'zhestkii, zhestokii chelovek'* (a cruel, merciless person) – does not express her own opinion of herself, but the opinion of the others, which she has adopted. As such, this self-characterisation poses a question to the reader: is she really such a 'cruel, merciless person', or is she not only a culprit but also a victim?

The theme of many of the short stories is the problematic relationship between the individual and the group.[5] In the story 'Rasskazchitsa' (The Story-teller),[6] the naïvety and gullibility of the main female character is exploited by her colleagues for their own amusement. The work collective, in which the female protagonist of Natal'ia Baranskaia's *Nedelia kak nedelia* felt she was understood and taken seriously with her everyday worries, here betrays the trust of the individual. The tears shed by the female protagonist at the end of the story, which her colleagues misinterpret as tears of emotion, are a sign that she has understood their rejection.

The dehumanisation of an environment governed by indifference and lack of compassion and consideration lead to the disregard and violation of human dignity. The women are part of this environment, and moulded by it – they can be victims, but also culprits, the oppressed, but also the oppressors, without ever realising how dependent they are on the norms of this microsociety which causes them so much suffering. One exception is the protagonist of 'Svoi krug', who consciously makes use of these mechanisms for her own purposes.

The Narrative Voice in Liudmila Petrushevskaia's Prose

Female self-sacrifice and guilt (perpetration of injustice), one could object, are nothing new in Russian literature. Iurii Trifonov's *Moskovskie povesti* (*Moscow Tales*) provide striking evidence of this. In *Obmen* (*The Exchange*, 1969), for example, Lena Luk'ianova is the one who forces the exchange of apartments, who seeks material gain at the expense of humanity and egotistically pursues her materialistic goals. Ol'ga Vasil'evna, the protagonist in *Drugaia zhizn'* (*Another Life*, 1975), yields to certain rituals in order to attain professional advantages for her husband – a trip abroad, a positive evaluation of his thesis. Both women feel compelled to such behaviour by the conditions of Soviet society, for any other conduct would achieve nothing. They have no qualms about acting so inconsiderately, even against the will of those directly affected, because they believe they know what is right. This makes them both victims and culprits at the same time.

Yet Trifonov does not leave the reader with an impression of complete despair. In each story there is within the narrative voice a vanishing point in which the moral authority is concentrated. Abandoning the authorial narrator of socialist realism, a narrator who classified and passed judgement while also conveying certain values, Trifonov turns to the personal style of narration. Although the narrator transmits a variety of figural viewpoints, he always makes quite clear to which values the text is appealing in the conscience of the reader.[7] The story *Drugaia zhizn'*, for example, is narrated from the perspective of Ol'ga Vasil'evna. Her train of thought, which, from the point of view of the heroine, is logical and therefore makes sense to the reader, is constantly being qualified. But in the encounter with her daughter, she is revealed as a woman who is trapped in a system of prefabricated opinions and prejudices without being aware of it, and is therefore unable to liberate herself from them. Her conflict with the girl reveals clearly her inability to respond to others, to understand their motives and generally to relate to people on an equal basis. She imposes her views on her daughter and attempts to do the same with her husband: her will to dominate and control others represses his desire to find his own way. In this confrontation of different points of view, the quintessence of

Trifonov's texts emerges: readers are made aware of the unconscious mechanisms of social intercourse, they come to realise what amoral behaviour is, and this realisation leads them to reflect on their own actions and encourages them to change. At the same time, though, in the person of Sergei, Ol'ga Vasil'evna's husband, Trifonov shows us a character in search of his own path, rejecting the conformist behaviour of his wife and setting out on his way towards a new and different life.

The use of a narrative persona as a focus of moral appeal to the reader is discredited by Liudmila Petrushevskaia. As Nina Kolesnikoff has demonstrated,[8] this is achieved by using the commentary of the narrator to create ambiguity through irony. This allows for varying interpretations, and in the end readers are left to their own devices. The story 'Takaia devochka' (A Girl like That)[9] is about the friendship between two women. The protagonist, who narrates in the first person, describes her relationship to her neighbour Raisa Ravilia, who does not live up to what is generally expected of a woman. She has no job, no children to take care of and leaves all of the housework to her husband. Consequently, she does not even come close to fulfilling any of the duties that the narrator expects of a *normal* woman. In contrast to this, the narrator herself, according to her own statements, meets all the requirements of the strong woman. She is just as competent in her career as she is in her household; she fulfils her duties as the lover of her husband in the same exemplary fashion as she does those as the mother of her son. Yet the high opinion in which the narrator holds herself is contradicted by the facts, which, reflected in the consciousness of the protagonist, are gradually unveiled. Her husband Petrov wants to leave her but is too weak to carry out his resolve. She tolerates his affairs imperturbably and with great composure. This fact alone suffices to cast doubts on the truth of the narrator's statements about herself, that is, on her reliability as a source. The motivation for the persistence with which she forges plans to get her husband back lies less in her selfless love for him than in the prospect of getting a bigger apartment, which would fall flat in the case of a divorce. The contradiction between her own opinion and her materialistic motivation renders her unreliable as a moral authority.

She projects herself as the positive antipode to Raisa Ravilia, whom she refers to as a 'prostitute' because she goes to bed with every man she meets. But here, too, mistrust arises. The heroine knows the girl's life story, which she relates in a few brief sentences, but fails to draw any conclusions from it. She leaves it to the reader to establish the connection between the girl's past and her current behaviour, in particular the fact that she feels no pleasure during sexual intercourse. Raisa, a victim of sexual abuse in her early youth, displays all the characteristics defined by psychologists as typical of women who have suffered from sexual abuse: physical stiffness, loss of a sense of her own identity, including bodily identity, existential dread and suicidal tendencies. The protagonist shows no understanding whatsoever of her neighbour's mental state and refuses help in the form of empathetic talks. When her husband Petrov takes advantage of the defencelessness of the girl, sleeping with her and afterwards making fun of her frigidity, she takes him, the culprit, back, while refusing solidarity with Raisa, the victim. It remains unclear whether this is an unconscious defence mechanism by which she attempts to protect her nest, her territory, or whether she deliberately does not want to endanger what she has achieved and therefore wards off opposition from outside. One thing is indisputable: her behaviour consolidates male (mis)behaviour.

The author's narrative technique forces the reader – and, for the Russian reader, in particular, this is a great challenge – to tackle a taboo topic, namely sexual violence against women and the effect it has on their psyches. The heroine's attitude toward her neighbour reflects the 'normal' reaction, that is, the reaction prescribed by social behavioural norms. The realisation that such behaviour is not justified in light of the facts prevents the reader from identifying with the heroine. Even the pitiable victim Raisa cannot serve as a character with whom to identify. Instead, readers have to find their orientation somewhere between these two poles. The narrative persona fails to provide a focal point of moral authority. In this story, Liudmila Petrushevskaia refuses to give any indication whatsoever as to morally and ethically correct behaviour. Putting forward a moral claim requires a narrator who relates the facts in a reliable and comprehensible fashion. In Liudmila Petrushevskaia's prose works the narrator has lost his/her directive function. The system of values attached to the narrator, functioning implicitly as a moral postulate in the works of *bytovaia proza*, is no longer a point of reference in the works of Liudmila Petrushevskaia. Her texts do not communicate even the slightest directions as to proper conduct, but rather leave her readers feeling helpless and perplexed, obliged to find their bearings by comparing the representation of the content in the stories and the actual content itself. The extra-textual, extra-literary system of values is not indicated in the text. The author foments scepticism with regard to the narrator's point of view and compels the reader to be critical in dealing with the facts presented. She thereby trains her readers to examine and judge the facts critically and challenges their critical and analytical faculties much more radically than the representatives of *bytovaia proza* – she leaves everything open, and readers can rely only on their own powers of judgement.

Conclusion

With her representation of private and not public life in an urban area – the implied place of action is Moscow, the author's home town – Liudmila Petrushevskaia stands firmly in the tradition of *bytovaia literatura*. What characterises the everyday literature of the 1960s and 1970s? One of the most important features, in contrast to socialist realism, is the retreat of the protagonists into the private sphere, remote from politics and economics. Social reality is represented with regard to its effect on people's consciousness, important questions are presented from the viewpoint of the individual, particularly of members of the so-called *nauchno-technicheskaia intelligentsiia* (scientific and technological intelligentsia). The theme of work is stripped of its ideological significance. Of central importance is the individual, who strives for self-realisation beyond the working world; his desire for harmony in personal relations finds all but ideal conditions in matrimonial and family bonds.[10]

Liudmila Petrushevskaia's prose is based on these premises. The female in everyday literature continues to be strong, that is, she adheres to the functions imposed upon her in private and public life and endeavours to fulfil the duties which arise in both spheres. As Trifonov demonstrates, she is also able to assert herself better than the male within the social canon of norms. Liudmila Petrushevskaia demolishes the notion of the strong woman and shows her female protagonists caught in and confused by circumstances. She also demonstrates how, depending on their situations and their own predispositions, they can be either victims or culprits, or both. Not one of her short stories contains a female figure conceived as a positive hero. In addition, the author does away with the narrative persona who serves as a point of reference and who implicitly imparts a moral authority. She portends the capitulation of the narrator.

The short story 'Doch' Ksenii' (Kseniia's Daughter)[11] deals with another taboo topic: the theory that prostitution is borne out of the demands and exigencies of the masculine part of society and is then cemented by it. In view of the horrifying details, which will not be discussed in depth here, the narrator expresses an inability to comment and pass judgement:

> The function of literature consists, it would appear, in showing all those who are usually despised as people worthy of respect and pity. Thus writers seem to raise themselves high above the rest of the world, taking upon themselves the function of the sole protectors of just these despised people, taking upon themselves the role of universal judges, taking upon themselves the difficult task of bearing the guiding idea and instructing others. (Petrushevskaia: 81–82)

In an environment determined by inability to communicate and by lack of understanding for others – for such is the world represented in Liudmila Petrushevskaia's short stories – there cannot be an objectively observing, reliable narrator. Moral competence does not exist in the world of her prose.

Finally, I should like to return to the opening question: what functions do these works fulfil? The answer can be derived from the textual analyses: the author merely wishes to pose questions, advance ideas, to portray, as a journalist once put it in an interview, 'the offensive, the unthinkable, that which one never shows outwardly, that which is usually hidden behind the mask of decency, not only in front of strangers, but also from oneself. That which is pushed away into the black corner of consciousness'.[12] She wants to ask questions without attempting to steer her readers in any way. They have to look for the answer themselves. And yet she does not want to leave them completely alone, she hands them over to their own goodness, as she once emphasised in an interview.[13] It can be seen that the author is not completely immune to the temptation of being 'the voice in the wilderness':[14] by believing in the good in human beings, she hopes to awaken this goodness in her readers.

Notes

1. The term was coined by Vera Sandomirsky-Dunham, 'The Strong-Woman Motif', in Cyril E. Black (ed.), *The Transformation of Russian Society: Aspects of Social Change since 1861* (Cambridge, MA: Harvard University Press, 1960), pp. 459–83.
2. Natal'ia Baranskaia, 'Nedelia kak nedelia', first published in *Novyi mir*, no. 11 (1969), pp. 23–55 (p. 29). (Editor's note: translated into English as Natalya Baranskaya, *A Week Like Any Other and Other Stories*, trans. Pieta Monks [London: Virago, 1989]).
3. Liudmila Petrushevskaia, 'Strana', in *Bessmertnaia liubov'. Rasskazy* (Moscow: Moskovskii rabochii, 1988), pp. 75–76.
4. Liudmila Petrushevskaia, 'Svoi krug', in ibid., pp. 196–218. (Editor's note: translated under the title 'Our Crowd' in Helena Goscilo and Byron Lindsey [eds.], *Glasnost: An Anthology of Russian Literature under Gorbachev* [Ann Arbor: Ardis, 1990], pp. 3–24.)
5. See Adele Barker, 'Women without Men in the Writings of Contemporary Soviet Women Writers', in Daniel Rancour-Laferrière (ed.), *Russian Literature and Psychoanalysis*, Linguistic and Literary Studies in Eastern Europe, no. 31 (Amsterdam and Philadelphia: J. Benjamins, 1989), pp. 431–49.
6. Liudmila Petrushevskaia, 'Rasskazchitsa', in *Bessmertnaia liubov'*, pp. 27–35.
7. See Georg Witte, *Appell-Spiel-Ritual. Textpraktiken in der russischen Literatur der sechziger bis achtziger Jahre*, Opera slavica, no. 14 (Wiesbaden, 1989), pp. 27ff.

8. Nina Kolesnikoff, 'The Narrative Structure of Liudmila Petrushevskaia's Short Stories', *Canadian Slavonic Papers*, vol. 32, no. 4 (1990), pp. 444-56.
9. Liudmila Petrushevskaia, 'Takaia devochka', in *Bessmertnaia liubov'*, pp. 144-58.
10. For a comprehensive account, see Dirk Kretzschmar, *Sowjetische Alltagsliteratur und ihre Rezeption durch die Literaturkritik. Dargestellt anhand ausgewählter Werke der sechziger und siebziger Jahre*, Bochumer Slavistische Beiträge, no. 13 (Hagen, 1988).
11. Liudmila Petrushevskaia, 'Doch' Kseni', in *Bessmertnaia liubov'*, pp. 81-86.
12. Ibid., pp. 81-82.
13. 'Augenblicke des Glücks. Mit der Moskauer Schriftstellerin und Dramatikerin Liudmila Petruschewskaja sprach Sonja Margolina', *Tageszeitung* (Berlin), 27 March 1990, p. 16.
14. Antje Leetz, 'Gespräch mit Ludmila Petruschewskaja', *Sinn und Form*, vol. 42, no. 3 (1990), pp. 533-44 (p. 535).
15. 'Augenblicke des Glücks', p. 9.

Chapter 13

CONTEMPORARY WOMEN POETS IN THE METROPOLIS AND DIASPORA

Marina Ledkovsky

The number of women poets writing in Russian at the present is remarkable. It seems that the air of freedom has given free rein to talents that either have been subdued or could not surface because of the well-known factors that held sway over this much tried and long-suffering nation. Both in the homeland and abroad, there are scores of women poets who keep 'the sacred craft' alive, no matter under what circumstances and in what conditions. This chapter will deal with four of those 'craftswomen', two from the metropolis and two from the diaspora, who are probably little known in the West, but whose names may perhaps be familiar to poetry lovers and to those scholars who keep watch over contemporary cultural developments. The poets are the émigrés Ina Bliznetsova and Elena Ignatova, the Muscovite Ol'ga Rozhanskaia and Irina Znamenskaia of St Petersburg.

All four poets belong to a generation which has grown up without any illusions about the failure of the Bolshevik revolution, distrusting their devious government, but nevertheless harbouring a profound devotion to their battered motherland. Only one of them managed to have a collection published during the so-called 'period of stagnation' (the Brezhnev era): Irina Znamenskaia in 1982; the others resorted to publishing in *samizdat* and abroad. Ina Bliznetsova chose not to publish anything in her homeland before her emigration.

A unifying characteristic of these four poets is their strikingly high level of sophistication, their command over their craft, which, of course, links them to a great number of sister poets at home and abroad. All four belong to the intellectual élite and hold university degrees; two symptomatically in mathematics, one in fine arts, and only Elena Ignatova actually has a literary-philological graduate education which qualified her to teach literature at Leningrad University until her family's first attempt to emigrate in 1979.

All four poets work within the tradition of Russian poetry, having mastered its classical poetics. They even frequently assume the persona of typical Russian *intelligenty* conversing with their precursors. While they are establishing a continuum of Russian *ars poetica*, they also seek to transcend it by creating totally novel imagery and metric forms through ingenious associative semantic twists, syntactic inversions and vibrant innovative rhythms. The poetry of both émigré writers, especially Bliznetsova's, is enriched by non-Russian poetic and cultural traditions, and that, as it seems at this point in time, to a higher degree than the work of their peers in the homeland. Yet, it would be only fair to assert that the poetry of all four women is impregnated with the civilisation of this planet in its most diversified forms, reflecting its achievements, failures and concerns in winged transcendence.

Noteworthy and symbolic are the titles of the various collections: Bliznetsova's painful themes in her first book *Dolina tenet* (Dale of Snares, 1988) are resolved in the second collection *Vid na nebo* (A View of the Sky, 1991). Similarly, Elena Ignatova's themes in the earlier *Teplaia zemlia* (Warm Earth, 1989) culminate in her latest book *Nebesnoe zarevo* (Heavenly Glow, 1992). The earthbound view changes direction towards the heavenly light. Rozhanskaia's *samizdat* collection *Dalee vezde* (From Now On It's Everywhere, 1978) and Znamenskaia's *Dolgii svet* (Long Light) echo their poetic sisters' longing for the glowing light to illumine their spirits and enlighten humanity's ephemeral existence in the 'dale of snares'.

These women poets certainly share the 'eternal themes' of love, life and death, but interestingly, with all four poets love recedes before more pressing and oppressing topics and is frequently treated with irony. Despondency and nostalgia, the pain of parting, loneliness, Russia's tragic destiny, the transience of time, the incongruity of city life, awe before the void of cosmic space, helplessness in face of life's constraints and yet trust, in spite of all, trust and faith in Divine Grace, are the major themes which fill these women's verses.

Ina Bliznetsova, the youngest and possibly the most original and intense lyricist among the four poets, is a professional mathematician. She draws on many currents of Russian and non-Russian poetic traditions. Her sources include Shakespeare, Keats, Auden, Tolkien, Lewis Carroll, Pushkin, Blok, Bely, Tiutchev, the Old and New Testaments, especially the Revelation, the Apocrypha, the Koran, the Scaldian tradition and others. Her complex verses seem to reflect inversions of Maiakovsky or even Trediakovsky and include elements harking back to Khlebnikov's ingenious devices, particularly the personification and dramatisation of primary elements; but all these seemingly borrowed techniques are transfigured into a totally idiosyncratic perception of God's creation, as, for example, when she speaks about a burning candle:

Согласное движение огня,
весь язычок не более окурка,
а в серцевине чёрная фигурка
поклоны бьёт и молит за меня.[1]

(Harmonious movement of the flame,/ the tongue not bigger than a cigarette stub,/ But in its core a little black figure/ Is bowing down and praying for me.)

The praying, little black figure is the candle's wick. In Bliznetsova's poetic realm the sun is feeling cold and its face turns white (*D.t.*: 119), leaves behave like humans in many different ways: they clap hands and whirl in Russian round dances in the garden behind the window.[2]

The tone of Bliznetsova's first collection *Dolina tenet* is overwhelmingly sombre. 'Memory' is a net for the soul, for life, it leads the soul by its will, darkens the light and causes days to blend, each worn to holes (*D.t.*: 117). By contrast, the mood of *Vid na nebo* is radiant and limpid: wind causes fire to change its face, and water (feminine in Russian) runs away from the wind, teasing it (him in Russian) like a flirtatious woman (*V.n.n.*: 9). Windows are eyes discovering the sun's pupil which blazes with a spoon bait (device to catch a fish) and lures the air to move closer to it (*V.n.n.*: 15); and 'memory [becomes] crystal clear; its mirrors need not reflect a face but simply admit it with the same ease as a hare moves his ears' (*V.n.n.*: 25).

One of Bliznetsova's themes is the myth of woman in Russia. In a 1979 poem dedicated to Akhmatova and written as an epistle to her in the other world (*D.t.*: 40), Bliznetsova uses Akhmatova's own coined word-images, such as '*besputnaia*' (dissolute) and '*nezabytaia*' (unforgotten), and spontaneously ascribes to Akhmatova a semi-folklore title of a princess reigning on Earth, and possibly in the other world as well: '*legko li tsarit'sia, tsarevna?*' (is it easy to rule, princess?). Bliznetsova's informal address to 'Akhmatova the poet', combined with her reverence towards her as 'a legendary woman', suggests the idea of a poetic sisterhood between the great predecessor and

Bliznetsova's lyrical heroine. In the long narrative poem *Apokrif shestogo dnia* (Apocrypha of the Sixth Day) (*D.t.*: 63–81), Bliznetsova traces the history of Shakespeare's, Pushkin's and others' poetic inspiration from Cleopatra to Lilith. The theme of the *femme fatale*, however, is underplayed. The most prominent topic of the poetic cycle is the role of feminine consciousness in the development of a universal poetic tradition.[3] The lyric persona appeals to Cleopatra as '*Porfirorodnaia!*' (Porphyrogeneta, or born in purple, that is, of imperial heritage/descent), and continues: '*pochti Latona – nepomnimaia mater' Apollona*' (almost Latona – the non-remembered mother of Apollo, *D.t.*: 66),[4] and then recalls several famous feminine figures including Euridice, Lilith, Lot's wife, Sarah, Mary, Psyche and the Lorelei, whose major acts are recorded for their power of love. Cleopatra responds to the woman poet speaking of Lilith's and her own love mysteries: '*po snegam tvoim nashi tainy raznes arap*' (the African [Pushkin] has spread/published our secrets all over your snows [*D.t.*: 64]). The contrast between Russian snow and Pushkin's Africanness emphasises the broad range of continuity existing between Cleopatra (and possibly Lilith) and Bliznetsova's poetic persona, who embodies here a contemporary link in a chain of feminine poetic consciousness.[5]

In 'Zhemchug' (Pearls, *V.n.n.*: 81), one of Bliznetsova's latest poems, with the parenthetic title 'Vermeer', she grasps almost at one stroke the Dutch master's accomplished hermetic art. She might perceive a kindred spirit in Vermeer. Like Vermeer, she is unique within a popular and much diffused art genre, in her case lyrical poetry. Like Vermeer, she withstands all possible influences, being preoccupied with a wholly personal direction unlike any other. Her art also expresses a knowledge of matter that is so sensitive as to be almost scientific. Each poem seems to be the sum of various analytic experiments with resources of the Russian language in vocabulary, syntax and rhythmical sequences. Bliznetsova concentrates on purely intellectual proliferations, writing basically for herself in an enclosure of her own created world, very much like Vermeer who is alleged to have painted his great works confined to his rooms. Vermeer recreated a closed universe in which gradations of natural and reflected daylight are rendered with infinite care. Bliznetsova's poems, like Vermeer's paintings, depict a refined existence, refinement understood as a sifting of reality designed to make it more accessible through intellectual perception. Her poems remind one of Vermeer's lavish surroundings filled with pearls, silk and ermine, embroidery and silver cutlery; they are gems in the heritage of pure art. Her work, hitherto regrettably little known, attests to a major poetic talent that promises unique and rich contributions to Russian literature.

Elena Ignatova, also an émigré since 1990, who lives in Jerusalem, is the oldest among the four chosen poets. She is also the most accomplished and mature artist who has full power over her poetic material. She was raised alternately in Grishko, a village in the Smolensk district, and in Leningrad. This background endows her perception with a sense of the unity between rural and urban cultures of all periods. Thus she deals with the myth of St Petersburg as a stone beast coming to life, as it does in Pushkin's *Mednyi vsadnik* (*The Bronze Horseman*, 1837) and in Andrei Bely's *Peterburg* (*Petersburg*, 1916), and juxtaposes '*prostoliudin antichnyi*' (the laziness and playfulness of the plebeians of antiquity, referring to the many classical statues in parks and on buildings) with the defencelessness of the city's inhabitants before the ominous dreams of herds of prancing horses on bared streets;[6] but in another poem, 'Gorod cheren i tochen beloi noch'iu' (The City is Black and Chiselled by the White Night [*T.z.*: 11–12]), those plebeians of antiquity become soldiers with rifles, workers with hammers and militant peasant women of socialist realism. In Ignatova's perception, the St Petersburg myth is continued and transformed into an more threatening mythology of Soviet Leningrad.[7]

The tragedy of Russian history is a major topic in Ignatova's poetry. It is interwoven with the Russian cultural myth, perceived in terms reminiscent of Zabolotsky, and further back, Nekrasov:

Сидят большие мужики,
Их бороды клинообразны,
В глазах зимуют светляки,
А руки праздны.

(*T.z.*: 30; see also 42.)

(Large peasant men are sitting [here],/ Their beards wedge-shaped,/ Glow-worms hibernate in their eyes,/ And their hands are idle.)

Ignatova uses folklore elements and models in following up the fates of Russia's cities and towns, alternating between regular and irregular metrics as well as accentuated lines:

И останется от меня грамотка,
Мол, жила баба в Суздале,
Хорошо ли, скудно ли – не вем.

(*T.z.*: 37; see also 38.)

(And a note will remain after me,/ Saying a peasant woman lived in Suzdal',/ I don't know whether in plenty or in poverty.)

Rather ominous associations in the poem 'Smutnoe vremia' (The Time of Troubles) bring the reader up to the present, when the 'infamous Stepan' (the rebel leader Sten'ka Razin) aims to become the autocrat of all Russia (*T.z.*: 40). The people's inhuman sufferings are intertwined with Russia's ordeals, and the lyrical persona desires to take part in Russia's regeneration in a moving metaphorical way:

я просила бы здесь умереть, чтобы семечком лечь;
в чернопахотной смуглой горсти.

(*T.z.*: 48-49)

(I would ask to die here, to lie down as a small seed/ in the dark palm of arable black earth.)

Ovid's presence is prominent in Ignatova's poetry. She refers to him in her poems about exile or internal exile. In poems about flight and exile Ignatova uses long Ovidian lines of up to nine feet, except that hers are iambic or trochaic and not dactylic. In a poem about exile from Russia, 'Iu. Kolkeru' (To Iu. Kolker), Ignatova uses consistently trochaic lines of nine feet to convey the laborious yet glorious 'Flight to Egypt' and its unsurpassed significance over the plight of the common man.[8] In an elegy to the memory of a friend, Ignatova uses, if somewhat inconsistently, Ovid's alternating irregular hexameter and pentameter. Each departure from the regular metric scheme contains a special message for the reader: the kenotic suffering of the lyrical persona at the painful parting from her friend. Thus, the truncated tetrametric line: '*Ton'she solominki stavshii liubimyi*' (The beloved who became skinnier than a straw [*T.z.*: 19]) conveys formally its kenotic solidarity with the visible disappearance of the emaciated beloved who becomes thinner than a straw. Ignatova uses stunning metaphors and similes and meaningful metric violations to convey various strong feelings: the utter exhaustion of survivors of the revolution or war on their flight from persecution (*T.z.*: 12–14), or rejoicing over miraculous happenings. In the poem 'Kogda volkhvy ne zazhigali svech' (When the Magi did not light candles), the regular iambic pentameter is interrupted by an important line in amphibrakh: '*Zemlia, kak rozhenitsa, syna zhdet*' (The earth awaits a son like a birth giver [*T.z.*: 54]) to express the earth's exultation over her own renewal; and the wondering of the earth, the second *rozhenitsa* (birth giver), over this miracle of her own renewal becomes a gift to the new-born son of Mary and, by that same token, comfort for Mary's premonition of her son's supreme sacrifice:

Смотри, Мария, видишь голубица,
Как счастливо земля себе дивиться,
И это чудо – Сыну Твоему.

(*T.z.*: 55)

(Look, Mary, do you see, my darling,/ How happily the earth is wondering at herself,/ And this miracle is [a gift] to your Son.)

In her verses about 'Lot's Wife' (*T.z.*: 52–53), Ignatova adduces an example of deep-seated memory: Lot's wife cannot forget her people; her implication in their sins forces her to turn around and suffer along with them. This partaking in a common plight turns into a blessing, as does suffering along with Christ, the Sinless One, in another poem, 'Strastnaia Nedelia' (Holy Week).[9] Ignatova turns frequently to the figure of memory. Memory is always present, it does not forget, and becomes a testimony to her cruel epoch (*N.z.*: 9). She speaks for the entire intelligentsia over the past seven decades in her harassed country when she announces in solemn anapaestic pentameter:

Ничего не проси у страны – ни любви, ни суда, ...
Но как тайный судья, соучастник судьбы, тугодум –
вывожу на полях неизвестное слово «свобода».

(*N.z.*, 10)

(Do not ask for anything of your country – neither love, nor judgement,.../ But as a secret judge, a participator in fate, a slow-witted person – / I trace in the margins the unknown word 'liberty'.)

The poem 'Nebo pomnit bol'she' (Heaven Remembers More [*N.z.*: 58]) confirms that time will preserve memory, that it will not erase it, but will return it to its sources in joining the heaven with its (everlasting) light. In other verses memory is a bond to the forebears (*N.z.*: 61). Ignatova further addresses fellow poets to establish an unceasing bond. In a sombre, Lermontovian mode ('Chto delat', brat?' [What's to be Done, Brother?, *N.z.*: 50]), she recalls the tragic fates of Khlebnikov, Tsvetaeva, Akhmatova, and the village Komarovo, the favorite abode of Petersburg writers and poets, in a covert appeal to remember the long line of poetic tradition and not let it fall into oblivion.

Ignatova has some remarkable love poems in which love appears in a generous and noble guise. 'There is fullness of light and regal bitterness in unhappy love', the poet exclaims, resigned to 'azure loneliness' (*N.z.*: 21). The feminine theme of mother love works in two ways: it is love of the poet's mother and love of her son. All tenderness is turned toward her mother ('Nezhnost' moia' [My Dearest One, *N.z.*: 35]). Ignatova blesses the happiness of having a child:

О будь благословенна, жизнь моя,
за то, что ты дала минуту эту
пронзительного счастья бытия!

(*N.z.*: 34)

(Be blessed, o my life,/ for granting me those minutes/ of intense happiness of existence!)

This attitude seems quite different from Mariia Shkapskaia's poetic vision of motherhood and adds a unique tonality to this prominent theme in Russian women's poetry. Elena Ignatova's poetry as well as her prose is presently being published in Russia. She hopes to publish another collection of poems in Russia as soon as circumstances will permit.

Ol'ga Rozhanskaia is a Muscovite by birth and presently resides in Moscow. She was trained in mathematics at the Faculty of Mathematics and Mechanics of Moscow University, but her interests ranged from mathematics to literature, music, art, civil and human rights. She became active in the dissident movement while also writing poetry. In 1974 she was expelled from the university for supporting Gabriel Superfin (a prominent archivist and librarian now residing and working in western Europe) before and during his trial. In 1975 she finally graduated from the department of mathematics of Kalinin University (now Tver'). In 1978 she published in *samizdat* her first collection of poems, *Dalee vezde* (From Now on It's Everywhere). Several of her poems were used as texts to music by the composer Anatoly Aleksandrov – one of them, 'Granadskaia pesnia' (The Granada Song), was published in 1978 in a collection that included music set to the words of Hölderlin, Tiutchev, Blok, Akhmatova and Pasternak. In 1988 Rozhanskaia started publishing many of her poems in Russian periodicals and almanacs both in Russia and abroad. In spring 1993 the volume *Stikhi po-russki* (Verses in Russian) was published in Moscow. Many of Rozhanskaia's poems are written as 'responses' to Russian poets ranging from Pushkin to Akhmatova, Pasternak, Mandel'shtam and Zabolotsky. Thus 'Na kladbishche' (At the Cemetery)[10] is written as a scene from Pushkin's 'little tragedy' *Kamennyi gost'* (*The Stone Guest*, 1830) that had been 'lost' and subsequently 'retrieved' by Rozhanskaia. It deals with the vanity of life and its pernicious corruption. Her short poem 'V Moskve stoit polupogoda' (It is Half-Weather in Moscow [*S.p-r.*: 13]) responds to two Russian poetic traditions of the beginning of this century. It combines the graphic clarity of the Acmeists with the typically Pasternakian fusion of Nature and the distinct human subject surrounded by it. The ratio of four enjambments per seven lines in this poem resembles the way Brodsky 'digests' both the Acmeist and the Pasternakian traditions. Hence, besides these two traditions Rozhanskaia also incorporates into this very short poem Brodsky's poetic world. The extremely colloquial '*nanesena na nichego*' (etched on nothing), instead of the more appropriate '*ni na chem*', or the awkward but still correct philosophical term '*na nichto*', is typical of Rozhanskaia's poetic persona, a Russian *intelligent* who uses colloquial kitchen Russian to describe even a natural phenomenon that may lead him or her to the 'learned' cartesian conclusion *ergo est.*. With the density of various poetic traditions reflected in this short poem, the style of the poem is nonetheless unique. It amalgamates elements which none of these poetic traditions would combine in the same context.[11]

Generally, Rozhanskaia combines with mastery the lofty and the lowly, vulgarisms with high style, and by this paradoxical blending embraces all of life's meaning, as in the following short piece:

> Где мы на праздник собрались,
> Там стаи ангелов вились
> И хрипло каркали. Теснима
> Печальным знанием душа.
> Как несказанно хороша
> Ты, жизнь! Как зла, как нелюбима ...
>
> (*S.p-r.*, 51)

(Where we gathered for a holiday,/ There circled flocks of angels/ And croaked hoarsely. The soul/ Is oppressed by sad wisdom./ How ineffably beautiful you are/ O life! How evil, how unlovable...)

Rozhanskaia operates comfortably and with ease within the classical tradition and, unlike Ignatova and Bliznetsova, only rarely attempts experimentation with blank verse, irregular metrics and rhyme. Yet within the strict confines of classical versification she creates innovative images by purely semantic elements. She reworks Mandel'shtam's 'Na lune ne rastet ni odnoi bylinki' ('Not One Blade of Grass Grows on the Moon')[12] and Zabolotsky's 'Ne pozvoliai dushe lenit'sia' ('Do not Allow the Soul to Loiter')[13] in her own variations, as if polemicising with them in a very witty way. She uses the exact Mandel'shtamian cadence of alternating anapaestic and trochaic lines to come to the ironic dismissal of Mandel'shtam's longing for a peculiar Eden:

> На луне не дома
> Просто голубятни.
> Голубые дома –
> Чудо голубятни.

(On the moon there are no houses/ There are simply dovecotes./ Blue houses – / Dovecotes just a marvel.)

To this idyll Rozhanskaia replies:

> Что прошло на Луне –
> Будто и не было.
>
> (*S.p-r.*: 103)

(What has gone by on the Moon – / Seems never to have existed.)

And to Zabolotsky's entreaties not to allow the soul to be lazy comes Rozhanskaia's conclusion:

Кто сулил нам труд и глад,
Верно, нынче Сам не рад.

S.p-r., 60)

(He who has promised us labour and hunger,/ Probably, now Himself is unhappy.)

The Creator Himself rejects humanity turned to insanity.
The poem 'Chto Rozhdestvo? –' ('What About Christmas? –' [*S.p-r.*: 59]) echoes several of Brodsky's Christmas poems, but especially the last lines of his '24 dekabria 1971 goda' ('24 December 1971') in *Chast' rechi* (*Parts of Speech*):

Возникает фигура в платке,
и Младенца, и Духа Святого
ощущаешь в себе без стыда;
Смотришь в небо и видишь – звезда.[14]

(There emerges the figure in a veil,/ and the Child, and you/ sense the Holy Spirit in yourself without shame;/ You gaze at the sky and you see – the star).

'The weary slave' in Rozhanskaia's poem, the Everyman and at the same time the Lord of the Universe, is stunned by the same visions of the Virgin, the Child, and the Star. Pushkin's frequently used metaphor *ustalyi rab* (weary slave) acquires in Rozhanskaia's line a new, profoundly spiritual meaning. Thus, the Russian poetic and cultural heritage kindles Rozhanskaia's fertile imagination to carry further the 'sacred craft' in constant spiritual communication with the greatest of Russia's poets.

The same can be said about Irina Znamenskaia who was born and raised in St Petersburg and still lives in the Northern Palmyra. She began writing poetry as a child, but her primary interest was in graphic arts. After high school she took up studies in graphic arts as well as painting. She worked primarily in watercolours. Only after meeting the poet Gleb Semenov did she decide to take up poetry full-time and give up painting. Znamenskaia began to publish her poetry in 1977, and in 1982 her first collection *Dolgii svet* (The Long Light) was released uncut and she was awarded the Gor'ky prize for literature. In spite of this award Znamenskaia could not publish again until 1989, because her poetry was not to the taste of the increasingly tense literary officials. Her verses were too sensitive to the uneasiness of human existence and were constantly questioning its absurdity and bemoaning the irretrievable passing of time, the discord between her winged dreams and the surrounding reality. Znamenskaia, like so many of her peers ever since the 1920s, had to support herself with translations and literary reviews.

Motifs of the transience of existence, of unhappy love, of loss of heart fill most of the pages of her two collections. Like her peers, she responds to the great precursors, claims descendance from Pasternak and Mandel'shtam and feels akin to Brodsky. Yet in her poetry you find reminiscences of Akhmatova and Tsvetaeva. She is very conscious of her deep links to the poetic brother- and sisterhood which she hopes to join in eternity. In her poem 'Al'ternativa' (Alternative), she exclaims: 'The way out of Russia is into heaven …/Its night stripe/ Raises dust in the constellations of the zodiac./ For now – it is the only way/ Where the echo calls back to you like a brother.'[15] Only in heaven does Znamenskaia expect to be accepted as an equal by her poetic predecessors. In another poem-prayer written after a disastrous earthquake in Mexico she appeals to the Lord for grace and mercy to grant safety for all sisters around the globe:

Господи! Сохрани Лауру, и дочерь её Либертад,
И младенца Светлану, русскую мексиканску!

(*O.n.t.*: 127)

(O Lord! Preserve Laura, and her daughter Libertad,/ And the baby Svetlana, the Mexican Russian girl! …)

At the end of the poem she implores the Lord: 'Turn all of us around that we may face each other …' (*O.n.t.*: 128), presumably to form a universal kinship.

Znamenskaia polemicises with her great poetic forebears in several poems. The distance receding like the sea and falling to an unknown bottom in 'Kak more – vglub' ukhodit dal'' (*O.n.t.*: 71) does not evoke Pushkinian serene sadness but rather seems to limit her memory. And the Lermontovian-inspired meditation on the stony road where space hearkens to God is exchanged for the screech of brakes and impudent headlights ('… O chem zhaleiu?' [What do I regret?, *O.n.t.*: 74]). Likewise, the poem 'Pora, moi drug, – parad/ Soshel na net postylo …' (It's time, my friend, the parade/ Has come to naught in an odious way [*O.n.t.*: 136]) reworks Pushkin's 'Pora, moi drug, pora! pokoia serdtse prosit' ('It's time, my friend, it's time! The heart begs for peace').[16] Each line is saturated with tropes. Metaphors carry the basic weight of meaning of each verse. Throughout the second collection the poet strives, successfully, to avoid clichés and banalities. The ironic search for peace in an unfamiliar freedom points to the major concern that still dominates the poetic world of many writers. Znamenskaia, like her sister poets, continues to develop and should expect well-deserved recognition of her talent.

The work of these four women is provocative and challenging, sophisticated and in many ways crosscultural. It may be that their poetry belongs to the future, and that only the coming generations will be able to appreciate fully their extraordinary contribution.

Notes

This article is based on research for a larger project, *Russian Women Writers 1760–1992*, supported by a grant from the International Research and Exchanges Board (IREX) and with funds provided by the Andrew W. Mellon Foundation, by a National Endowment for the Humanities Travel to Collections award, a travel grant by the American Philosophical Society, as well as several associateships at the Summer Research Laboratory of the Russian and East European Center at the University of Illinois, Champaign-Urbana. Neither of these organisations is responsible for the views expressed. It is also the result of collaboration with Olga Meerson, Columbia University, whose thoughtful contribution to the discussion of the poetry of Ina Bliznetsova, Elena Ignatova and Ol'ga Rozhanskaia is deeply appreciated.

Gratitude is due to Ina Blizetsova, Elena Ignatova, Ol'ga Rozhanskaia and Irina Znamenskaia for permission to quote from their work. All translations are mine unless otherwise indicated.

1. Ina Bliznetsova, *Dolina tenet* (Tenafly: Hermitage, 1988), p. 22. Additional examples from this book will be identified by *D.t.* and the page number in the text.
2. Ina Bliznetsova, *Vid na nebo* (Tenafly: Hermitage, 1991), p. 12. The shortened title *V.n.n.* and page number will be used for further citations in the text.
3. Olga Meerson, 'Bliznetsova, Inessa Viktorovna', in Marina Ledkovsky, Charlotte Rosenthal and Mary Zirin (eds), *Dictionary of Russian Women Writers 1760–1992* (Westport, CT: Greenwood Press, 1995), pp. 87–89.
4. Note the uncommon, yet perfectly appropriate passive participle '*nepomnimaia*': according to Greek mythology Latona bore the god of the sun, and as legend has it, Cleopatra's and Anthony's son was the sun whereas their daughter was the moon.
5. Meerson, 'Bliznetsova'.
6. Elena Ignatova, *Teplaia zemlia* (Leningrad: Sovetskii Pisatel', 1989), p. 7. The shortened title *T.z.* and page number will be used for further citations in the text.
7. Olga Meerson, 'Ignatova, Elena Alekseevna', in Ledkovsky, Rosenthal and Zirin, *Dictionary of Russian Women Writers*, pp. 252–54. Meerson's important ideas are integrated in the overall discussion of Ignatova's poetry.
8. Elena Ignatova, 'Iu. Kolkeru', in *Nebesnoe zarevo* (The Heavenly Glow) (Jerusalem: Prisma-Press, 1992), p. 63. *N.z.* and page number will be used for additional citations in the text.

9. Elena Ignatova, 'Strastnaia Nedelia' (Holy Week), in *Stikhi o prichastnosti* (Verses of Belonging) (Paris: Ritm, 1976), p. 12.
10. Ol'ga Rozhanskaia, *Stikhi po-russki* (Moscow, 1993), p. 76. *S.p-r.* and page number will be used for citations in the text.
11. Olga Meerson, 'Rozhanskaia, Ol'ga Vladimirovna', in *Dictionary of Russian Women Writers*, pp. 545–46.
12. Osip Mandel'shtam, *Collected Works in Two Volumes*, ed. G.P. Struve and B.A. Filipoff (Washington: Inter-Language Literary Associates, 1964), vol. 1, p. 36.
13. Nikolai Zabolotskii, *Poems*, ed. Gleb Struve and Boris Filipoff (Washington: Inter-Language Literary Associates, 1965), p. 204.
14. Iosif Brodskii, *Chast' rechi* (Ann Arbor: Ardis, 1977), p. 6.
15. Irina Vladimirovna Znamenskaia, 'Al'ternativa', in *Obrashchaius' na "ty"* (I Address You as 'Thou' [Leningrad: Sovetskii pisatel', 1989]), p. 155. In following citations the abbreviation *O.n.t.* with page number will be used in the text.
16. A.S. Pushkin, *Polnoe sobranie sochinenii v desiati tomakh* (Moscow: Akademiia Nauk SSSR, 1962–1966), vol. 3, p. 278.

Part Four

THE IMAGE OF WOMEN IN TWENTIETH-CENTURY RUSSIAN LITERATURE

Chapter 14

GAPS IN THE COSMOGONY: WITCHCRAFT IMAGERY IN ANDREI BELY'S *KOTIK LETAEV*

Peter I. Barta

Andrei Bely intended to write a history of his spiritual life to be entitled 'Moia zhizn" (My Life). He managed, however, to complete only the first volume of this project, the novel *Kotik Letaev*. The highly innovative use of form and style, not to mention the unconventional symbolism, are an attempt to create his 'poetic word' which, in turn, will give rise to a 'new world'.[1] In other words, he sets out to develop the idea expressed in the words of Tolstoy's Natasha Rostova in the epigraph of *Kotik Letaev*:

> – Знаешь, я думаю, – сказала Наташа шёпотом ... – что когда вспоминаешь, вспоминаешь, до того довспоминаешься, что помнишь то, что было ещё прежде, чем я была на свете ...
> (L.Tolstoy, *Voina i mir*, in *KL*: 428).

('You know, I think', Natasha said in a whisper ..., 'that when you remember and remember, you see so far back in the past that you recall what happened even before you were born.')[2]

Bely's 'pseudo-autobiographical' narrator aims at attaining a transcendental level of consciousness:[3] Kotik Letaev's adult self traces the journey of the mind from a supposedly atemporal, eternal condition, through the development of an emerging human consciousness, towards a union with Christ in which the transhistorical condition is regained. Inspired by Steiner's anthroposophy, Bely's autobiographical narrative intends to re-enact an act of 'cosmogony' as it outlines the soul's journey into time and space.[4] Throughout the journey, significantly, the child encounters frightening old women.

Jungian archetypal criticism uses the categories of the positive and negative elementary characters of the feminine. According to this view, the positive aspects of woman spring from the visible mother-child relationship, whereas the negative side of woman arises from the inner experience of fear and anguish. These cannot be derived from any specific attributes, but from a projective ring of symbols.[5] While the archetypal approach is itself sexist, in that it considers the positive aspect of femininity to be the child-bearing vessel, without taking into account such factors as discourse and ideology when arguing about supposedly 'universal' concepts, it proves to be a helpful analytical tool in investigating how Bely's text creates the world of the *'uzhasnaia pramat"* (dreadful female ancestor) and the witches.[6]

This chapter does not seek to analyse how Bely's symbolism is designed to reveal his system of gnosticism. Instead it will consider how the portrayal of the witch in the history of European culture functions to underpin the novel's ideology. This covert discourse in the text illustrates how the values shaping the author's culture taint the philosophical views which inform his account of the child's 'cosmogonic' journey. In Kotik's pre- and post-natal memories we find a consistently negatively valorised 'feminine principle' at work. This chapter will investigate the cultural archetypes of a decidedly misogynistic culture which buttress the self-conscious gnostic symbolism of the surface. In order to substantiate our claims, it will be necessary to study aspects of both Russia's medieval and popular culture which are informed by the archetypes of the feminine. As transcendental memories are retrieved from a little boy's childhood experiences, the historical imagery of the witch occupies a marked presence in the novel's consciousness. The symbolic 'darkness' that wicked old women supposedly represent stands in contrast to the light in which Christ's figure is bathed.

Kotik Letaev might be described as a *Bildungsroman* of sorts, in that its theme depicts the maturation of consciousness as the protagonist travels on a journey of the mind from 'innocence' to 'experience'. 'Experience' means the loss of pre-natal consciousness: the adult narrator is ready to return to the eternal world of innocence from which the child supposedly came.[7] This is the realm of real maturity. The journey of the protagonist in *Kotik Letaev* is reminiscent of the initiation rite in the world of tales of the miraculous. The event marks the boy's turning into a man and during its course the hero 'dies' temporarily in order to be resurrected as a 'new man'. The process also has analogies with the Romantic yearning for transcendental purity and light which the child loses upon entering society, as in Wordsworth's *The Prelude* and his ode 'Intimations of Immortality'. Kotik's grown-up self knows that he will regain the happiness and knowledge he left behind at the end of his passage through human life, and the adult persona acquires the ability to recreate the child's memory of its beginnings.

Bely introduces mythological references to bridge the gap between Kotik's physical world and a transcendental world of essences. Characters and events are integrated into a mythological and cosmic system. Bely is typical of his generation of Symbolists in his desire to find a path from the external, superficial manifestations of the physical world to a supposedly eternal, higher reality. History is also present, however, albeit only in the text's subconscious. Supposedly, behind the multiple forms of symbols lies universal truth and both the unborn child, before his journey, and the adult, after his journey, are at one with this force to which, during one's lifetime, access can only be gained by searching one's soul.[8] Essential knowledge is hidden inside the self: the narrator says, *'pravdu vyskazat' nevozmozhno – ona gorit v serdtse'* (It is impossible to articulate the truth; it burns in one's heart).[9]

In an appraisal of the substantial artistic merits of *Kotik Letaev*, the interrelated imagery of the novel will, no doubt, be of greater interest than its incongruities. If we wish to study the text's mooring in history, however, we will need to focus primarily on the differences. Such pairs of binary opposites as light and darkness, thought and body, eternal and temporal, father and mother and, finally, Christ and witch-like women can all be ultimately reduced to the male-female opposition.

Kotik's parents are the most important characters within the child's physical-temporal reality. The depiction of their conflict, on one level, summarises the treatment of gender in the text at large.[10] Clearly, Kotik's father seems to be more involved with the child than his mother. '*S papoi mne legko i prosto*' (With daddy it is simple and easy), says Kotik. Importantly, the father teaches the child about religion, a certain kind of '*stroi*' (order), as opposed to the maternal, swarm-like '*roi*' (chaos).[11] Firmly entrenched in the story of Adam and Eve, the serpent and the tree, which the father tells the child, is the ideological bias according to which woman is the destructive force in creation. It is, then, hardly surprising that while they are praying together, Kotik wishes for the sake of family harmony that his mother should not wake up, since she would probably not be happy seeing him worship with his father. According to the mother, the child resembles his father; she says '*[on] bol'shelobyi – v ottsa*' (he has got a big forehead – he is like his father).[12] The mother complains that the father is developing the child into his own image. The child senses that she resents him: '*mamochka menia ottolknet ot sebia*' (Mummy pushes me away).[13]

Whereas the mother is depicted as a silly and self-centred woman, Kotik's father is the one who settles disputes, chiefly those involving women. He attempts to stop the servants' quarrel and he tries to prevent the old women from setting Kotik's mother up against the child's governess, Raisa Ivanovna. Furthermore, he warns his wife about her friend Bleshchenskaia's bad influence: '*ia vsegda govoril: pustota zhizni Bleshchenskikh ne byla napolnena nikakim soderzhaniem*' (I have always said that the emptiness of the life of the Bleshchenskys was not informed by any meaning).[14] The narrative strongly suggests, of course, that the mother's association with Bleshchenskaia indicates that she, too, is contemplating adultery. The father's words advocate the superiority of masculine virtue over the shallow feminine values which ultimately lead to trouble, as in the archetypal story of Adam and Eve.

A recurrent motif in the narrative is the inability to resolve the parental conflict: Kotik keeps saying '*Ia ne mamin, ne papin*' (I am not either mummy's or daddy's). It has been suggested that the synthesis of the two forces – that of the mother ('*roi*') and that of the father ('*stroi*') – appears in the figure of the son who follows in Christ's footsteps.[15] Kotik resembles his father, however; certainly, according to his mother he does. In addition, the narrative of his adult self clearly privileges the father. Kotik's association with Christ further strengthens the bias of the text in favour of the male. Thus, Kotik can hardly offer the synthesis capable of annulling the opposition between his parents.

If the story favours the fathers, what then is the role of the feminine principle? One critic has postulated that *Kotik Letaev* is 'expressly a book of women'.[16] While not all the female characters of the novel are endowed with the attributes of the misogynistic stereotypes of European Christian culture, it is important to note that none of the women is as positively portrayed as the figures of patriarchal authority, notably Professor Letaev, the father, and ultimately, Christ. Of all the females, the repulsive and frightening '*starukha*', the old woman, leaves the strongest impression on the narrative.

The ecclesiastic and didactic literature of the Russian Christian heritage, which proclaims that a good woman fully subjects herself to male-dominated interests, reveals a hierarchy similar to that in *Kotik Letaev*. Indeed, a chapter in *Domostroi* (*Book of Household Management*, a sixteenth-century Russian manual) deals with praiseworthy women, but it quickly asserts that hardly any of them exist. Another chapter in *Domostroi*, however, is entitled 'Message and Warning from Father to Son' (also referred to as the 'Conversation') and is more in keeping with social practice in medieval Russia.[17] The paternal advice contains a list of commonly held beliefs, suggesting, for example, that woman is the original tempter, responsible for the Fall, and that woman's sexual attraction is associated with sin. Stupid, evil and treacherous, women were considered physically unclean, and even the food they prepared was suspect.[18] Some Russian monasteries apparently went so far as to ban female animals from the premises.[19]

The ideological foundations of *Domostroi* are implied in *Kotik Letaev*. The *starukha* – the frightening old woman – represents the unpredictability, difference and 'evil' of women in general: not only the witch-like old women, but the young females, too, place obstacles in the male child's passage towards his goal. The old woman first appears in the beginning of the first chapter.[20] She chases Kotik as he sets out on his pre-natal journey, trying to grab the child to catch him. In Russian folklore – well known to Russians of all social classes – the female witch, Baba-Iaga, is believed to hover over the infant's place of entry into the world and threaten to 'steal it', to take it back to her domain.[21] According to A.N. Afanas'ev, Baba-Iaga was also believed to steal children after birth: she would fly up with the baby and then kill it by dropping it on the roof from on high.[22] Both eastern and western folklore are full of images of the flying witch: according to some beliefs, witches even do their laundry in the sky.[23] In Russian tales of the miraculous, witches were believed to ride on a pestle and mortar. The concept of the witch riding a broom across the sky at dusk or in the dark came to Russia with Romanticism in the early nineteenth century. But whether it is a broom, a poker or a pestle and mortar, the equipment used for flying was a utensil common in peasant households.

The narrator of *Kotik Letaev* dwells on the possibility of locating correspondences between retrieved early-childhood memories and physical realities. It is suggested, for example, that the 'lion' in the baby's inner world corresponds to a dog called Lion; similarly, the frightening encounters with the old woman correspond to various encounters with Afrosin'ia, the cook. At the end of the novel, 'recognition' dawns on Kotik that his grandmother *is* the old woman of his nightmarish world of visions. For the purposes of discussing the feminine principle in the text, it is of secondary interest how the novel's mythical and 'real' characters are fused: more important is the fact that the description of old women in the narrative is rooted in the historical image of the evil and ugly female witch. The *starukha* and the actual old women surrounding the child are depicted in the same terms. We read that the *starukha 'opisyvaia v prostranstve dugu, rushilas' … priamo v spinu'* (having described an arc in space, she fell straight on to my back), [24] that Afrosin'ia, the cook, '*opisyvaet kochergoiu dugu*' (describes an arc with the poker), and that her action over the fire terrifies the child.[25] In Russian folk belief the grandmother is often understood to be the 'priestess' of Baba-Iaga in the home.[26] Certainly, Kotik's grandmother and the *starukha* are depicted identically; the grandmother's evil eyes and chewing mouth are recurrent images in the text, only to remind us of the *starukha*'s '*belo-kalenaia golova s zhuiushim rtom i ochen' zlymi glazami*' (white-hot head with a chewing mouth and very evil eyes). Although to a lesser extent than in Germany, in Russia cannibalism became associated with female witchcraft (hence the frequent use of the term *liudoedka*, or man-eater). Propp suggests that the hero of the tale encounters the cannibalistic witch or her agents: rats – which want to tear him to pieces – or snakes – which want to swallow him up.[27] In many Russian tales of the miraculous, the witch devours human meat: no wonder that her hut is imagined to be surrounded by a fence built of human bones and skulls.[28] In *Kotik Letaev*, cannibalism is explicitly associated with Afrosin'ia, the cook. Like the *starukha*, she also has '*belo-kalenaia golova i ochen' zlye glaza*' (a white-hot head and very wicked eyes). In tales of the miraculous, witches are particularly keen on little boys' and girls' meat; they lure them to their hut to bake them in their oven.[29] But cannibalism is not limited to children: it is, therefore, hardly surprising that we learn from Kotik's recollections that '*Afrosin'ia davno zagryzaet Petrovicha; kidaetsia na nego s ostrym nozhikom ... i vyrezaet nozhom iz Petrovicha ... rostbify*' (Afrosin'ia has been tearing Petrovich apart for a long time; she throws herself on him with a sharp knife and carves slices of roast beef out of him).[30] Likewise, Serafima Gavrilovna, an old woman from grandmother's circle, '*zagryzet shcheniatok*' (tears puppies to pieces).[31]

The witch-like women are repulsively ugly and old. Both in Europe and in Russia, witches believed to practise *maleficia* were normally thought of as old unmarried women or widows over the age of fifty. Accusations were also levied against young married women or young widows but, apparently, never against girls. The older the women were, the greater their power was supposed to be.[32] Features of the witch's female sexuality tend to be strongly exaggerated in tales: the size of her breasts is often described as huge.[33] Their unpleasant appearance was understood to signify the darkness of their souls. Afrosin'ia in *Kotik Letaev* is described as follows: '*[u nee] likhaia ruka, borodovka pod nosom, podozritelen vspuchennyi podborodok, kak zob indiuka*' (a brutal hand, a wart under her nose, her raised chin is suspect like the crop of a turkey).[34] Incidentally, the phrase '*dryablyi zob indiuka*' (withered crop of a turkey) is also used to refer to the old woman, the *starukha*.[35] Apart from their looks, these women are also physically terrifying. Not only is the grandmother bald-headed, but Kotik also complains: *'babushka...mne grozitsia rukoiu'* (grandmother threatens me with her hand).[36] Similarly frightening is Aunt Dotia who appears with a carpet-beater in her hands: *'khudaia, nemaia, blednaia...tetia Dotia'* (thin, dumb, pale...aunt Dotia).[37] Like threatening black-horned women who appear from the air, Aunt Dotia also turns up from the shadows or steps out of the mirror.[38]

In conventional depictions, the witch is frequently contrasted with the virginal, pure woman. While there are a few traces of the idealised feminine figure in *Kotik Letaev*, by and large all the women share some diabolic features. It is, of course, undeniable that the sweet, young women Kotik loves – Nanny Aleksandra and Raisa Ivanovna – and also Kotik's mother, differ sharply from the *'vechnyi tetia-dotin mir'* (eternal Auntie-Dotia-world).[39] Evil old women are duly hostile to young women; they even chase away the child's governess – a loss from which he never completely recovers.[40] Although to a lesser extent than the old women, the young and pretty female characters are also outside male control and thus threaten a male-centred ideology. This threat is expressed in the novel's symbolism. Nanny Aleksandra and Raisa Ivanovna keep knitting like grandmother. Because of the shape of the wool and its quick and sudden movement, the yarn and the activity of knitting conjure up the image of the snake.[41] Through its biblical and folk connotations, the snake can imply woman's undoing of harmony and her aggressive and dominant sexuality. In some Russian folk beliefs, witches have tails, remnants of their former bodies as serpents.[42] Witches in Russian tales often take the shapes both of old women and animals.[43] This is the case in the Siberian version of 'The Ballad about the Slaying of the Slandered Wife': the mother-in-law is transformed into a vicious snake.[44] Baba-Iaga is frequently depicted with the spindle;[45] in western European folklore and medieval literature the witch's needle is a diabolical sacrament which can erase sins and restore lost maidenhood.[46] Any manifestation of female sexuality is frightening and distressing for Kotik; it causes disharmony and contributes significantly to the text's general bias against women. Even the sweet governess, Raisa Ivanovna, is shown to be carnal. The child is concerned about the consequences Raisa Ivanovna might suffer for exposing her naked body to him as she undresses, and for taking him into her bed. In Slavic tales, female sexuality, the snake and the witch are consistently associated with each other. Furthermore, in many tales the snake and Baba-Iaga appear as identical figures.[47] As the pure female figure is missing, the image of the evil old woman is all the darker.

The main function of witch-like old women in *Kotik Letaev* is to prevent Kotik's progression on his journey from pre-natal unity through human life, to the '*ogromnyi mir*' (the immense world) which he aspires to attain. It is hardly surprising that the old woman is so prominent in the initial stage of Kotik's journey: in tales of the miraculous, the Baba-Iaga's hut — which is the centre of her realm — is on the border between two worlds.[48] The witch denies the possibility that the hero will ever return to the place whence he originates: '*Kuda idesh, dobryi molodets, kuda put' derzhish'? Tuda mnogo narodu idet, a nazad eshche nikto ne vorotilsia*' (Where are you going, my fine lad, which road are you taking? Many have gone that way but none has ever returned).[49] Similarly, in *Kotik Letaev* the *starukha* and the other old women do everything in their power to divert Kotik from his course and to obstruct his eventual reunion with trans-historical harmony.

As was suggested earlier, Kotik seems to be undergoing a process akin to the initiation rite in the tale of the miraculous. His eternal condition is supposed to be regained through Christ. '*On pridet i voz'met; uvedet; vremena na iskhode*' (He will come and take me; he will lead me away; time is nearing its end), the narrator says.[50] Surrounded by light in the text, Christ stands diametrically opposed to the shadow from which the old women appear and the fiery world in which the *starukha* is mistress.[51] In the initiation rite, which can occur at various stages of human development, the hero has to undergo an experience with fire.[52] Christ's cathedral offers protection against the *starukha*: '*razbivaiutsia o nego okeany krasnogo mira: tam sklonilas' starukha; ona ne mozhet voiti*' (he breaks up the oceans of the red world: the old woman stoops there; she may not enter).[53] Kotik is convinced that the evil old women hate the Christian 'logos' which he first heard from his father.[54] It is the women who kill him by nailing him to the cross. Yet, even as they kill him, they cannot avoid fitting into the greater scheme of order which is Christ's will. Death is temporary and resurrection follows. For all her attempts, the witch cannot prevent the happy ending according to Christian specifications.

The reason why the feminine principle of the novel is so negative has a great deal to do with placing the mother in the background, minimalising and trivialising her role, and foregrounding the old woman, the grandmother and Aunt Dotia. While these figures are richly symbolic, they are quite vaguely delineated. It will, therefore, be beneficial to examine some of the cultural, social and psychological underpinnings of the type.

The figure of the evil female witch became widespread in oral and written discourse in the late Middle Ages. This was thanks to one of the most insane documents the Roman Catholic church ever produced — *Malleus Maleficarum* (*The Hammer of the Witches*, 1486), written by two zealous German clergymen, the Dominican monks Heinrich Krämer and Jacob Sprenger, at the same time as the invention of printing. Because of the printed page, the compiled 'information' about witches was spread across Europe.[55] Witch-hysteria was initiated and kept alive for centuries largely by the male-dominated Christian churches – Catholic, Protestant and Orthodox. (It is interesting to note that outside the Christian tradition, males are at least as likely to be considered witches as females. This is generally the case in African, Asian and native American societies.) In Russia, nevertheless, the situation was slightly different: the Russian Orthodox church fought against the remnants of paganism mainly in the cities, while in the village Christian and pagan traditions coexisted more peacefully.[56] The pre-Christian veneration of strong, divine, female figures was converted partially into the cult of the Virgin Mary. Tat'iana Mamonova, however, claims (not too convincingly) that the mysterious and magical female figure of the matriarchal tradition of pagan Russia was turned into the image of the evil and disgusting old sorceress through the introduction of the Christian tradition by pagan-hunting, misogynistic monks.[57] Fortunately, better researched publications than Mamonova's also draw on an impressive range of literature on the subject and, while they cannot conclude unequivocally that there was a stage in pagan Europe when women dominated in society,[58] they do not rule out the possibility that the large corpus of evidence in favour of the historical primacy of matriarchy could be valid.[59] If matriarchy, whose vestiges can be found in Russian and Czech folklore, ever existed, it presumably preceded the arrival of the Slavs in Eastern Europe.

It appears that the figure of *mat' syra zemlia* (Mother Damp Earth) was pivotal in pagan Slavic civilization.[60] The veneration of such a goddess indicates that women were seen to possess an organic bond with nature. They were endowed with qualities of strength and/or magical power. Of course, maternal power is most clearly marked when the child's descent is registered on the mother's side. Matrilineal social bonding in some pre-historic societies is well established, and the reason for it is quite evident: the ties between mother and child are spontaneous and obvious while the relationship between father and child must be learned.[61] Folklore provides some evidence for a period when women were depicted as strong and powerful. It is of some interest to note that the Amazon myth has been associated with the Slavs, albeit with little credence. This society of female warriors was, supposedly, related to the Sarmatians and the Scythians in what later became southern Russia, between the Caucasian region in the east and the river Don in the west.[62] According to some scholars, the Amazons offer evidence of the existence of a matriarchal society in the region.[63] The Russian female warriors, the *polianitsy*, might have been the successors of the Amazons, although unless they submitted to male authority, married and settled down, they were killed. The *rusalki* were nymphs who, like the Amazons, were believed to be young women living without men. They were magical creatures, in control of fertility and the seasons. Furthermore, *rusalki*, like the Sirens of classical Greek mythology, were believed to lure men with their songs to destroy them.[64]

Importantly, according to early Russian folklore, women – believed to have access to the world of the supernatural – could use their power for good and evil purposes.[65] One of the vital distinctions between pagan figures endowed with supernatural powers and the witch of the medieval Christian period has to do with the question of choice. The pagan figure is born with supernatural powers, whereas the medieval witch is generally believed to choose evil and the devil's company to obtain magical power. Witchcraft came under the church's jurisdiction in the Middle Ages. In Vladimir the Great's *ustav* (legal code) it is designated as a crime to be dealt with by ecclesiastical courts.[66] While in the sixteenth century the Russians produced *Domostroi* – that highly misogynistic document – they certainly never laid down anything so rigorously systematised as *Malleus Maleficarum*. *Malleus Maleficarum* was less well known in eastern Europe than in the central and western parts of the continent,[67] but that is certainly not to say that misogyny in the Slavic east was less intense.[68] *Malleus Maleficarum* argues that as Jesus was male, it is clear that providence preserved men from the sin of witchcraft.[69] The document considers it self-evident that witches, by definition, are female.[70] Clearly, eastern Slavic cultures adhered to both of these assumptions as well. According to some historians, Russia saw proportionally fewer executions of witches than did the heartland of Europe. However, the view that Russia in its treatment of witches was somehow more enlightened than western Europe is refuted by Shashkova in *Istoriia russkoi zhenshchiny* (History of Russian Women, 1879).[71] Indeed, the persecution of women may well have started in Russia centuries before it did in Europe, and it certainly lasted longer than in the West.[72] In contrast with Russia, the Church in western Europe until the late Middle Ages refuted beliefs that women had magical power for evil purposes.[73] The major wave of persecution started in Russia in the middle of the seventeenth century, by which time the executions and accusations in Germany, France and Belgium had been officially stopped. But executions of witches among the eastern Slavs started as early as the beginning of the thirteenth century and continued sporadically until the nineteenth century.[74] It should be noted that witches in Russia, unlike those in the West, were connected primarily with paganism rather than the devil.

To be sure, the image of the evil old woman, sustained and perpetuated in *Kotik Letaev*, was in previous centuries responsible for the torture and murder of at least one hundred thousand women.[75] The women who were most likely to be tried and punished for being witches greatly resemble the old females in Bely's symbol-laden novel. The French feminist critic, Xavière Gauthier, argues that 'if the figure of the witch appears wicked, it is because she poses a real danger to phallocratic society, built on exclusion and oppression of female strength'.[76] Clearly, women who did not fit the categories of mother and wife, who appeared to be independent from man's world and who were endowed with power – such as midwifery or some other form of medical knowledge – were obvious violators of the social order.[77] To suggest that they were evil and to remove them from society restored the 'balance' required for uncontested male dominance.

Bely has been rightly praised for creating a highly innovative and original form of expression in his novels. As far as his 'feminine principle' is concerned, however, he is deeply rooted in the conventions of a notably intolerant brand of discourse. Undoubtedly, *Malleus Maleficarum* is unusually extreme in its explicitness, but its impact, together with other misogynistic Christian writings, has been pervasive in European culture. The image of the lustful, wicked old woman is most common in the traditional tales of the miraculous which are read to children. The ideological moorings of much of folklore go back to the feudal, Christian Middle Ages. As the patriarchal institution of serfdom lasted well into the end of the nineteenth century in Russia, it is hardly surprising that in that underdeveloped society folk beliefs survived almost unchanged. According to late nineteenth-century published sources, the belief in witches was widespread in 1883 even in Russian university towns.[78] It is more than probable that in the tales Raisa Ivanovna read out to little Kotik, besides kings and knights, the European wicked witch as well as the Slavic Baba-Iaga also loomed large. Behind her dark and ominous figure lurks intolerance and persecution, leaving a marked gap in the midst of Bely's 'cosmogony' to be filled by history.

Notes

The author would like to express his gratitude for successive Honorary Visiting Fellowships at the School of Slavonic and East European Studies, University of London, which made it possible for him to utilise the School's outstanding library collection for the writing of this article. Many thanks are due to Faith Wigzell and David Larmour for reading the manuscript and offering useful comments and suggestions.

1. Andrei Belyi, 'The Magic of Words', in Steven Cassedy (ed.), *Selected Essays of Andrei Belyi* (Berkeley, CA: University of California Press, 1986), p. 98.
2. Andrei Belyi, *Kotik Letaev*, in *Staryi Arbat* (Moscow: Moskovskii rabochii, 1989) (henceforth *KL*), p. 428. All translations are mine.
3. Andrew B. Wachtel, *The Battle for Childhood* (Stanford, CA: Stanford University Press, 1990), p. 175.
4. Leonid Dolgopolov, *Andrei Belyi i ego roman 'Peterburg'* (Leningrad: Sovetskii pisatel', 1988), pp. 348–49.
5. Erich Neumann, *The Great Mother*, transl. Ralph Manheim (Princeton: Princeton University Press, 1963), p. 147.
6. *KL*, p. 433.
7. Barta, 'Childhood and the Autobiographical Novel. An Examination of Tolstoy's *Childhood*, Joyce's *A Portrait of the Artist as a Young Man* and Belyi's *Kotik Letaev*', in Wolfgang Zach and Heinz Kosok (eds), *Literary Interrelations: Ireland, England and the World*, vol. 2 (Tübingen: Gunter Narr Verlag, 1987), pp. 52–53.
8. J.D. Elsworth, *Andrei Belyi: A Critical Study of the Novels* (Cambridge: Cambridge University Press, 1983), p. 17 discusses how, according to Bely's anthroposophy, studying the self paves the way towards understanding the outer world: 'the individual soul ... reveals itself as the locus of all cultural forces'.
9. According to Carol Anschuetz, 'Word creation in *Kotik Letaev* and *Kreshchenyi kitaets*' (unpublished Ph.D. dissertation, Princeton University, 1972), pp. 22–23, the action of *Kotik Letaev* is about the acquisition of language. The better the child's mastery of language is, the worse are his 'recollections' of pre-natal experiences.
10. The conflict between Kotik's parents symbolises the duality at work in the world, according to Elsworth, *Andrei Belyi*, p. 130.
11. Barta, 'Childhood', p. 53; Gerald Janacek, 'An Acoustico-Semantic Complex in Belyi's *Kotik Letaev*', *Slavic and East European Journal*, vol. 19 (1974), p. 154.
12. *KL*, p. 552.
13. *KL*, p. 531.
14. *KL*, p. 552. Tolstoy's *Anna Karenina* occupies a marked intertextual presence both in *Kotik Letaev* and in *Petersburg*. Both Senator Ableukhov and Professor Letaev share analogous features with Karenin, and the wives of both men allude to Anna Karenina. The friendship between Kotik's mother and Bleshchenskaia, for example, reminds us of Anna's friendship with Princess Betsy.
15. Janacek, 'Acoustico-Semantic Complex', p. 154.
16. Michael Molnar, *Body of Words: A Reading of Belyi's 'Kotik Letaev'* (Birmingham: Birmingham Slavonic Monographs, no. 17, 1987), p. 29.
17. Joan Delaney Grossman, 'Feminine Images in Old Russian Literature and Art', *California Slavic Studies*, vol. 11 (1980), p. 51. (Ed.: for a new edited translation, see Carolyn Pouncy, *The Domostroi: Rules for Russian Households in the Time of Ivan the Terrible* [Ithaca, N.Y. and London: Cornell University Press, 1994])
18. In the chapter entitled 'Den' Kotika Letaeva', food is brought to the child, prepared, naturally by female domestics: '*raz prinesli mne kusochek cherstvogo khlebika ... iz nego delat' greshnika, to est' obmakivat' v chai; razlomili kusochek, a tam-to – v kusochke to! – murashki: – krasnye! – polzaiut!*' (once they brought me a mouldy piece of stale bread ... to make a 'sinner' out of it, in other words to dip it into tea; they broke the slice into bits and there in the slice – there were ants – red ones – creepy ones) (*KL*: 479). Importantly, it is the father among the adults who notices the insects and, presumably, takes the bread away from the child.
19. S.S. Shashkova, *Istoriia russkoi zhenshchiny*, 2nd edition (St Petersburg, 1879), p. 78. Shashkova's and Efimenko's articles are insufficiently documented and the reliability of some of the research is dubious. I have used these articles and Afanas'ev's book as sources of information and not as a basis for evaluation.

20. Molnar, *Body of Words*, p. 31 writes that the '*starukha*' stands for a principle rather than a character in the plot: she represents an 'extra-corporeal state' for the narrator. She appears in several embodiments, notably as Afrosin'ia and Malinovskaia.
21. Joanna Hubbs, *Mother Russia. The Feminine Myth in Russian Culture* (Bloomington: Indiana University Press, 1988), p. 46.
22. A.N. Afanas'ev, *Poeticheskie vozzreniia slavian na prirodu*, vol. 3 (Moscow: Izdanie K. Soldatenkova, 1869), p. 587.
23. Ibid, p. 468.
24. *KL*, p. 436.
25. Fire is an important component in the mythology of witchcraft. Witches were believed to fly up through the fireplace and they were also depicted in stories roasting human meat over the fire. The '*starukha*' – the old woman – comes from a 'fiery world'.
26. Hubbs, *Mother Russia*, p. 46.
27. V.Ia. Propp, *Istoricheskie korni volshebnoi skazki* (Leningrad: Izdatel'stvo leningradskogo universiteta, 1986), p. 63.
28. Afanas'ev, *Poeticheskie vozzreniia*, p. 590.
29. Ibid., p. 586. 'Hansel and Gretel' was popularised by the Grimm brothers. Kotik Letaev, the son of a Moscow professor, was certain to be familiar with the tale as a little child. In the homes of the upper echelon in Russian society, the most popular way of keeping children occupied, particularly in inclement weather, was the reading out loud of tales of the miraculous (Wachtel, *Battle for Childhood*, p. 106).
30. *KL*, p. 533.
31. *KL*, p. 557.
32. Norman Cohn, *Europe's Inner Demons* (London: Sussex University Press, 1975), p. 248.
33. Propp, *Istoricheskie korni*, p. 75.
34. *KL*, p. 533.
35. *KL*, p. 435.
36. *KL*, p. 439.
37. *KL*, p. 451.
38. *KL*, p. 534. In folklore, mirrors can be endowed with magical significance. They can conjure up images of events taking place elsewhere or ones which will happen in future (W.F. Ryan and Faith Wigzell, 'Gullible Girls and Dreadful Dreams. Zhukovskii, Pushkin and Popular Divination', *Slavonic and East European Review*, vol. 70, no. 4 [October 1992], p. 658). Furthermore, the Old Believers considered mirrors to be the devil's invention (M. D. Chulkov, *Abevega russkikh sueverii idolopoklonnicheskikh zhertvoprinoshenii svadebnykh prostonarodnykh obriadov, koldovstva, shamanstva i proch.* (Moscow, 1786), p. 199; cited from Ryan and Wigzell, 'Gullible Girls', p. 658).
39. *KL*, p. 467.
40. In the Belorussian and Trans-Carpathian versions of 'The Ballad about the Slaying of the Slandered Wife', the husband's mother – a witch – suggests to him before he reaches their house after a long absence that his wife has chased the child's nannies away, in addition to leading a wasteful, immoral and generally irresponsible life. To punish her, as soon as the husband arrives home he kills his innocent wife, only to find out that his mother had misinformed him out of malice (D.M. Balašov, *The Ballad about the Slaying of the Slandered Wife*, ed. and trans. Felix J. Oinas and Stephen Soudakoff [The Hague: Mouton, 1975], p. 263).
41. Molnar also associates the image of knitting with that of the snake. He suggests that the needles transform the snake-like wool into garments and that this process resembles the way the growing body is filled with consciousness (Molnar, *Body of Words*, p. 30).

42. Afanas'ev, *Poeticheskie vozzreniia*, p. 422; Sergei Maksimov, *Nechistaia, nevedomaia i krestnaia sila* (Moscow: Kniga, 1989), p. 83. According to other beliefs, a witch who did not have a tail had not been born one, but had turned into one. Thus, she was particularly 'bad' (P.I. Efimenko, 'Sud nad ved'mami', *Kievskaia starina*, vol. 7 (Nov. 1883), p. 378). This kind of reasoning offered a useful caveat for proving that a woman was a witch even if she had no 'tail'; in short, any woman accused of the crime of witchcraft could be proven guilty without any evidence.
43. Propp, *Istoricheskie korni*, p. 107.
44. Balashov, *The Ballad*, pp. 263, 266.
45. Hubbs, *Mother Russia*, p. 38.
46. Javier Herrero, 'Celestina: The Aging Prostitute as Witch', in Laurel Porter and Laurence M. Porter (eds), *Aging Literature* (Troy: International Book Publishers, 1984), pp. 31-47 (p. 36).
47. Afanas'ev, *Poeticheskie vozzreniia*, p. 586. Arguable as it may be, Afanas'ev suggests that the Russian word *iaga* is etymologically related to the Sanskrit word for snake, *aki*. He claims that in Greek and Albanian tales, the role of the Slavic Baba-Iaga is taken by the mythical snake (ibid., pp. 255, 256).
48. Maria-Gabriele Wosien, *The Russian Folk-Tale* (Munich: Otto Sagner, 1969), p. 136; Propp, *Istoricheskie korni*, p. 60.
49. Ibid., p. 136.
50. *KL*, p. 513.
51. *KL*, p. 441.
52. Propp, *Istoricheskie korni*, pp. 82, 98, 100. Prince Tamino and Pamina have to walk across fire as part of their initiation into Sarastro's empire in Mozart's *The Magic Flute*.
53. *KL*, p. 442.
54. *KL*, p. 575.
55. Literacy, even before the discovery of printing, contributed towards the subjugation of women. This process culminated in the witch hysteria in Europe in the fifteenth and sixteenth centuries. In the Middle Ages, literacy remained largely within the domain of the Church. Centuries before the Church produced its misogynistic documents about evil female witches, literacy had supplied biblical and classical cultural stereotypes about the social and biological inferiority of women (Bonnie S. Anderson and Judith P. Zinsser, *A History of Their Own*, 2 vols (London: Penguin, 1988), vol. 1, p. 4.
56. Linda J. Ivanits, *Russian Folk Belief* (Armonk, NY: M.E. Sharpe, 1987), p. 87.
57. Mamonova demonstrates the misogynistic attitude of a fifth-century Orthodox monk when she discusses the case of St Kiril, archbishop of Alexandria. Kiril burned all the scholarly works of Hypatia, a woman scholar (Tatyana Mamonova, *Russian Women's Studies* [Oxford: Pergamon Press, 1989], p. 3).
58. Anderson and Zinsser, *History of their Own*, vol. 1, p. xxii; Dorothy Atkinson, 'Society and the Sexes in the Russian Past', in Atkinson et al. (eds), *Women in Russia* (Hassocks: Harvester Press, 1978), p.4.
59. For further reference, see J.J. Bachofen, *Myth, Religion and Mother-Right* (London: Routledge and Kegan Paul, 1968), and R. Briffault, *The Mothers* (London: Allen and Unwin, 1927). For a more contemporary analysis, see Merlin Stone, *When God was a Woman* (New York: Harcourt Brace Jovanovich, 1978).
60. Ivanits, *Russian Folk Belief*, p. 15.
61. Atkinson, 'Society and the Sexes', p.4.
62. Ibid., p. 3.
63. See George Vernadsky's *Ancient Russia* (New Haven: Yale University Press, 1943), pp. 54, 113, and his *Kievan Russia* (New Haven: Yale University Press, 1948), p. 155. For some interesting observations on ideology surrounding the myth of the

Amazons, see Page du Bois, *Centaurs and Amazons: Women and the Pre-History of the Great Chain of Being* (Ann Arbor: University of Michigan Press, 1991). (Editor's note: recent archaeological discoveries of burial sites of women warriors in southern Russia give greater credence to this tradition.)

64. Hubbs, *Mother Russia*, pp. 27–28, 35, 37, 52.
65. Anderson and Zinsser, *History of their Own*, vol. 1, p. 162; Atkinson, 'Society and the Sexes', p. 16.
66. Russell Zguta, 'The Ordeal by Water (Swimming of Witches) in the East Slavic World', *Slavic Review*, vol. 36, no. 2 (June 1977), pp. 220–30 (p. 224).
67. Ibid., p. 220.
68. Shashkova cites misogynistic propaganda from the eleventh century, suggesting that 'eastern', patriarchal, hostility against women pervaded all classes of Russian society (*Istoriia*, pp. 79–80).
69. Sela R. Williams and Pamela J. Williams, *Riding the Nightmare* (New York: Atheneum, 1978), pp. 38–39.
70. Russell Zguta, 'Witchcraft Trials in Seventeenth-Century Russia', *American Historical Review*, vol. 82, no. 5 (Dec. 1977), pp. 1187–1207 (p. 1196) has argued that the number of women standing trial for witchcraft in Muscovy did not exceed the number of males as dramatically as in western Europe. Efimenko, 'Sud', p. 287, however, asserts that men were seldom considered to be witches in Russia.
71. Shashkova, *Istoriia*, p. 84.
72. Zguta, 'Ordeal by Water', p. 222.
73. Anderson and Zinsser, *History of their Own*, vol. 1, p. 167.
74. Maksimov, *Nechistaia*, p. 84; Shashkova, *Istoriia*, pp. 84, 88; Zguta, 'Ordeal by Water', p. 228.
75. According to some estimates, as many as eight million women may have been burnt at the height of the hysteria in the fifteenth, sixteenth and seventeenth centuries. See Xavière Gauthier, 'Why Witches?', in Elaine Marks and Isabelle de Courtivron (eds), *New French Feminisms* (Brighton: Harvester, 1980), p. 201.
76. Ibid. p. 203.
77. Hubbs, *Mother Russia*, p. 252.
78. Efimenko, 'Sud', p. 375; Shashkova, *Istoria*, p. 84. Efimenko lists numerous examples demonstrating how strongly people believe in witches, even at the end of the nineteenth century. In the 1970s I met university-educated people in Moscow who believed in the ability of old women to put the 'evil eye' on children. In the last five years, there has been a great revival in folk beliefs concerning witches and wizards.

Chapter 15

THE ROMANTIC PRESENTATION OF THE HEROINE IN SELECTED WORKS OF ALEKSANDR GRIN

Anna Darmodekhina

In 1880 Russia gave birth to at least two outstanding writers – Aleksandr Blok and Aleksandr Grin. The latter experienced a life full of hardship: before the Revolution he was exiled and had to live under various false names, then after the Revolution he experienced homelessness and lack of appreciation. Literary critics throughout the Stalin period accused Aleksandr Grin of being insufficiently attached to his motherland, of ignoring the great achievements of Soviet society and trying to imitate authors in the West.

It is true that the author abandoned the entire socialist world in order to create an alternative world for his readers and himself. In Grin's 'unreal' world, behind the foreign sound of the characters' names and the names of various cities and villages (Liss, Zurbagan, Poket), real Russian (now Ukrainian) sea-ports can easily be distinguished – Sebastopol', Yalta, Odessa, and so on. As for the foreign names of the 'strange' personages in his books, Grin used to reply: 'I don't think your attitude to Hamlet, say, would change if someone told you he didn't come from Denmark but from New Zealand'.[1] This statement, along with Grin's creative writing, demonstrates that it is the unreal world which gave him a chance to escape from what was unfair and unkind, providing a better opportunity to search for the ideal, to reach wider social conclusions and attempt to decide what universal values should function in any society. But before he could do that in his best novels there was a long way to go.

The early heroines of Grin's short stories had Russian names, lived in Russian society with its eternal problems, and in most cases they possessed some romantic features. In 'Tikhie budni' (Quiet Weekdays, 1913), Evgeniia virtually stops having any inner life of her own because of her despotic father, who never gives her a chance to make her own decisions. She regains her colourful individual perceptions only after she overhears a soldier who has deserted from the army speaking to a bird, addressing it as if it were a human being. Liza, the heroine of the longer story 'Tainstvennyi les' (Mysterious Forest, 1913), has to make her choice between the practical and reliable, but boring Ryleev, and a romantic vagrant, a typically Russian 'superfluous' figure, Tushin. We can safely say of these two early works by Aleksandr Grin that they express one of his most important ideas: that a woman's love can totally change the fate of a man.

In the story 'Sto verst po reke' (A Hundred Versts along the River, written in 1912; first published in 1916), a woman's love saves the man not only spiritually, but also literally. This work actually reflects the writer's own tragic attempt to escape from exile. Vera Kalitskaia, Grin's first wife, became the prototype of the heroine. In order to escape, Nok, the main character in the story, tries to buy a boat, but, as he has insufficient money, Gelli (who provides the money) has to travel with him. Sincere and open-hearted, she has the rare quality of being able to listen to another person, and, what is more, to hear him. As Nok himself admits, he is a man with a dead soul: he categorises women in such terms as: 'When a woman is asleep, she can't do any harm'.[2] Women for him represent evil; only men can create. Gelli tries to argue against his view: 'It's true Shakespeare has Lady Macbeth. But there are also Juliet and Ophelia' (*A.p.*, 107). Gelli has no experience of life – on the one hand, she is horrified when she realises that she is in a boat with a convict, and on the other, she cannot help respecting him for his fearless struggle against his dangerous fate. In this short story Grin uses his favourite technique – contrast, which is here one-sided. Gelli's feelings, actions and inmost thoughts are shown in detail, whereas the 'evil in the shape of a human being', that is, the woman who actually made Nok a criminal, is depicted briefly through a few remarks from the hero and the author. Eventually, Gelli finds the right words and does the right thing to save the lost soul. They part for a short while, but, afterwards, will never part again.

Spiritually, the heroine of the story 'Pozornyi stolb' ('The Pillory', 1911) is close to Gelli, but otherwise she represents an extremely different character. Goan, the protagonist, is put in the pillory for trying to run away with Daisy, the girl he loves. (Using biblical parallels is another feature of Grin's romantic presentation of life.) Goan has been tortured mercilessly. The poor girl, afraid of village gossip, only comes to see him late at night and it seems then that all she cares about is not to be noticed by neighbours. But in the morning when they banish Goan she decides to follow him, which is not at all an easy decision. Thus, Grin states, 'Two loves joined together like a little stream in the forest and a big river' (*A.p.*, 91). It should be pointed out that both stories end in the same way: 'They lived for a long time and died on the same day' (*A.p.*, 91, 129). Grin's romantic formula suggests that dying on the same day was a just reward given to a couple for a happy and loving life. To some extent, Gelli and Daisy can be seen as precursors of the noblest women characters in Grin's best works. In the story 'Pierre and Surine' (1929), we can see another variant of the same type of heroine, for her love brings her beloved back to life after his death. The same approach to a similar problem can be found in Anthony Minghella's film *Truly, Madly, Deeply* (1991).

Whether they have Russian names and surroundings or not, the heroines of Grin's early short stories are firmly in the mainstream of the ideals of Russian literature and develop its best Romantic traditions. He is even more successful in depicting female characters in his later works *Alye parusa* (*Scarlet Sails,* 1923) and *Begushchaia po volnam* (She Who Runs on the Waves, 1928).

Grin never approached his characters in the way many Soviet writers did in the 1930s and 1940s – that is, showing the poor as automatically good, whereas the rich are by definition bad. In *Scarlet Sails* Arthur Grey's mother is an arrogant aristocrat whose beauty repels people rather than attracts them. With her dear boy, however, she 'became just a mother who spoke in a loving and gentle tone those trifles coming from the heart which are impossible to describe because their strength lies in their feeling and not at all in themselves' (*A.p.*, 28). His mother's attitude helps Grey to find his own world of romantic ideas, despite the feudal family castle and a distinguished father who demands from his son common sense and a normal, aristocratic way of life. After running away from home Grey decides to become a sailor, or, if possible, the captain of a ship. On his journey he will confront prosaic reality and hardship, but will manage to preserve that rare aspect of his character: the capacity to expect a miracle in life. Beautiful lines are composed by Grin in tribute to a mother's love. When after many years her grown-up son comes back home for a short time, his mother recognises him at once. She calls him 'my dear, my little one', and for a moment Captain Grey ceases to be an adult. But Arthur's aristocratic mother fails to understand her son or his ideas. She does not argue with him when he speaks of his values and principles, but thinks about them as if they were toys with which he plays – even though he 'plays' with 'continents, oceans and seas'.

Only a few details are mentioned about Assol''s mother's tragic life. These are remarks made by her husband, by a woman neighbour and by the author himself. Her father Longren thus becomes both a mother and father to the girl. He is an ordinary sailor, but understands his daughter much better than Her Ladyship, Grey's mother. The fact that Longren has never forgiven the owner of the local tavern for his wife's death, and as a result does not save his life, affects Assol''s entire childhood. The village children are not allowed to play with her. Sarcastically, the author classifies the girl's crying, scratches and bruises as the expression of public opinion. 'Why don't they like us?', she asks her father. The answer is: 'One has to know how to love, but they just cannot' (*A.p.*, 13). To compensate for the child's lack of love he tells her numerous stories about the sea and sailors, sea legends. She plays with toys he has made to sell, and now and then she takes them to the shop in the nearest town. On one such day Assol' meets a miracle created by a human being. Grin introduces the device of combining the real and the unreal, describing how Assol' meets an old folklorist, Egl', who after looking into her innocent eyes tells her a wonderful story. He describes a beautiful white ship with scarlet sails and a handsome prince on its deck coming to their village for Assol': ' "Is it all for me?", asked the girl quietly. "What would you do then?" ..."I ...would love him", she answered quickly. "Unless he starts fighting with me"' (*A.p.*, 20). This was the quality in a woman's character which Aleksandr Grin admired so much: his best heroines, while fully grown-up, remain somewhat childlike. Assol' does not just wait for a prince on a white ship or a white horse like any other young woman of her age – she awaits a miracle. The dream story enters her life and changes it. Some Russian critics regard the village name, Caperna, as symbolic, associating it with the old Palestinian city Capernaum, for whose citizens Jesus Christ predicted severe punishment on account of their dishonesty. This may be so. But it is certain that a dream becomes almost a religion for Assol'.

The compositional structure of this book is based upon time shifts, revealing either Grey's or Assol''s childhood or youth (another device typical of Romantic literature). Poetic details are carefully chosen to show the inner world of the hero and heroine. The unusual world she has created gives Assol' a chance to see more than others. She speaks to plants and insects as if they were alive, and shows great understanding, sympathy and humour in so doing. To depict the woman's complex character in different dimensions, Grin describes her from the point of view of 'double vision': 'One is just a sailor's daughter, the other – a living poem with all the miracles of its sounds and images' (*A.p.*, 47). When she works hard making toys for sale just like her father, she dreams of making them like those that can only be found in fairy tales: 'It is as hard for us to enter a fairy tale as it was for Assol' to emerge from its power and charm' (*A.p.*, 66). Only a woman like this could help the protagonist to realise that one has to create a miracle with one's own hands. The author's view is: 'If you can, try to create a miracle for your beloved with your own hands'; 'But there are miracles that are no less than this: just a smile, cheerfulness, forgiveness, and a much-needed word said at the right time' (*A.p.*, 74). The book portrays the parallel development of two good-natured young people who seek perfection. In this work good triumphs over evil – it is the most optimistic of Grin's novels, and Assol' became one of the most dearly loved female characters in Soviet literature of the period.

The same type of heroine is developed in the novel *Begushchaia po volnam* (1928). If in *Scarlet Sails* the reader finds numerous unreal but tangible events, in *Begushchaia po volnam* there are many layers of unreality that are mystical and inexplicable. The principle of mixing the real and the unreal is used here on a higher level. Although the hero, Thomas Harvey, is with several other people in a restaurant, only he can hear a mysterious voice saying 'She who runs on the waves'. His friends try to explain his 'hallucination' from the point of view of logic and psychoanalysis. But there are more distant associations in the novel. When Thomas meets and falls in love with Daisy, her voice reminds him of a voice from the past. The phrase serves as a kind of introduction to what will become the beautiful mystery of a woman who can run on the waves saving people after shipwrecks, while he who sees her will think about her for the rest of his life.

The ghost Frezi Grant was once an ordinary girl, but the time came when she had to leave her loved ones and her motherland to live in the sea, which became her new home; the people she saved became her new family. The sea is present in almost all of Grin's novels and short stories as a most important image, but in *Begushchaia po volnam* it becomes a symbol. Another symbol in the novel is the monument to Frezi Grant. By depicting the contrasting attitudes of various people to the monument, Grin is able to evoke their attitudes to life, revealing the characters of those with abundant common sense but unable to dream of anything, and those who see the world through a mist of beautiful romantic perceptions. Alongside these mystic and fantastic aspects of the novel there is also an element of the detective story: the murder of Captain Gez, the ship's change of owner, and so on.

It is not at all easy to define the heroine of this novel. On the level of reality in the book, one could possibly refer to a 'collective' image of the female character. Biche is common sense itself, she is self-confident and knows exactly what she is doing. Her view of life is: 'If I don't understand, then it doesn't exist'.[3] One of Grin's friends recalls that the writer often used to say: 'To forbid dreams means not to believe in happiness, and not to believe in happiness means not to live at all'.[4] Daisy is a girl who believes in happiness, and is open to everything fine and wonderful. Whereas there is a polite smile on Biche's lips, Daisy smiles broadly and openly. The girls are contrasted in the novel, but they are by no means antipodes. Daisy is very often shown privately among her friends and relations, whereas Biche is depicted as larger than life. To some extent, the effect of 'disappointed expectation' works here, for Harvey's attention is focused on Biche most of the time, but it is Daisy he chooses. If we regard these two women as the 'collective' character of Grin's heroine, we could analyse her as sincere and rational, intellectual and poetic, emotional and reserved.

Some commentators suggest that Grin's first wife was the prototype of Biche. Vera Kalitskaia was by his side during the long years of his exile and illegal wanderings, but nevertheless could not understand why he was unable to write a 'realistic' novel. Daisy is undoubtedly Nina Nikolaevna Grin, the writer's second wife, who would take care of a wounded hawk or look for weeks on end for a proper name to suit a character in one of her husband's short stories.

It is hard to overestimate the value of Grin's female characters. His heroines are portrayed without detailed descriptions of sexual relationships – unlike the fashionable trend in the 1920s and 1930s (which is even more evident today). The author's heroines are so fine because they are able to dream, to believe in miracles, and to love.

Aleksandr Grin's life was not an easy or a happy one, but there was a great love in it which helped him to create unforgettable images of women, making a deep impression on several generations of Russian teenagers. The author once wrote to his wife, Nina Grin: 'You gave me so much happiness, love, tenderness, and even good reasons to change my attitude to life ... that I stand here now as if amidst flowers and waves with a flock of birds above my head. In my heart there is joy and light'.[5]

Notes

1. V. Rossel's and A.Grin, *A. Grin. Iz neizdannogo i zabytogo* (Moscow: Nauka, 1965), vol. 74, pp. 645–46.

2. A. Grin, *Alye parusa* (Moscow, 1979), p. 101, hereafter *A.p.* followed by the page number.
3. A.S. Grin, *Sobranie sochinenii v shesti tomakh* (Moscow: Pravda, 1965), vol. 5, p. 181.
4. N. Verzhbitskii, *Vospominaniia ob Aleksandre Grine* (Moscow, 1972), p. 214.
5. Grin's letter to his wife, RGALI, op. 1, ed. khr. 69, l. 9.

Chapter 16

IS VILLAGE PROSE MISOGYNISTIC?

David Gillespie

The question of the title may seem purely rhetorical, as many people are undoubtedly aware that the surviving *derevenshchiki* (village prose writers) became notorious in the late 1980s for their chauvinistic and xenophobic statements on the state of Russia and their reactionary stance on social and political affairs. Indeed, the prospect of reclaiming such writers as Vasily Belov, Viktor Astaf'ev and Valentin Rasputin in the 1990s for an intellectually and morally respectable place in a democratic Russia do not look good, for a variety of reasons. In the first place, village prose, of which they are the most prominent living representatives, is written exclusively by men, almost all of them born and raised in the countryside; secondly, their works are written in a traditional and conservative realistic style, with stock characters and fairly representative plots, and generally reflect a conservative and/or chauvinistic world view; thirdly, their treatment of women is usually within a traditional patriarchal framework.

However, there is a distinction between the explicit intentions of the *derevenshchiki*, and the actual texts of *derevenskaia proza* (village prose). It does not necessarily follow that just because the writers are chauvinists and reactionaries, their writings exhibit the same views. By focusing exclusively on the texts, we can save *derevenskaia proza* from the *derevenshchiki*.

The plot of what Kathleen Parthé calls 'canonical village prose'[1] is usually based on a comparison and a conflict of opposites: old and new, male and female value systems, tradition and progress, town and village, asphalt and forest, one-family wooden huts and multi-storey communal housing, tranquillity and movement, stability and disruption. Village prose is about the end of a world, which is being replaced by something less wholesome, morally unsound and 'un-Russian'. Indeed, the parameters of village prose perfectly correspond to those of the pastoral, as defined by Peter Marinelli:

> The movement from the garden to the city implicit in Christian mythology is a direct result of the Fall, and while every bosom returns an echo to Samuel Johnson's statement that when a man is tired of London he is tired of life, the more orthodox view is stated by Cowper: 'God made the country and man made the town'. The omnipresent desire to escape from town is really the desire to escape from the circumstances into which we were plunged by the Fall and of which the city is, however glorious, really the result. Ultimately, therefore, the dominant idea of pastoral is a search for simplicity away from a complexity represented by a specific location [...], from which the refuge is a rural retreat to Arcadia; or from a specific period of individual human existence (adulthood), from which the refuge is in the visions of childhood. All pastoral is in search of the original splendour, but the different ways in which it conceives of that splendour are the ground of its fertility and its multiple variations.[2]

Village prose, a particularly Russian version of pastoral, is written by men who recall their own rural childhood and youth (Belov and Rasputin in several short stories, Astaf'ev in *Poslednii poklon* [The Final Bow, 1968–1987]). As a result of war and collectivisation, we find that the dominant relationships in village prose are between mothers and sons, since most of the adult menfolk are absent from the village. It is thus not surprising that in 'canonical village prose', representing the traditions of the pastoral, little attention is paid to sexual relationships (the work of Fedor Abramov is an exception to this rule). The main oppositions and contrasts of village prose are between those who represent the hearth and those from outside (*svoi* and *chuzhie*), but, as opposed to urban prose, very little sexual activity takes place at all. Moreover, in most works of village prose the dominant and strong characters are women, while the male characters are weak, confused or tainted by city life.

The dominant relationship in village prose is not between husband and wife, or between lovers, but rather between parents – and often grandparents – and children, in particular, as mentioned above, the relationship between mother and son. This is true of all the major 'canonical' works of village prose: Solzhenitsyn's 'Matrenin dvor' ('Matrena's Home', 1963), Rasputin's *Poslednii srok* (*Borrowed Time*, 1970), Astaf'ev's *Poslednii poklon* (although in this work the figure of the grandmother is the central one), Rasputin's *Proshchanie s Materoi* (*Farewell to Matera*, 1976). Even the relationship in Belov's *Privychnoe delo* (*That's How It Is*, 1966) between Ivan Afrikanovich and his wife Katerina is more akin to that of a mother and her son, and the same could be said about the relationship between Liuba and Egor in Vasily Shukshin's *Kalina krasnaia* ('Snowball Berry Red', 1973). Village prose is fundamentally concerned with individual people, particularly older characters who have outlived their time and feel unable to comprehend the new reality. Fedor Abramov has said that the village is Russia's *'materinskoe lono, gde zarozhdalsia i skladyvalsia nash natsional'nyi kharakter'* (the maternal bosom which gave birth to and formed our national character). Furthermore, village prose represents the country's filial gratitude to the women of the village who fed Russia and kept it going through its darkest hours of the Second World War.[3]

Most of the leading authors of village prose (Belov, Boris Mozhaev, Abramov, Vladimir Tendriakov, Sergei Zalygin) are preoccupied with history, particularly with the collectivisation of Soviet agriculture in the late 1920s, and the injustices perpetrated in its name. Significantly, and in contrast to the *povesti* (novellas) and *rasskazy* (short stories) about the contemporary village, in two long novels, Mozhaev's *Muzhiki i baby* (Peasants and their Women, 1976; 1987) and Belov's *Kanuny* (The Eves, 1972; 1987), the main women characters actually do very little: rather, they represent the home or notions of honour that are about to be turned upside down by dekulakisation and the ensuing upheavals. Other writers do not stop there, but go on to describe the disaster that collectivisation wrought on agriculture, the village way of life and the country's social and economic development in subsequent years. In works dealing with the post-war years, moreover, village prose looks at the process of change and modernisation from the point of view of those directly affected: the peasants. Their way of life is changing, and in many respects disappearing, not because of new economic relationships or the natural social processes prevalent in all industrial societies, but rather as a result of Party decisions, governmental decrees and the violence of local activists determined to transform the countryside. It is no wonder that the 'enemy' in village prose (apart from the works on collectivisation) is a faceless bureaucrat, accountable only to those higher up, sitting in a comfortable office somewhere in Moscow or the regional capital, and the closest we get to him, if ever, is the lowly local official (almost always male) who has to carry out the agreed policies.

In times of change and disruption, the mother figure offers warmth, humanity, stability and also a link with the past, a past of tradition and certainty. This has been particularly true of the recent history of Russia, with its many upheavals which have had a profound impact on the countryside. The distinctive contribution of village prose to the image of the mother is the symbolic importance attached to it. Much recent research has been done on the importance and prevalence of the mother figure in Russian culture and folklore, and one motif which stands out is the mother as a symbol of fertility.[4] Certainly, the mothers of village prose have many children, but the emphasis is not on their fertility, but rather on their suffering: many of these women have lost most, if not all, of their children through war, famine and hardship. These mothers command their authors' sympathy and highest respect, and are themselves indicators of the great harm done to the countryside and the centuries-old village way of life by Soviet rule.

Given the dominance of the mother motif in village prose, can we really talk about misogyny? Discussions of misogyny in Russian literature generally focus on sexual relationships (or potential ones), where the threat of female sexuality is effectively neutralised by the death of the woman (Dostoevsky's *Idiot* [*The Idiot*, 1868], Lermontov's *Geroi nashego vremeni* [*A Hero of Our Time*, 1840]), or where female sexuality is seen as grotesque and evil (as in short works by Gogol', and Olesha's *Zavist'* [*Envy*, 1927]).[5] In village prose, male dominance is associated with progress, disruption and disaster; the female values of stability, tradition and warmth are the only positive ones. The focus here is on the village as the moral soul of the country, and the female becomes an embodiment not only of Mother Nature, but also of Mother Russia (the symbolism of the names 'Matrena' and 'Matera', with motherhood – *mat'* – at their root, is an obvious example of this). This is in effect a Romantic notion of woman's capacity to save the world. In village prose, though, the ugly nature of contemporary reality dashes this potential and when the modern world intrudes into the village, or when the rural woman goes into the town, we get an entirely different type of woman, who will be discussed later.

Significantly, village prose has more in common with folklore than with classical Russian literature, both in the structure of its conflicts between 'us and them', based as they are on the struggle of opposing sides for the soul and the land of Russia, and its glorification of the mother figure. Adele Barker has noted the significance of the mother-son relationship in Russian folklore:

> Male-female interactions in Russian epic were often strained because the females took an aggressive stance thought appropriate only to males. This male aggressiveness made itself felt not only in marriage relation-

ships, but in those between sons and mothers as well. The mother-figure, in the father's absence, took on many of the characteristics that would have been appropriated by the father in the normal family situation. She became the authority figure and the one who, when necessary, employed physical force in order to restrain her son from violence. She became phallic in the sense that she served as an object of both power and fear in her son's life... Russian epic dismisses the physical father altogether. Along with the image of the aggressive phallic mother went another, a softer one, more in conformance with traditionally held notions of woman as a maternal, succoring being. The phallic mother on Russian soil contained both qualities. At best, she provided a necessary check on the hero in shielding him from harm and his own ill-judgment. At worst, her power over him was felt by the hero to be so formidable that it led to regression in the warrior's development. In order to mature the hero had to break free.[6]

There are several points of interest as well as divergence here. Firstly, as we have seen, the son-mother relationship is the dominant one in village prose. The father is absent, either because he has been killed in the war or during collectivisation. However, perhaps more important is the fact that the mother in village prose does not compel her son to act, nor does she necessarily protect him; but rather carries out the action *instead of* him. The son has either lost his will to resist (as in Rasputin's *Proshchanie s Materoi* or his more recent work *Pozhar* [*The Fire*, 1985]), or drunk himself into a state where he no longer has a will (*Borrowed Time*). In Rasputin's work in particular, the son betrays his mother first and his land second. To borrow a phrase used to characterise the dissidents in Iuliia Voznesenskaia's *Zhenskii dekameron* (*The Women's Decameron*, 1986), men 'too have not been spared by the times'. Continuing the themes of Voznesenskaia's work, we can see that in village prose, too, the woman has been made strong by the times.[7]

Rasputin claims that he glorifies women in his works,[8] but, of course, the women he portrays in glowing colours, such as Nastena in *Zhivi i pomni* (*Live and Remember*, 1974), Dar'ia in *Proshchanie s Materoi*, Anna in *Poslednii srok*, Alena in *Pozhar*, are all idealised and saintly figures, explicitly associated with the land and with motherhood. Indeed, a striking feature of Rasputin's portrayal of women is that they are not described physically: we get little idea of their external appearance, only of their inner moral qualities. Solzhenitsyn also does not describe Matrena's appearance in any detail, but she exudes spirituality. She is frail and has few material possessions, betrayed by the State which refuses her a pension, and exploited by her neighbours. And it is exactly on such spiritual and moral paragons as Matrena that Russia stands. Solzhenitsyn's views on the role of women in society have not changed significantly: in his pamphlet *Kak nam obustroit' Rossiiu?* (*Rebuilding Russia*, 1990) he urges the Russian government to increase the pay of men so that the women of the household need not go out to work: *'zhenshchina – dolzhna imet' vozmozhnost' vernut'sia v sem'iu dlia vospitaniia detei, takov dolzhen byt' muzhskoi zarabotok'* (the woman should have the opportunity to return to the family to bring up her children, if her husband's pay allows it).[9] For him, as for Rasputin, woman's natural role in life is essentially that of a patriarchal age and a rejection of modern notions of equality. Neither accepts that women may actually want to work as a means of professional or vocational satisfaction.

Women as sexual partners are vilified in a way that is not too far removed from the male Russian nineteenth- and early twentieth-century tradition mentioned above. Men are also categorised in terms of *svoi* and *chuzhie:* those who belong are hard-working, honest, and downtrodden (Ivan Afrikanovich, Mozhaev's Fedor Kuz'kin, Abramov's Mikhail Priaslin); the men from the outside (usually the town) are threatening, aggressive and rational (for example, in Rasputin's *Pozhar, Proshchanie s Materoi*, Astaf'ev's *Tsar'-ryba* [*Queen Fish*, 1976] and novels by Belov, Mozhaev and Sergei Antonov on collectivisation). It would not be an exaggeration to say that in village prose the state and its policies are embodied by men.

The affirmation of the mother figure as the link with the past and the custodian of the hearth conceals a mistrust and a fear of female sexuality. When sexual relationships are introduced into village prose, we see its dark side. There are no idealised heroines exuding spiritual light and guidance here. This glorification of the mother figure by necessity excludes the sexual partner, be she based in the town, or in the village (Shukshin's wives, for instance). In Belov's early 'urban' work 'Vospitanie po doktoru Spoku' (Upbringing According to Dr Spock, 1968–1979: note the irony inherent in the title), all the women – that is, wives or possible sexual partners – are negative characters, having lost their moral integrity in moving from the village. In the cycle *Plotnitskie rasskazy* (*Carpenter's Yarns*, 1968), the young hero Konstantin Zorin returns to his native village and, as he admires the stillness of the summer night, he is approached by the daughter of a neighbour, also visiting from the town. She promptly invites him to spend the night with her. Zorin is filled with disgust that shame and decency seem so easily lost. Later the same night he comes to the conclusion that his own wife back in the town is probably no different, and despises her all the more. The story 'Moia zhizn'' ('My Life', 1974) is a detailed account of a woman's gradual degradation and descent into moral purgatory after she leaves the security of the village. In this cycle, set both in the village and in the town, only the older women, who either still live in the village or retain links with it, are warm, compassionate and generally moral beings. Belov undoubtedly uses his main character Zorin to bemoan the absence of uncorrupted and demure young maidens in modern Russia:

> Он, Зорин, всегда был верен своей жене. Он любил её. Ему всегда становилось гнусно от дамских штучек, он терпеть не мог этих откровенных намёков, взглядов встречных, совершенно незнакомых женщин, этих прищуров, полуулыбок. Нормальные, неиспорченные женщины не смотрят в глаза незнакомых мужчин. Они идут по улице нормально. Мерзость и грязь самих мужчин не пристаёт к ним, они чисты даже в самой отвратительной обстановке. Много ли их, таких? [10]

(He, Zorin, had always been faithful to his wife. He loved her. He always felt sickened by female flirting, he couldn't stand these open hints and the glances of women he didn't know and whom he met briefly, these grimaces and half-smiles. Normal, uncorrupted women do not look men they do not know in the eye. They have a normal way of walking down the street. The vileness and filth of men do not cling to them, they remain pure even in the most disgusting environment. Are there many such women?)

In the later, urban novels of Belov and Astaf'ev, *Vse vperedi* (*The Best is Yet to Come*, 1987) and *Pechal'nyi detektiv* (The Sad Detective, 1986), the modern, urbanised women are painted in black colours as sexually aggressive, promiscuous, self-opinionated, and morally irredeemable. Similarly, the wives or partners of the male characters in Shukshin's short stories are almost always portrayed as interested only in material things, thwarting the spiritual searchings (*'prazdnik dushi'*) of their men.

In other words, the *derevenshchiki* neutralise the threat of female sexuality by domesticating and idealising their women, thus conforming to a cultural stereotype that is not the sole preserve of the Russians, but which has been appropriated by them. Moreover, the ideal, 'normal' woman they construct is nothing more than a projection of their longing for a more ordered, stable world run along conservative and patriarchal lines. They reject the modern, urban world, associated as it is with western ways, and yearn for a return to what they see as a uniquely Russian way of life, based on the rural community, its customs and moral values. Conversely, the counter stereotype is the creation of an aggressive and immoral younger woman who has lost her link with the village, and therefore also lost her soul (Abramov's Al'ka, for instance). Such a model reveals the fear felt by these authors of female sexuality, and of the threat posed by the younger generation as a whole.[11]

Yet woman is also the symbol of Russia's purity and innocence: Astaf'ev's story 'Liudochka' (1989) offers a clear indication of what happens to a simple country girl (Liudochka of the title) who moves to the town: exploitation, rape and suicide. It is, moreover, through the image of the mother figure that the village writers have deplored the ravages wrought on the countryside since collectivisation, and it is in these works that the historical record has been put straight (and often before the official historians have been permitted archive access to do so).

So there is a clear contradiction here when considering the problem of misogyny in village prose. On the one hand it is there, but probably no more than in other works of Soviet and non-Soviet Russian literature (we find similarly prejudiced depictions of women in the works of more 'progressive' writers such as Iury Trifonov, Andrei Bitov, Evgeny Popov, and even Tat'iana Tolstaia). On the other hand, the women of the village have to work hard to feed their children in the absence of male figures. Also, the male glorification of motherhood serves two ends: to symbolise the human and moral cost of the destruction of the peasantry and to retreat from uncomfortable modern realities into safe havens of domesticity and security. The elevation of motherhood may be a male fantasy, but this fantasy does not necessarily denigrate or deny the place and status of women in the community. There is no evidence in their fictional writings that the village writers hate or fear all women; rather, the woman in the form of the mother is both the focus of resistance to the state and a more abstract, metaphysical symbol of strength and purity lacking in the modern, urbanised world.

In conclusion, it should be stressed that village prose remains one of the clearest condemnations of historical injustice and tyranny to emerge in post-war Soviet literature. At a time of cultural conformity and considerable repression – the era of 'stagnation' – it managed to inform the Soviet reading public of grave miscarriages of justice, state terrorism and vast ecological damage. Its role in forming Soviet public opinion on these issues in the 1960s and 1970s should not be undervalued. Its preoccupation with the resilience and inner strength of the peasant – especially the peasant woman – is not only a testament to the harshness of ordeals suffered, it is also a reminder of values now lost. Village prose relies heavily on Russian (as opposed to western) cultural models, in particular traditional and symbol-laden images of mother figures. All the more wonder, then, that these writers place their women in the forefront of opposition to male-inspired state policies, and thereby elevate them to positions of moral leadership and guidance that men in the Soviet age have been unable to occupy.

Notes

1. Kathleen Parthé, *Russian Village Prose: The Radiant Past* (Princeton, NJ: Princeton University Press, 1992).
2. Peter Marinelli, *Pastoral* (London: Methuen, 1971), pp. 10–11.
3. See, for example, his speech to the Sixth Writers' Congress in 1976, 'O khlebe nasushchnom i khlebe dukhovnom', in F. Abramov, *O khlebe nasushchnom i khlebe dukhovnom* (Moscow: Molodaia gvardiia, 1988), pp. 16–17:

    Вспомним, к примеру, только один подвиг русской бабы в минувшей войне. При этом я ни на минуту не забываю о подвижничестве женщин других народов нашей великой страны. Но говорю о русской бабе, потому что о русской прозе веду речь. Ведь это она, русская баба, своей сверхчеловеческой работой ещё в сорок первом году открыла второй фронт, тот фронт, которого так жаждала Советская Армия. А как, какой мерой, каким мерилом измерить подвиг всё той же русской бабы в послевоенную пору, в те времена, когда она, зачастую сама голодная, раздетая и разутая, кормила и одевала страну, с истинным терпением и безропотностью русской крестьянки несла свой тяжкий крест вдовы-солдатки, матери погибших на войне сыновей!

    (Let us recall, for instance, just one heroic deed by the Russian peasant woman in the last war. At the same time I do not forget the heroism of women of other nationalities of our great country. But I speak of the Russian peasant woman, because I am speaking about Russian prose writing. For it is she, the Russian peasant woman, whose superhuman capacity for work back in 1941 opened up the second front, the front the Soviet army so yearned for. And how, by what yardstick, can we measure the heroism of the Russian peasant woman in the post-war period, at a time when she, often herself going without food, clothing or footwear, fed and clothed the country, and with the true endurance and forbearance of the Russian woman of the soil carried her heavy cross, as a woman who had lost her husband or had her children killed at the front!).

4. See, for example, Adele Marie Barker, *The Mother Syndrome in the Russian Folk Imagination* (Columbus, OH: Slavica, 1985), and Joanna Hubbs, *Mother Russia: The Feminine Myth in Russian Culture* (Bloomington and Indianapolis, IN: Indiana University Press, 1988).
5. For a discussion of the misogyny of these works, see Barbara Heldt, *Terrible Perfection: Women and Russian Literature* (Bloomington and Indianapolis, IN: Indiana University Press, 1987), especially pp. 25–37. See also Rosalind Marsh's chapter, this volume.
6. Barker, *The Mother Syndrome*, pp. 54–5.
7. Julia Voznesenskaya, *The Women's Decameron*, translated by W.B. Linton, (London, Melbourne, New York: Quartet, 1986), p. 154.
8. See Pieta Monks, 'An Interview with Valentin Rasputin', *Anglo-Soviet Journal*, vol. 43, no. 2 (Spring 1983), p. 14:

    It is not true that I have a limited attitude towards women, I glorify them, and it is right that I should do so ... But it is true that a woman should put her home, the upbringing of her children and the domestic duties first. After all, an awful lot of problems arise nowadays from the fact that the woman has left the home. Emancipation makes life very difficult for her, although it has its own attraction, makes her the legal equal of men, but she finds it difficult to cope with her new role, and yet she doesn't want to return to her former way of life, she has abandoned her basic role in life. And, after all, what kind of freedom can she really have when she has liberated herself from precisely those obligations that nature has placed upon her ... It is more like desertion than liberation.

9. Aleksandr Solzhenitsyn, 'Kak nam obustroit' Rossiiu?', *Komsomol'skaia pravda (Spetsial'nyi vypusk. Broshiura v gazete)*, 18 September 1990, p. 4.

10. 'Svidaniia po utram', in *Roman-gazeta*, nos 13–14 (947–48) (1982), p. 111.
11. The fear of the present and the feeling of loss in the modern, post-Soviet world can be gauged in the fiction published by Rasputin and Belov in recent years. See Rasputin's somewhat pained and sad short stories 'Sania edet' (Sania is on his Way), 'Rossiia molodaia' (Young Russia) and 'V odnom sibirskom gorode' (In a Siberian Town), *Moskva*, no. 7 (1994), pp. 3–20; Belov's angry, vitriolic and fiercely nationalistic play *Semeinye prazdniki* (Family Celebrations), *Moskva*, no. 9 (1994), pp. 9–41.

Chapter 17

REAL AND UNREAL WOMEN IN THE WORKS OF CHINGIZ AITMATOV

Natal'ia Zhuravkina

This chapter is based on the following works by Chingiz Aitmatov: *Pegii pes, begushchii kraem moria* (*The Piebald Dog Running Along the Shore*, 1977) and *Belyi parokhod* (*The White Steamship,* 1970), with additional references to *Proshchai, Gul'sary!* (*Farewell, Gul'sary!*, 1966), and *I dol'she veka dlitsia den'* (*The Day Lasts Longer than a Hundred Years*, 1980; original book title *Burannyi polustanok* [Railway Halt in a Snowstorm, 1980]). The female images in these works are significant because they are so extraordinarily vivid and poetic.

Although the terms 'myth' and 'legend' are often used loosely and interchangeably in modern English, for the purposes of this chapter 'myth' will be used in its narrower, primary definition to refer to a purely fictitious narrative, often involving supernatural persons and embodying popular ideas on natural phenomena, whereas 'legend' will be used to denote a traditional story popularly regarded as historical. The term 'epic' will be used to mean a work of heroic scale or 'national significance', embodying 'the history and aspirations of a nation in a lofty or grandiose manner'.[1]

In *Pegii pes*, myth is the main narrative feature.[2] The work is explicitly mythological both in form (the author himself calls it a 'mythological poem') and content. It is based on two myths of the

Translated by David Gillespie

Nivkh (or Giliak) people in north-east Siberia who inhabit the coast along the Sea of Okhotsk – the Luvr bird and the Fish Woman – it combines epic legend with epic narration, and its mythology is entirely that of the Giliaks. The plot concerns four Giliaks caught in the open sea in a dense, potentially dangerous fog. According to Giliak legend, the Luvr bird created the world – the land within the boundless ocean of water – and the great Fish Woman begat the line of Ruiingun. The legend of the origins of the Kyrgyz people (descendants of Ruiingun still live in the mountains by Lake Issyk-Kul'), the Great Deer Mother, the founder of the nation, and the epic tale of the Siberian deer that Aitmatov uses in *Belyi parokhod* – all form part of the consciousness of the characters in *Pegii pes*.

The depiction of female figures contributes to our understanding of the place and role of national traditions in Aitmatov's work. In this respect, Aitmatov's own bilingualism is a most important factor, for it not only allows the writer to convey the scope of his ideas freely in both languages, but also enables the Russian reader to gain a full and deep understanding of Kyrgyz culture. Aitmatov's early works such as *Materinskoe pole* (*Mother Earth*, 1963) were written in Kyrgyz and translated by him into Russian, while his later works *Proshchai, Gul'sary!*, *Belyi parokhod, Pegii pes* and *I dol'she veka dlitsia den'* were written initially in Russian and then translated by the author into Kyrgyz.

Aitmatov's bilingualism is significant because it constitutes such a fundamental aspect of his own talent. He is able not only to grasp all the meanings and the subtlest nuances of words and phrases, but also the rhythm, the music of another language in order to create a work of literature that can retain its own distinct national flavour, whether Russian or Kyrgyz. As he himself says:

> I write my books in Kyrgyz and Russian. If it is initially written in Kyrgyz, then I translate it into Russian, and vice versa. That gives me the greatest pleasure. It is an immensely fascinating work of the mind which leads to greater stylistic accomplishment and the enrichment of the language's store of images.[3]

Aitmatov's description of the Fish Woman is particularly poetic and colourful: 'A fish in the shape of a woman, of unparalleled beauty: a smooth body shining like silver pebbles in the moonlight, dark nipples on a gleaming bosom, green eyes flashing with fire …'.[4] He also gives a lyrical depiction of the Horned Deer Mother:

> Her eyes are large, full of reproach and sadness. The Deer herself is white, her horns an image of pure beauty as they are spread out like the branches of trees in autumn. Her udder is clean and smooth, like the breasts of a mother feeding her child.(*R.z.*, 226)

Although *Pegii pes* contains no such poetic portrayal of the boy Kirisk's mother, we know from his memories that she is a loving and caring woman, a devoted wife and mother, in contrast to the mother in *Belyi parokhod*. The boy cannot remember his mother, as his parents parted when he was two years old. Since that time she has lived in another town and he has not seen her. She has another family: two daughters, who are brought up in a kindergarten and whom she sees only once a week. She lives in a large house, but her room is small – so small, there is no room even to turn round. When she and her husband get a new flat, she promises old Momun that the boy will go to live with her. If, of course, her husband agrees. As she relates all this, she herself is crying and begging forgiveness.

Aitmatov writes *Pegii pes* as an epic: that is to say, for him myth *is* reality and the most absolute of life's truths.[5] Indeed, dream is a companion that often visits the clan elder Organ, bringing him joy, sadness and spiritual torment. What is surprising about this sense of dream is that each time it occurs, it impresses Organ because it is endless and contains a multitude of allusions within its various configurations and transformations. As he reflects on this and attempts to grasp the secret of all secrets – the inexorable and ever-changing link between dream and reality, whose very enigma and portent are forever the source of man's anxieties – Organ realises that, no matter how confused his spirit, it always longs for the return of dream, and yearns with a constant hunger to meet the great Fish Woman. Myth in *Pegii pes,* with all its limitations, is a form of perception of the world. Aitmatov may describe the past as legend, but the reader still perceives it as the concrete past, because, although Aitmatov wishes to create legend and myth, he does away with the conventions of myth. Immersing the reader in the world of reality, he explodes the myth.

In *Pegii pes*, myth lives only in the consciousness of the protagonists, especially in Organ's fantastic dreams, which help the reader to understand the soul of the Elder, a soul which aspires to greatness because of its unassuming simplicity.

> He waited for the Fish Woman, as one who had lost his senses, with the passion and ferocity of a drowning man clutching at a straw. He knew that only the Fish Woman could give him happiness and so, with all his might, he waited. The mysterious Fish Woman glided along the waves, delighting the eye with the pearl-like warmth, sleekness and dexterity of her body, and drawing him further and further into the ocean. She could banish ordinary dreams forever. Organ could never forget her, he thought about her as something of actual importance in life. Therefore meeting her and parting from her were real events. (*R.z.*, 298)

In *Belyi parokhod* too, myth is ever present and is correlated with everyday life: the old grandfather relates a tale to his grandson and the boy believes it to be true. Aitmatov portrays the inner world of his young protagonist and shows its rich poetic potential. The boy is always creating tales of wonder in his imagination – with binoculars, stones or flowers – and the tale of the Horned Deer Mother also lives in his imagination. The boy's belief in the Deer Mother is not so significant in itself, as every child needs a sense of the wondrous; the important thing is that the boy comes from Aitmatov's world, a world with a very particular relationship to nature.

In *Pegii pes*, the boy Kirisk is lying on the bottom of the boat, almost dead from thirst, and he recalls his childhood. When he was younger he had fallen seriously ill with fever, and was consumed by just such a desire to drink. His mother did not leave his side and thought up a tale about a blue mouse. She taught him to repeat: 'Blue mouse, bring me some water', assuring him that 'it will bring you water and you will get better' (*R.z.*, 324). The miracle happened and the illness subsided. Now that Kirisk is again on the brink of death, he thinks of his mother and the hope she instilled in him and the incantation 'Blue mouse, give me some water' becomes his last hope.

There is a similar incident in *Belyi parokhod*. Here the boy also falls ill, but he is without a mother's warmth and affection, and so turns to the Horned Deer Mother: 'Help me, Deer Mother, help me, I am also your son' (*R.z.*, 250). He sees the Deer Mother, with her dark, warm, moist eyes, running along behind him on the shore, running so fast that the wind whistles through her antlers. And the boy immediately feels better. He has returned to the world of his imagination, where he was 'the son of the sons of the Horned Deer Mother'. This adds considerable force to the end of Aitmatov's story, when Old Momun, who had told the boy the history of the Deer Mother as the founder of the Kyrgyz people and who had himself believed it, kills a female deer. For him, too, the Deer Mother had been not simply a legend, but an object of worship.

Aitmatov employs a variety of stylistic devices to create his beautiful and graceful feminine images. In *Pegii pes* a musical quality is evoked by refrain and chant, as in the following:

> Where are you, great Fish-Woman?
> The warmth of your womb begets life
> The warmth of your womb gave us life by the sea
> The warmth of your womb is the best place on earth.
> Where are you, Great Fish-Woman?
> The white of your breasts is like the heads of seals
> The white of your breasts gave us food by the sea.
> Where are you, Great Fish-Woman?
> The strongest man swims to you
> To give fruit to your womb
> To people the earth with your stock. (*R.z.*, 297)

Such chants are sung at festivals to celebrate the progenitor of the nation. With each refrain, the repeated phrase assumes a different nuance and comes to resemble a musical theme, a leitmotif which brings a musical dimension to the narrative. The image of the Great Fish Woman is thus infused with a poetic and musical quality.

On the other hand, in *Belyi parokhod* and *I dol'she veka dlitsia den'* the musical motif takes second place to the mythic. In the former novella, the boy's poetic and lyrical voice (for instance, his tale of the Siberian deer) alternates with the author's narrative voice. The authorial voice is laconic, devoid of any folkloric elements, but it has a structure, rhythm and musicality that find echoes in the boy's narrative voice, thus creating a stylistic unity which brings the novel closer to the epic story-telling of yore. Here is the boy's tale:

> The Siberian deer were no more. The mountains were empty, the deer couldn't be heard at midnight, nor at dawn, they couldn't be seen in the forest, nor in the clearing. People say that when the bullets and the hounds had completely exterminated the deer, then the Horned Deer Mother climbed the highest mountain peak, bade farewell to Issyk-Kul' and led the last of her line beyond the great pass into another land and other mountains. (*R.z.*, 230)

This is the authorial narrative that immediately follows:

> It was once more autumn in the mountains. Once more, after the tumult of summer, life was becoming attuned to the quiet of autumn. The herds had gone for the winter. The people had gone. The mountains were empty. (*R.z.*, 231)

The poetic intonation comes from the sustained rhythm of repetition and refrain.

In *Proshchai, Gul'sary!* song is also important: it is the natural form of expression of the characters' feelings, thoughts and emotions. Thus, after Biubiudzhan has told him that their relationship is doomed, Tanabai, although he realises in his mind that she is right, cannot in his heart imagine life without her. Only in the song that he sings can the reader see the pain of his soul: 'Quietly and indistinctly, in time with the measured tread of his horse, Tanabai sang of the sufferings of people long since dead.' The word 'sufferings' reveals to the reader the protagonist's own inner state.

Song as a spiritual need is explained in *Proshchai, Gul'sary!*:

> Travelling alone, one sings for oneself. When he is alone, a man sings of his unrealised dreams, of his life and his loves. A man likes to pine for the times when he still had ambition. And sometimes he likes to think about that, to feel himself.[6]

Song is thus important as a means of self-perception and self-discovery. It also serves to show how vital the tradition of song is in the Kyrgyz artistic consciousness. Song as lament and song as story-telling are both evident in *Proshchai, Gul'sary!*, but it is associated with other motifs in *Pegii pes*: love, desire, passion, hope and longing. It occurs spontaneously, without interrupting the narrative flow, but rather, like all music, imbues it with mood. Both song and story-telling as used by Aitmatov acquire an allegorical function. If song as lament in *Proshchai, Gul'sary!* communicates loss, then in *Belyi parokhod* the tale of the ancient line of the Kyrgyz people offers a different motif.

In *Pegii pes* Aitmatov assumes the role of a writer in the epic style: myth becomes both reality and absolute truth, and is used to reveal the psychology behind the characters' actions. Organ's fantastic dreams about the Fish Woman have a realistic function, as the author helps the reader to understand the soul of the Elder. Aitmatov himself claims to subject the morality of his characters to 'the ultimate test – the test of death'. He shows how difficult it is on the final threshold to remain a man, suggesting that it is just as important to think of someone else as of oneself. This is the ultimate test of one's humanity – a humanity which also emanates from the folkloric tales that the characters in *Belyi parokhod* create and inhabit, and from the song as story-telling in *Proshchai, Gul'sary!*

Aitmatov's images stem from nature and the life based on the natural world. The half-real, half-mythological image of the Fish Woman, the image of the Horned Deer Mother, the image of the horse Gul'sary, are all natural, simple images of Mother Nature. Lev Tolstoy may tell his tale 'Kholstomer: Istoriia loshadi' ('The Story of a Horse', 1886) from the point of view of the horse itself, giving it his own ideas and thoughts, but Aitmatov makes no attempt to humanise his horse. Gul'sary is important as a being which embodies the world of nature to which it inseparably belongs.

Myth is also present in the novel *The Day Lasts More than a Hundred Years*. Aitmatov tells the tale of a mother, Naiman-Ana, who has lost her son, but refuses to believe that he is dead and sets out to look for him. It turns out that he has been imprisoned by fierce tribal enemies, the Zhuan-zhuany (a nomadic tribe ethnically related to the Mongols, who in the third and fourth centuries AD waged war against the Turkic peoples of Central Asia). He has been deprived of his memory, and given the name '*mankurt*'.[7] According to Central Asian legend, *mankurts* were prisoners who had been turned into slaves by having their heads wrapped in camel skins which under the hot sun dried as tight as a steel band. A *mankurt* did not remember his tribe, his family, or even his own name.[8] Naiman-Ana finds her son and tries to restore his memory, but under the influence of his captors he shoots and kills her. Her white headscarf slips from her head and as it falls to the ground becomes transformed into a bird. As it flies off, it calls out: 'Remember who you are and what is your name.'[9] The place where Naiman-Ana is buried comes to be called the cemetery of Ana-Beiit: Mother's Repose. Thus, real women may assume many features of unreal women. As Irena Maryniak observes: 'Through her death, the mother figure is transformed into a totem of the people – the symbol of a common ancestry'.[10]

In *Burannyi polustanok* one of the 'real' women, Zaripa, is described by Aitmatov as resembling a bird which attempts to shelter its nest from the storm with its wings, and she possesses all the classical female characteristics of splendour, self-sacrifice, devotion and beauty. The female image thus comes close to an image from legend, and like many other female characters in Aitmatov's work, provides a significant illustration of his view that a woman cannot be loved in an ordinary, earthly manner.

Notes

1. J. A. Cuddon, *The Penguin Dictionary of Literary Terms and Literary Theory*, 3rd edition (Harmondsworth: Penguin, 1992), p. 284.
2. Irena Maryniak defines myth in relation to recent Russian literature: 'While presenting a textual model by which life may be understood, the mythological narrative makes demands. On the one hand it sets something apart as sacred: the text itself, something or someone within it, or an idea. It creates a polarity between that which is set apart as absolute, inviolable, and that which is profane. On the other hand it calls for an unconditional suspension of disbelief, a revision of one's sense of life's linkages and, finally, action: the endeavour to bring the sacred quality into the profane world': Irena Maryniak, *Spirit of the Totem: Religion and Myth in Soviet Fiction, 1964–1988*, MHRA: Text and Dissertation Series, 39 (London: W.S.Maney & Sons Ltd, 1995), p. 6.
3. Chingiz Aitmatov, *Sobranie sochinenii v trekh tomakh* (Moscow: Molodaia gvardiia, 1982–1984), vol. 3, p. 348.
4. Chingiz Aitmatov, *Rannie zhuravli* (Alma Ata: Zhazushy, 1988), p. 295. In-text references will be styled *R.z.* followed by the page number.
5. Joseph P. Mozur writes that Aitmatov in this story 'demonstrates that his theme is not Nivkh civilization at the turn of the twentieth century, but modern humankind at the turn of the twenty-first century, caught in the paradoxes of the atomic age'. Joseph P. Mozur, *Parables from the Past: The Prose Fiction of Chingiz Aitmatov* (Pittsburgh and London: University of Pittsburgh Press, 1995), p. 95.
6. Chingiz Aitmatov, *Izbrannoe* (Minsk: Iunatstva, 1981), p. 30.
7. Aitmatov's treatment of the *'mankurt'* legend is discussed in detail in Mozur, *Parables from the Past*, pp. 107-15. (Editor's note: Aitmatov himself coined the term *mankurt*, which means 'I-worm'.)

8. Editor's note: the image of the *mankurt* was frequently used by critics and publicists in the Gorbachev era as a symbol of the collective loss of memory of the Soviet people: see, for example, G.Volkov, *Sovetskaia kul'tura*, 4 July 1987. It has also won a permanent place in the idiom of Central Asian intellectuals.
9. Chingiz Aitmatov, *I dol'she veka dlitsia den'* (Frunze: Kyrgyzstan, 1988), p. 125.
10. Maryniak, *Spirit of the Totem*, p. 107.

Chapter 18

THE IMAGE OF WOMEN IN THE PROSE OF SERGEI DOVLATOV

Boris Lanin

Sergei Dovlatov was born in 1941 in Ufa, but his family later moved to Leningrad, where his father worked as a theatre administrator, and his mother as an actress.[1] After working in a factory for a short while, Dovlatov went to Leningrad State University, where he studied Finnish. Two years later he was expelled from the university and called up into the army. He spent his term of national service in the camps of Komi, an experience described in his first collection of stories and novellas, *Zona: Zapiski nadziratelia (The Zone: A Prison Camp Guard's Story)*, published in 1982. As the critic Lev Loseff has remarked: 'The stories in *Zone* are rich in detail and colourful in language, with military and criminal jargon abundant; however, the author focuses not on the exotically violent life in the camps, but rather on the psychological analysis of his characters'.[2]

For Dovlatov, *Zone* became an original visiting card. Who likes to be labelled a camp guard? But in Dovlatov's case, this gave him the right to write sincerely and openly about the camps, and in his stories the brutality of camp life is supplemented by tales about the brutality of the guards' lives. This text is structured as a frame narrative. The literary notes of the guard Alikhanov, inserted into the main narrative, are distinguished both by italic script and the rhythm of the text. We sense a new dimension as soon as Alikhanov takes up the pen.

Translated by Rosalind Marsh

The only nurse in the barracks is Raia, a young girl whom it would be difficult to describe as pretty: she had 'thick ankles, small blackened teeth and oily skin'.[3] When a new soldier appears – the Estonian Pakhapil' – the first thing he asks is whether there are any women in the barracks. He is assured that there are, and even that there are many of them:

> 'There are Solokha, Raia, and eight "Dun'kas" …'.
> This answer made Pakhapil' very happy. He didn't know that Solokha was the horse that carried the groceries, and that 'Dun'ka' was the name given to the camp pederasts …
> However, Raia made up for ten. After his first date with her Pakhapil' came back again the same night and found another man with her. Raia rejected Pakhapil''s indignation. 'What if I love you both?',[4] Raia said, 'What then?' (1: 60)

The search for a woman – and subsequent disillusionment – is always a feature of Dovlatov's heroes.

In the camp zone women are not in the habit of working. Sex is their chief work and way of life. *'Tiazhelee khrena v ruki ne beru'* (I won't take in my hands anything heavier than a cock), says Zina, one of the characters in the story. It is the narrator himself who has pretensions to being some kind of moral focus of the life depicted here. Significantly, even his peccadilloes do not prevent this, but make the hero appear more human, kinder, closer to the reader.

After his demobilisation in 1965, Dovlatov became a journalist and continued writing stories. He achieved the kind of popularity which was quite typical of writers later to become part of the third wave of emigration – popularity in *samizdat*. He was saved from reproaches and accusations of leading an anti-social way of life by the well-known Soviet writer Vera Panova, who hired Dovlatov as her literary secretary. In 1974, in search of a more liberal atmosphere, Dovlatov moved to Tallinn, where he got a job on the Party newspaper. In 1975 his first book was in press with the publishing house 'Eesti Paamat', but suddenly the KGB launched a new anti-dissident campaign (the so-called 'Soldatov case'). Dovlatov's relations with Estonian nationalists and well-known dissidents in Tallinn attracted the attention of the KGB, and his book was dropped from the programme of the publishing house. This is how Elena Skul'skaia, daughter of the writer Grigory Skul'sky, describes this episode in his life: 'In 1975, imperceptibly, as if doctors were taking leave of a patient after convalescence, in the editorial offices of *Sovetskaia Estoniia* the writer Sergei Dovlatov had his throat cut'.[5]

In 1978, at the height of the authorities' anti-dissident campaign, Dovlatov was forced to leave the USSR. In the autumn he moved to the United States. The lyrical hero of his cycle *Chemodan* (*The Suitcase*, 1986) later recalled that OVIR (the bureau which issued visas for foreign travel) allowed him to take only three suitcases, and this distressed him terribly. However, he became even more distressed when he discovered that he managed to fit all of his possessions into just one suitcase which he had kept since his trips to pioneer camp as a child.

The popularity of non-fiction literature in the United States at the time of his immigration proved very welcome. 'I gambled on this, trying to make my stories like documentaries, but they are essentially "fiction", inventions disguised as documentary episodes'.[6] Dovlatov arrived in the United States at a time when there was a renewed interest in stories with concealed meanings and veiled irony. An English translation of one of his stories was published in the *New Yorker*, one of the most prestigious U.S. journals, rocketing Dovlatov to instant fame. Up to then, Vladimir Nabokov had been the only Russian writer to have been published in this journal. The fact of Dovlatov's popularity is evident, if only from the fact that he received about sixty reviews for his books in English translation, all of which were positive. Dovlatov is, perhaps, the most 'Chekhovian' writer since the death of the great short story writer. In his prose Chekhov's motifs of 'non-meetings', 'non-romances' and 'non-dénouements' are developed in a talented manner.

In emigration, woman is the hero's chief support. First the women get settled, then their husbands get up off Oblomov's sofa and reluctantly drag themselves around in search of a wage. Female naïvety proves to be useless in situations which demand vigour and enterprise – this idea forms the basis of Dovlatov's story *Inostranka* (*A Foreign Woman*, 1986). The main female protagonist of the story, Marusia, discovers that all her woman friends are already married, in possession of a hearth and home:

> Of course, not all her friends were living well. Some were unfaithful to their husbands. Some were rudely bossed about by them. Many had to put up with infidelity themselves. But still – they were married. The very presence of a husband gave them value in the eyes of people around them. A husband was absolutely essential. It was necessary to have one, if only as an object of hatred. (3: 26).

In Dovlatov's work this object of hatred often turns out to be the narrator himself. For Dovlatov's narrator, writing from a masculine point of view, masculinity is associated with transgression, the sense of another world, and death, whereas femininity is associated with restlessness, bustle and the impossibility of attaining fulfilment.

There are three themes which permeate the whole of Dovlatov's work: firstly, the absurdity of life; secondly, the loneliness of the suffering, ironic intellectual; and thirdly, the theme of drunkenness, which for Dovlatov proves to be the only escape from the absurdity of life and the only means of overcoming loneliness. Almost all of Dovlatov's male characters drink. People who do not drink seem to him to be false, hollow, peevish, or hopelessly moralistic.

In *Zapovednik* (The Preserve, 1983), this weakness makes intimacy with a woman much easier:

> 'Do you know', I said, 'what I regret? There's a lot of drink left ... Over there, in the studio ...'
> At the same time I stepped over the threshold, as if by chance.
> 'I've got some wine', Tania said. 'I'm hiding it from my brother. He drops in with a bottle, and I put half in the cupboard. He's got a bad liver ...'
> 'You intrigue me', I said.
> 'I understand you', said Tania. 'I've got an uncle who's a chronic alcoholic'. (1: 370–71).

Wine and women are the two passions of Dovlatov's heroes, as they were for the legendary hussars of the past. However, in life women are far more stable creatures. Dovlatov's heroes wear themselves out between women and drink.

A woman has to persuade a man to enter into a relationship with her. In *Kompromiss* (*The Compromise*, 1981) – a collection of novellas linked by one hero-narrator who tells us about his work in the Tallinn Party newspaper – not one single date ends in a happy, natural way. Women are even prepared to pay their lovers! This would have been inconceivable in the Soviet Union. The narrator has to beg for mercy, under pressure from a sexually curious woman who insists on experimentation, and to ask her for a postponement, at the very least. But Tiina Karu cannot wait, and asks him to introduce her to one man at least who might be worthy of her experiments in this new phase of her sexual education. The narrator does make an introduction but even with the man he suggests to her, Os'ka Malkiel', who 'had had more women than the narrator had had hot dinners', not everything succeeds immediately, only at the third attempt. However, when the woman's satisfaction is attained and her curiosity is satisfied, the 'hired lover' receives ten roubles and the narrator, who has turned pimp against his will, gets some chocolate and a bottle of 'Long John' whisky. When in Dovlatov's work a man is faced with the choice of drink or sex, the problem is resolved very quickly. For Dovlatov's heroes, drink is the main value in life. And even the 'girls for export' specially offered to correspondents in the capital cannot tear them away from their favourite occupation: 'You can't have sex without it', Evi whispers as a parting shot.

The origin and development of this image in Dovlatov's work can be traced through the following series: *Solo na Undervude* (Solo on an

Underwood, 1980), 'Literatura prodolzhaetsia: Posle konferentsii v Los-Andzhelese' (Literature Continues: after the Conference in Los Angeles, 1982) and *Filial* (Branch institution, 1989). *Solo* relates incidents which have been recorded, but reworked according to the laws of the anecdote genre. In the article about the conference these anecdotes are arranged into something like a series of topics, but real people remain themselves and appear under their own names. In *Filial* they all change their names: for example, the writer Viktor Nekrasov becomes Panaev (the namesake of the legal husband of Avdot'ia Panaeva, the common-law wife of the nineteenth-century poet Nikolai Nekrasov), Naum Korzhavin becomes Ruvim Kovrigin, and Dovlatov becomes Dolmatov. This enables him to introduce the profoundly personal theme of his former wife Tasia, who unexpectedly appears at the conference, a wild but vivacious, exceptional, fascinating feminine woman for whom, as it turns out, the narrator's feelings have not yet died.

However, women are, at best, good friends and nothing more. Dovlatov's hero has not experienced a happy, mutual, requited love:

> I rummaged in my notebook. I phoned. It was Nelli who answered:
> 'Oh, it's you?! I thought you'd completely forgotten about me ...'
> 'Can I come round?' I asked.
> There was a pause. And then she said:
> 'I'm sorry, I'm not alone'.
> 'All right', I said, 'next time'.
> She replied:
> 'There won't be a next time. Everything is over between us. You have a wife and daughter. It's high time I thought about myself...'.
> And Nelli hung up.
> At this point I sank into thought. Everyone is cruel in different ways. For example, men are rude and lie. They twist and turn as much as they can. But even the cruellest man will not shout at you: 'Go away! Everything is over between us!...'. As for women, they say all this easily, even with some pleasure:
> 'Go away, you disgust me! Don't ring me any more!...'
> At first they weep and sob. Then they find someone else and shout: 'Go away!'
> Go away! I'm not even capable of saying such a thing...[7]

And what do his heroines look like? This is the radio journalist Lida Agapova:

> Imported rubber boots. Her heavy brown skirt does not emphasise her seat. Her synthetic zipped jacket crackles. A blue-topped cap in the uniform of the Tallinn polytechnic. She has a face which is resolute, always frozen. No traces of make-up. A missing tooth at the side of her smile. [It was only later, in the United States, that he was to write: 'in America the only women I have met with missing front teeth have been Slavs'.[8]] Only her eyes express astonishment; her brows are as motionless as a finishing tape. (1: 213)

However, 'a free woman exudes some kind of special fluids' (3: 47), and a woman to whom everything has already happened, happened and passed by, becomes fascinating and irresistible, like Tasia in *Filial*:

> I went out on to the balcony. The panorama of Los Angeles lay spread out before me. Down below, cars piled up on the cross-roads hooted in desperation. A woman walked across the road, taking her time, ignoring the drivers' irritation. She was in wide trousers of some transparent, gauzy material, with a purple turban on her head.
> I understood that the drivers had braked of their own accord. And they were signalling out of the fullness of their hearts.
> It was Tasia, of course. (3: 163)

The meeting with Tasia turns out to be the moment to draw, in the words of the writer Iurii Trifonov, 'preliminary conclusions':

> I could not make out what had happened. We had parted twenty years ago. We had not seen each other for fifteen years. I had a wife and children. Everything was normal.
> But suddenly this unbalanced woman, to put it mildly, had appeared. She was bringing a measure of the absurd into my life. She was bringing back the long-forgotten past. And as a result she was making me suffer ... (3: 192)

There is only one medicine for this pain, and the good doctor arrives just in time: the door opens wide, and a waiter brings a brandy ordered by an invisible person.

Sergei Dovlatov died unexpectedly early, in 1990, without even reaching his fiftieth birthday. His ironic, sad prose still awaits detailed analysis. His heroines are by no means Turgenevan maidens. They are daughters of the twentieth century which brought them up to love life, to be strong and independent, although, like all Dovlatov's protagonists, they often feel unhappy too.

Notes

1. Editor's note: for a sympathetic memoir on Dovlatov, see A. Zverev, 'Zapiski sluchainogo postoial'tsa', *Literaturnoe obozrenie*, no. 4 (1991), pp. 65–70.
2. Lev Loseff, 'Dovlatov, S. D.', in *The Modern Encyclopedia of Russian and Soviet Literatures,* vol. 5, ed. Harry B. Weber (Gulf Breeze, FL: Academic International Press, 1981), p. 240.
3. S. Dovlatov, *Zona*, in Dovlatov, *Sochineniia*, 3 vols. (St Petersburg: Limbus-Press, 1993), vol. 1, p. 59. Hereafter, references to the volume and page numbers of this edition will be given in the text.

4. Translator's note: the Russian is *'A chto, esli mne vas oboikh zhalko'* – 'So what if I love [or, take pity] on you both?'. In peasant speech, the verb *zhalet'* is frequently used as a synonym of 'to love'.
5. E. Skul'skaia, 'Kniga ob ottse', *Raduga* (Tallinn), no. 5 (1990), p. 14.
6. John Glad, *Besedy v izgnanii* (Durham and London: Duke University Press, 1990), p. 90.
7. S. Dovlatov, 'Na ulitse i doma', *Zvezda*, no. 1 (1995), p. 73.
8. *Zvezda*, no. 3 (1994), p. 155.

Chapter 19

IN THE SHADOW OF A PROMINENT PARTNER: EDUCATED WOMEN IN LITERATURE ON THE *SHESTIDESIATNIKI*

Svetlana Carsten

In the second half of the 1980s a debate took place among Soviet literary critics about the *shestidesiatniki*, a large group of Soviet intellectuals who had participated in the liberal movement of the late 1950s and early 1960s. This debate reached its peak at the beginning of the 1990s. The focus of discussion was the *shestidesiatniki*'s role in the liberalisation process of the late 1950s and early 1960s, their aspirations, political struggle, and ultimate defeat. In sociological terms, some attempt was made to define the similarities and differences within this group. The classifications that emerged centred on the moral and aesthetic values of this generation, their ideology and politics – the latter taking the form of political scepticism or apolitical procrastination. Literary criticism has also taken a great deal of interest in their lives, their literature, and literature about them.[1] It is the latter that is the focus of attention here, and specific reference will be made to two novellas of 1987 – Vladimir Makanin's *Odin i odna* (*All Alone*)[2] and Nikolai Shmelev's *Pashkov dom* (Pashkov House).[3] These two short novels have been singled out in Soviet literary criticism as addressing problems common to the *shestidesiatniki*.[4]

The two novels in question depict members of that generation in the late 1970s, in the case of *Pashkov dom*, and the mid-1980s in Makanin's *Odin i odna*. *Pashkov dom* is written by an author who is himself a *shestidesiatnik*. Shmelev is perhaps better known as an economist who became an ardent supporter of Gorbachev's reforms. However, his few literary attempts (his earliest go back to the 1960s) are of high quality and deserve their place on the long list of the best Soviet fiction. *Pashkov dom* falls into the category of delayed literature, written a few years before it could be published.[5] While most of that literature addressed historical issues connected with the Stalin period, *Pashkov dom* dealt with the more recent past – the stifling reality of what became known as the 'period of stagnation' (the Brezhnev era). It should be stated, however, that Shmelev does not offer us a meticulous description of various aspects of Soviet *byt* (everyday life) or social conditions. The end result of the novel is the creation of a social type, a representative of a particular group of the Soviet intelligentsia, the group that by the second half of the 1980s became known as the *shestidesiatniki*. The protagonist, Aleksandr Gort, is, like the author, in his early fifties (he would be in his sixties by Gorbachev's time). His youth and his prime (or *'sezon dushi'*, the prime time of the soul, to use the words of Makanin's character, Goloshchekov) coincide with Khrushchev's thaw. He is intoxicated by the fresh breeze of liberalisation; he is a young, talented and promising academic specialising in Chinese history, who is admired by his students and colleagues alike, and above all he is a reformer. He spends a good part of his youth in the library writing a work of philosophy and politics (*traktat*) on 'charity as the most profitable policy in a commercial sense'. But with the end of the thaw comes the end of Gort's prime (a fate shared by many other intellectuals). His work is not accepted for publication because it does not conform to the ideology of the new situation. Gort now devotes his entire life to his translations from Chinese and to his research, going straight to the library after his daytime work. He keeps a low profile in politics and refuses to take up promotions in order to preserve his academic and personal freedom and honesty. Like many *shestidesiatniki*, Gort does not embark on the path of open dissent, but does not turn into a conformist either.

A similar social type, a portrait of a *shestidesiatnik*, is drawn by Vladimir Makanin in his novel *Odin i odna*. Makanin is about Shmelev's age. He is a prolific writer of the 'Moscow school' who became known in the 1970s. Although most of his writing takes us to his native Urals, there are some works that he devoted to the Moscow intelligentsia – *Odin i odna*, a reworking of an earlier novel *Portret i vokrug* (A Portrait and its Surroundings, 1978), is among them. *Odin i odna* was written in 1986 when the debates on the *shestidesiatniki* began. At that time the younger generation of Soviet writers, *sorokaletnie* and *tridtsatiletnie* (the so-called 'thirty-year-olds' and 'forty-year-olds') started voicing their criticism of the *shestidesiatniki* for their apparent conformism and Marxist politics.[6] Makanin distanced himself from the *shestidesiatniki* (although he is of an age that should qualify him as one), but his attitude to them is not hostile, as some critics believe it to be. A master at portraying various social types, he turned to a *shestidesiatnik* character in *Odin i odna*, describing him from the position of an outsider, unlike Shmelev who identifies with his hero. The protagonist in *Odin i odna*, Igor', is a writer of Makanin's age who is writing two portraits, one of a single man, Gennady Pavlovich Goloshchekov and the other of a single woman, Ninel' Nikolaevna. He forms a friendship with them and regularly visits them, relating his observations to the reader as if making notes on the spot. The picture that emerges is of two single people whose lives are so similar that according to Igor''s expectations they should immediately take to each other when they meet. But this expectation is not fulfilled. Makanin's (and Igor''s) attitude to them is ironic and somewhat patronising, with a note of reproach, which is not surprising because they constantly moan about loneliness and yet do nothing to change their lifestyles. Their malady is total apathy, or a 'paralysis of the will', as the critic Sergei Chuprinin describes it.[7] Gennady, just like Gort in *Pashkov dom*, is very nostalgic about his past – he was also active and brilliant during the thaw years. But at present all that remains are his books and his intellect. Ninel' also lives in a world of dreams, reminiscent of her youth. On the whole Makanin's attitude to his characters is ambivalent. On the one hand he is critical of their lack of will-power, but on the other hand he sympathises with them for the constraints imposed on them by society, which might explain their passive existence. Goloshchekov declares that he is an 'unfulfilled man' ('*chelovek nesostoiavshiisia*'), but the reader is made to understand that the potential to serve his society is there. Goloshchekov is described as being in a state of constant expectation that 'one day he will be called upon and he will immediately go, if there is such an opportunity'.[8]

This ambivalent position of the Russian intellectuals in both novels provoked a wave of controversy among literary critics. Sergei Chuprinin, for example, in his article 'Lishnie liudi' (Superfluous Men) condemns Gort's 'paralysis of will' in *Pashkov dom* (not an uncommon post-thaw syndrome among Soviet intellectuals), thus criticising the author for creating such a 'weak' character.[9] Igor' Dedkov, a prominent *shestidesiatnik* himself, claims that, by presenting portraits of *shestidesiatniki* as lacking the will-power to get on with their lives, Makanin in his novella has ridiculed a whole generation of noble people.[10] Similarly, Natal'ia Ivanova reproaches Makanin for excessive use of 'merciless irony' in relation to his characters who in fact, according to her, 'achieved quite a lot' in their 'prime'.[11] On the other hand, Alla Latynina insists that despite Makanin's irony and Shmelev's portrayal of a social outcast, the characters in the two novellas emerge as positively attractive and should be admired for their personal and intellectual integrity. Latynina claims that in a conformist society it is an honorary status to be an 'outsider' ('*lishnii chelovek*', '*autsaider*'), as these two characters perceive themselves to be.[12]

There was one discrepancy in the critics' polemics, which they may possibly not have been aware of themselves. The general arguments were centred mainly on *shestidesiatniki* (masculine gender) and not *shestidesiatnitsy* (feminine gender). When discussing Makanin's *Odin i odna*, most of the focus was on Goloshchekov and only very occasionally on Ninel'. However, the assumption was that *shestidesiatniki* in the plural were being addressed. And yet, a closer examination of Ninel' reveals that there is little of a *shestidesiatnitsa* about her. She was not even of the same generation as Goloshchekov, being almost ten years his junior, so even on this score she is too young to qualify as one. As for *Pashkov dom*, it is not clear whether Gort's female partners have ever been understood as *shestidesiatnitsy*, either by the author or by literary critics. On closer analysis, they do not seem fit to fulfil the criterion of progressively thinking reformers, or rather their characters are not developed in this light. Moreover, the obvious question that may arise in the reader's mind is: why does this enlightened, progressive *shestidesiatnik* have such a negative perception of the women he comes close to? It may even seem rather symbolic that the crowning work of his life, his *traktat*, which describes the best way to run or govern the state, is modelled on the ideas of *Domostroi*, a work written by the sixteenth-century monk Silvester, which 'offers meticulous instructions on the manner in which husbands must beat their wives ("privately", "politely")', as the American novelist and essayist Francine Du Plessix Gray puts it in her book on Russian women.[13] This aspect of *Domostroi* is not Gort's concern and does not receive any mention by him – a fact ignored by the critics.

While the male figures in both novels represent skilfully drawn social types, we cannot say the same about the female characters, whose composite features amount to no more than the usual selection of stereotypes. If the political and cultural reforms of the late 1950s marked a distinctive departure for many artists (the future *shestidesiatniki* among them) from socialist realism, and in many ways liberated the fictional hero or the protagonist from social and political conformism, they did very little to emancipate the heroine from stereotypes imposed on her by society's prejudices. The heroine of Viktor Nekrasov's *Kira Georgievna* (1961) perhaps came closest to an apolitical emancipated type, but she was too involved in her private affairs to be a *shestidesiatnitsa* heroine. Unlike Kira Georgievna, real-life heroes were in the vanguard serving the cause of liberal reform and seizing every opportunity to express their new ideas in public. It is enough to recall the cultural atmosphere of the late 1950s and early 1960s when these charismatic figures, predominantly men, appeared on the podiums at public gatherings. Such were Shmelev's and Makanin's male characters in their youth: charismatic, bold and daring. However, their female partners are denied any prominence. By comparison even their socialist realist sisters achieved a lot more on the social ladder.[14]

Could such ostracism of women from the public sphere be a true reflection of life? Ol'ga Voronina, a scholar from Moscow and a feminist, has commented on the stereotype of people in power in Soviet society, arguing that they had to be middle-aged men, of Russian nationality as a rule, and Party members.[15] Similarly, the stereotype of a *shestidesiatnik* would be a man, an intellectual, in his late fifties or early sixties, prominent during the time of Khrushchev's reforms and emerging again during Gorbachev's glasnost era – somebody like Shmelev or Gort, or Goloshchekov. Is it correct then to typify the *shestidesiatnik* as only being male? The answer is: yes and no. Yes, because the whole movement of *shestidesiatnichestvo* is strongly associated with male culture.[16] However, it would be wrong to assume that women stood by and watched passively as their male colleagues broke the ice. Although their absence was noticeable in political and economic reform (where Shmelev and his fictional *alter ego* were involved), a lot of women came to the forefront in the arts in the early 1960s. The issue is perhaps not so much about how accurately fiction reflects reality. Rather, the question of female representation in literature amounts to the same old problem – society's perception of woman's social role, or rather lack of it, narrowing her functions down to domestic and personal concerns.

As was pointed out earlier, Soviet literary critics, for their part, while addressing the problem of the *shestidesiatniki* in the two works, failed to clarify whether they saw the female characters as *shestidesiatnitsy*. Later discussion of the texts will indicate that the women may not have the necessary qualities of a *shestidesiatnik* type; they are simply not good enough to attain a status equal to that of their male partners. An examination of these female characters reveals that, regrettably, they fulfil the stereotypes of educated women as perceived by Soviet society, including educated men. Gender bias in

Soviet male prose is not an uncommon phenomenon.[17] A particularly unattractive gallery of educated women appear in Trifonov's works, especially his *Moskovskie povesti* (*Moscow Tales*). Shmelev's and Makanin's novels thematically follow Trifonov's tradition in depicting the Moscow intelligentsia (although Trifonov was not concerned with the *shestidesiatniki*), and there are strong similarities in the characteristics of the women in the works of the three authors. In Shmelev's and Makanin's works four points can be identified which fit the category of literary clichés on educated women in male-authored literature:

1. Women's intellectual inferiority and, on the whole, their philistine nature.
2. Their tendency to betray.
3. Their practicality to the point of pettiness, and their domineering role at home.
4. The recognition of male superiority.

According to the nineteenth-century Russian tradition of progressive thinking, which, one might assume, would also be a natural characteristic of the twentieth-century *shestidesiatniki*, these learned men (*prosveshchennye liudi*) should perceive their female partners to be their equal match, on both the domestic and the intellectual levels. But in these works the women fail to attain the status of the man's intellectual equal either because of social stereotypes, rooted too deeply in the author's consciousness, or because of the author's vanity and consequent need to protect his male characters. *Pashkov dom* appears to get the highest score on a gender bias scale. A considerable part of the novella is devoted to women. There are two women characters: Lelia, Gort's first love, and Tania, his wife. Gort meets Lelia for the first time in the library, in Pashkov dom (the old part of what became known in the Soviet period as the Lenin Library), a respectable enough place for an educated man and an educated woman to meet. But, while throughout the novel the author depicts the process of Gort's intellectual evolution and subsequent maturity, his women fail to reach the same intellectual heights, and in fact do not achieve much. Lelia's lack of intellectualism is observed early in their lives, while they are still students:

> Even then he started getting involved in serious work: he was trying to do some extra reading in addition to the compulsory list. He was trying to read Chinese authors in the original and was also learning Japanese little by little. All this provoked sincere amazement and admiration in her. She herself preferred to read fiction, detective stories and memoirs of great people.[18]

Gort ends up as a scholar, a historian, an assistant professor (*dotsent*) at Moscow University. Lelia can only make it to being a librarian.

Of his wife's profession and talent we learn even less, although he has spent a good part of his life with her (twenty-five or thirty years). We know that she studied at the university at the same time as Gort, but we do not know what subject and how her career developed. Although Gort cannot deny the fact that she is, after all, an educated woman and is allowed to have some interests outside her family and home, he nevertheless regards such interests (such as acquiring friends, her need to go to the theatre or a concert) as superficial emancipation. His opinion of his wife is summed up quite eloquently in the following way:

> She is quite a nice person, simple, like any other woman, healthy, beautiful in her own way, sometimes clever, sometimes not. Her understanding of life is also straightforward: there should be home, a family, the children should be fed, the husband should be the breadwinner. (p. 110)

Being a practical woman, Tania fails to perceive and accept his uncompromising integrity: for example, she finds it hard to understand his refusal to take up the offer of a diplomatic post which would bring prosperity to her family. This tendency to show a strong preference for things practical rather than intellectual can be observed in Lelia to an even greater degree. She betrays him with other men on several occasions for nothing more than material comforts and wealth (Sergei Chuprinin terms such betrayals one of the most common clichés in Soviet fiction).[19] When they unite for the third time after Lelia's final betrayal (Gort obviously forgives her each time), he is already a married man with children. However, Gort's wife is not aware of his affair and he himself does not give any thought to the fact that he has betrayed her.

Similarly, there is a world of difference in Makanin's *Odin i odna* between Gennady Goloshchekov and Ninel' Nikolaevna (we do not even know her surname in the novel). Not only does Goloshchekov score much higher than Ninel' intellectually, he turns out to be a much nicer, more subtle personality. As with Gort, Goloshchekov's heyday coincides with Khrushchev's thaw. He used to be a kind of intellectual leader among his peers at the university; he was a great connoisseur of the arts and was constantly invited to give talks on poetry and literature. Soon after graduation he becomes a leading economist, a reformer. No wonder that he should be so nostalgic about his past, his *'sezon dushi'* (springtime of the soul). The author's protagonist meets him during the years of stagnation when Goloshchekov whiles away his time in intellectual isolation (*'intellektual'noie podpol'e'*, or the intellectual underground).[20] Igor' is attracted to him for his challenging ideas, and throughout the novel we observe the development of Goloshchekov's theory of *roinost'* (the hive mentality), according to which the human community operates like a beehive in which an individual is rejected by society after his productive life is over. Igor' is meant to understand that Goloshchekov is rejected by his society, but here we should be aware of the ambivalence of Goloshchekov's words: is it society that rejects such individuals as Goloschekov and Gort or is it the individuals who reject conformist society?[21]

The portrayal of Gort, and especially of Goloshchekov in the novels' present time may lead us to believe that they are drawn in the Russian tradition of 'superfluous men' – noble in spirit and intentions, but alienated from a society that does not allow their aspirations to develop. The critics Sergei Chuprinin and Igor' Dedkov unhesitatingly term Gort and Goloshchekov the 'superfluous men' of twentieth-century Soviet/Russian literature.[22] But to agree completely with such an assumption would be to misinterpret the way the authors conceived these characters and to deny broader traditional trends that can be traced in their portraiture. First of all, both characters' lives are clearly marked by a definite sense of purpose which, as they are fully aware, cannot lead to fruition. Secondly lack of will-power, which is more pronounced in Makanin's depiction than in Shmelev's, is not an innate condition of their spirit or mind. Goloshchekov and Gort are 'new men' of the 1960s, turned 'superfluous men' in the 1970s, whose purposeful ideas we find suspended in the period of *bezvremen'e* (timelessness) that restricts their freedom to deliver. Shmelev's protagonist, Gort, is a 'superfluous man' only by the standards of the outside world. For the author he is a positive hero and the author's *alter ego*, even bearing some resemblance to Chernyshevsky's 'new man', Rakhmetov from *Chto delat'?* (*What is to be Done?*, 1863). He is a *razumnyi egoist* (rational egotist) whose obsessive devotion to his scholarly pursuits makes him adopt a kind of ascetic way of life. This devotion compels him to sacrifice the pleasures of life, even his family. The fact that he is no longer a radical reformer now allows us to place him in the category of 'superfluous men'. He once had inspiring dreams but they have not been fulfilled because of political circumstances. If Shmelev wants us to perceive Gort's predicament as the tragedy that afflicted thousands of other Soviet intellectuals, Makanin for his part shows us, with subtle irony but not without sympathy, a breed of men whose time has passed, but whose ideas could nevertheless have been useful to society if the conditions to implement them had been right. But because the conditions are not there, they while away their time philosophising and day-dreaming in a 'sybaritic' manner, as Turgenev would describe it.

There is, however, one nineteenth-century literary tradition that was lost somewhere in the passage through socialist realism and Soviet existentialism: the preoccupation with the question of women's emancipation typical of the nineteenth-century *shestidesiatniki* (the radical young intelligentsia of the 1860s, particularly those sympathetic to populism). What is wrong with the women of the contemporary *shestidesiatniki* is that by contrast with the emancipated women of the nineteenth-century *shestidesiatniki*, they sink into complete domesticity. As suggested earlier, the partial return to artistic freedom in the early 1960s had a strong masculine feel about it. The ivory tower was by now crowded with exceptionally clever and talented men, and the notion of a 'room of one's own' for both sexes (according to Barbara Engel, a concept introduced into Russian literature by Chernyshevsky)[23] had now been redefined. In *Pashkov dom* no one in the family is allowed to disturb Gort in his room while he is working. Woman had been evicted from the 'room of her own' and was never really welcomed into the exclusive circles of the Soviet artistic world. The male rationale for such treatment, as Natal'ia Malakhovskaia remarks, was that 'there's never been and cannot be a female Mozart, the Lord God didn't create you for that'.[24] Viktor Nekrasov's most famous (I would be inclined to say notorious) fictional woman artist was shown as not deserving a 'room of her own'. Kira Georgievna was too flippant to sustain devotion to her art in the way that Gort, for example, did. Access to high culture remains a man's prerogative, and the retreat to the ivory tower away from the domestic drudgery of everyday existence (which is the world where woman reigns) is a necessary condition for artistic fulfilment.

Following the stereotype of women's domesticity in Russian literature, family and home is shown as the domain of power for Gort's wife Tania in *Pashkov dom* and the secondary female character in *Odin i odna*, Igor''s wife Ania. Although both Igor' and Gort acknowledge that their wives have not achieved anything because they have to run their homes (in a typically Russian phrase, *'na nei dom i deti'* [the house and children are her responsibility]), they nevertheless expect this to be their natural role. The function of these women is not only to look after children and home, they are also expected to provide conditions where their intellectual partners will be able to work successfully. We can imagine that, when Gort goes to the library after his work at the university, Tania goes shopping. Similarly, Igor', who periodically feels an urge to run away from domestic routine which is important for his creativity, always has a comfortable home to return to. Both women recognise that this is important to their partners. Gort's Tania declares in the end that she is prepared to carry on as before because she understands that spending all his time in the library is Gort's mission ('Who knows? Maybe it is your function to spend all your time over there [at the library]?', p. 138).

Any endeavour at true emancipation on a woman's part is doomed to failure. In *Pashkov dom*, deserted by her husband, lonely Tania (Gort has given her up for the library) tries to acquire her own circle of friends. And, indeed, she succeeds in attracting a large group of people, possibly the cream of Moscow's intelligentsia – artists, famous linguists, economists, and so on. However, Gort is not able to accept them, detecting signs of *besovshchina* (devilry) in their way of thinking, but probably most of all because, like Goloshchekov, he cannot belong to *roi* (a swarm). An unpleasant confrontation with one of the group's representatives puts an end to Tania's role as the hostess of this bohemian circle. A man, a famous linguist (whom Gort suspects of being the subject of his wife's admiration), almost physically attacks Gort, apparently because Gort does not agree with his ideas. Thus Tania has been put to shame for making the wrong choices and having the wrong preferences. In her husband's eyes Tania deserves only such humiliation. Her function in life as he sees it is to guard and protect his muse from the outside world. There is no feeling of remorse on his part as regards his wife's intellectual, professional, social and spiritual sacrifices. This sacrifice can only be one-sided and she is totally excluded from his own intellectual life. In fact, he admits that his marriage was not his own choice but the choice that fate had imposed on him:

> Now, looking back, he realised that Lelia, his marriage to Tania, his postgraduate course, were all part of his youth, a sweet light mist in the morning. All this was just a stream of events in which he had played some kind of subordinate part or maybe just the part of an external observer, as if none of it were happening to him: there was one woman who disappeared, then another – who stayed ... No, he han't made a choice, life had made it for him ... But life is life, and he had to make his own choice. This had happened during the second year of his postgraduate course when, after passing his first set of exams, he had started working seriously on his thesis ... And maybe this was the only real choice in his life ... (p. 98)

It is not because the theme of love takes up a secondary place in Shmelev's novel that we find women's personalities so underdeveloped and presented in a one-sided, almost typically Soviet, masculine way. The theme of love and of married life, sketchy though it appears to be, occupies a good part of the novel. But, as we read on, we come to realise that the protagonist's relationship with his women serves a very specific purpose – that of nurturing his male vanity, especially his intellect, and assisting in the fulfilment of his ego. Shmelev does not give a satisfactory explanation as to what makes

Tania, Gort's wife, consent in the end to the role of servant to his muse. This is simply the way he sees her role. We can also speculate as to why the Lelias of this world keep running away from the Gorts. Perhaps they do not want to see themselves as people whose only function in life is to boost the male ego.

In *Odin i odna* the protagonist time and again tries to convince the reader that the two lonely people, Gennady and Ninel', are so similar that they should immediately recognise each other and feel an afffinity when they meet. However, the characters fail to do so. Either they lack the will-power to make an effort to come together or they are too selfish to consider the feelings of others. One Soviet critic, Karen Stepanian, explains that the relationship between them was impossible due to their innate spiritual incompatibility (*'iznachal'noe odinochestvo dush'*).[25] But in actual fact it is their incompatibility in character more than anything else that prevents them from coming close. The characters that are depicted are so different that a perplexed reader would have every right to ask 'but why should they recognise each other?' Why should the artistic, gentle, subtle and on the whole positive Goloshchekov recognise the aggressive, unfriendly and grumpy Ninel'? Igor' describes her as somewhat abrupt, and the author comments on differences even in their manner of speaking:

> Ninel' always shouts, not because she is arguing with someone but just out of lack of restraint in her behaviour, out of her boisterous temperament, which like a stream bubbles noisily and is unable to direct its flow in a soft and graceful manner, the way Gennady Pavlovich directs his conversation. (p. 53)

At first when they meet there seems to be some hint of a common interest – they end up talking about poetry. But Ninel''s knowledge of poetry cannot stretch to Gennady's level, which is not surprising because she does not spend all her free time reading as he does – in her free time Ninel' knits in front of the television: 'Knitting is not only a way out of solitude, knitting is [her] way of life. Ninel' Nikolaevna continues to knit even when the television utters its final words' (p. 33). Very often throughout the novel, Igor' finds Ninel' just knitting. On the other hand, he always finds Gennady reading ('As usual, Gennady Pavlovich reads a lot, addictively', p. 33). Ninel''s collection of books is extremely modest ('she does not have piles of books or fine collections of works', p. 40), whereas Gennady is in possession of a unique and enormous collection. You could find piles of books everywhere on the floor arranged in some meaningful manner ('Like any bibliophile, Gennady Pavlovich when buying books liked to sort them out first, spread them, study them and then read', p. 26). Ninel' prefers to collect furniture (a clear sign of practicality), and of that only mirrors have a symbolic importance. Their meeting ends up with Ninel''s rude remark that Goloshchekov has exceeded his time limit – overstayed his welcome. Ninel' does not leave much of an impression on Goloshchekov either. In her past, although a bright student and a great lover of poetry, Ninel' showed a lack of scholarly inclination. We are told that she used to revolt against the academic sterility of the lectures she attended (exactly where Goloshchekov's and Gort's talents would shine) and used to incite her fellow students to take up hiking instead (p. 35). Unlike Goloshchekov or Gort, who had at one time acquired some academic fame, Ninel' ends up as a statistician in some dull statistical centre, 'number crunching', as the author describes her duties. Ninel' is intensely disliked by her colleagues in the small unit that she supervises because of her bossiness and lack of sensitivity. She does not have a family, but it is easy enough to imagine her in the role of a bossy, domineering matriarch. Her behaviour at work is just a projection of her would-be behaviour at home, another widely used stereotype in literature.

Ninel', an emancipated woman by circumstance rather than choice, constantly talks to Igor' about her desire to acquire a partner or a husband. In Goloshchekov's understanding, she thus condemns herself to *roinost'*. Goloshchekov himself does not marry because he cannot accept *roinost'*, although in his middle age he sometimes, out of loneliness, dreams of acquiring a wife, some woman who could take care of his immediate needs – a woman of much lower social status, a waitress, for example, a wife for an Oblomov:

> 'Maybe I should marry a shop-assistant or a waitress', Gennady Pavlovich sometimes thought. He could not interact well with the sober-minded and practical people of the younger generation who had taken hold everywhere. But maybe a simple woman could understand him, a middle-aged (and unentrepreneurial) intellectual ... (p. 54)

Ninel''s problem is her inability to find her ideal in life – a kind of romantic, 'Odoevsky-like', figure, 'an army officer of the imperial wars in the Caucasus' (p. 32). The irony of Ninel''s dream is that such young officers of the imperial wars were outsiders (*lishnie liudi*) in Russian society and at the same time quite a noble breed, and yet she did not recognise these qualities in Goloshchekov. We are aware that Ninel''s sexual fantasy has no chance of realisation – she is in love with an image of a young man who existed 150 years ago, as one critic put it.[26] Goloshchekov is no longer young enough for Ninel' to fall in love with. But if Ninel' had met Goloshchekov in his younger days, she would have barely attracted his attention. The best she could have done was to be among five or six of Goloshchekov's female student admirers, dear memories of whom keep feeding his male vanity in his older age. He, of course, never considered having an affair with any of them: it was beneath his dignity. Yet he derived intense pleasure from the fact that he was so much admired. Ninel' for her part has never been admired – we are told only of some dull love affair that led nowhere.

Makanin's novel invites various interpretations of his characters' inability to become friends. The author's own philosophy leads us to believe that it is man's self-centred nature and his egotistic preoccupation with his own world that leaves him with a sense of being out of place and a feeling of anomie. And yet Goloshchekov's isolation has a tremendously beneficial effect on him – it nurtures his intellectual toil. His flat is his metaphorical ivory tower where he hides from the crude reality of the outside world, from that 'swarm', the knowledge of which he is happy to acquire through his books. Ninel''s isolation on the other hand gives her a strong sense of imprisonment. She longs for company, for romantic love, and she is prepared to embrace the 'swarm', that is, society, but it is too late, as she sinks deeper into that category of society's outcasts known as spinsters.[27] Of all the adverse old patriarchal traditions, the one that assigns a shameful status to an unmarried woman remains very strong in Russia. The status of bachelor on the other hand would arouse respect and often admiration as a kind of privileged position synonymous with man's free spirit. Ninel' is not shown as one who cherishes her independence. She does not regard her habitat as a place of refuge but rather as a prison, and to avoid the loneliness she fills it up with mirrors so as to create a false sense of company when her own reflection moves along with her.

In *Odin i odna*, the portrait of Goloshchekov, drawn with a touch of irony, presents a fairly realistic and quite typical character in its fully realised, complete version. The final impression created in the novel is the image of a man who is positive in many respects, but his female opposite, Ninel', is in no way as fully developed as Goloshchekov. So one-dimensional, negative and irritating is her persona that it would not be an exaggeration to charge the author with psychological failure in creating this character. Her lifestyle, her behaviour, her manner of speaking should not only repel any intelligent person, all these characteristics would qualify Ninel' as the antithesis of an educated woman. And yet, as we learn from the author's protagonist, Igor', that was not the initial intention. The intention was to draw two portraits of a similar kind.

Fortunately, fiction is not always a true reflection of life, but it is remarkable that even some women writers do not challenge the stereotype of female virtue as based on woman's moral and spiritual superiority. In this respect, Alla Latynina, writing about female characters in contemporary women's prose, said:

> Desperately sad is the realisation in life of the gradual loss of illusions and hopes. A clever, gifted schoolgirl, a brilliant student – what happens to this early feminine talent? How is this talent and enthusiasm, thirst for self-realisation in everything – creativity, love, and life – subsequently dispelled down the drain of domestic drudgery?[28]

It is not that life does not provide enough examples for literature to emulate. The problem appears rather to be symptomatic of Soviet Russian literature as a whole (perhaps with the exception of memoirs), where one group in society is either under-represented or presented with a totally biased slant. One might argue that it is only natural that male writers would sympathise or identify with their male protagonists. Yet it is regrettable that the female partners of generally noble and progressive thinking male protagonists should appear in such an inferior light. A strong, educated female character, on a par with Aleksandr Gort, and perhaps more in the tradition of the best nineteenth-century heroines, is yet to emerge in Russian literature. I. Grekova's minor work 'Bez ulybok' ('World Without Smiles', 1986)[29] is perhaps an exception, but in general such a character has not been created in fully fledged form.

Notes

1. See, for example, Natal'ia Ivanova, 'Legko li byt'? ...', *Druzhba narodov*, no. 5 (1987); Alla Latynina, 'Kolokol'nyi zvon – ne molitva', *Novyi mir*, no. 10 (1988); Igor' Zolotusskii, 'Krushenie abstraktsii', *Novyi mir*, no. 1 (1989); Viktor Erofeev, 'Pominki po sovetskoi literature', *Literaturnaia gazeta*, no. 27, 4 July 1990; Mikhail Lipovetskii, 'Sovok-bluz: Shestidesiatniki segodnia', *Znamia*, no. 9 (1991); Lev Anninskii, 'Shestidesiatniki, semidesiatniki, vos'midesiatniki ... K dialektike pokolenii v russkoi kul'ture', *Literaturnoie obozrenie*, no. 4 (1991); Andrei Nemzer, 'Strast'' k razryvam', *Novyi mir*, no. 4 (1992).
2. Vladimir Makanin, 'Odin i odna', *Oktiabr'*, no. 2 (1987).
3. Nikolai Shmelev, 'Pashkov dom', *Znamia*, no. 3 (1987).
4. It would be prudent to clarify here that the aim of the discussion is not *any* work on the intelligentsia. For that purpose Iury Trifonov's works could have been chosen as well, especially as Trifonov, in the eyes of some critics (Mark Lipovetsky, for example), can be considered as a *shestidesiatnik*. What makes principal characters in Makanin's and Shmelev's novellas different from Trifonov's fellow intellectuals is, firstly, the fact that Trifonov's characters are not shown as partic-

ipants in the liberalisation process of the 1950s and 1960s, and secondly, that they are not demoted as a result of such involvement and do not have to retreat into the kind of intellectual exile that a lot of the liberal intellectuals were forced into (as is the case with Makanin's and Shmelev's characters). However, one should not exclude the possibility that some of Trifonov's characters could have sympathised with, if not joined, the ranks of the liberals. We can come across a *shestidesiatnik* type among the dissident circles in Vladimir Kormer's 'Nasledstvo' (Inheritance), *Oktiabr'*, nos 5-8 (1990), but this work is primarily about dissidents (with a small 'd') and not *shestidesiatniki*. Viktor Erofeev's 'Pis'mo k materi' (A Letter To Mother), *Iunost'*, no. 11 (1988) is, on the other hand, a portrait of a liberal *shestidesiatnik*, but it is a parody, which is consistent with the author's generally negative attitude to the *shestidesiatniki*.

5. On delayed literature see, for example, Julian Graffy, 'The Literary Press', in Julian Graffy and Geoffrey A. Hosking (eds), *Culture and the Media in the USSR Today* (Basingstoke: Macmillan, 1989). See also Svetlana Carsten, 'The Writer in Society', *Scottish Slavonic Review*, no. 17 (Autumn 1991).
6. See, for example, Nina Agisheva, 'Nuzhna li nam svoboda?', *Teatr*, no. 10 (1989); Andrei Nemzer, 'Strast'' k razryvam', *Novyi mir*, no. 4 (1992); Aleksandr Terekhov, 'My vpitaiem vsiu pyl' ...', *Literaturnaia gazeta*, no. 24, 13 June 1990; Erofeev, 'Pominki po sovetskoi literature'.
7. Sergei Chuprinin, 'Lishnie liudi', *Literaturnaia gazeta*, no. 13, 25 March 1987.
8. Vladimir Makanin, 'Odin i odna', *Oktiabr'*, no. 2 (1987), p. 50. This version of the text is the one cited hereafter.
9. Chuprinin, 'Lishnie liudi'.
10. Igor' Dedkov, 'Spor o pokolenii', *Moskovskie novosti*, no. 16 (1987).
11. Natal'ia Ivanova, 'Illiuziia obreteniia', *Literaturnaia gazeta*, no. 14, 1 April 1987.
12. Alla Latynina, 'Autsaidery', in *Za otkrytym shlagbaumom* (Moscow: Sovetskii pisatel', 1991), p. 269.
13. Francine Du Plessix Gray, *Soviet Women: Walking the Tightrope* (London: Virago, 1991), p. 117.
14. Xenia Gasiorowska gives a detailed study of the socialist realist heroine in her book *Women in Soviet Fiction 1917-1964* (Madison: University of Wisconsin Press, 1968).
15. Ol'ga Voronina, *Moskovskie novosti*, 11 June 1989.
16. On attitudes to women artists after the thaw see, for example, Alison Hilton, 'Feminism and Gender Values in Soviet Art', in Marianne Liljeström, Eila Mäntysaari and Arja Rosenholm (eds), *Gender Restructuring in Russian Studies*, Slavica Tamperensia, no. 2 (Tampere: University of Tampere, 1993).
17. Note, for example, Vasilii Belov, *Vse vperedi* (1986), Fazil' Iskander, *Chegemskaia Karmen* (1986), Anatolii Afanas'ev, *Bol'no ne budet* (1986), Evgenii Tuinov, *Fil'm* (1987).
18. Nikolai Shmelev, 'Pashkov dom', *Znamia*, no. 3 (1987), p. 94. This version of the text is the one cited hereafter.
19. Sergei Chuprinin, 'Lishnie liudi', *Literaturnaia gazeta*, no. 13, 25 March 1987.
20. Ibid.
21. As discussed in the polemical articles by Ivanova, Latynina and Chuprinin cited earlier.
22. Chuprinin, 'Lishnie liudi'; and Dedkov, 'Spor o pokolenii'.
23. Although Barbara Engel describes how Chernyshevsky's wife had never accepted the idea of the 'room of her own'. See Barbara Alpern Engel, *Mothers and Daughters: Women of the Intelligentsia in Nineteenth-Century Russia* (Cambridge: Cambridge University Press, 1983), p. 80.

24. Natal'ia Malakhovskaia, *Woman and Russia: First Feminist Samizdat* (London: Sheba Feminist Publishers, 1980).
25. Karen Stepanian, '... Golos, letiashchii v kupol', *Voprosy literatury*, no. 2 (1988), p. 86.
26. S. Piskunova and V. Piskunov, 'Vse prochee – literatura', *Voprosy literatury*, no. 2 (1988), p. 60.
27. On Soviet society's attitude to marriage see 'Marriage, Mother, and Divorce', in Gray, *Soviet Women*.
28. Alla Latynina, *Znaki vremeni* (Moscow: Sovetskii pisatel', 1987), pp. 289–90.
29. I. Grekova, 'Bez ulybok', *Oktiabr'*, no. 11 (1986).

Chapter 20

RUSSIAN WOMEN IN ANATOLY KURCHATKIN

Arch Tait

'Earth moving for you, then?', she heard him crowing from somewhere above. Her teeth clenched, her eyes shut, her legs twined round his, she pressed herself up into him until she arched his back. She was completely convulsed, incapable of answering.

'Getting it where you want it, eh?', his condescending, conqueror's voice broke in on her again, and, sinking down spent together with him, disentangling her legs which had suddenly lost all their strength from his, the bird still fluttering unpredictably within her but already less frequently, less wildly, she managed to half-open her eyes. His face was right beside hers, making it difficult to focus on him.

'You did it', she gasped blissfully, her breath irregular, her voice hoarse, and shut her eyes again.

He chuckled in the same triumphant way.

'Any girl who gets me goes like a rocket, any of them.'

Again she made no reply, switching herself off as soon as she realised what he was saying, blanking it out.

'More. Please. Again', she begged, becoming sensation incarnate in order to savour within herself his slightest movement.[1]

Anatoly Kurchatkin's *Strazhnitsa* (The Watchwoman), published in an expurgated version in *Znamia*, numbers 5–6 (1993), is a new departure. Kurchatkin, not usually unduly flattering in his representation of female characters, has placed a female consciousness at the centre of this, his second full-length novel. How successfully he imagines his heroine's experience of sex with her ex-Afghanistan lover the reader may judge from the passage above. Pigeon-holed in the late 1970s as one of the 'forty-year-old writers', Kurchatkin's fiction combines sensitive chronicling of the Russia contemporary to him with a strong vein of fantasy, and both these features are much in evidence in *Strazhnitsa*.

Anatoly Kurchatkin's first, politically controversial novel, *Vechernii svet* (Light of Evening) was completed in 1981, rejected by *Oktiabr'* when he refused to re-write it, and finally published only in 1989, well into the era of glasnost.[2] It is firmly centred on an elderly male hero whose inner integrity enables him to live a charmed life in the midst of the cynicism and corruption of the Brezhnev years. In *Vechernii svet* the female characters are relatively peripheral: a dutiful wife who reflects the innate goodness of her husband, a wilful daughter corrupted by the system, and a son's monstrous lover who seems to attain an almost metaphysical status as the embodiment of traditional notions of the manipulative and materialistic female who drags down and defiles the spiritual aspirations of her man.[3] *Vechernii svet* nevertheless presents the Soviet Union as a matriarchy where guileful women on the whole find their niche more readily than naïve men, who either walk straight into trouble with authority or are forced to keep their heads down for the whole of their lives.

Kurchatkin does have one earlier major work in which women are central. This is *Babii dom* (Houseful of Women) a novella written from 1982 to 1985, and set a few years earlier.[4] Here his misgivings about the female characters are positively Chekhovian. *Babii dom* is in fact quite reminiscent of the prototypical Chekhovian play, and was originally conceived as a piece for the theatre. Almost without comment, it depicts the lack of communication between those closest to each other, and the horrendous philistinism and heartlessness of society at large. More often than not the victims in Chekhov are female characters whose misfortunes seem attributable to a lack of male guidance, not infrequently personified by a dead or absent father or husband. Thus, Chekhov's *Tri sestry* (*Three Sisters*, 1901) opens on the first anniversary of father's death, and ends as the army, embodying virile purposefulness, marches off into the distance. In *Babii dom* dead grandfather's elaborately inlaid hunting rifle (phallic shades of *Hedda Gabler*) hangs nostalgically on the wall of a flat in which Nina, aged fifty, lives with her daughters Lida, thirty, and Ania, eighteen. Like Chekhov's Ol'ga, Masha and Irina, they incarnate three ages of woman, long for happiness, but are battered to the ground by the forces of *poshlost'* (philistine vulgarity). They either allow less admirable characters to take even what little happiness they might have had away from them or blindly cast it aside themselves. The surviving men in the novella are either themselves infected with *poshlost'* or their masculinity is neutralised by it.

Kurchatkin's work retains not a few dramatic attributes: it is divided into parts separated in time, in effect acts; a large washbasin, symbolic of female impracticality, lies centre-stage waiting to be installed by a plumber; and grandmother, paralysed by a stroke, lies off-stage in an adjacent room.

The mother, Nina, is, like not a few of Kurchatkin's heroines, more a bearer and protagonist of *poshlost'* than a victim. She and her younger daughter row incessantly, and as the novella opens she is more than usually on edge because she is expecting a gentleman caller at 10 o'clock in the morning. She calculates they will have three hours for sex before she has to be off to her job as a museum guide. Evgeny is a romantic provincial (in the writing of Kurchatkin, himself from Ekaterinburg, the relative worth of Moscow versus the provinces is the reverse of that in Chekhov). He is in Moscow on a training course and is taken aback by the matter-of-factness with which, as soon as he sets foot in her flat, Nina sets about converting her divan into a bed. Romance is in any case thwarted, first by his tripping over the washbasin in the middle of the floor, then by the crash of grandmother's upturned bedpan, and finally by the arrival of the plumber. Nina laughs him out of the flat.

Lida, the elder daughter, is a decent person torn between going off on holiday to the Caucasus with her married lover Andrei and staying for the censor's preview of the latest play in which her father is acting. (Her mother had left her father when he insisted on pursuing his acting ambitions rather than taking a dull job with a good and secure income.) Father wins, and the Caucasus trip will have to be postponed. Lida's friend Marina has a vast wardrobe of dresses, collected from a string of lovers whom she ably manipulates. She disapproves of Lida's indulgence of Andrei, and decides to discredit him. She flirts with him and succeeds in turning his head, later entrapping him by having Lida listen in on an amorous telephone conversation.

The younger daughter, Ania, fares little better. She is picked up by the police after being discovered wandering half-naked in a block of flats. She had been tricked into parting with her Finnish jeans by her supposed friend Svetka. Ania's decent and conventional young man, Misha, idealises the immature and selfish Ania and aspires to marry and settle down with her. Ania's father, an insufferable and aggressive barrister, is summoned by Nina for a family conference on how best to work the system to get Ania off the hook with the police. Evgeny inopportunely arrives, bearing brandy, apples and flowers for Nina and is thrown out. A true *femina sovietica*, Nina values guile above true love. Young Misha breaks off the romance with Ania, having been untruthfully told by the racketeering Svetka that his would-be fiancée is a prostitute. The discredited Andrei shamelessly slanders Misha to Ania in a misguided attempt to soften the blow until she threatens to shoot this emblem of Soviet manhood with grandfather's rifle. He flees.

The plumber now comes back to this rudderless houseful of women, drunk but with the right size of wall brackets for fitting the washbasin, and expecting vodka and a sex orgy for him and his mate in return. Repulsed, he threatens to disfigure Ania with the brackets, and succeeds in wounding Lida before he is thrown out. During the night Ania inadvertently knocks grandfather's rifle, which goes off with a loud bang, restoring grandmother's power of speech. She muses on the eternal hunt for happiness, when what is really needed is only to work well and love while there is still time.

The novella ends with a breath of fresh air, a lyrical evocation of the outer suburbs of Moscow in the small hours of the morning where a lone (male) wanderer, faced with a long walk home, is rescued from misfortune by the compassionate driver of a passing truck: a redemptive man-to-man relationship which defeats the Soviet *poshlost'* all around. The message of *Babii dom* seems to be that the Soviet state has disastrously undermined lawful matrimony, the primacy of men, and the tried and tested institution of the family, to the misfortune of those who believe themselves to have been thereby liberated.

Strazhnitsa continues Kurchatkin's preoccupation with female psychology, but without the irony which distances the personages in *Babii dom*. The heroine is a schizophrenic whose experiences and innermost thoughts are related in a narrative which covers the years from 1985 to 1991, and follows the rise and fall of Mikhail Gorbachev through the eyes of Al'bina, the wife of a highly placed Communist official. In 1985 she has a secure job in the local rural soviet. From childhood she has had a recurrent dream that she must safeguard a distant figure she sees wandering along a road through a wilderness. In May 1985 she sees Gorbachev on television for the first time and realises that the Communist Party's new Secretary-General is the figure in her dream and that, consequently, it is he she has a mission to protect and his work she must see through to fruition. As her ability to concentrate on the political situation improves or deteriorates so do his fortunes, which are related in documentary but at the same time nightmarish detail. A sign of the times, perhaps, the novel sees Kurchatkin, who has always favoured realistically colloquial speech, now presenting remorselessly realistic bad language and a boldly explicit treatment of sex and violence.

Al'bina begins to note unnerving small changes in the life around her, such as the women who have always delivered eggs and milk to her door for a pittance asserting their rights and requiring her to collect them herself. As she finds her sympathy for Gorbachev increasingly at odds with her husband's total hostility towards him, she suddenly refuses to tolerate any longer the routine boorishness and infidelities she has been accustomed to. When one night her husband shouts at her to come to him in the bathroom to soap his back, she rebels:

> She put the loofah to his back and was about to start rubbing when, to her own surprise, she moved it more comfortably to the other hand and, bending down, slipped the other, free hand covered in lather, under his paunch to the gorge between his legs. [She immediately had his fat flabby pestle in her hand, but that was not what she was after, and she merely tweaked the pointed empty fold of skin. She went for his balls, cupping the oval testicles dangling in the wet warm bag of his scrotum and making him jump on the seat when she gave them a hard squeeze.]
> 'Why don't I tear them off? That'd put a stop to your whoring!', she said, looking at him eyeball to eyeball, and was taken aback to see the fear in them. He really was scared she was going to do it. The loose bag of his scrotum contracted in her hand from the relaxed looseness of a tobacco pouch to become dense and thick, rapidly retracting his balls back to the root of his penis.[5]

She is bowled over by a twenty-year-old soldier back from the war in Afghanistan, to whom she succumbs with a passion such as she has never experienced before. When he abandons her she suffers a mental blackout, and is referred for the first time to a psychiatrist. She is subjected to a brutal regime of insulin injections which reduce her to a comatose state, and awakes to find that during this period when she has been unable to exercise her guardianship over the new leader there has been an earthquake in Armenia with the loss of seventy thousand lives.

As the stormclouds of political and natural disasters, such as Chernobyl', gather over Gorbachev, her mental health deteriorates until she leaves the family home to live in a shack in the forest for a time, and is returned to the mental hospital when she confides to her best friend that her baby grand-daughter is a vampire and that she is going to kill her. She succeeds in escaping from the asylum, and goes to live with a former (female) inmate in an underground dugout, making a living as a a fully fledged beggar, complete with a minder to whom she is obliged to hand over 400 roubles a week. Her former lover and a gang of his ex-Afghan friends attempt to rape her and she is left for dead, recovering only to learn of the attempted coup of August 1991. She is now found to be suffering from terminal cancer and dies on the day Gorbachev hears from the meeting of republican leaders in Alma-Ata that they foresee no future role for him. For a moment the apparently self-confident Gorbachev seems to see himself wandering blindly along a road through a wilderness. He shrugs. It is hardly the end of everything, he supposes.

In the increasingly demented Al'bina, Kurchatkin creates an extraordinary 'correspondence' for the nightmarish sense Russians following the news on television or in the newspapers had of a link between the disasters (reported thanks to glasnost) and the ups and downs in Gorbachev's and the nation's political fortunes. His most prominent female personage to date is not merely a passive spectator but, like Dame Fortune or Lady Luck, exercises an unpredictable, and ultimately lunatic, influence on the destiny of Russia in the Gorbachev years.

Notes

1. Anatolii Kurchatkin, 'Strazhnitsa', *Znamia*, no. 5 (1993), pp. 56–57.
2. A. Kurchatkin, *Vechernii svet. Roman* (Moscow, 1989).
3. I discuss *Vechernii svet* at greater length in 'The Russian Disease: Kurchatkin's Diagnosis', *Slavonic and East European Review*, vol. 71, no. 1 (January 1993), pp. 14–34.
4. A.Kurchatkin, 'Babii dom,' in *Zvezda begushchaia* (Moscow, 1986), pp. 220–334.
5. *Znamia*, no. 5 (1993), p. 14. The section in square brackets has been cut by the editors of *Znamia*, and is quoted from the manuscript, p. 20.

NOTES ON CONTRIBUTORS

Joe Andrew is Professor of Russian at Keele University, where he has worked for the last twenty-four years. His main research interests are in nineteenth-century literature, especially images of women and women writers in this period. His main publications in this field are *Women in Russian Literature, 1780–1863* (Macmillan: Basingstoke and London, 1988) and *Narrative and Desire in Russian Literature, 1822–1849* (Macmillan: Basingstoke and London, 1993) and he is the editor of *Russian Women's Shorter Fiction: An Anthology 1835–1860* (Oxford: Oxford University Press, 1996). He is co-chair of the Neo-Formalist Circle, as well as co-editor of the Circle's journal *Essays in Poetics*, now in its twenty-first year of publication.

Adele Barker is Associate Professor of Russian and Comparative Cultural and Literary Studies at the University of Arizona. She is the author of *The Mother Syndrome in the Russian Folk Imagination* (Columbus, OH: Slavica, 1986) and co-author of *Dialogues/Dialogi: Literary and Cultural Exchanges between (ex)Soviet and American Women* (Durham and London: Duke University Press, 1994). She is currently working on a book entitled *Configurations of Exile: Soviet Women's Writing since the 1960s* and is co-editor of *A History of Russian Women's Writing*, to be published by Cambridge University Press.

Peter I. Barta, Senior Lecturer in Russian Studies in the Department of Linguistic and International Studies at the University of Surrey since 1994, previously taught at the University of Illinois at Champaign-Urbana and was Associate Professor in the Department of Classical and Modern Languages and Literatures at Texas Tech University. He has co-edited *The Contexts of Aleksandr Sergeevich Pushkin* (Lewiston, NY: Edwin Mellen, 1988); edited *The European Foundations of Russian*

Modernism (Lewiston, NY: Edwin Mellen, 1991); co-edited *Russian Literature and the Classics* (Newark, NJ: Harwood Press, 1996) and published *Bely, Joyce and Döblin: peripatetics in the city novel* (Gainesville: University Press of Florida, 1996). He is currently co-editing *Carnivalizing Difference: Bakhtin and the Other* for Harwood Press.

Svetlana Carsten is a Lecturer in Russian Studies at the Department of Modern Languages, University of Bradford. In 1996/1997 she was Max Hayward Fellow in Russian culture at St Antony's College, Oxford. She is the co-author of *Glasnost: advanced Russian interpreting course* (Bradford: University of Bradford, 1993). Her current research is in Soviet literature from the 1960s to the 1980s, with particular interest in the literature on and by the *shestidesiatniki* (members of the 1960s generation).

Neil Cornwell, Professor in the Department of Russian Studies at the University of Bristol, formerly taught in the New University of Ulster and The Queen's University of Belfast. He has written extensively on Russian and comparative literature, and his books include *The Life, Times and Milieu of V. F. Odoyevsky, 1804–1863* (London: Athlone Press, 1986); *Pasternak's novel: perspectives on 'Doctor Zhivago'* (Keele: Essays in Poetics, 1986); *Daniil Kharms and the poetics of the absurd: essays and materials* (New York: St Martin's Press, 1991); *James Joyce and the Russians* (Basingstoke: Macmillan, 1992); *Pushkin's 'The Queen of Spades'* (Bristol: Bristol Classical Press, 1993); and *Vladimir Odoevsky and Romantic Poetics: Collected Essays* (Oxford and Providence, RI: Berghahn Books, 1998).

Julie Curtis is a Lecturer in Russian at the University of Oxford, where she is a Fellow of Wolfson College. She formerly taught at the Universities of Leeds and Cambridge. She is the author of *Bulgakov's Last Decade: the writer as hero* (Cambridge: Cambridge University Press, 1987) and the compiler and translator of *Manuscripts Don't Burn: a Life in Letters and Diaries* (London: Harper Collins, 1991). She is currently working on a study of Evgeny Zamiatin.

Anna Darmodekhina is Head of the Department of English Language Translation at Kuban State University. She graduated from Kuban State University and received her PhD in the Department of Twentieth-Century Western Literature at the Academy of Sciences Institute of World Literature in Moscow. From 1990 to 1993 she taught in the Department of Russian Studies of the University of Bristol. She has published more than seventy articles, mostly on modern English and American literature, and has translated Gordon McVay, *Isadora and Esenin* (Ann Arbor: Ardis, 1980). Her current research focuses on a comparison between modern trends in British and Russian poetry.

David Gillespie is Reader in Russian Studies at the University of Bath. He is the author of *Valentin Rasputin and Soviet Russian Village Prose* (London: MHRA, 1986); *Iurii Trifonov: Unity through Time* (Cambridge: Cambridge University Press, 1992); *The Twentieth Century Russian Novel: An Introduction* (Oxford and Providence, RI: Berg, 1996); the editor of *The Life and Work of Fedor Abramov* (Evanston, IL: Northwestern University Press, 1997) and the author of numerous articles on village prose, contemporary literature and film.

Sheelagh Graham, formerly Senior Lecturer in Russian Studies at the University of Strathclyde, is a specialist on nineteenth-century and early twentieth-century Russian literature. She is the author of *The Lyric Poetry of A.K. Tolstoi* (Amsterdam: Rodopi, 1985); the co-editor of N. Gumilev, *Neizdannoe i nesobrannoe* (Paris: YMCA Press, 1986); editor of *New Directions in Soviet Literature* (London: Macmillan, 1992) and has published articles on Akhmatova, Gumilev, Bulgakov and Aitmatov.

Diana Greene is Slavic librarian at New York University's Bobst Library. She is the author of *Insidious Intent: An Interpretation of Fedor Sologub's 'Melkii bes'* (Columbus, Ohio: Slavica, 1986); the co-editor with Toby W. Clyman of *Women Writers in Russian Literature* (Westport, CT: Greenwood, 1994) and has written on Anastasiia Chebotarevskaia, the Strugatsky brothers, and Karolina Pavlova. She is currently writing a book on twenty Russian women poets of Karolina Pavlova's generation.

Katharine Hodgson, Lecturer in Russian at the University of Exeter, formerly held a Postdoctoral Research Fellowship at St Catherine's College, Cambridge. She is the author of *Written with the Bayonet: Soviet Russian Poetry of World War Two* (Liverpool: Liverpool University Press, 1996), has written articles on Ol'ga Berggol'ts and Russian women writers during the Second World War, and is currently working on a study of Ol'ga Berggol'ts.

Monika Katz studied Russian and Polish literature and history in Paris and Berlin, and until 1995 she taught Russian literature at the Freie Universität, Berlin. She is co-editor of *Zwischen Anpassung und Widerspruch: Beiträge zur Frauenforschung am Osteuropa-Institut der Freien Universität Berlin* (Wiesbaden: Hartassowitz, 1993). She is writing her PhD on Russian vaudeville in the nineteenth century.

Irina Kazakova is a literary scholar who studied at the Philological Faculty of Moscow State University, and since 1985 has taught in the Department of Russian Language at RGMU, Moscow. In 1990 she completed her graduate studies at Moscow State University, and is currently working on a dissertation entitled 'The woman question and the theme of women in the work of women writers at the end of the nineteenth and the beginning of the twentieth century'. She has written numerous articles, including entries on women writers of the Silver Age for the bibliographical dictionaries *Russkie pisateli* (Moscow, 1990); Marina Ledkovsky, Charlotte Rosenthal and Mary Zirin (eds), *Dictionary of Russian Women Writers* (Westport, CT: Greenwood, 1994) and *500 russkikh pisatelei XX veka: Slovar'* (Moscow, 1995).

Natasha Kolchevska, Associate Professor of Russian at the University of New Mexico, is currently completing a book on Russian women's autobiographical writing in the twentieth century. Her most recent article, 'Mothers and Daughters: Variations on Family Themes in Tsvetaeva's *The House at Old Pimen*', appeared in Pamela Chester and Sibelan Forrester (eds), *Engendering Slavic Literatures* (Bloomington: Indiana University Press, 1996).

Boris Lanin is Professor and Head of the Department of On-Line and Distance Learning at the Russian Academy of Education, Moscow. He studied in Baku and Moscow, in 1994 was awarded the degree of Doctor of Philology and has three times received Cyrus Clark and British Academy Fellowships for research in the UK. He has published numerous books and articles on twentieth-century Russian literature, notably on Evgeny Zamiatin, the Russian literary anti-utopia, Vasily Grossman, and Russian émigré literature. His most recent works include *Russkaia literaturnaia antiutopiia* (Moscow: Open University of Russia, 1993); 'Images of Women in Russian Anti-Utopian Literature', *Slavonic and East European Review*, vol. 71, no. 4 (December 1993), pp. 646–55 and *Proza russkoi emigratsii (tret'ia volna)* (Moscow: Novaia shkola, 1997).

Marina Ledkovsky, formerly Professor of Russian at Barnard College, Columbia University, New York, has published numerous articles on major topics in Russian literature and culture. She is the author of *The Other Turgenev: From Romanticism to Symbolism* (Würzburg: Jal-Verlag, 1973); the editor of two anthologies of women's writings in Russian and English, *Rossiia glazami zhenshchin*; transl., *Russia according to Women* (Tenafly, NJ: Hermitage, 1989; 1991) and co-editor of the *Dictionary of Russian Women Writers*, which in 1994 won the Heldt Prize for the 'Best Book in Slavic Women's Studies' from the American Association of Women in Slavic Studies. In December 1995 she received an Award for Outstanding Achievement in Scholarship from the American Association of Teachers of Slavic and East European Languages. Her current research is focused on the writings of Russian émigré women, concentrating on memoirists and autobiographers of the 'first wave' and poets of the 'second wave'.

Rosalind Marsh is Professor of Russian Studies and former Director of the Centre of Women's Studies at the University of Bath. She became President of the British Association of Slavonic and East European Studies in 1997. She previously taught at The Queen's University of Belfast and at the University of Exeter, where she was Director of the Centre for Russian, Soviet and East European Studies from 1989 to 1991. She is the author of *Soviet Fiction since Stalin: Science, Politics and Literature* (London and Sydney: Croom Helm, 1986); *Images of Dictatorship: Stalin in Literature* (London and New York: Routledge, 1989); *History and Literature in Contemporary Russia* (London: Macmillan, 1995); the editor of *Women in Russia and Ukraine* (Cambridge: Cambridge University Press, 1996) and *Gender and Russian Literature: New perspectives* (Cambridge: Cambridge University Press, 1996); and has published articles on the position of women and women writers in Russia.

Catherine Schuler is an Associate Professor of Theatre History at the University of Maryland, College Park. She is the co-editor of *Theatre and Feminist Aesthetics* (Madison, WI: Fairleigh Dickinson University Press, 1995); the author of *Women in Russian Theatre: The Actress in the Silver Age* (London: Routledge, 1997); and has published articles on Russian theatre and feminist performance in *The Drama Review, Theatre Survey, Theatre History Studies,* and *Theatre Topics*. In 1994, she won the Heldt Prize for the 'Best Article in Slavic Women's Studies'.

Arch Tait is Senior Lecturer in the Department of Russian Language and Literature, University of Birmingham. He is the author of *Lunacharsky: poet of the revolution, 1875–1907* (Birmingham: Birmingham University Press, 1984); the co-editor of the journal *Glas: New Russian Writing,* and the translator of Evgeniia Kirichenko, *The Russian Style* (London: Laurence King, 1991), Anatolii Smeliansky, *Is Comrade Bulgakov Dead?* (London: Methuen, 1993), and Vladimir Makanin, *Baize-Covered Table with Decanter* (London: Readers International, 1995).

Natal'ia Zhuravkina is Lector in Russian at the University of Bath. She is a graduate of the Lenin Pedagogical Institute, Moscow, and taught Russian to foreign students at the Pushkin Institute in Moscow from 1979 to 1991. She has written several articles on Russian literature and film, and is currently engaged in research at the University of Bath on 'Images of women in the drama of Aleksandr Ostrovsky'.

INDEX

For texts in English translation, see under relevant author

Aberdukh, N.I., 115, 117
Abramov, Fedor, 235, 236, 240, 242 n. 3
Abramovich, N.Ia., 100
Acmeism, 130, 205
actresses (of Silver Age), xiii, 108-29
Adams, Abigail, 82
Afanas'ev, Aleksandr, 216, 223 n. 19, 225 n. 47
Aitmatov, Chingiz, xv, 244-51
   The Day Lasts Longer than a Hundred Years, 244, 248
   Farewell, Gul'sary!, 244, 248, 249
   Mother Earth, 245
   The Piebald Dog Running Along the Shore, 244-45, 246, 249
   'Railway Halt in a Snowstorm', 244, 250
   The White Steamer, 244, 245, 248, 249
Akhmatova, Anna, x, xii, 16, 27, 34 n. 26, 50, 52, 124-33, 164, 200, 204, 205, 208
   'About poetry', 131
   'Craft Secrets', 125
   From Six Books, 133 n. 5
   'He left me at the new moon', 126
   Requiem, 27
   diaphor in, 124-33
Aksenov, Vasily, 155, 162 n. 24
   The Burn, 162 n. 24
alcohol, 24, 181, 255
Alcott, Louisa May, 15

Aldington, Richard, 131
Aleksievich, Svetlana, 181
Alexander I, 82, 83
Amazons, 220, 221, 225-26 n. 63
Amfiteatrov, Aleksandr, 102
Andreev, Leonid, xiv
   'The Abyss', xiv
   'In the Fog', xiv
Andrew, Joe, ix, 2
Antonov, Sergei, 239
Aplin, Hugh, 70, 76 n. 34
Asmus, Valentin, 169
Astaf'ev, Viktor, 234, 235, 239, 240, 241
   The Final Bow, 235
   'Liudochka', 241
   Queen Fish, 239
   The Sad Detective, 240
Auerbach, Nina, 12, 36 n. 59
Austen, Jane, 7, 44, 61
autobiography, xiii, xviii n. 24, 8, 148-50, 160 n. 5, 163-4, 182, 183
   camp memoirs, 16, 21, 43, 148-59, 161-62 n. 17, 177-78, 252
   memoirs of Pasternak, 164-72
   war memoirs, 142-44, 181
Azimirova, M.N., 102

Bakhtin, Mikhail, 51-52, 57 n. 25, 153, 156
   Rabelais and His World, 51

Baranskaia, Natal'ia, 28, 29, 181, 185, 189, 190, 191
  A Week Like Any Other, 28, 29, 181, 189, 190, 191
Barker, Adele, 237
Bashkirtseva, Mariia, 34 n. 26, 110, 119 n. 6
Belinsky, Vissarion, ix, 16, 19, 22, 80
Belov, Vasily, 16, 234, 235, 236, 239-40, 243 n. 11
  The Best is Yet to Come, 16, 240
  Carpenters' Tales, 239-40
  The Eves, 236
  Family Celebrations, 243 n. 11
  'Upbringing According to Dr Spock', 239
Bely, Andrei, xiv, 200, 202, 212-26
  Kotik Letaev, 212-26
  Petersburg, 202, 223 n. 14
Berggol'ts, Ol'ga, xii, xiii, 16, 27, 134-47
  'About Myself', 134-35
  'The Blockade Bath-House', 142-44
  Daytime Stars, 142
  'In Memory of the Defenders', 140
Bernhardt, Sarah, 110, 111, 119 nn. 6, 9
Bildungsroman, 6-7, 148, 153, 213
Bitov, Andrei, 241
Blair, Juliet, 109
Bliznetsova, Inessa, xii, 198, 199-201, 206
  Dale of Snares, 199, 100-201
  A View of the Sky, 199, 201
Blok, Aleksandr, xiv, 200, 227
Bloom, Harold, 50
Boborykin, Petr, 102
Boccaccio, Giovanni, 180, 183, 187 n. 19
Brezhnev, Leonid
  Brezhnev era ('stagnation'), 27, 40 n. 123, 198, 265, 276
Britain/British, ix, 12, 62, 76 n. 44, 78, 81, 83, 89, 94 nn. 15, 16
  English literature, 12, 44, 125, 131, 200, 201
Brodsky, Iosif, 205, 207, 208
Brontë, Charlotte, 12, 15, 31, 35 n. 46, 37 n. 72
  Jane Eyre, 15, 35 n. 46
  Villette, 12
Brontë, Emily, 44
Brownstein, Rachel, 4
Bulgakov, Mikhail, 14, 25
  The Master and Margarita, 14

Butler, Charles, 90
Byron, George Gordon, 69

Catherine the Great, 79
censorship
  post-communist, 280 n. 5
  Soviet, 48, 53, 96 n. 37
  tsarist, xv n. 2, 45, 88
Chekhov, Anton, 4, 17, 22, 31, 32, 119 n. 6, 190, 254, 276, 277
  'The Betrothed', 25
  'His Wife', 25
  'The Lady with the Dog', 17
  Three Sisters, 276
  Uncle Vania, 4-5
Chernobyl', 182, 183, 184, 279
Chernyshevsky, Nikolai, 7, 29, 61, 89, 97 n. 37, 266, 267, 273 n. 23
  What is to be Done?, 29, 61, 266
Chodorow, 20, 39 n. 93, 149
Chukovskaia, Lidiia, 8, 16, 27, 43, 164
  Going Under, 8
  Notes on Anna Akhmatova, 164
  Sof'ia Petrovna, 8, 27, 43
Chukovsky, Kornei, 143
Chuprinin, Sergei, 261, 265, 266
Cixous, Hélène, 12
conduct books, xiii, xviii n. 27, 79, 83, 89, 90, 92-93 n. 9
Conquest, Robert, 157
Costlow, Jane, 3
costume (of Silver Age actresses), xiii, xviii n. 28, 108-18, 120 nn. 13, 22, 121 n. 44
criticism
  of Silver Age women writers, 98-105
  western, x, xvi n. 6, 42, 44, 45, 48-49
  see also Bakhtin; cultural studies theory; feminism; postmodernism
cultural studies theory, xii, 42, 43-44, 53-54, 56 n. 15, 58 n. 31

Dashkova, Ekaterina, 7
Decembrism, 31
Dedkov, Igor', 261, 266
Derrida, Jacques, 44
diaphor, 124-33
Dickinson, Emily, 44, 125, 128
  'After Great Pain', 125
Dictionary of Russian Women Writers, x
Dmitrieva, Valentina, 21, 27, 33-34 n. 15, 104

Clouds, 21
'Dimka', 33-34 n. 15
Dobroliubov, Nikolai, ix
domestic ideoloogy, xiii, 78-97
   domesticity, 87, 267
   piety, 84
   purity, 85
   submissiveness, 86-87
Domostroi, 215-16, 221, 262
Dostoevsky, Fedor, ix, 3-4, 9, 10, 11, 12, 14, 17, 22, 23, 25, 30, 31, 32, 33 n. 7, 61, 237
   The Brothers Karamazov, 4, 6, 7, 17
   Crime and Punishment, 13, 14, 17
   The Devils, 13, 31
   Diary of a Writer, 13
   The Gambler, 11, 25
   The Idiot, 4, 11, 12, 17, 237
   'The Meek One', 12, 13, 31
   Netochka Nezvanova, 6, 61
Douglas, Ann, 88
Dovlatov, Sergei, 24, 252-58
   Branch institution, 256, 257
   Compromise, 255
   A Foreign Woman, 254
   'Literature Continues: after the Conference in Los Angeles', 256
   The Preserve, 255
   Solo on an Underwood, 255-56
   The Suitcase, 254
   The Zone, 252
Druzhinin, Pavel, 30, 89
du Maurier, George, 7
   Trilby, 12
Durova, Nadezhda, 7, 23, 34 n. 26, 63, 69, 70, 72, 89
   The Cavalry Maiden, 7
   The Sulphur Spring, 63, 70
Duse, Eleonora, 110, 111, 113, 119 nn. 6, 8, 9

Edmondson, Linda, 89, 92 n. 6
Efron, Ariadna, 164, 167
Eikhenbaum, Boris, 61, 125
Eliot, T.S., 125, 126-27, 128, 130
   'Sweeney among the nightingales', 125
Ellis, Sarah, 79, 80
Ellman, Mary, 125
Elshtain, Jean Bethke, 135, 136
Emerson, Caryl, 10
émigrés/emigration, xiv, 15, 179, 181, 184
   as literary theme, 174-75, 181, 182, 183, 184, 203, 254
   émigré literature, xiv, 15, 184-85
   émigré poets, 198, 199-205
   émigré writers, 253-54
Engel, Barbara, 64, 75 n. 28, 267, 273 n. 23
Erofeev, Venedikt, 24
   Moscow to the End of the Line, 24
Erofeev, Viktor, 6, 23, 28, 273 n. 4
   'A Letter to Mother', 273 n. 4
   Russian Beauty, 6, 28
everyday literature (*bytovaia literatura*), 188, 189, 194, 195

fashion (for Silver Age actresses), 108, 110, 111-12, 113, 114, 115
Fedin, Konstantin, 14, 170
   Cities and Years, 14
Felman, Shoshana, 26
feminism, x, xi, xii, xiii, xviii nn. 21, 23, 12, 20, 21, 23, 25, 26, 31, 32, 42, 43-44, 104
   French, 33 n. 13, 62, 222
   American, 88, 96 n. 36
   feminist criticism, x, xi, xii, 30, 31, 32, 42, 43-44, 48, 55-56 n. 7, 104
   feminist psychology, 20
   feminist theory, xiii-xiv, xviii nn. 21, 23, 12, 26, 28, 31, 32, 43-44, 48, 52, 55 n. 2, 104
   feminist writings, 17, 18, 21, 27, 30, 104, 108, 109
   in Russia, 15, 21, 23, 27, 30, 89, 107, 108, 109, 173, 185, 263
   see also feminist critique; images of women; 'woman question'; women; women writers
feminist critique, ix, x, xi, 2, 21-24, 29-31, 32
First World War, 135, 146 n. 13
folklore, 19, 75 n. 33, 202, 216, 217, 218, 220-21, 222, 224 n. 38, 237-38
Fonvizin, Denis, 61
   The Minor, 61
France/French, 62, 78, 79, 81, 82, 83, 86, 89, 94 nn. 16, 17, 149, 221
   see also feminism, French

Gan, Elena, 7, 21, 22, 60, 61, 62, 63-64, 69, 73, 75 n. 28, 89
   A Futile Gift, 7, 62, 69

The Ideal, 7, 21, 62, 63, 70
The Locket, 21, 62, 63, 70
Society's Judgement, 7, 62, 64, 70
Ganina, Maia, 16
Garshin, Vsevolod, 3
Gelfand, Elissa, 149
gender, x, xi, xii, 31, 32, 45, 46, 48, 54, 107, 108, 109, 111, 133, 136, 153, 214, 263-64
  in Bely, 214
  in Evgeniia Ginzburg, 153
  in Grekova, 45, 46, 48
  in masculine prose, 263-64
  in poetry, 133, 136
  see also feminism; images of women; men; misogyny; patriarchy; sexuality; stereotypes; women; women writers
Germany/German, 78, 79, 81, 83, 89, 217, 221
Gilbert, Sandra, 44, 45, 46, 55-56 n. 7
  The Madwoman in the Attic, 44, 46
Gilligan, Carol, 149
Ginzburg, Evgeniia, xviii n. 24, 16, 43, 148-62, 164
  Into the Whirlwind, 148-62
Ginzburg, Lidiia, 164
Gizhitskaia, L., 103
Gladkov, Fedor, 18-19
  Cement, 18-19
glasnost, x, 15, 27, 263, 276, 280
Gogol', 10, 20, 24-25, 39 n. 95, 61, 65, 69, 72, 94 n. 13, 237
  Dead Souls, 24
  Evenings on a Farm near Dikanka, 72
  The Inspector General, 20, 24
  'Ivan Fedorovich Shpon'ka and his Auntie', 25, 61, 69, 94 n. 13
  Marriage, 25, 94 n. 13
  'Old-World Landowners', 65
  St Petersburg Stories, 61
  Taras Bul'ba, 61
Golovin, K.F., 99, 103
Goncharov, Ivan, 3, 30
  Oblomov, 254, 270
Goncharova, Natal'ia (Pushkin's wife), 24, 39-40 n. 109
Gorbachev, Mikhail, 23, 278, 279-80
  Gorbachev era, 263, 280
Gor'ky, Maksim, 6
  Mother, 6
Gouges, Olympe de, 82

Gray, Francine du Plessix, 262
Grekova, I., xii, 28, 45-48, 272
  'Ladies' Hairdresser', 46-48
  Ship of Widows, 28
  'World Without Smiles', 272
Grin, Aleksandr, xv, 227-33
  'A Hundred Versts along the River', 228
  'Mysterious Forest', 228
  'Pierre and Surine', 229
  'The Pillory', 228
  'Quiet Weekdays', 228
  Scarlet Sails, 229-31
  She Who Runs on the Waves, 231-2
Grinevskaia, Isabella, 107, 114, 115, 116
Groys, Boris, 51, 56-57 n. 19
Gubar, Susan, 44, 45, 46, 55-56 n. 7
  The Madwoman in the Attic, 44, 46
Gumilev, Nikolai, 125, 126, 131
  'The Animal Tamer', 126
gynocritics, x, xi, 60, 62

Haggard, Rider, 12
  She, 12
Hale, Sarah, 88
Heldt, Barbara, ix, 2, 9, 31, 149
Herrman, Claudine, 153, 155
Herzen, Aleksandr, 20, 30, 76, 89
  Who is to Blame?, 20, 72
Hippel, Theodor Gottlieb von, 82
Hoisington, Sona Stephan, 2, 3, 4, 9
Hölderlin, Friedrich, 205

Iavorskaia, Lidiia, 111, 120 n. 13
Ignatova, Elena, xii, 198, 199, 202-205, 206
  Heavenly Glow, 199, 204-205
  Warm Earth, 199, 201-204
images of men, 22, 29, 154, 272
  in Bely, 213, 214-15
  in Berggol'ts, 138, 139
  in Kurchatkin, 275, 276, 277, 278, 279
  in Makanin, 261-62, 263, 264-65, 266, 269-70
  in Shmelev, 262, 263, 265, 266, 267, 268
  in village prose, 239
images of women, x, xi, xiii, xiv, xv, 2-41, 156
  as beauty, 5, 14-15, 37 n. 71

as ideal, xv, 8-9, 23, 35 nn. 32, 36, 156, 218, 228, 230, 231, 232, 238, 239-40, 241, 250
as mystery, 11
as plain, 5, 15, 16, 36 n. 56, 37 n. 75, 271
as victim, xiv, 11-13, 192
as witch, 14, 215-26
educated woman (Soviet), 263-64, 267, 269-71
emancipated woman (Russian), 16-19, 22, 38 n. 81, 264, 267
feminine archetypes, 132, 200-201, 213
in Aitmatov, 244-51
in Bely, 212-26
in Berggol'ts, 134-35, 138-9, 141-45
in Bliznetsova, 200-201
in Dovlatov, 252-58
in Evgeniia Ginzburg, 150, 155, 156-59
in Gan, 62, 63-64, 69-70, 73
in Grekova, 46-48
in Grin, 227-33
in Kurchatkin, 276, 277, 278-80
in Makanin, 262, 264, 265-66, 267, 269-71
in Petrushevskaia, 189-92
in Shmelev, 264-65, 267-9
in village prose, 234-43
in Voznesenskaia, 180-86
in wartime, 135-37, 138-39, 140, 141, 142
in Zhukova, 60, 62, 64-69, 70-73
in Znamenskaia, 208
lack of centrality of, 3-8
new woman, 18-19, 22, 103
unmarried woman, 15-16, 36 n. 56, 37 n. 75, 271
see also older women; misogyny; mothers; stereotypes; witches; women's literature
Ivanova, Natal'ia, 262
Ivinskaia, Ol'ga, 164-68, 169, 170, 171

Jameson, Frederic, 50, 55 n. 2, 58 n. 29
Jardine, Alice, 128
journals
children's magazines, 79, 84-87, 92 n. 7, 95 n. 23, 96 n. 33
U.S., 88, 96 n. 33
women's, xiii, 79, 83, 92 n. 7, 96 n. 37

Kammer, Jeanne, 124, 125, 126, 128
Karamzin, Nikolai, xv, n. 1, 6, 9, 10, 11, 12, 83
Poor Liza, 6, 9, 10, 11, 12, 83
Kelly, Catriona, 60, 65, 73, 186 n. 2
Khlebnikov, Velemir, 200, 204
Khrushchev, Nikita,
Khrushchev era, 48, 260, 263, 265
Khvoshchinskaia, Nadezhda, 7, 45, 56 n. 9
Kogan, P., 103
Kollontai, Aleksandra, 18, 30, 101, 103
'The New Woman', 101, 103
Vasilisa Malygina, 18
Kolodny, Annette, 31
Koltonovskaia, Elena, 100, 102, 103-4
Women's Silhouettes, 100, 103
Kommissarzhevskaia, Vera, 111
Kornilov, Boris, 139
Korzhavin, Naum, 256
Kovalevskaia, Sof'ia, 103
Kovrov, A., 102
Kozhevnikovaa, Nadezhda, 16
'Vera Perova', 16
Krandievskaia, Anastasiia, 103
Krestovskaia, Mariia, 101, 104, 120 n. 10
Lelia, 120 n. 10
Kristeva, Julia, 5, 155, 159
Kruchenykh, Aleksei, 170, 171
Krylov, Viktor, 111, 112
Kunin, Vladimir, 9
Hard Currency Prostitute, 9
Kurchatkin, Anatoly, 16, 28, 275-80
Houseful of Women, 276
Light of Evening, 16, 276
The Watchwoman, 28, 275-76
Kushner, Aleksandr, 129-30
Kuzmin'sky, Konstantin, 174, 181

Lacan, Jacques, 44
La Roche, Sophie von, 82
Latynina, Alla, 262, 272
Leningrad, siege of, xii, 16, 134, 135, 137, 143, 145
Lermontov, Mikhail, 3, 6, 12, 24, 32, 39 n. 95, 76 n. 47, 204, 208, 237
'Bela', 6, 12, 76 n. 47
A Hero of Our Time, 3, 6, 12, 39 n. 95, 76 n. 47, 237
'Princess Mary', 6
lesbianism, 17, 38 n. 81
Letkova, Ekaterina, 104

Index

Limonov, Eduard, 23, 179
 It's Me, Eddie, 179
Loseff, Lev, 252

Maegd-Soëp, Carolina de, 26
Maiakovsky, Vladimir, 200
Makanin, Vladimir, 259, 260, 261, 262, 264, 267, 269-71, 272-73 n. 4
 All Alone, 259, 260, 261, 265-66, 267, 269-71
 A Portrait and its Surroundings, 260
Makarov, Mikhail, 82
Malakhovskaia, Natal'ia, 267
Mallarmé, Stéphane, 124
Malleus Maleficarum, 219-20, 221, 222
Mamonova, Tat'iana, 15, 173, 178, 185, 220, 225 n. 57
Mandelker, Amy, 5, 31, 37 n. 76
Mandel'shtam, Nadezhda, xviii n. 24, 34 n. 26, 164, 167
Mandel'shtam, Osip, 127, 167, 169, 171, 205, 206, 208
Margol'm, Laura, 100-101, 102
Mariia Club, 173, 179, 180
Marinelli, Peter, 235
Maryniak, Irena, 250, 250 n. 2
matriarchy, 220, 276
 benevolent, 60, 68-69, 71, 72-73
McCarthy, Mary, 40 n. 126, 53
men/masculinity
 and alcohol, 24, 255
 and conduct books, xiii
 and war, 135, 136, 137-38, 144
 'little man', 8
 male bonding, 21, 39 n. 95, 278
 male writers, xii, xiv, 9, 14-15, 16, 20-21, 23, 24-26, 30, 32, 136, 272
 masculine culture, xii, xiv, 2, 3, 6, 20, 21, 27-28, 31, 156, 263, 267, 268
 masculine sexuality, xiv, 6
 masculine values, 144, 156, 184, 194, 215, 254
 masculinities, x, 41 n. 139
 'new man', 213, 266
 'superfluous man', 21, 22, 189, 228, 266, 270
memoirs, *see* autobiography
Michurina-Samoilova, Vera, 116
Mikhailov, Mikhail, xv n. 2, 89, 97 n. 37
Mikulich, Vera (Lidiia Veselitskaia), 103, 104

Minghella, Anthony, 229
misogyny
 in Europe, 222, 225 nn. 55, 57
 of Russian culture, xiv-xv, 2, 4, 21, 22-26, 27, 29-30, 31, 32, 39 n. 103, 40 n. 120, 108-109, 213, 220, 234, 237, 241
modernism, xiv, xix n. 35, 128, 130
Morozova, Boiarina Feodosiia, 132
Morson, Gary Saul, 5
Mother Damp Earth, 220
Mother Nature, 237, 249
Mother Russia, xv, 19, 136, 139, 140, 144, 237
mothers/motherhood
 Empresses as mothers, 92 n. 7
 images of, xv, 5, 14, 18, 19-20, 37 n. 67, 63, 65, 69, 158-59, 190, 204-205, 215, 219, 236-39, 241, 250
 matrophobia, 74 n. 11
 mothers and daughters, 19-21, 38 n. 91, 38-39 n. 92, 75 n. 28, 158
 mothers and sons, 237-38
 see also matriarchy
Mozhaev, Boris, 236, 239
 Peasants and their Women, 236
Mulvey, Laura, 12
myth, 220, 245, 246-48, 249, 250 n. 2

Nabatnikova, Tat'iana, 29
 'The Bus Driver Astap', 29
Nabokov, Vladimir, 15, 254
 Lolita, 15
Nadezhdin, N., 99, 102
Narbikova, Valeriia, 28-29
 The Equilibrium of Diurnal and Night-time Stars, 28-29
Neigaus, Genrikh, 166, 168
Nekrasov, Nikolai, 30, 89, 92 n. 9, 202, 256
Nekrasov, Viktor, 256, 263, 267
 Kira Georgievna, 263, 267
Newcomb, Harvey, 90
Newcomb, Sarah, 90
Nicholas I, xv n. 2, 45, 83, 88, 92 n. 7
Nikolaeva, Galina, 53, 146 nn. 3, 9

Odoevsky, Vladimir, 6, 37 n. 75, 39 n. 95, 61, 270
 Katia, or The Story of a Young Ward, 72
 New Year, 39 n. 95

Princess Mimi, 6, 37 n. 75, 61
Princess Zizi, 6
older women, xiv, 13-14, 28, 37 n. 67, 60-73, 74 n. 3, 76 n. 44, 213, 215-22, 224 nn. 20, 25, 239-40
see also witches
Olesha, Iury, 10, 15, 237
Envy, 10, 15, 237
Orthodox Church, 19, 80, 93 n. 12, 215, 220
Ostrovsky, Aleksandr, 3, 11-12
The Storm, 11-12
Ostrovsky, Nikolai, 19
How the Steel was Tempered, 19
Ovid, 203

Palei, Marina, 28, 29
'Evgesha and Annushka', 28
'Cabiria from the Bypass', 29
Panaeva, Avdot'ia, 63, 76 nn. 36, 37, 89, 256
The Young Lady of the Steppes, 63, 76 nn. 36, 37
Panova, Vera, xii, 45, 53, 56 n. 11, 253
The Factory, 56 n. 11
Span of the Year, 56 n. 11
Pascal, Jacqueline, 84
Pasternak, Boris, xxiii, 9, 10, 20, 21, 25, 37 n. 70, 50, 205
Doctor Zhivago, 9, 10, 20, 221, 37 n. 70, 164, 165, 167, 168, 169, 170, 171, 172 n. 6
memoirs of, 164-72
Second Birth, 168
Pasternak, Zinaida, 21, 164, 165, 166, 167, 168-71
pastoral, 235
patriarchy, xiii, 7, 9, 12, 21, 27, 45, 75 n. 29, 76 n. 46, 222
of Russian cultural tradition, x, 11, 12, 27, 68-69, 215, 222, 239, 240, 271
Pavlova, Karolina, 7, 89
Petrushevskaia, xii, 16, 28, 52-53, 58 n. 32, 185, 188-97
'Country', 191
'A Girl like That', 193-94
'Kseniia's Daughter', 195
'The New Robinsons', 58 n. 32
'Our Crowd', 28, 190-91
'The Story Teller', 191
The Time: Night, 28, 58 n. 32

Pil'niak, Boris, 169, 171
Pirogov, N., 89, 96 n.37
Pisarev, Dmitry, ix
poetry, women's, xix n. 35, 8, 124-33, 134-45, 174-75
contemporary women poets, 198-210
Pokrovskaia, Mariia, 102-103
Ponomarev, S.I., 99
Popov, Evgeny, 241
popular culture, 34 n. 26, 50, 51, 53-54, 58 n. 30
and élite culture, 50-51
and official culture, 49-50, 53, 56 n. 17, 58 n. 30
post-communist period, xiv, 15, 16, 23, 27
postmodernism, xii, 42, 43-44, 55 n. 2
Potapenko, Ignaty, 102
Pound, Ezra, 127
prostitutes
in literature, 9, 195, 255
Silver Age actresses as, 108, 113, 115, 116, 118, 120 n. 17
women writers as, 95-96 n. 30
Protopopov, M., 100, 103
Pushkin, Aleksandr, ix, 3, 6, 9, 10, 11, 13-14, 22, 24, 32, 34 n. 18, 39 n. 95, 39-40 n. 109, 61, 72, 200, 201, 205, 207, 208
The Bronze Horseman, 202
The Captain's Daughter, 6
Evgenii Onegin, 3, 6, 9, 10, 23, 34 n. 18, 39 n. 95, 61
Prisoner of the Caucasus, 11, 39 n. 95
The Queen of Spades, 13-14, 61, 72
Roslavlev, 40 n. 109
The Stone Guest, 205
Tales of Belkin, 72

Rabelais, François, 51, 52
rape, xiv, xv, 16, 18, 19, 23, 24, 25, 29, 81, 157, 162 n. 22, 181, 241, 279
Rasputin, Valentin, 14, 234, 235, 236, 238, 239, 242 n. 8, 243 n. 11
Borrowed Time, 238
Farewell to Matera, 14, 236, 238, 239
The Fire, 238, 239
Live and Remember, 238
Ratushinskaia, Irina, 16, 183
revisionism, xii, 2
Rich, Adrienne, 26, 38 n. 91, 39 n. 93
Romanticism, 6, 154

romantic presentation of heroine, 227-33
Rosenholm, Arja, 26
Rosenshield, Gary, 2, 8, 26, 29, 31
Rostopchina, Evgeniia, 23, 31, 45, 56 n. 9, 128-29, 132
  'The Dream', 31
  'How women should write', 129
  'To the Sufferers', 31
Rousseau, Jean Jacques, 82, 89
  Emile, 82, 89
Rozhanskaia, Ol'ga, xii, 198, 199, 205-207
  From Now On It's Everywhere, 199, 205
  Verses in Russian, 205-207
Rubinshtein, M., 101
Rybakov, Iul', 175, 176, 184

Sand, George, 30, 38 n. 81
Savina, Mariia, 111-12, 114, 119 n. 9, 120 nn. 12, 13, 121 n. 34
Schweik, Susan, 135
Second World War, xiii, 27, 134, 181, 236
Semenov, Gleb, 207
Sentimentalism, 6, 11, 63
sex/sexuality
  absence of, 232, 235
  and alcohol, 24, 255
  and death, 11, 33 n. 10
  in camps, 157, 162 n. 22
  in literature, xiii, 28-29, 179, 181, 193-94, 217, 218, 237, 240, 255, 275, 277, 278
  masculine, xiv, xv, 24, 179, 275
  pornography, 23, 24
  sexual abuse of women, 6, 23, 181, 194
  women's, 11, 16, 18-19, 20, 22, 28-29, 36 n. 51, 128, 181, 216
  see also rape
Shakespeare, William, 73, 200, 201, 228
Shapir, Ol'ga, 27, 101, 103
Shchepkina-Kupernik, Tat'iana, 27
Shashkova, S.S., 221, 223 n. 19, 226 n. 68
Shelgunov, Nikolai, 26
Shelley, Mary, 44
shestidesiatniki, 259-73
  shestidesiatnitsy, 262, 263
Shkapskaia, Mariia, 205
Shmelev, Nikolai, 259, 260, 261, 262, 263, 264-65, 266, 267, 272 n. 4

Pashkov House, 259, 260, 261, 262, 263-64, 266, 267
Showalter, Elaine, ix, 44, 45, 62, 75 n. 29
Shukshin, Vasily, 236, 240
  Snowball Berry Red, 236
Silver Age, xii, xiii, xiv, xix n. 35, 16, 34 n. 26
  actresses of, 107-21
  criticism of women writers, 98-106
Siniavsky, Andrei, xviii n. 24, 9, 24, 149
Smith, Sidonie, 149
Skabichevsky, Aleksandr, 103
Skul'skaia, Elena, 253
socialist realism, xiii, xiv, 23, 48, 50, 51, 56-57 n. 19, 154, 189, 195, 262, 263
Sokhanskaia, Nadezhda, 21, 23, 63, 69, 70, 75 nn. 28, 33
  A Conversation After Dinner, 21, 63, 70, 75 n. 28, 76 nn. 38, 39
Sologub, Fedor, 3
Solzhenitsyn, Aleksandr, xviii n. 24, 10, 14, 15, 25-26, 43, 50, 149, 150, 157, 161 nn. 8, 10, 179, 235, 238-39
  August 1914, 25-26
  Cancer Ward, 10
  The First Circle, 15, 157
  March 1917, 17
  'Matrena's Home', 14, 25, 235, 238
  'Nobel Lecture', 43
  Rebuilding Russia, 239
Sommer, Doris, 150
Sorokin, Vladimir, 23
Soviet system, xiii, xiv, 48, 49, 50
Spacks, Patricia Meyer, 44
Staël, Germaine de, 82
Stalin, Iosif, ix, 43, 52, 150, 158, 159, 169
  Stalin era, xii, 16, 27, 43, 44, 48, 50, 51, 53, 54, 132, 139, 148, 151, 152, 169, 227, 260
  Stalinist culture, 19, 45, 48, 54, 56 n. 10
  post-Stalin culture, xii, 20, 45, 48, 54, 241, 260
Stepanian, Karen, 269
stereotypes, female, xiv, 4, 10, 14, 15, 22, 26-29, 31, 32, 36 n. 87, 225 n. 55, 262, 263, 267, 270, 272
Strepetova, Polina, 111, 120 n. 9
suicide, 11, 12, 13, 22, 241

Surkov, Aleksei, 170, 171
Suslova, Apollinariia, 25, 37 n. 72
Symbolism, xiv n. 35, 15, 18, 27, 130, 214

Tarasova, Elena, 16
Tarlovskaia-Rastorgueva, Iuliia, 112, 117
Tendriakov, Vladimir, 236
theatre (in Silver Age), 107-21
Tikhonov, Nikolai, 140
Tiutchev, Fedor, 205
Tolstaia, Tat'iana, 15, 185, 241
  'Hunting the Woolly Mammoth', 15
Tolstoy, Aleksei, 17, 32
  'The Viper', 17
Tolstoy, Lev, 4, 5, 9, 10, 11, 12-13, 15, 17, 25, 30, 31, 36-37 n. 62, 37 n. 76, 74 n. 14, 223 n. 14
  Anna Karenina, 4, 5, 6, 11, 12, 15, 31, 37 n. 76, 66, 129, 223 n. 14
  Family Happiness, 12, 61
  The Kreutzer Sonata, 17, 30
  Resurrection, 13, 15
  War and Peace, 10, 13, 15, 36-37 n. 62, 39 n. 95, 212
Trediakovsky, Vasily, 200
Trotsky, Lev, 23
Trifonov, Iury, 190, 192-93, 195, 241, 257, 264, 272-73 n. 4
  Another Life, 192
  The Exchange, 192
  Moscow Tales, 192-93, 264
Tsvetaeva, Marina, x, 34 n. 26, 50, 52, 164, 167, 204, 208
Tur, Evgeniia (Elizaveta Seilhas de Tournemire), 23, 39 n. 102, 45, 56 n. 9
  'Antonina', 56 n. 9
Turgenev, Ivan, ix, 3, 4, 7, 10, 12, 17, 20, 22, 25, 30, 38 n. 81, 39 n. 102, 61
  Fathers and Sons, 3, 17, 20, 38 n. 81
  First Love, 4, 12, 21, 61
  Nest of the Gentry, 9, 10, 30
  On the Eve, 7, 12, 30
  Rudin, 7, 20, 30
  The Torrents of Spring, 4
  Virgin Soil, 17, 30
  'Turgenevan maiden' (moral paragon), 30, 61, 57, 257

Ulitskaia, Liudmila, 29

'Bron'ka' 29
'Gulia', 29
'Lialia's House', 29
underground
  literature, xiv, 15, 21, 27
  of Brezhnev era, 21, 174-76, 265
Unger, Friederike Helena, 82
United States of America, ix, xiii, xviii n. 27, 254, 256
  American literature, 7, 39 n. 98, 89, 125, 131
  American 'New Woman', 110
  domestic ideology in, 78, 81, 83, 87-88, 90, 91 nn. 1, 3
  see also feminism, U.S.
urbanisation
  and culture, xiv, 51
  urban prose, 189
  urbanised women, 240

Vasil'eva, N.S. 113, 117
Verbitskaia, Anastasiia, 7, 17, 21, 27, 34 n. 26, 103
  First Signs, 7
  In a New Way, 17
  The Keys to Happiness, 34 n. 26
  She Was Liberated!, 7
  Story of a Life, 7
  To my Reader, 21
Vermeer von Delft, 201
Viardot, Pauline, 25, 38 n. 81
Vigdorova, Frida, 48
village prose, 28, 189, 234-43
Voronina, Ol'ga, 263
Vovchok, Marko (Mariia Markovich), 27, 38 n. 81
Voznesenskaia, Iuliia, xii, 16, 21, 29, 173-87, 238
  Letters of Love, 184
  The Star Chernobyl', 177, 182-84, 185, 186
  The Women's Decameron, 21, 29, 173, 177, 179-82, 183, 185, 186, 187 n. 19, 238

war
  and men, xiii, xiv, 16, 135, 146 n. 20
  and women, 135, 136-37, 138-39, 146 n. 13, 181, 236
  and women writers, xiii, 16, 134-47
Weininger, Otto, 23, 100, 101
  Sex and Character, 23, 100

Wheelwright, Philip, 124, 126, 130
Whitman, Jason, 90
witches/witchcraft, xiv, 37 n. 67
  witchcraft imagery in Bely, 212-26
Wolf, Christa, 184
  Accident, 184
Wollstonecraft, Mary, 82
'woman question' (*zhenskii vopros*), ix,
  xv n. 2, 26, 98, 105, 108, 136
women
  and death, 11-13
  and war, 135, 136-37, 138-39,
    146 n. 13, 181, 236
  in Russian society, xi, 28, 80,
    162 n. 23
  in Soviet society, 136-37, 144,
    162 n. 23
  'new woman', 24, 110
  psychology of, 99, 109-10
  revolutionaries, 26, 30, 162 n. 23
  women's history, 80-3, 98, 225 n. 55
  women's movement, 27-28, 29, 83,
    88, 89, 98-99, 107
  see also feminism; images of women;
    women writers
women writers, x, xi, xii, xv, 7-8, 15, 16,
  20, 21, 22-23, 33-34 n. 15, 52-53,
  57 n. 26, 57-58 n. 27, 61-62, 69-71,
  86-87, 89, 128-29, 148, 173, 271-72
  foreign, 30-31, 44, 55-56 n. 7
  scorn of, 7, 39 n. 103, 52-53, 86-87,
    95-96 n. 30, 128, 187 n. 30
  'women's writer', 185, 187 n. 30
  see also feminism; images of women;
    misogyny; women; women's litera-
    ture
women's literature, x, xi, xii, 7-8, 15, 16,
  20, 21, 26-29, 33-34 n. 15,
  41 n. 127, 42, 44, 52, 54, 56 n. 12,
  62
  contemporary women's prose, 272
  criticism of, 98-105
  female solidarity in, 21, 29, 63, 64,
    75 n. 28, 180-82, 186, 200
  see also matriarchy
  in wartime, xiii, 16, 134-37, 146 n. 9
Woolf, Virginia, 3
Wordsworth, William, 214

Zabolotsky, Nikolai, 202, 205, 206, 207
Zalygin, Sergei, 236
Zamiatin, Evgeny, 4, 33 n. 10

We, 4, 33 n. 10
Zhdanov, Andrei, 23
Zhirmunsky, Viktor, 126
Zhukova, Mar'ia, 15, 16, 22, 33-34 n. 15,
  61, 62, 63, 64-73, 75 n. 28, 76 nn.
  34, 36, 77 n. 51
  'Baron Reikhman', 33-34 n. 15, 65-66
  Dacha on the Peterhof Road, 60, 62, 67-69
  Evenings by the Karpovka, 60, 62, 64,
    70, 77 n. 51
  'The Final Evening', 71, 73
  'The Locket', 15, 66, 67, 72
  'The Monk', 64, 65, 71, 72
  My Acquaintances from Kursk, 16
  'The Provincial Girl', 66
  Self-Sacrifice, 72, 75 n. 19, 76 n. 36
Zhukovsky, Vasily, 83
Znamenskaia, Irina, xii, 198, 199, 207-
  209
  I Address You as 'Thou', 208-209
  Long Light, 199, 207

New from *Berghahn Books*
Volume 3
Studies in Slavic Literature, Culture, and Society

Russian Postmodernism
New Perspectives on Post-Soviet Culture
By Mikhail N. Epstein, Alexander A. Genis, and Slobodanka M. Vladiv-Glover

The last ten years were decisive for Russia, not only in the political sphere, but also culturally, for this period saw the rise and crystallization of Russian Postmodernism. The essays, manifestos, and articles gathered here investigate various manifestations of this crucial cultural trend. Exploring fiction, poetry, art, and spirituality, they provide a point of departure and a valuable guide to an area of contemporary literary-cultural studies which is currently insufficiently represented in English-language scholarship. Conceived as a "textbook," *Russian Postmodernism* provides a broad and coherent overview of the main aspects of Russian Postmodernism, including its historical roots, its relationship with Modernism and Socialist Realism. A brief but useful "Who's Who in Russian Postmodernism" as an appendix renders this collection essential reading for scholars and students of Russian Literature, History, and Politics, Slavic Languages and Culture, Literary Criticism, and Postmodern Studies.

December 1998
520 pages, bibliography, index
ISBN 1-57181-028-5 hardcover
ISBN 1-57181-098-6 paperback

To Order: 1.800.540.8663

Berghahn Books
55 John Street, 3rd Floor, New York, NY 10038 • Tel 212.233.1075 • Fax 212.791.5246

Volume 1
Studies in Slavic Literature, Culture, and Society

Vladimir Odoevsky and Romantic Poetics
Collected Essays
By Neil Cornwell

Vladimir Odoevsky (1804-1869) was a fascinating and encyclopedic figure in nineteenth-century Russian culture, in his day he was mentioned in the same breath as Pushkin and Gogol. Thinker, pedagogue, musicologist, amateur scientist, and public servant, he is now undergoing a revival as a virtually rediscovered writer of Romantic and Gothic fiction. The author, a leading specialist on Odoevsky, analyzes his contribution to Russian prose fiction and in particular his influential approach to Romanticism, his Gothic novellas, and his proto-science fiction, as well as his critical reception.

December 1997
288 pages, bibliography, index, LC: 97-28787
ISBN 1-57181-913-4 Hardcover

To Order: 1.800.540.8663
Berghahn Books
55 John Street, 3rd Floor, New York, NY 10038 • Tel 212.233.1075 • Fax 212.791.5246